Charles B. Weinstock and
John Rushby (eds.)

Dependable Computing for Critical Applications 7

Dependable Computing and Fault-Tolerant Systems

Edited by
A. Avižienis, H. Kopetz, J.C. Laprie

Volume 12

Charles B. Weinstock and
John Rushby (eds.)

Dependable Computing for Critical Applications 7

Los Alamitos, California

Washington • Brussels • Tokyo

IEEE Computer Society Order Number PR00284
ISBN 0-7695-0284-9
ISBN 0-7695-0285-7 (case)
ISBN 0-7695-0286-5 (microfiche)
Library of Congress Number 99-63959

Additional copies may be ordered from:

IEEE Computer Society
Customer Service Center
10662 Los Vaqueros Circle
P.O. Box 3014
Los Alamitos, CA 90720-1314
Tel: + 1-714-821-8380
Fax: + 1-714-821-4641
E-mail: cs.books@computer.org

IEEE Service Center
445 Hoes Lane
P.O. Box 1331
Piscataway, NJ 08855-1331
Tel: + 1-732-981-0060
Fax: + 1-732-981-9667
mis.custserv@computer.org

IEEE Computer Society
Asia/Pacific Office
Watanabe Bldg., 1-4-2
Minami-Aoyama
Minato-ku, Tokyo 107-0062
JAPAN
Tel: + 81-3-3408-3118
Fax: + 81-3-3408-3553
tokyo.ofc@computer.org

Editorial production by Bob Werner

Cover art production by Alex Torres

Printed in the United States of America by Technical Communication Services

In Memoriam

Since the Conference was held last January, one of our distinguished colleagues and friends, Flaviu Cristian, passed away on April 27, 1999 at the age of 47, after a long and courageous battle against cancer.

Flaviu was born in Romania in 1951, and moved to France in 1971 to study computer science. He received his Ph.D. from the University of Grenoble, France, in 1979, where he carried out research in operating systems and programming methodology. He went on to the University of Newcastle Upon Tyne, UK and worked in the area of specification, design, and verification of fault-tolerant software. He then joined IBM Almaden Research Center in 1982. While at IBM, he received the Corporate Award, IBM's highest technical award, for his work on the Advanced Automation System for air traffic control. He subsequently joined UC San Diego as Professor in the Department of Computer Science and Engineering in 1991. He was nominated an IEEE Fellow in 1998 for his contributions to the theory and practice of dependable systems.

Flaviu's work on the design and analysis of fault-tolerant distributed systems was fundamental, and he was widely regarded as one of the technical leaders in his field. The impact of his work was felt both in the theory and in the practice of fault-tolerance. He actively contributed to both FTCS and DCCA; in particular, he was the General Chair for DCCA-4 held in San Diego in January 1994. He continued to be active in his work and his advising of students throughout his illness.

He was also interested in poetry, and turned to it as a form of therapy when diagnosed with cancer. His poems were published as two books "52 Poems" and "At the Crossroads" in 1995 and 1996, respectively. The following poem (reproduced with permission), reveals another facet of Flaviu's inspiring talent and provides an additional reason to remember him.

Perpetual Life
At the beginning a spark that bursts
from a man's flint and a woman's stone
Then a fire that burns alone
or merges with other fires
producing new sparks
As years pass the fuel that sustains each fire
is consumed and the fire dies out
Despite this the earth is lit each moment
by the billions of fires that burn

Flaviu Cristian (1951-1999)

CONTENTS

Page

Foreword   xi

Organizers   xii

Assessment of COTS Components

Microprocessor Entomology: A Taxonomy of Design Faults in   3
COTS Microprocessors
Algirdas Avžienis and Yutao He (UCLA)

Assessment of COTS Microkernels by Fault Injection   25
J.-C. Fabre, F. Salles, M. Rodríguez Moreno, J. Arlat (LAAS-CNRS)

Coping with COTS

Minimalist Recovery Techniques for Single Event Effects in   47
Spaceborne Microcontrollers
Douglas W. Caldwell and David A. Rennels (UCLA)

Building Fault-Tolerant Hardware Clocks from COTS Components   67
Christof Fetzer and Flaviu Cristian (UCSD)

Formal Methods

A Methodology for Proving Control Systems with Lustre and PVS   89
S. Bensalem, P. Caspi, C. Parent-Vigouroux, C. Dumas (VERIMAG)

Prototyping and Formal Requirement Validation of GPRS: 109
A Mobile Data Packet Radio Service for GSM
Laurent Andriantsiferana, Brahim Ghribi, Luigi Logrippo (University of Ottawa)

Formal Description and Validation for an Integrity Policy Supporting Multiple   129
Levels of Criticality
A. Fantechi, S. Gnesi, L. Semini (Università di Firenze)

Distributed Systems

Proteus: A Flexible Infrastructure to Implement Adaptive Fault Tolerance in AQuA   149
Chetan Sabnis, Michel Cukier, Jennifer Ren, Paul Rubel, William H. Sanders,
David E. Bakken, David Karr (University of Illinois and BBN)

Improving Performance of Atomic Broadcast Protocols using the   169
Newsmonger Technique
Shivakant Mishra and Sudha M. Kuntur (University of Wyoming and MINC Inc.)

Time-Triggered Architecture

The Transparent Implementation of Fault Tolerance in the
Time-Triggered Architecture
Hermann Kopetz and Dietmar Millinger (Technische Universität Wien) — 191

Formal Verification for Time-Triggered Clock Synchronization
Holger Pfeifer, Detlef Schwier, Friedrich W. von Henke (Universität Ulm) — 207

Fault Tolerance and Safety

PADRE: A Protocol for Asymmetric Duplex REdundancy
D. Essamé, J. Arlat, D. Powell (LAAS-CNRS) — 229

Experimental Validation of High-Speed Fault-Tolerant Systems using
Physical Fault Injection
*R.J. Martínez, P.J. Gil, G. Martín, C. Pérez, J.J. Serrano
(Universitat and Politécnica de València)* — 249

Models of Partitioning for Integrated Modular Avionics

A Model of Cooperative Noninterference for Integrated Modular Avionics
Ben L. Di Vito (NASA Langley) — 269

Invariant Performance: A Statement of Task Isolation Useful for
Embedded Application Integration
Matthew M. Wilding, David S. Hardin, David A. Greve (Rockwell Collins) — 287

A Model of Noninterference for Integrating Mixed-Criticality Software Components
Bruno Dutertre and Victoria Stavridou (SRI International) — 301

Dependability Evaluation

Dependability Modeling and Evaluation of Phased Mission Systems:
A DSPN Approach
*I. Mura, A. Bondavalli, X. Zang, K.S. Trivedi
(University of Pisa, CNUCE/CNR, and Duke University)* — 319

Dependability Evaluation using a Multi-Criteria Decision Analysis Procedure
Divya Prasad and John McDermid (University of York) — 339

Probabilistic Guarantees

Probabilistic Scheduling Guarantees for Fault-Tolerant Real-Time Systems
*A. Burns, S. Punnekkat, L. Strigini, D.R. Wright
(University of York and City University)* — 361

Fault Detection for Byzantine Quorum Systems   **379**
Lorenzo Alvisi, Dahlia Malkhi, Evelyn Pierce, Michael Reiter
(University of Texas at Austin, AT&T Labs, and Bell Laboratories

Panel: Certification and Assessment of Critical Systems

Dependable Computing System Evaluation Criteria: SQUALE Proposal   **397**
Yves Deswarte (LAAS-CNRS)

FOREWORD

Welcome to the Seventh International IFIP Working Conference on Dependable Computing for Critical Applications. DCCA is a unique conference both because of its focus — Can We Rely on Computers? — and its format, which allows ample time for consideration and discussion of the work presented.

Like the six previous conferences in the series, DCCA-7 addresses aspects of dependability, a broad term connoting the extent to which reliance can justifiably be placed in the service provided by a computer system. Topics presented at DCCA include attributes of dependability such as security, safety, and reliability, with a special interest in issues involving combinations of these attributes. The session on Models of Partitioning for Integrated Modular Avionics provides an excellent illustration of this focus. Integrated modular avionics must support multiple critical applications in such a way that faults cannot propagate from one application to another; the concern is safety, but the techniques for enforcing and modeling partitioning have much in common with those in computer security. Each field is enriched by studying techniques developed for the other.

This volume contains all 20 of the papers that were presented at the conference, plus a position paper for the panel on the certification and assessment of critical systems. For the first time at DCCA, papers were submitted to the conference electronically. We believe this simplified the process for authors, reviewers, and the organizers, and may have been partly responsible for the excellent response to the call for papers: a total of 62 papers were received from 16 countries. (The distribution was USA 22.5, UK 10, France and Germany 6 each, Italy 3.5, Austria, Japan, and Spain 2 each, and 1 from each of Canada, Finland, Macau, Malaysia, Poland, Portugal, South Africa, and Sweden.) The final program was selected from this very strong field through the diligent efforts of the program committee and many outside referees. Their careful scrutiny and thoughtful reviews ensured the high standard of quality and originality in the papers gathered in this volume.

Cordial thanks are due to all those who submitted papers to DCCA-7, and to the members of the program committee and the external reviewers listed on the following pages. It is only through their hard work that this conference is brought to you. Special thanks are due to all those who attended the program committee meeting in Alexandria, and to Cathy Meadows for enabling the vast amount of material distributed and considered at that meeting to be printed locally.

Finally, John Rushby would like to record his deep appreciation for the contribution of his administrative assistant, Dr. Judith Burgess, over the last 10 years, including the early stages of organizing this conference. Judith died in October 1998 and is sadly missed by all who knew her.

John Rushby, Program Committee Chair
Charles B. Weinstock, General Chair

ORGANIZERS

General Chair
Charles B. Weinstock
Software Engineering Institute
Carnegie-Mellon University
Pittsburgh PA 15213 USA

Program Committee Chair
John Rushby
Computer Science Laboratory
SRI International
Menlo Park, CA 94025 USA

Ex Officio (IFIP WG 10.4 Chair)
Hermann Kopetz
Real-Time Systems Group
Technische Universität Wien
A-1040 Vienna, Austria

PROGRAM COMMITTEE

Kathy Abbott, FAA, USA
Jacob Abraham, University of Texas at Austin, USA
Ozalp Babaouglu, University of Bologna, Italy
Alan Burns, University of York, UK
Flaviu Cristian, UCSD, USA
Ben Di Vito, NASA LaRC, USA
Danny Dolev, Hebrew University, Israel
Kevin Driscoll, Honeywell, Minneapolis, USA
Marie-Claude Gaudel, LRI, Paris, France
Friedrich von Henke, University of Ulm, Germany
Gerard Holzmann, Bell Labs, USA
Ravi Iyer, University of Illinois, USA
Yoshiaki Kakuda, Hiroshima City University, Japan
Peter Kearney, SVRC, Brisbane, Australia
Carl Landwehr, NRL, USA
Bev Littlewood, City University, UK
Cathy Meadows, NRL, USA
David Powell, LAAS-CNRS, France
Brian Randell, University of Newcastle upon Tyne, UK
Mike Reiter, Bell Labs, USA
Bill Roscoe, Oxford University, UK
William H. Sanders, University of Illinois, USA
Rick Schlichting, University of Arizona, USA
Roger Shaw, ERA Technology Ltd., UK
Paulo Verissimo, University of Lisbon, Portugal

REFEREES

Rajeev Alur
Joffroy Beauquier
Jayanta Bhadra
Ramesh Bharadwaj
Nadia Busi
Antonio Casimiro
Miguel Correia
Michel Cukier
Paul Ezhilchelvan
Colin Fidge
Michael Goldsmith
Carl Gunter
Nevin Heintze
Brian Hicks
Doug Howe
Kenji Ishida
Zbigniew Kalbarczyk
Shmuel Katz
Maciej Koutny
David Leer
Gavin Lowe
Bruno Marre
Jon Millen
Paul S. Miner
Alberto Montresor
Fabrice Mourlin
Rodolphe Ortalo
Larry Paulson
Rob Pike
Anuj Puri
Jon Riecke
Marco Roccetti
Luis E.T. Rodrigues
Sascha Romanovsky
Jose Rufino
Jian Shen
Graeme Smith
Neil Speirs
Guy Vidal-Naquet
Axel Wabenhorst
Philip Wadler
Jie Xi
Avelino Zorzo

Assessment of COTS Components

Microprocessor Entomology:
A Taxonomy of Design Faults in COTS Microprocessors

Algirdas Avižienis and Yutao He
Dependable Computing and Fault Tolerance Laboratory
Computer Science Department
University of California, Los Angeles, CA 90095-1596
E-mail: {aviz,yutao}@cs.ucla.edu

Abstract

The rapid increase of the complexity of high-performance COTS (Commercial Off-The-Shelf) microprocessors has led to continuing post-design discoveries of numerous design faults, called "errata" by the manufacturers. This paper presents a systematic framework, the Design Fault Taxonomy, for the study of such design faults. Based on the proposed methodology, an in-depth analysis of design faults uncovered in the Intel Pentium [†] II microprocessor since its initial release is presented in detail. The results raise concerns about the use of such processors in high-confidence systems and point to potential solutions.

Keywords: **COTS microprocessors, design faults, errata, fault taxonomy, high-confidence systems, microprocessor entomology**

1 Introduction

The rapid increase in complexity of high-performance COTS (Commercial Off-The-Shelf) microprocessors (abbreviated μp) has led to continuing post-design discoveries of numerous design faults. As shown in the following section, the Intel Corporation has published eight lists that enumerate 535 μp-design faults (called "errata") uncovered in Pentium and P6 family processors from February 1995 to April 1999 [1–8].

It is evident that high-performance COTS microprocessors that contain these μp-design faults will have to be used in high-confidence systems, since errata-free units are not known to exist. The task facing the designers of fault-tolerant high-confidence systems is to assure that the known μp-design faults will not lower the dependability of the system below acceptable bounds.

[†]Pentium is a registered trademark of Intel Corporation.

The problem is compounded by the continuing discovery of new μp-design faults that may be first announced after the high-confidence system design has been completed. Every new fault implies the need for a new assessment of system dependability and even the possibility of mandatory modifications. And how do we establish confidence in a system that depends on microprocessors that are very likely to contain several as yet undiscovered μp-design faults?

Design diversity by multichannel computation using different microprocessors in each channel is one possible and costly solution, but even here each microprocessor has its own set of μp-design faults, which may produce similar errors, although the faults are distinct [9]. The analysis of such possibilities is much more complex than the case of non-diverse implementation.

The goal of this paper is to review the publicly available information about the "errata", or μp-design faults, and to present a taxonomy of these faults that should lead to an informative classification and facilitate the analysis of their effects on a given system.

The rest of the paper is organized as follows: Section 2 summarizes the published "errata" information. Section 3 describes the methodology of the proposed *Design Fault Taxonomy (DFT)* in detail. An in-depth DFT analysis of μp-design faults (errata) uncovered in the Pentium II microprocessors is presented in Section 4. Section 5 summarizes the key results and offers our conclusions and some recommendations.

2   The "Errata" Phenomenon in COTS Microprocessors

In a previous study [10] we looked into the applicability of high-performance COTS microprocessors in high-confidence (critical) applications. A review of the Web sites of major manufacturers revealed that Intel Corporation allowed public access to very comprehensive documentation of their microprocessor designs at the architectural level. In early 1996 the Pentium Pro was documented in a three-volume *Developers Manual* [11], totaling over 1400 pages, although the information on error detection and recovery features was widely scattered and difficult to organize [10].

2.1   "Errata": Documentation of Design Faults by Intel

An interesting discovery during our study was the existence of monthly *Processor Specification Update* publications for Intel microprocessors, which listed "errata", defined in the documents [1–8] as follows:

"Errata are design defects or errors. Errata may cause the Pentium II processor's behavior to deviate from published specifications. Hardware and software designed to be used with any given processor must assume that all errata documented for that processor are present on all devices unless otherwise noted" [3, p. vii].

As of April 1999, separate *Processor Specification Update* publications are available at the Intel Corp. Web site *http://developer.intel.com/design/processor/* for the Pentium and all succeeding Intel P6 family microprocessors: Pentium (96 pp.) [1], Pentium Pro (99 pp.) [2], Pentium II (72 pp.) [3], Mobile Pentium II (55 pp.) [4], Celeron^{TM} (37 pp.) [5], Pentium II Xeon^{TM} (43 pp.) [6], Pentium III (35 pp.) [7], and Pentium III Xeon^{TM} (39 pp.) [8]. The *Updates* usually appear monthly, except when there are no changes to report.

Each *Update* has a "General Information" part followed by four sections titled "Errata", "Documentation Changes", "Specification Clarifications", and "Specification Changes". The errata are listed for every "stepping", which is an Intel term used to designate a distinct variant of the given microprocessor.

Every stepping contains a subset of the total (cumulative) set of errata. The discovery of previously unknown errata is almost a monthly occurrence. For example, the January, 1999 *Pentium II Processor Specification Update* listed three new errata (A67, A68, A69) that are present in all seven existing steppings, but were not known (listed) in December, 1998, or earlier.

The steppings are released consecutively in time. Some errata are eliminated ("fixed") in a later stepping; for example, Pentium II erratum A42 is present in the first four steppings, but is not present in the next three steppings.

The tabulation of errata has a "Plan" column. The entry "Fix" indicates that "*this erratum is intended to be fixed in a future stepping of the component*"; "NoFix" indicates that "*there are no plans to fix this erratum*", and the entry "Fixed" means "*this erratum has been previously fixed*", i.e., it is not present in the most recent stepping, or in more than one of the most recent steppings. There is no indication why the "NoFix" decision has been made for a given erratum.

Table 1 summarizes the errata information in the eight *Updates* listed above.

Processor Model	No. of Step- pings	First Update		After 1st Update		April 1999		
		Mo. & Yr.	No. of Errata	No. of Months	New Err.	Total Err.	Presently	
							NoFix	Fix
Pentium	17	2/95	40	47	79	119	42	0
P. Pro	5	11/95	30	38	71	101	60	0
P. II	7	5/97	27	23	46	73	44	5
Mob. P. II	7	8/98	37	8	10	47	31	13
Celeron	5	4/98	25	12	20	45	30	6
P. II Xeon	2	5/98	36	11	20	56	47	6
P. III	1	3/99	44	1	1	45	42	3
P. III Xeon	2	3/99	47	1	2	49	44	5

Table 1: Errata reported for Intel processors (to April 1999)

2.2 Recurrence of Errata in the Intel P6 family

As new members of the P6 family of processors reach the market, it is interesting to note that they share a common subset of errata with Pentium II, while other Pentium II errata are absent (fixed), or Not Applicable (N/A) because of different designs. Some new errata that were not present in Pentium II also appear. A comparison of the errata in five recent models to the 73-errata set of Pentium II is presented in Table 2. The data are from the April, 1999 *Updates* [4–8], and each model is being compared to Pentium II [3].

Processor Model	Reported Errata in April 1999			
	Absent or N/A	Common	New	Total
Mob. P. II	26	44	3	47
Celeron	28	45	0	45
P. II Xeon	17	50	6	56
P. III	28	40	5	45
P. III Xeon	24	40	9	49

Table 2: Errata in the P6 Family of Processors, Compared to Pentium II

2.3 Documentation of Errata by Other Manufacturers

To gain a better understanding of the errata problem, we have searched for errata information at the Web sites of other microprocessor manufacturers: Motorola (MC680x0, MC683xx, MPCxxx); SGI, formerly MIPS Technologies (R10000, R8000, R4xxx); Compaq, formerly DEC (Alpha); Sun (UltraSparc); IBM (PowerPC); and HP (PA-RISC). As of April, 1999, the Web site of Intel Corp. provides comprehensive (35 to 100 pages per processor) monthly *Specification Updates* that contain listings of errata in the Pentium and P6 families of microprocessors. Motorola supplies relatively short errata listings for the processor families listed above. The MPC860 errata list (46 pp.) is the most complete and up-to-date (March, 99) of the set, yet it is still far behind Intel in its organization and comprehensiveness. The SGI/MIPS site has "MIPS R4400 MC Errata" (4 pp.) last revised 1/24/1995. We were not able to locate similar errata lists at other manufacturers' Web sites, but it is likely that they exist in restricted publications.

3 A Taxonomy of Microprocessor Design Faults, or "Errata"

The preceding section shows that contemporary high-performance microprocessors contain extensive sets of design faults that are called "errata" in the manufacturers' literature. We will conform to this usage in the discussion of specific examples. In general discussion the term "design fault" is more appropriate, since the "errata" are not a list of typographical errors with their corrections inserted in a book (as defined in *Webster's New World Dictionary of the American Language*,

Simon and Schuster, 1980), but potentially very harmful "bugs" in the logic of microprocessors. An errata list in a book completes the correction, while the errata list for a microprocessor only raises an alarm: "What do we do about them?"

The existence of the errata raises three fundamental questions on design and verification:

(1) Can we use the microprocessors in dependability-critical applications, i.e., how do we show that the errata (design faults) can be tolerated in a high-confidence system?

(2) How can design processes be refined so that the errata are either avoided or tolerated in future designs?

(3) What improvements in the verification techniques would have led to the discovery of the errata prior to manufacturing?

The first step in answering the above questions must be a thorough understanding of the properties and manifestations of the errata. The Intel *Updates* [1–8] list the errata in the chronological order of their discovery, and no further classification is provided.

In this paper we present a *Design Fault Taxonomy (DFT)* that classifies the microprocessor design faults (abbreviated as "μp-design faults", and called "errata" by the manufacturers) with respect to a set of orthogonal properties. We expect that the DFT will provide a foundation for answers to the three questions raised above.

An important reference point for our work has been the Orthogonal Defect Classification for software [12]. The main difference is that the published data about the errata does not provide any insight about at what point in the design process the fault (erratum) was introduced, and fault types are determined according to the kind of errors that the fault produces. Design faults in state-of-the-art COTS microprocessors seem thus far to have received little attention. The references we have located are a study of development of a VLIW super-minicomputer architecture [13], a brief study in [14], and a discussion in the context of security [15].

The security study [15] identifies architecture properties and "implementation errors" (i.e., "errata") of the Intel 386, 486 and Pentium processors that may cause undesirable results in secure computer systems. Only the early steppings of the Pentium are included in the discussion. The errata are also called "flaws" and are classified according to their impact on security in the order of decreasing severity as: (1) hardware protection flaws; (2) system instruction flaws; (3) denial of service flaws; and (4) others, that are not directly security-relevant. The subsequent discovery of many more Pentium errata and their continuing appearance in the P6 processor family evidently pose a security problem as well.

3.1 General Issues of DFT Methodology

This section discusses some general issues that we consider essential in development of the proposed taxonomy. Our objective is to gain an understanding of the properties of μp-design faults that have eluded the rigorous verification process and were discovered after the design was completed. Three fundamental questions are:

1. **Where do design faults occur in microprocessors?**

   With the increase of complexity of VLSI chips, the probability of occurrence of design faults has also increased. The different functional units of a VLSI chip are of different complexity and thus have differing difficulties of verification. As a result, a systematic study of the distribution of design faults in terms of functional subsystems within the VLSI chip should identify those "dark spots" that are more likely to elude the verification process.

2. **What are the triggering conditions of design faults?**

   The essential and challenging issue of verification is to find a test stimulus that leads to activation of an existing design fault. It is complicated further by the increase in the configurations and operation modes of today's state-of-the-art COTS microprocessors. As a result, characterizing the triggering conditions of design faults that are uncovered will help to derive better tests.

3. **What consequences do design faults cause?**

   Design faults in different locations cause errors that have different effects on system performance and dependability. In COTS-based fault-tolerant systems, the adverse effects of design faults in the COTS building blocks have to be analyzed, tolerated, or eliminated.

3.2   Overall Structure of The DFT

The DFT requires a set of *μp-design faults*, a *target system model*, a *design fault model*, and a *classification procedure* that is applied to analyze the μp-design faults in terms of the fault model, each of which is discussed in the following sections.

3.3   Definition of μp-Design Faults

In conformity to the definition in [16], *μp-design faults* in the DFT are defined as human-made faults that are created during the design of microprocessors but discovered only after the chips have been designed, i.e., during the post-silicon stage. As a result, a μp-design fault can be either a fault in the specification (eg., a deadlock in communication protocol), or a fault in the implementation (eg., omission of a specified feature). The μp-design faults are interesting because they have eluded extensive pre-silicon verification processes and their presence has to be accounted for in high-confidence designs that employ the given COTS microprocessors.

3.4   The Target System Model

There exist different models of microprocessors. For example, distinct abstractions of a microprocessor at instruction-set-architecture level, microarchitecture level, register-transfer level, gate level, and transistor level reflect the process of building a microprocessor from its high-level specification to its final implementation and have been used by different communities for various purposes.

In the DFT, at the highest level of abstraction a microprocessor is divided into two logic units: *Performance Delivery Architecture (PDA)* and *Confidence-Assurance Architecture (CAA)*. Further partitioning is performed in a hierarchical manner, down to function level, subfunction level, and instruction level, etc., according to the needs of analysis and the information that is available.

Performance Delivery Architecture (PDA) The PDA is the logic part of a microprocessor that aims to deliver the desired performance and has been the primary topic of modern computer architecture research. For example, the floating-point unit is an element of PDA.

Confidence Assurance Architecture (CAA) The CAA is the logic part of a microprocessor that aims to assure the ability of the PDA to deliver the expected performance. For example, the BIST logic and the error-correcting code logic are elements of the CAA.

It is important to note that the DFT system model is partitioned into logic units rather than physical units as implemented on the chip. The reasons for using logic partitioning are: (a) essential implementation information is considered confidential by the manufacturers and is generally not available; (b) the record of design faults provided by the manufacturers is also based on a logic model.

3.5 The μp-Design Fault Model

A design fault can be characterized on the basis of many different attributes. The goal of the DFT is to choose a subset of most representative attributes that characterize design faults. In particular, the classification criteria should be orthogonal to eliminate ambiguity and inferential to disclose cause-effect relationships. With this in mind, the following set of attributes has been chosen for the DFT:

- **Logical location**: It is defined by the logic partitioning of a microprocessor and consists of the PDA, the CAA and their logic elements that can be identified from system manuals provided by the manufacturer. The granularity depends on the technical information available. Note that a *logical* location is not necessarily equivalent to the *physical* location where a function is actually implemented. In essence, it is the hypothesized logic unit that contains the μp-design fault.

- **Type**: This attribute describes what kind of error is caused by the fault. Faults are divided into: (1) *data faults*, (2) *timing faults*, and (3) *control faults*. A data fault is a μp-design fault that causes an incorrect value in a data/address register, or at a data/address bus; a timing fault is a μp-design fault that causes incorrect timing; a control fault is a μp-design fault that causes any other incorrect behavior, for example, change of execution flow of the microprocessor, failure to set a flag, etc.

- **Triggering condition**: This attribute characterizes the operational environments under which a μp-design fault is activated and includes:

  - **Configuration**: It describes how the system is configured when a μp-design fault is activated, for example, the uniprocessor or multiprocessor configuration.

  - **Operation mode**: It describes the operational mode of the system such as: normal operation, test, or recovery mode.

  - **Triggering dependency**: This attribute describes events that activate a μp-design fault. A fault can be triggered by either a *single event*, or *multiple events*, i.e., a combination of two or more events.

- **Effect**: This attribute describes the errors caused by a μp-design fault and can be divided into two categories:

  - **Severity**: The following effects are used to designate severity: (1) *crash*: a fault causes either a shutdown, a corrupted state, or any unpredicted behavior. (2) *hang*: a fault causes a microprocessor to hang (stop operation); (3) *service denial*: a fault causes the denial of service of one or more functions; (4) *lesser*: a fault causes an effect that is less critical than the preceding three.

  - **Affected elements**: The logic element(s) such as function, instruction, etc., that are affected by a μp-design fault. The effect is described by both extent and latency of errors produced. Note that one fault may affect two or more logic elements.

The attributes discussed above are summarized in Figure 1. The attributes at the leaves are chosen to be mutually exclusive and are used to characterize a μp-design fault orthogonally.

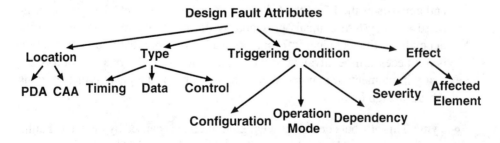

Figure 1: Attributes of μp-design faults in the DFT

3.6 Classification Procedure

The classification procedure consists of four steps:

1. **Collection of data.** The initial step is to obtain a record of design faults that have been uncovered and documented for a microprocessor. The record should be detailed enough to provide the relevant information for the analysis.

2. **Acquisition of the system model.** The manufacturer's documentation is used to acquire a representation of the microprocessor at the level of abstraction detailed enough for the purpose of analysis, as outlined in Section 3.4.

3. **Refinement of the μp-design fault model.** The attributes are identified that are specific to the microprocessor under analysis, for example, the logic locations, the operational modes, etc.

4. **Analysis of μp-design faults.** The evaluation procedure is conducted by partitioning the collected set of design faults according to the refined μp-design fault model.

4 Application of the DFT: A Taxonomy of the Errata in Pentium II

We chose Intel microprocessors for this study because Intel Corporation allows public access to a complete up-to-date record of the errata [1–8] , as well as to extensive documentation (about 2000 pages) of microprocessor design at the architectural level [17–26]. The documents are accessible to the public at the Intel Corporation Web site: *http://developer.intel.com/design/processor/*.

The fundamental rule of this study has been that only publicly distributed Intel documentation would be used. We have not made further inquiries or signed any non-disclosure agreements. The needed information has not always been easy to find and to interpret. Some of our difficulties are explicitly noted in the following discussion. We also wish to note that we do not preclude future collaboration with Intel researchers if mutually beneficial goals can be established. At the present time we alone are responsible for the interpretation of the documents accessed at the Intel site. The term "errata" will be used for "μp-design faults" in this section of the paper, since it is the accepted usage in Intel literature.

To illustrate the proposed DFT, the 73 errata reported for the Intel Pentium II microprocessor from May, 1997 to April, 1999 [3] have been analyzed. The results are presented subsequently in detail.

4.1 Source of Pentium II Design Fault Data

The source of the data used in this study is the *Pentium II Processor Specification Update* published by Intel [3] [‡]. From May 1997 to April 1999, 7 steppings of Pentium II have been released.

[‡]It has been noticed that there exist some other sources that describe design faults in Intel microprocessors [27,28]. Because they have not been officially confirmed by Intel in the *Specification*

The description of an erratum has four parts: *Problem, Implication, Workaround,* and *Status. Problem* describes the symptoms of an erratum and its triggering conditions; *Implication* describes potential consequences (error or failure) the erratum could cause. *Workaround* gives possible solutions to avoid activating the erratum or to eliminate errors caused by the erratum. *Status* indicates the processor stepping(s) affected by the erratum. The tabulation of errata has a "Plan" column. The entry "Fix" indicates that *"this erratum is intended to be fixed in a future stepping of the component"*; "NoFix" indicates that *"there are no plans to fix this erratum"*, and the entry"Fixed" means *"this erratum has been previously fixed"*, i.e., it is not present in the most recent stepping, or in more than one of the most recent steppings.

The cumulative total of all errata as reported in the monthly *Updates* (May 1997 to April 1999) for Pentium II is presented in Figure 2. Note that the first *Update* reported 27 errata, apparently discovered since the manufacturing of the first stepping began. Out of the 73 errata reported up to January 1999, 24 have been fixed, 5 are to be fixed in future steppings, and 44 will remain unfixed. One erratum (A34) is marked "fixed", but is not shown to have been present in any one of the seven steppings. We cannot explain this anomaly.

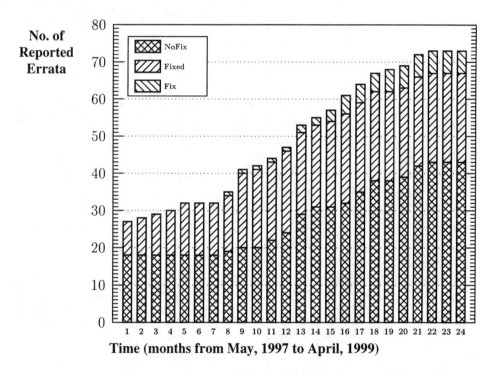

Figure 2: Total errata reported for Pentium II vs. time (all steppings)

Figure 3 presents the number of errata for each one of the seven steppings of Pentium II as of April 1999. The number of errata ranges from 63 to 49 (out of

Updates, they are excluded from our study.

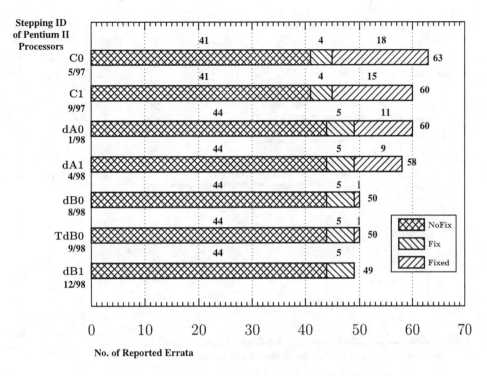

Figure 3: Errata reported for the steppings of Pentium II (April 1999)

72 total, not including A34) and decreases in the more recent steppings as some errata are fixed. New errata have appeared only once: there are 9 new errata in the third stepping (dA0), which were not present in the previous steppings C0 and C1. However, 9 errata that existed in C1 were fixed in dA0, leaving the total unchanged between C1 and dA0. On the other hand, 3 of the new errata were NoFix, raising the NoFix number from 41 to 44, and one new erratum was Fix, raising the Fix number to 5. The Fixed number shows how many errata that were present in the given stepping had been fixed prior to the release of the dB1 stepping.

4.2 The Target System Model of the Pentium II Processor

The target system model of the Intel Pentium II processor has been compiled from publicly available technical documents [17–26].

4.2.1 The Performance Delivery Architecture (PDA) Pentium II is a member of the Intel P6 processor family and employs the so-called *Dynamic Execution* microarchitecture which combines multiple branch prediction, data-flow analysis and speculative execution to boost its performance. In addition, it uses dual independent busses, of which one is the dedicated external system bus and the other is the dedicated internal high-speed cache bus. It also provides on-chip support for MMX^{TM} technology.

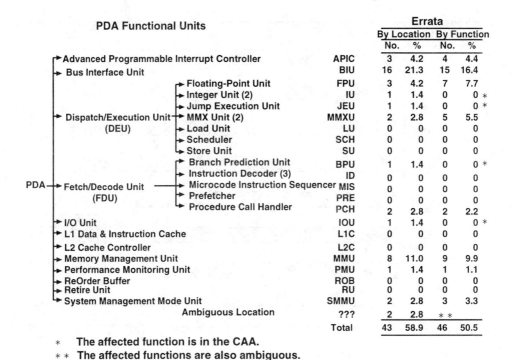

PDA Functional Units		Errata			
		By Location		By Function	
		No.	%	No.	%
Advanced Programmable Interrupt Controller	APIC	3	4.2	4	4.4
Bus Interface Unit	BIU	16	21.3	15	16.4
Floating-Point Unit	FPU	3	4.2	7	7.7
Integer Unit (2)	IU	1	1.4	0	0 *
Jump Execution Unit	JEU	1	1.4	0	0 *
Dispatch/Execution Unit MMX Unit (2)	MMXU	2	2.8	5	5.5
(DEU) Load Unit	LU	0	0	0	0
Scheduler	SCH	0	0	0	0
Store Unit	SU	0	0	0	0
Branch Prediction Unit	BPU	1	1.4	0	0 *
Instruction Decoder (3)	ID	0	0	0	0
PDA Fetch/Decode Unit Microcode Instruction Sequencer	MIS	0	0	0	0
(FDU) Prefetcher	PRE	0	0	0	0
Procedure Call Handler	PCH	2	2.8	2	2.2
I/O Unit	IOU	1	1.4	0	0 *
L1 Data & Instruction Cache	L1C	0	0	0	0
L2 Cache Controller	L2C	0	0	0	0
Memory Management Unit	MMU	8	11.0	9	9.9
Performance Monitoring Unit	PMU	1	1.4	1	1.1
ReOrder Buffer	ROB	0	0	0	0
Retire Unit	RU	0	0	0	0
System Management Mode Unit	SMMU	2	2.8	3	3.3
Ambiguous Location	???	2	2.8	* *	
Total		43	58.9	46	50.5

*   **The affected function is in the CAA.**
* * **The affected functions are also ambiguous.**

Figure 4: The Performance Delivery Architecture of the Pentium II

The PDA implementation utilizes about 95% of the transistors in Pentium II, leaving only 5% to the CAA implementation [29]. The logic decomposition of the PDA used in our study is shown in Figure 4. The figure also shows the number of errata discovered in each logic unit, along with affected functions. Note that the number of affected functions (46) is greater than the number of errata (43), since some errata affect more than one function. This comment also applies to Figure 5. Further discussion follows in Section 4.5.

4.2.2 The Confidence Assurance Architecture (CAA) The Pentium II processor has a sophisticated set of CAA-related features. It provides parity checking for many on-chip storage elements such as instruction and data caches, translation look-aside buffer, and microcode storage arrays. It protects the system bus with parity checking, error-correcting codes, and protocol features. It also has a "Machine Check Architecture" (MCA) that provides comprehensive error logging and reporting functions for every on-chip internal physical component. In addition, Pentium II has introduced the System Management Mode to handle system-wide functions and added on-chip debugging support. The master/checker duplexing technique has been implemented as the Functional Redundancy Checking mode. To increase its testability, Pentium II contains the Test Access Port architecture which is compatible with the IEEE 1149.1 JTAG Boundary Scan standard. Some other features

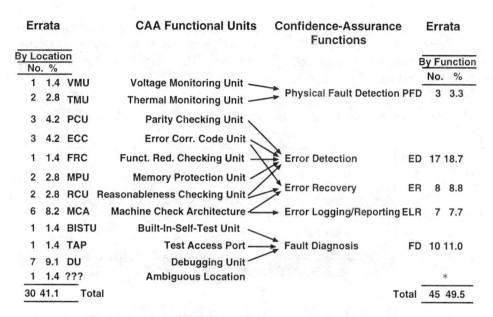

Errata		CAA Functional Units	Confidence-Assurance Functions	Errata	

By Location · By Function

No.	%				No.	%
1	1.4	VMU	Voltage Monitoring Unit			
2	2.8	TMU	Thermal Monitoring Unit	Physical Fault Detection PFD	3	3.3
3	4.2	PCU	Parity Checking Unit			
3	4.2	ECC	Error Corr. Code Unit			
1	1.4	FRC	Funct. Red. Checking Unit	Error Detection ED	17	18.7
2	2.8	MPU	Memory Protection Unit			
2	2.8	RCU	Reasonableness Checking Unit	Error Recovery ER	8	8.8
6	8.2	MCA	Machine Check Architecture	Error Logging/Reporting ELR	7	7.7
1	1.4	BISTU	Built-In-Self-Test Unit			
1	1.4	TAP	Test Access Port	Fault Diagnosis FD	10	11.0
7	9.1	DU	Debugging Unit			
1	1.4	???	Ambiguous Location	*		
30	41.1	Total		Total	45	49.5

* **The affected functions are also ambiguous (A10)**

Figure 5: The Confidence Assurance Architecture of the Pentium II

such as memory protection, and invalid instruction detection are also employed. Finally, it also provides temperature and voltage monitoring features to detect faulty physical conditions.

Figure 5 shows the CAA functional units and the corresponding confidence-assurance (CA) functions. The numbers of errata occurring in each location and affecting each function are also shown, which are discussed in Section 4.5.

4.3 The μp-Design Fault Model

The attributes that are specific to the Intel Pentium II are as follows:

1. **Configuration.** In the Pentium II, three configurations are supported in terms of number of used processors: (1) Uniprocessor (UP), (2) Multiprocessor (MP), and (3) Functional-Redundancy-Checking (FRC). The FRC is a master/checker duplex configuration that may be substituted for a single processor in UP or MP configuration.

2. **Operation mode.** There are five operation modes available: (1) Start; (2) Test; (3) Normal, including both real-address and protection modes; (4) System Management Mode, and (5) Recovery.

3. **Affected Element.** While the logic units of the PDA are identified in Figure 4, the affected logic units of the CAA are also identified by the functions

that they provide. This improves the convenience of understanding and analysis. The affected CAA functions could be any one of the following: Error Detection, Error Logging/Reporting, Error Recovery, Fault Diagnosis, and Physical Fault Detection.

4.4   Classification of the Errata of Pentium II

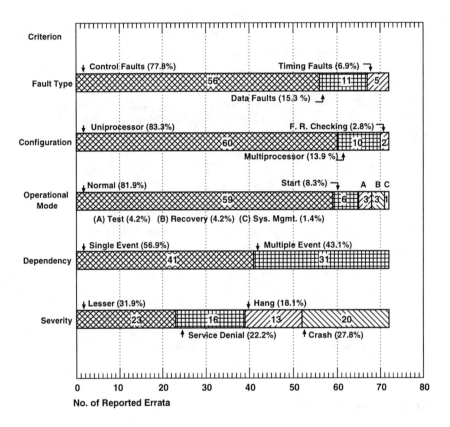

Figure 6: Classification of errata according to five criteria

Using the DFT, 73 errata reported in [3] have been classified as shown in Figures 4, 5, and 6. The numbers (e.g., A7) in the following discussion refer to the erratum numbers used in [3]. Three comments apply to the classification:

1. In Figures 4 and 5, an additional category, labeled "Ambiguous location", has been added for both the PDA and the CAA. This is used to indicate those errata whose location cannot be uniquely decided with the information provided in the errata list. The best we can do is to decide its location at the highest level (PDA or CAA).

   For example, A45 occurs under 3 distinct conditions that involve a memory load instruction, a floating-point instruction, and a MMX instruction, respectively. It is clearly located in the PDA. However, it is not certain whether the erratum occurs in the MMU, the FPU, or the MMXU.

Another example is A10. It is an erratum causing the BIST to behave improperly under the FRC mode. Again, it is not clear if it is due to an erratum in the BIST unit, or one in the FRC unit. The only conclusion that can be drawn is that it is located in the CAA.

2. Figures 4 and 5 show that the total number of PDA and CAA functions affected by 73 reported errata is 91. This is due to the fact that some errata have "global" effects and affect more than one function.

   For example, A7 occurs in the System Management Mode Unit. However, it affects not only the SMM unit, but also the Debugging Unit with a stale value of instruction address that is subsequently used by the DU.

3. Figure 6 shows the distribution of the 73 errata by configuration of the system. While an erratum that affects a UP configuration will also affect a MP configuration, the MP errata are unique to MP configuration.

4.5 Analysis

4.5.1 By Location. Figure 4 shows that 43 (about 59%) errata occur in the PDA, where over half of these errata cluster in the Bus Interface Unit and the Memory Management Unit. These functional units are inherently more complex. For example, the BIU is an interface between three internal units of the microarchitecture (the FDU, the DEU and the RU), the L2-cache and the system memory. It has been designed to support a sophisticated synchronous latched bus protocol with pipelining and parking features.

It is also observed that 5 errata affect the Floating Point Unit. 2 of them lead to incorrect results, 2 cause control errors, and one causes early execution of an instruction. Given that similar FPU designs have been used since the Pentium processor, it is surprising that these errata still occur.

Figure 5 shows that 30 (about 41%) errata occur in the CAA, fewer than in the FDA. This does not imply that the CAA is better verified than the PDA. On the contrary, when the relative size of the CAA (about 5%) [29] is taken into account by defining the *fault density* as the number of faults per unit of size (measured by the number of transistors), it is seen that the CAA has the fault density of $30/.05 = 600$, over 13 times that of the PDA ($43/.95 \approx 45.3$)! The vulnerability of the CAA is a very serious problem for high-confidence systems.

4.5.2 By Type. In Figure 6, 3 of the 5 timing faults are located in the BIU. As mentioned earlier, the BIU employs a sophisticated high-performance bus protocol with pipelining and parking features. All 3 BIU-related timing faults cause timing violations of the protocol. Specifically, A29 causes early deassertion of the lock signal; A42 causes missing a required cycle; and A53 causes incorrect order of two bus transactions. The 2 remaining timing faults cause either a late signaling of a floating-point exception (A31), or an early execution of an instruction (A45).

11 errata are data faults that occur in various locations and cause incorrect values in an address register (A1), in a data register (A23), etc. In particular, 4 of them occur in the MCA and the DU. For example, A13 causes an error in L2 cache to be incorrectly logged with a code indicating an error in L1 cache.

Figure 6 shows that the majority of 73 errata are control faults . While they can be basically divided into two classes: *missing* and *incorrect* control functions, our study finds that control faults exhibit more complicated scenarios and can be better characterized by such semantic patterns as: "it does not do function A" (A3), "it only does part of the specified function A" (A2), or "it should do A but instead it does B" (A5), etc.

4.5.3 By Triggering Condition.   The analysis of the errata in the CAA reveals that the majority of them (22 out of 30) are activated by a single event. For example, the BIST always signals *"fail"* regardless of whether the test actually passes or fails (A35).   Another example is that in the Functional-Redundancy-Checking (FRC) mode, if the checker encounters a hard failure while running the BIST, the checker will tri-state all of its outputs without raising an error signal (A10). The results indicate that verification of the CAA has not been as good as that of the PDA. We note that the verification of CAA requires exercising its functions under the expected abnormal conditions through fault injection - a difficult task.

In addition, Figure 6 shows that 32 errata are activated by a sequence of events, and 41 errata are activated by a single event. For example, the erratum A23 in the L2 cache performance monitoring counter causes an incorrect count value due to a retried request. In addition, 24 errata are activated during normal operation mode in the uniprocessor configuration by a sequence of two or more events. This suggests that verification of a single processor still remains a challenge with the increase in its complexity, and that verification of the multiprocessor configuration has a very long way to go.

4.5.4 By Effect.   Figure 6 indicates that 50 (about 68%) errata have severe consequences, causing either denial of a function, a hang, or a crash. It should be noted that the analysis is based on the *Implications* part of [3] which only gives the direct effect.   As a result, those errata that seem to cause only *lesser* errors could lead to more severe consequences. For example, due to A25, when the floating-point instruction, FIST, is executed, some out-of-range operands will not be detected as invalid. What if this undetected erroneous result is used to make a crucial decision in mission-critical applications?

Figure 5 shows that about 50% of all functions affected by errata are CAA functions. For example, the Error Detection function is affected by 17 errata, some of which cause a false alarm (A20), a failure to raise a detection signal (A10), etc. It appears that built-in CAA-related functions themselves, that are supposed to provide trustworthiness, cannot be trusted in the first place!

Out of 73 errata, 44 are labeled with "NoFix", which according to the definition by Intel, means that "there are no plans to fix this erratum" [3]. While some of them have appeared in recent steppings, there are 15 errata (A1-A15) that were reported in the first release of the Specification Update (May, 1997) and have remained un-fixed. The reasons behind the decision have not been provided but it would be helpful to know, whether it is due to failure to find the root cause of the errata, or to the cost of modification.

A further analysis of *Workarounds* provided by Intel makes the case even worse. 15 errata are not provided with a *workaround* at all and most of them affect the CAA-related functions. For example, A12 causes that the Machine Checking Ex-ception handler may not always execute successfully, which essentially limits the MCA's role in error recovery. In case of those errata for which *workarounds* are pro-vided, some need compensation from the BIOS, or the operating system, and some only suggest "not to use the affected function". For example, due to A9, break-point trap and branch trace messages will not work together. The only makeshift *workaround* available is not to use both simultaneously. It is evident that the er-rata not only degrade the high performance of COTS microprocessors, but also pose tremendous challenges for building COTS-based fault-tolerant systems. Con-sequently, the trustworthiness of these COTS microprocessors cannot be taken for granted and needs to be assessed carefully in a fault-tolerant system.

5 Summary and Conclusions

5.1 The Main Results

The study has revealed several significant facts about the state of the art in high-performance microprocessor design. First, it is evident that regardless of all veri-fication efforts, significant design faults ("errata") of varied nature are discovered after production has begun. The discoveries continue to occur at a fairly steady rate even years after the first stepping of the processor has reached the market, as shown in Table 1 and Figure 2.

Second, while there is no doubt that the manufacturers are doing their best to eliminate the errata in the steppings released after their discovery, more than half of all errata are in the "NoFix" category, i.e., the decision has been made to let them remain in all subsequent steppings until the end of production. There is even the unusual case of nine new errata appearing in a new stepping. Figures 2 and 3 illustrate this observation.

Third, the effects of the errata are frequently catastrophic - nearly half cause a crash or hang of the entire processor, as shown in Figure 6. The workarounds provided with the errata list are costly. They usually involve the BIOS or operating system, or simply suggest that the affected function should not be used. Over 20% of the errata have no suggested workaround at all.

Fourth, it has been our experience that in order to identify and to understand the attributes of the errata it was necessary to acquire a thorough understanding of the logic structure and the functions of the processor. The information is contained within some 2000 pages of manuals and is not always easy to locate. Especially, the description of the CA functions is scattered throughout the vast bulk of the literature. In spite of our intensive effort, some ambiguities of location and effect were left unresolved and are so noted in Figures 4 and 5.

Fifth and worst, Figures 4 and 5 show that the CA functions which utilize about 5% of the transistors are affected by 50% of the errata manifestations. That is about 20 times higher vulnerability (per unit of size) than that of performance delivery functions that utilize the remaining 95% of the transistors. The defenses are by far the most likely part of the processor to fail when the errata manifest themselves!

5.2 Conclusions of this Study

Several conclusions can be drawn from the results of our work. First, the existence of the errata list and the continuing discovery of new errata that were there since the initial release of the COTS processor exert a severe stress on the designers who employ the processor in critical applications, especially in embedded systems. Can they adequately verify that none of the known errata will cause catastrophic failures? And what do they do about errata that are discovered after the system has been put into operation? How many system failures that were attributed to software bugs or human error were actually caused by the previously unknown (or even known, but not circumvented) errata? Such questions are challenges that did not exist just a few years ago, when the microprocessor was a trustworthy foundation for a high-confidence system. Now they pose an additional demand that cannot be deferred or ignored.

The second conclusion is that currently the information on "errata" is hard to find and difficult to use. Only two of seven major manufacturers (listed in Section 2.3) offer information on the errata in their processors at their Web sites. They are Intel and Motorola. The errata information is presented quite differently, with Intel offering a more comprehensive and better organized document; yet even this document is not adequately user-friendly. It is evident that the best interests of the customers demand that the *Errata Updates* should follow a standard, user-friendly format that could evolve from the Intel *Updates*. We intend to continue our search for the errata lists of the other five manufacturers - are they treated as confidential information? That remains to be discovered.

The final conclusion is that the rapid proliferation of μp design faults ("errata", or better: "microbugs") as the complexity of the processors keeps following Moore's Law is likely to lead to a chaotic situation caused by unmanageable errata lists and the existence of numerous as yet undiscovered errata. Even worse, the CA functions have been shown to be most vulnerable to the effects of errata. To avoid this crisis, it is necessary to change the design of the CA infrastructure of the processors. A rigorous and comprehensive design approach that makes design faults less probable (as outlined in [10]) must replace the current *ad hoc* introduction of more CA functions as the processors become more complex. The next step is even more challenging - the CA infrastructure must be augmented to be able to cope with the manifestations of the "microbugs", and to circumvent their effects after they have been located. Such capabilities are still beyond the state-of-the-art, but they will be indispensable within a few years, when the 100 million transistor, one gigahertz chips arrive on the scene.

5.3   Continuation of Our Research

This exercise in microprocessor entomology was started with the hope that our taxonomy of the "microbugs" would contribute to three objectives. First, it should help to design high-confidence systems containing processors with known and yet unknown errata. Second, it should provide the impetus to devise advanced design methodologies to avoid the "microbugs", and advanced fault-tolerance techniques to tolerate the effects of the inevitable left-over ones. Third, it should provide insights that lead to more powerful verification techniques that would have found the surviving "microbugs" prior to production.

We have confidence that the results are definitely supportive of the first two objectives and we are working in both areas. In the first, we investigate means of external detection and recovery support to assist in recovering from the effects of "microbugs". We also work on errata-oriented fault injection experiments to evaluate the effectiveness of such external support.

In the second, the design paradigm for the systematic design of fault-tolerance infrastructure [10] is being augmented to deal with the effects of "microbugs" in the PDA as well as within the CAA (fault-tolerance functions) themselves.

In the area of verification, we hope that our colleagues in that community will find our work useful and come back with suggestions of what additional work would benefit them most.

Finally, as an interim solution to the errata problem, we suggest that a tiny label be stuck on every high-performance microprocessor that reads: "Handle with Care! Microbugs Inside".

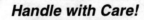

Figure 7: An Interim Solution

References

[1] Intel Corporation. *Pentium Processor Specification Update*, January 1999. Order No: 242480-041.

[2] Intel Corporation. *Pentium Pro Processor Specification Update*, January 1999. Order No: 242689-035.

[3] Intel Corporation. *Pentium II Processor Specification Update*, April 1999. Order No: 243337-025.

[4] Intel Corporation. *Mobile Pentium II Processor Specification Update*, April 1999. Order No: 243887-009.

[5] Intel Corporation. *Intel Celeron^{TM} Processor Specification Update*, March 1999. Order No: 243748-013.

[6] Intel Corporation. *Pentium II Xeon^{TM} Processor Specification Update*, April 1999. Order No: 243776-012.

[7] Intel Corporation. *Pentium III Processor Specification Update*, April 1999. Order No: 243776-002.

[8] Intel Corporation. *Pentium III Xeon^{TM} Processor Specification Update*, April 1999. Order No: 243776-002.

[9] A. Avižienis and J. P. J. Kelly. Fault tolerance by design diversity: concepts and experiments. *Computer*, 17(8):67–80, August 1984.

[10] A. Avižienis. Toward systematic design of fault-tolerant systems. *Computer*, 30(4):51–58, April 1997.

[11] Intel Corporation. *Pentium Pro Family Developers' Manual*, 1996. Volumes 1, 2, 3.

[12] R. Chillarege et al. Orthogonal defect classification - a concept for in-process measurement. *IEEE Trans. Software Eng.*, 18(11):943–956, November 1992.

[13] R. P. Colwell. Latent design faults in the development of Multiflow's TRACE/200. In *Digest of FTCS-22*, pages 468–474, June 1992.

[14] B. A. Wichmann. Microprocessor design faults. *Microprocessors and Microsystems*, 17(7):399–401, September 1993.

[15] O. Sibert, P. A. Porras, and R. Lindell. An analysis of the Intel 80x86 security architecture and implementations. *IEEE Transactions on Software Engineering*, 22(5):283–293, May 1996.

[16] J. C. Laprie, editor. *Dependability: Basic Concepts and Terminology*. Springer-Verlag, 1992.

[17] Intel Corporation. *Intel Architecture Software Developer's Manual, Vol. 1: Basic Architecture*, 1997. Order No. 243190.

[18] Intel Corporation. *Intel Architecture Software Developer's Manual, Vol. 2: Instr uction Set Reference Manual*, 1997. Order No. 243191.

[19] Intel Corporation. *Intel Architecture Software Developer's Manual, Vol. 3: System Programming Guide*, 1997. Order No. 243192.

[20] Intel Corporation. *Addendum - Intel Architecture Software Developer's Manual, Vol. 1: Basic Architecture*, 1997. Order No. 243691-001.

[21] Intel Corporation. *Addendum - Intel Architecture Software Developer's Manual, Vol. 2: Instruction Set Reference Manual*, 1997. Order No. 243689-001.

[22] Intel Corporation. *Addendum - Intel Architecture Software Developer's Manual, Vol. 3: System Programming Guide*, 1997. Order No. 243690-001.

[23] Intel Corporation. *Pentium II Processor Developer's Manual*, October 1997. Order No. 243502-001.

[24] Intel Corporation. *P6 Family Of Processors Hardware Developer's Manual*, September 1998. Order No. 244001-001.

[25] Intel Corporation. *Datasheet - Pentium II Processor at 233 MHz, 266 MHz, 300 MHz, and 333 MHz*, January 1998. Order No. 243335-003.

[26] Intel Corporation. *Datasheet - Pentium II Processor at 350 MHz, 400, and 450 MHz*, August 1998. Order No. 243657-003.

[27] R. Collins. Intel secret. http://www.x86.org/.

[28] Intelligent Firmware Ltd. The Intel x86 processor performance flaw. http://www.intelligentfirm.com/, 1998.

[29] A. Yu. The future of microprocessors. *IEEE Micro*, 16(6):46–53, June 1996.

Assessment of COTS Microkernels by Fault Injection

J.-C. Fabre, F. Salles, M. Rodríguez Moreno, J. Arlat
LAAS-CNRS
7, Avenue du Colonel Roche, 31077 Toulouse cedex, France

Abstract

This paper addresses the problem of using COTS microkernels in safety critical systems. As the behavior in the presence of faults of such basic components is seldom established, it is questionable whether they can be used to develop operating systems for critical applications. The approach proposed for the assessment of a COTS microkernel relies on fault injection as a means to obtain objective insights for the provision of upper layer services. A specific tool (MAFALDA) has been developed to implement this approach. We present and discuss the results obtained when applying the tool to the Chorus ClassiX r3 microkernel. Finally, some lessons learnt from these experiments and plans for future work are described.

1. Introduction

Mainly motivated by economic reasons, the use of COTS (*Commercial Off-The-Shell*) microkernels appears today as an increasingly attractive design alternative in many application fields, including safety critical systems as well (e.g., on-board aerospace systems, railway signaling control systems, etc.).

Microkernels correspond to the last generation of real-time executives. From an engineering viewpoint, this technology is very appealing for flexibility reasons. A dedicated operating system (OS) can be developed on top of the very basic functions provided by a microkernel as a set of basic system services. These services can provide the application programmers with either a standard API (*Application Programming Interface*) such as POSIX, or a proprietary interface as in the ELEKTRA railway signaling system (for being able to run legacy software) [1]. All processes implementing these services run as a microkernel application and thus rely on its capability to detect faulty situations.

The flexibility of this technology is even more convincing when considering open microkernels. Indeed, in this case, the microkernel can be tailored to fit a specific objective or an application field, because it is organized as a set of modules, each instance of which can be selected according to the specific requirements. For example, a given form of scheduling policy (e.g., rate monotonic, earliest deadline first, etc.) can be specified as an off-the-shelf module, during the generation process of a dedicated microkernel. Moreover, a user-defined module can be used instead of a standard one (e.g., a two-level scheduler as in the ARINC 653 standard for aircraft on-board control systems [2]).

The use of microkernels has an additional advantage. Because their specifications are often simple, their behavior can be more easily understood (from available documents). This can be used to define complementary error detection.

The development of safety critical applications often relies on a development process following *de facto* standards such as DO178-B [3]. Beyond the departure from standard requirements, the use of off-the-shelf software is a challenge for many developers of critical systems [4]. The concerns are even more crucial when considering the use of a COTS microkernel, since all applications running on top of it (including OS software) rely on its correct behavior. An error at the application level (either due to a physical fault or a design fault) should not propagate to the microkernel and prevent other applications to run. Conversely, errors affecting the microkernel itself should not propagate uncontrolled to the application level.

This paper elaborates on the challenges and objectives identified in [5]. Here, we describe and apply a methodology that helps one better characterize the behavior of a standard microkernel in the presence of faults. As long as such a behavior is known and —to some extent— predictable, errors can then be handled at the microkernel application level by several fault tolerance strategies. Either generic strategies (e.g., replication in case of microkernel crash) or more application dependent strategies can be defined and developed, when an error status or an exception is returned to the application level. Although timing and scheduling faults are of high interest in real-time applications, currently they are only partially addressed in this paper; work is in progress to address these issues in a more comprehensive way.

The remainder of the paper is organized into 4 Sections. Section 2 describes the motivations and the fault injection-based approach we have adopted for this work, as well as its position with respect to related research. The results presented in this paper have been obtained with a fault injection tool, called MAFALDA (*Microkernel Assessment by Fault injection AnaLysis and Design Aid*) which has been designed and implemented to these aims. The main features of MAFALDA are described in Section 3. A sample of the distributions for faulty behaviors observed for the Chorus ClassiX microkernel distributed by Sun are presented in Section 4. Finally, conclusions and directions for future work are given in Section 5.

2. Behavior analysis of COTS OS

2.1 Motivations

The use of COTS OS poses serious certification problems. It is noteworthy that recent specific efforts for developing the OSE real-time executive [6] have succeeded in its certification according to the IEC 1508 [7]. Although certification aspects are beyond the scope of this paper, we claim that the framework we propose provides a more general and promising approach for the assessment and improvement of the behavior of microkernel-based executives in the presence of faults, and can thus contribute to the certification process.

Because microkernels are not usually designed according to a development methodology recommended for critical software, their behavior may be weak from a dependability viewpoint. This is not surprising at all since their normal usage is often general. Because their size is to be kept small and they are a basic support for OS services, their error detection mechanisms must be enhanced at upper layers. Furthermore, microkernels are used in different target environments with different application profiles, so some classes of primitives may seldom be activated or even not activated at all. Accordingly, some error propagation channels could remain unknown. Finally, because software versions have usually a very short lifetime, it is difficult to improve our confidence on the basis of statistics from field experience.

Clearly, the confidence one can have in a microkernel depends on the impact of its failure modes on the upper levels. The origin of a fault can be physical or due to design or implementation.

2.2 Microkernel fault pathology and validation objectives

As for any software, an activated fault in the microkernel can propagate and lead to various types of failures layers (according to the causal chain fault ➡ error ➡ failure [8]), which may impair temporarily or permanently the delivered services. These failures can be classified according to their severity.

The simpler case is when the microkernel enters an infinite loop or waits for a fictitious event. This can only be handled by external mechanisms, i.e., fault tolerance strategies based on (preferably diversified) replication. Even if of high severity, this situation corresponds to a "fail-silent" behavior of the microkernel, which has benefits from a dependability viewpoint [9].

Alternatively, the fault can lead to an error that is detected by internal error detection mechanisms, either by software mechanisms (assertions, consistency checks, etc.) or by the underlying hardware (illegal memory access, illegal instruction, etc.). The error, notified either by an interrupt or by a returned error status, can respectively be handled at the upper layer, either by exception handling mechanisms or by analyzing the error status. The resulting error processing depends on the severity of the failure of the module: abort or automatic restart of the application software, cold-start of the entire system

Unfortunately, internal error detection mechanisms are not always able to confine an error within the executive software. Indeed, the invocation of a module often relies on complex operations that may involve many synchronous and asynchronous interactions between microkernel components within the same supervisor address space. The error can thus propagate to several modules. When the behavior of the executive no longer matches the functional semantics associated to the microkernel modules, errors may propagate to upper layers software components and remain undetected. This is the highest severity level.

2.3 Overall methodology

As it allows for a detailed analysis of faulty behaviors, fault injection has long been recognized as a pragmatic and efficient means to assess the behavior of complex fault-tolerant computer systems (e.g., see [10,11]). Thus, fault injection is very much suited to help characterize the faulty behavior of COTS executives.

Following our preliminary work presented in [5], we consider that a microkernel is composed of several basic modules. Each module operates on a set of input parameters *In_params* (*I*) and on the current internal state (persistent data structures) of the executive software, called the (executive) *Context* (*Contex_In: Ci*). The invocation of the module impacts the *Context* itself (*Context_Out: Co*), produces output parameters *Out_params* (*O*) and (possibly) returns an error *Status* (*S*). A fault occurring (or being activated) during the execution of a module may affect any of the output attributes *Co*, *O* and *S*. Our interest focuses here on the analysis of the consequences on the output attributes of a fault having led to the alteration of either *I* and *Ci.*

Hence, two forms of fault injection have been selected for the tool we have developed to analyze the behavior of a microkernel in presence of faults: (i) injection on the input parameters, and (ii) injection on the state of the microkernel.

Complementary forms of fault injection such as specific alteration of the functional activity of a module or injection on the output parameters have also been identified (see [5]). For example, the first form can be (i) a wrong sequence of kernel operations invocation, or (ii) additional invocations of kernel operations. The first form is not part of the current implementation of MAFALDA. The second form would be rather suited to the *analysis of the consequences of the faulty behavior* of the microkernel on the upper layers; this case is not considered here.

The objectives of the analyses carried out in this paper are twofold:

1) Statistics obtained can be used to assess the coverage of the error handling mechanisms.

2) Deficiencies can be revealed in the microkernel (including in the error handling mechanisms), thus providing guidance for design improvements; this also encompasses the definition of an appropriate fault tolerance upper layer.

2.4 Related work

Several studies have addressed the assessment of COTS software in the presence of faults [5,12,13]. FINE [14] is a pioneering fault injection tool addressing the assessment of a COTS OS by corrupting the kernel address space.

The main objective of most recent studies is to evaluate the robustness of the application interface: the idea is to observe the behavior of the operating system when input parameters of a given type are corrupted. Among these studies, BALLISTA [13,15] has been developed as an automated tool to analyze several well known POSIX-compliant OS; mainly, system/application crashes or hangs are observed. Comparative results have been obtained. The tool uses the so-called *SoftWare-Implemented Fault Injection* technique (SWIFI for short).

Our approach shares a similar black-box testing philosophy and the same interface robustness evaluation objective. Nevertheless, two main expansions can be identified. First, besides input parameters corruption, fault injection applies also on the internal address space of the executive (both code and data segments). Second, and what is more important, the monitored events extend beyond system and process crashes or hangs; they encompass various exceptions and application failures as well, the latter being the most severe case from our viewpoint. This increased observability allows for a wide range of error cases to be evaluated (e.g., error propagation from the executive to the application level, error propagation within the microkernel itself (covert channels), etc.). These results constitute objective data (i) for characterizing the efficiency of the internal error detection mechanisms of a microkernel and (ii) for assessing the suitability of using such basic software layers in a safety critical application.

3. MAFALDA

The primary objective of MAFALDA is to analyze the behavior of a microkernel in the presence of faults[1]: interface robustness with respect to external faults, error detection coverage of the internal error detection mechanisms, error propagation

---

[1] The *design aid* features supported by MAFALDA are not detailed in this paper.

channels between microkernel internal components and the impact of its faulty behavior on upper layers. MAFALDA is a fault injection tool running on Solaris providing features for the description of a fault injection campaign, the execution the experiments (re-boot, loading, fault injection, etc.) and the collection of observed results for later analysis.

MAFALDA is based on the idea of a modular workload [16] matching the componentized architecture of a microkernel. Most of off-the-shelf microkernels can be seen as composed of several internal modules, each dedicated to a specific class of functionalities: synchronization, task management and scheduling, memory and communication management. Except for basic hardware-dependent machine code, all these modules provide an interface to the applicative level as a set of kernel operations, called primitives. All the primitives related to a given internal module are said to belong to a given class (synchronization class, memory class, tasking class, communication class). A workload process is suitable for exercising the microkernel functionalities corresponding to a given class. Each workload process implements a simple application using almost all available primitives from a given functional class.

The corruption of input parameters aims at evaluating the inherent robustness properties of the microkernel interface. It consists of corrupting a selected parameter before its delivery to the microkernel interface. Such a fault can be interpreted as the consequence of the propagation of an error from the application level to the executive level.

The corruption of memory cells within the memory image of the microkernel at runtime simulates either hardware or software faults. It consists of corrupting a randomly selected memory location of one functional internal module of the microkernel; this aims at characterizing the microkernel behavior in the presence of faults, but also at evaluating error propagation over their internal modules. This form of injection can lead to the propagation of errors from the microkernel to upper layers, thus affecting user application processes. The modular workload approach is an efficient way to activate kernel internal modules selectively, but also to observe inter-module error propagation by analyzing the behavior and the results of each dedicated workload process.

Finally, such results are also expected to be very much useful for focusing on the development of pertinent and cost-effective error handling mechanisms (wrappers) aimed at increasing the dependability properties [12,13]. Moreover, once the failure profile of the candidate microkernel is well established then complementary error detection mechanisms can be developed and fault tolerance strategies can be defined at the upper layer, as suggested in [5]. MAFALDA can further be used to assess objectively the benefits provided by the integrated wrappers (see Section 5).

3.1 Architecture of MAFALDA

MAFALDA is based on a "classical" architecture that integrates three sets of components: components that form the workload to activate the various microkernel functional classes, components that perform fault injection either at the interface or within the microkernel address space, and components monitoring the experiments and devoted to results analysis.

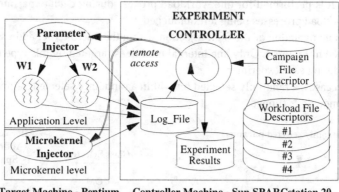

Target Machine - Pentium   Controller Machine - Sun SPARCstation 20
(Chorus/ClassiX r 3.1)   (Solaris 2.5.1)

Figure 2. MAFALDA architecture

Figure 2 depicts these components and their interaction with the Target Machine. A fault injection campaign consists in a loop of individual fault injection experiments. The `Experiment Controller` located in the Controller Machine is responsible for the execution of a fault injection campaign. It is able to reboot the target machine, load the microkernel with a given configuration and interpret the `Campaign File Descriptor`. This file describes (using a specific description language) the type of fault injection experiments that will be performed during the campaign and the workload processes (`Workload File Descriptor`) used to exercise the microkernel functional classes.

The behavior of the `Experiment Controller` depends on the type of fault injection. For a parameter fault injection campaign the `Experiment Controller` loads the `Parameter Injector` on top of the microkernel on the target machine and the various workload processes (`W1`, `W2`, etc.). For a microkernel fault injection campaign the `Experiment Controller` loads the `Microkernel Injector` within the address space of the microkernel on the target machine and the various workload processes. For each experiment, the same workload process is loaded for every microkernel components. During the execution of each experiment, traces are collected and saved in the Log_File and the results of each workload process is stored in Experiment_Results files.

3.2 Fault model

The fault model currently implemented by MAFALDA corresponds only to two types of fault injection. The corruption of the input parameters is described in Figure 3. It is performed for one workload process during each experiment, the others workload processes being left untouched.

The implementation of the fault injection within the microkernel address space is described in Figure 4. Only one internal module is targeted by this type of fault injection during each experiment.

In both cases, a randomly selected bit within a randomly selected parameter or byte in a module is flipped.

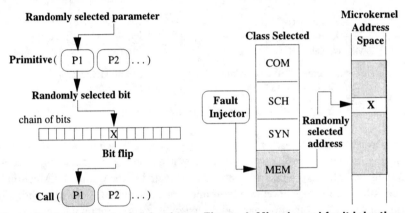

Figure 3. Parameter fault injection   Figure 4. Microkernel fault injection

3.3 Fault injection techniques

Several *SWIFI* techniques have been investigated and led to many fault injection tools like FIAT [17], DOCTOR [18], FERRARI [19], FINE/DEFINE [14,20], SOFIT [21], XCEPTION [22], etc. As in XCEPTION, MAFALDA uses processor debugging facilities to inject both permanent and transient faults. This approach allows monitoring the activation of the faults and also limits the interference with the target executive. This fault injection technique is thus less intrusive than in the previous cases where fault injection is performed by inserting software traps. Because most likely faults are transient, MAFALDA emulates such faults by programming the processor debug registers to stop execution when the control flow reaches the selected location (instruction or data). Then, the fault is injected and a breakpoint is set up to detect the instruction execution or the data access. Finally, the fault is removed by the trace handler routine which resumes execution. Permanent faults are injected in the same way; because they are not removed by the handler routine, the wrong value is kept at the memory location.

MAFALDA uses both spatial and temporal fault triggers: (i) the fault is injected when execution flow accesses a specified memory location either for data read/write access or for instruction fetch; (ii) regarding temporal aspects, a delay from the beginning of the application is set before the fault is injected.

3.4 Experiment description, expected results and analyses

A fault injection campaign with MAFALDA consists in a sequence of actions as described by Figure 5.

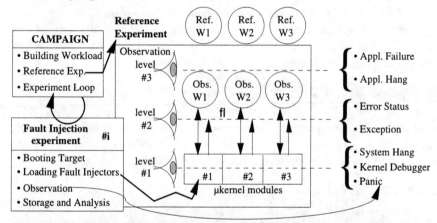

Figure 5. Fault injection campaign with MAFALDA

First, the workload requested in the Campaign File Descriptor is built (step 1) and a Reference Experiment launched without fault injection to obtain the correct results of the application software (step 2). These results will be later used in the analysis as an *Oracle* for the identification of errors propagated to the application level. Then, the loop of individual experiments is launched (step 3). Depending on the type of Fault Injection experiment, memory locations are corrupted either within one single workload process (parameter fault injection) or within one single microkernel internal component (microkernel fault injection). During an experiment round, all workload processes (W1, W2, W3 – one for each microkernel functional class) are executed concurrently and their results collected. These results are always compared to the *Oracle* to identify if one workload process was corrupted (either the injected workload process or a different one). This means that an error has propagated through the microkernel.

Indeed, the various faulty situations that can be identified are observed at three different levels. The upper level (#3) concerns the *application failure*, i.e. wrong application behavior or results (denoted APPFAIL or AF) or the *application hang* (denoted APPHANG). The second level (#2) relates to errors successfully detected by the microkernel error detection mechanisms, *error status* (denoted ERROR STATUS or ES) and *exception* (denoted EXCEPTION or EX). The last observation level (#1) corresponds to low level failures : *system hang, kernel debugger, panic* (denoted respectively SYSHANG, KDB, PANIC) The kernel debugger is activated by internal microkernels built-in mechanisms able to detect some erroneous internal state. This handler enters an infinite loop and provides the user with few basic functions enabling the internal state to be visualized and some simple corrective actions to be carried out. Panic corresponds to a system hang with basic exceptions providing the error location and some state information.

The final result provided by MAFALDA is the distribution of events (error propagation or various error detection events) observed during a fault injection campaign and also the latency of the various exceptions raised.

4. Experiments with a COTS microkernel

The experiments reported in this section have been performed using the Chorus ClassiX r3 microkernel. The various fault injection campaigns are run in parallel on a rack of 10 PC-Pentium machines in order to speed-up the campaign.

4.1 The Chorus ClassiX r3 microkernel

The Chorus ClassiX microkernel [23,24] is an open version of previous versions of this microkernel [25]. It is composed of various internal modules following the categories given below and providing or not primitives at the microkernel interface:
- *Core (COR):* set of primitives for the management of threads and actors (Chorus multi-threaded processes) and hardware related basic functions (e.g., interrupts, timers, traps, MMU, etc.), some of which not belonging to the interface.
- *Synchronization (SYN):* set of primitives for the management and the use of semaphores including mutexes, real-time mutexes, event flags, etc.
- *Memory Management (MEM):* set of primitives for the management and the use of memory segments including functions for flat memory, protected address spaces management policies, address space sharing, etc.

- *Scheduling (SCH):* various off-the-shelf schedulers are available including priority-based FIFO preemptive scheduling or with fixed quanta, Unix Time Sharing or Real-Time policies, etc. This module does not provide directly visible primitives although it handles running threads and actors and is thus indirectly activated by the creation of threads and actors.
- *Communication (COM):* set of primitives for local and remote message passing.

A customized microkernel can be generated from the available off-the-shelf instances of the above internal modules. Also, some of them can be user-defined (a specific scheduler, for instance) and can be used during the generation process, providing thus the users with various options to specialize the microkernel for a given application context. The microkernel and the application processes have separated address spaces; the microkernel is running in supervisor mode while application processes are (normally) running in user mode.

The various fault injection campaigns have been performed using MAFALDA on Chorus ClassiX r3 with the following configuration:
- *SYN:* standard module handling semaphores;
- *MEM:* protected address space management policy;
- *SCH:* priority-based FIFO preemptive scheduling policy;
- *COM:* standard module for local and remote communications.

We report in the sequel of this section the results obtained from the fault injection campaigns. In our experiments, fault injection was applied to the SYN, MEM and COM modules either using microkernel fault injection, in both code (Section 4.2) and data segments (Section 4.3), or using parameter fault injection (Section 4.4). However, fault injection has not yet been carried out directly within the core and scheduling modules. Nevertheless, our workload processes (holding a pre-determined number of threads) have been designed to be deterministic and their scheduling to be known in advance (in the reference execution). Then, corrupting the execution of synchronization primitives (either using microkernel or parameter fault injection) may have an impact on threads scheduling. Such occurrences have been reported in the results presented. Errors like *thread hang* or *deadlock* correspond to *application hang* in the figures, errors like *illegal access to shared resources* and *wrong threads sequencing* leading to incorrect results correspond to the *application failure* case.

4.2 Microkernel fault injection: *code segment*

Distribution of errors. We present here the results obtained by injecting into the code segment of various microkernel modules of our candidate microkernel. The first internal module considered in these experiments is SYN. More than 16000 faults have been injected from which 66% led to non activated faults.

Although such a figure shows the intrinsic difficulty in carrying out significant tests, it is worth noting that the same problem has been found in related work. For instance, in FERRARI such outcomes (labeled "*no error*") were directly excluded from the statistics. In FINE, a similar issue has been observed: 68% of the faults injected have not been activated (labeled "*very long latency*").

Several explanations can be given for such a high percentage of non significant tests:

- the activation of the software module under test does not lead to an internal control flow accessing the injected location;
- the latency is very long and the resulting error cannot be observed during the duration of the experiment;
- the injection applies to unused fields in data structures or in instruction format.

Because of the fault injection technique used in MAFALDA (processor debug registers and handlers), we are sure whether the fault has been activated or not. This allows the first case to be identified although it is still difficult to make the distinction between the two latter, which is a classical concern in fault injection experiments. In the results given below, these two cases are aggregated into a single label, called "*no observation*" (fault activated, but no observed effect). It is clear that only activated faults are of interest and thus subsequent results presented in this section only consider such cases.

About 3000 observed errors led to the following results (see Figure 6-a) . Among these errors, 9% have led the application to fail: i.e. the results obtained were different from the reference results and no detection signal was raised. This means that the error has not been detected by internal error detection mechanisms and has propagated to the application level, corrupting its final results. At the other end, 28.5% of the activated faults fall into the "*no observation*" category.

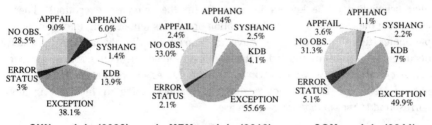

a. SYN module (2986)   b. MEM module (2918)   c. COM module (2944)

Figure 6. Distribution of errors - code segment

Similar experiments have been performed on the memory and communication management microkernel modules (see Figures 6-b, 6-c). With about the same number of errors, slightly different results have been observed, since more exceptions have been raised and less application failures have been observed.

Error propagation. MAFALDA also allows observation of error propagation channels within the microkernel. Indeed, some errors propagate from the injected module to some companion internal modules. For instance, when SYN was the injected module, the propagation has affected the COM and the MEM internal module. Similarly, when MEM and COM are the injected modules, some errors propagate to the two other companion modules, as illustrated in Figure 7.

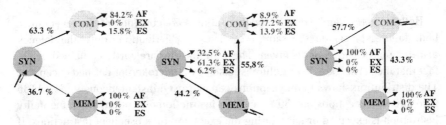

a. SYN module (30/3010)   b. MEM module (181/2924)   c. COM module (26/2970)
Figure 7. Evaluation of error propagation channels - code segment

The results show that a fault injected into a given internal module that propagates to a different module may lead to the following observed events: application failure, error status, exception raised. This means that these events have been observed first in a workload process different from the workload process focusing on the injected internal module. For instance, among the faults that propagated when MEM was the injected module, 44.2% affected SYN and 55.8% affected COM. The propagation has been detected because workload processes for SYN and COM produced wrong results. Additionally, many errors have propagated when the injection was performed into the MEM module (181/2924). Clearly, due to internal dynamic memory allocation, an error in this module strongly affects the behavior of microkernel companion modules.

Exception coverage and error latency. In all experiments, most of the exceptions raised (83%) led to a segment violation (*segFault* exception) when the fault was injected in the code segment of the module. The other exceptions are invalid instruction code (*InvOpCode* in 10%) and co-processor error (*copError* 7%). The same distribution was obtained with all three modules since exception mechanisms are common to all of them.

Error latencies can also be obtained with MAFALDA (see Figure 8).

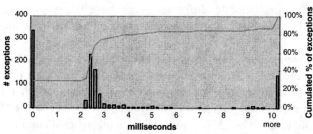

Figure 8. Exception latency - code segment (Example of SYN module)

Both *exceptions* and *kernel debugger* failures are considered. However, since both failures presented the same error latency distribution, only the latency distribution for *exceptions* is given. These similarities are partly explained by the fact that the *kernel debugger* failure is raised by a microkernel-defined exception. The distribution shows that exceptions can be raised instantaneously (340/1135 zero latency exceptions, i.e. 30% - current instruction execution) when the faulty instruction is executed or later during the execution of subsequent instructions. If not raised immediately, 80% of the exceptions are raised with a latency of less than 4 ms. Finally, we can also observe from experimental results that few of them (142, i.e. 12%) are raised with a latency beyond 10 ms. Among them, 42 have been raised before 30 ms and the remaining have been raised beyond 4.5 s. The latter depends very much on the control flow activated by our workload processes.

4.3 Microkernel fault injection: *data segment*

For each microkernel modules, faults are now injected into their data segment. In this case, less faults have been injected and thus less errors have been observed. Clearly, it is very difficult in this case to predetermine the access to data locations because it is very dependent on the control flow activated within the microkernel by the corresponding workload process. On the contrary, when injecting into the code segments, the segment implementation table (address of module primitives) is available at generation time and MAFALDA is able to identify the control flow (trace mode) within the injected module: these elements have been used to speed-up the experiment by selecting specific injected locations.

The number of errors depends also of the size of the data segments and the probability of activation which cannot be known in advance, in this case. Another important parameter is also the duration of the campaign (weeks). For these reasons, the number of observed errors is smaller in this case.

Distribution of errors. The results presented in Figure 9 are slightly different from those obtained in section 4.2. Among 1990 faults injected in the SYN module, 692 errors have been observed. We obtained even less errors for MEM and COM.

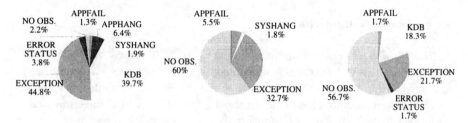

a. SYN module (692/1990)   b. MEM module (56/1986)   c. COM module (60/1985)
Figure 9. Distribution of errors - data segment

Error propagation. In the experiments carried out, no error propagation to other modules was observed when injecting into the COM module data segment. Figure 10 shows the error propagation results for the SYN and MEM modules.

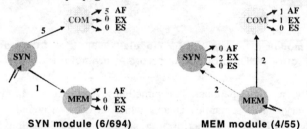

SYN module (6/694)   MEM module (4/55)
Figure 10. Evaluation of error propagation channels - data segment

Exception coverage and error latency. The results obtained in this case are different from those given previously in section 4.2. It is worth noting that no immediate exceptions are observed in this case, as shown in Figure 11.

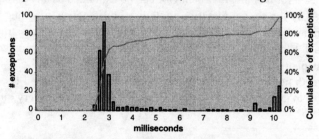

Figure 11. Exception latency - data segment (Example of SYN module)

This is not surprising since a wrong data value, when injected, does not have an immediate effect but later in the program execution. Also, less than 80% of exceptions were raised before 4 ms. Some exceptions have been raised beyond 10 ms (27/310, i.e. less than 10%). Again, this depends on the workload activity.

4.4 Parameter fault injection

Distribution of errors. Flipping a single bit at the interface of a primitive should enable the control checks performed by the microkernel on parameters delivered during the call to be evaluated. Although all injected faults have been activated, some did not lead to an observed effect. This type of injection was performed on the three modules leading to the results presented in Figure 12.

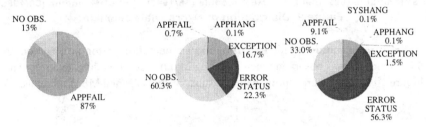

a. SYN module (994)   b. MEM module (1968)   c. COM module (1999)
Figure 12. Distribution of errors - parameter fault injection

Actually, a faulty parameter is sometimes very difficult to detect since it requires very clever semantics checks which are not provided by a standard microkernel. For instance, performing such type of injection in primitives parameters of the synchronization module leads to the application failure in 87 % of the cases (illegal access to a critical section, resources no longer accessed, thread hang). The remaining 13% correspond to an unobserved effect (fault masked, or very long latency).

The reason for this *singular* behavior can be explained as any parameter value is accepted by the synchronization module[2]. For instance, a wrong semaphore queue number leads to the creation of a new semaphore queue data structure in the microkernel. When the number of token of a release request is corrupted, the value of the semaphore is just changed without any additional control..

It is worth noting that the above results have been observed for the use of semaphores in user mode with Chorus ClassiX r3 and could be very different with

---

[2] Roughly speaking, the parameter of several primitives of the SYN module is a single data structure composed of three fields (queue_key, blocked_threads, semaphore_count) plus some unused bytes.

another candidate microkernel; this is very implementation dependent. In particular, the use of semaphores in supervisor mode leads to different results (see Figure 13). The reason for this is that the control flow of the primitives in supervisor mode is very different. Input parameters are not processed in the same way by the primitives: for instance, a corrupted identifier of a semaphore queue (unknown queue id.) leads to the creation of a new queue when running in user mode while it leads to an error detection when running in supervisor mode (exception, panic, KDB, system hang). The reason for this is that the kernel is confident with the given parameters and makes a straight usage of them. The proportion of undetected failures is still very high in this case, strengthening the need for additional checks (see [5]).

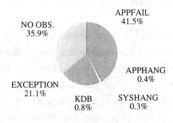

(987)

Figure 13. Distribution of errors - SYN primitives in supervisor mode

Error status coverage, exceptions, error propagation and latency. The most important outcomes provided by the microkernel regarding parameter fault injection is an error status returned to the user application, such as *K_INVAL* (some inconsistent process id) or *K_UNKNOWN* (process not reachable), etc. The type of exceptions that we observed are very limited and only one was raised in these experiments, *segFault* (segment violation). Also, few errors propagated from one module to another. In this case also, most propagated errors have been observed when injecting within the memory module which is a central one often used by internal companion modules (dynamic memory allocation).

Finally, latencies in this case showed a different distribution for the memory module (see Figure 14); three populations can be observed centered at 3, 5, 7 ms, these values being related to the way our workload uses the different memory primitives. For example, a faulty memory buffer allocation will be detected when a data structure in the workload process are mapped into the memory buffer. Also some exceptions have a very high latency and are over 10 ms.

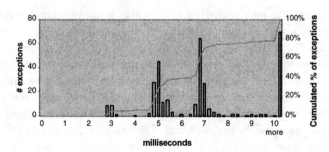

Figure 14. Exception latency - parameter fault injection (MEM module)

5. Conclusion and future work

The decision to include COTS microkernels in safety critical systems clearly calls for specific environments for evaluating they behavior in the presence of faults. A clear understanding of their failure modes enables the operating system software built on top of their basic functionalities to take into account such events, either for placing the system in a safety state or trying to tolerate the fault. However, in many safe critical systems, it is mandatory customizing even the very basic functions of the COTS microkernel. Thus, it is unlikely that relevant statistical figures can be obtained due to the limited number of *instances* in use.

Indeed, the primary interest of MAFALDA is to obtain quantitative results on a *single instance of a given microkernel*, whatever are its functionalities and composition in terms of standard, customized and user-defined modules. These results enable the designer of a safety critical system to take appropriate decisions regarding the use of the microkernel in a system. In order to understand whether or not a given candidate can be used, one has also to define the profile of the workload activity for a given application domain. This profile can change the activation of the microkernel and could lead to different results; according to our experience, changing the profile of workload processes does not impact very much the results. The same internal error detection mechanisms are used whatever the control flow is within the microkernel. However, this has to be confirmed by more intensive experiments. It is worth noting that running applications in supervisor mode (as illustrated in Section 4.4) may have a strong impact on the behavior of the microkernel.

Although reasonably good for off-the-shelf microkernels not designed to deal with all possible faulty situations, it is worth noting that the results we obtained may not be acceptable for safety critical systems and applications. Of course, different results could be obtained for a different candidate microkernel. A comparison of these results with several microkernels (e.g., VxWorks) is one of our next objectives. This involves updating MAFALDA with a Virtual Microkernel Interface, *VMI* (like the VOS in Eternal [26]), to be mapped onto any microkernel interface. This would enable the same workload processes to be used. Nevertheless, some additional features of the new target microkernel involve revisiting the workload processes. In this case different results could be obtained.

Our current work focuses on performing fault injection into the core and scheduling modules, in order to extend the preliminary study of the impact of a fault on processes scheduling sketched in this paper. The main difficulty is to design a specific workload able to detect faulty situations.

The main insight from this work is that the use of a COTS microkernel in a safety critical system requires additional semantic checks to achieve better error processing efficiency. This point is currently being investigated by implementing fault containment wrappers able to perform these checks. These wrappers are based on a formal specification of the various functional classes corresponding to the microkernel modules. Such specification can be easily extracted from the available documents as the semantics of the few microkernel functions is often simple and well known. Nevertheless, the black box approach is a very limiting factor and we are currently investigating a reflective approach to facilitate the implementation of wrappers. According to our first experiments with this approach [5], the results obtained are far better in some cases (the high proportion of application failure with parameter fault injection in the synchronization module can be significantly reduced) and give more confidence in a COTS microkernel for use in safety critical systems. This is why MAFALDA is also a good tool for *Design Aid.*

Acknowledgment. This work was partially supported by ESPRIT Project 20072, Design for Validation (DeVa).

6. References

[1]   H. Kantz and C. Koza, "The Elektra Signalling System: Field Experience with an Actively Replicated System with Diversity", in *Proc. 25th IEEE Int. Symp. on Fault-Tolerant Computing,* Pasadena, CA, USA, 1995, pp. 453-458.

[2]   ARINC-653, "Avionics Application Software Standard Interface (ARINC Specification 653)", ARINC Working Group (www.arinc.com/home.html), Annapolis, MA, USA, 1997.

[3]   DO-178B, "Software Considerations in Airborne Systems and Equipment Certification", DO178B/ED12B, Radio Technical Commission for Aeronautics (RTCA), European Organization for Civil Aviation Electronics (EUROCAE), 1992.

[4]   IEE, "Colloquium on COTS and Safety Critical Systems", Digest no. 97/013, Inst. of Electronical Eng., Computing and Control Division, 1997.

[5]   F. Salles, J. Arlat and J. C. Fabre, "Can We Rely on COTS Microkernels for Building Fault-Tolerant Systems?", in *Proc. Sixth IEEE Computer Society Workshop on Future Trends of Distributing Computing System),* Tunis, Tunisia, 1997, pp. 189-194.

[6]   OSE, "OSE Realtime Kernel", ENEA, P.O. Box 232, Nytorpswagen 5B, SE-183 Taby, Sweden (see http://www.enea.se/ose/products/RTK.htm), 1997.

[7]   IEC-1508, "Functional Safety: Safety-Related Systems", International Electronical Commission SC65A, 1995.

[8]   J.-C. Laprie, "Dependable Computing: Concepts, Limits, Challenges", in *Proc. 25th IEEE Int. Symp. on Fault-Tolerant Computing. Special Issue,* Pasadena, USA, 1995, pp. 42-54.

[9]   D. Powell, G. Bonn, D. Seaton, P. Veríssimo and F. Waeselynck, "The Delta-4 Approach to Dependability in Open Distributed Computing Systems", in *Proc. 18th IEEE Int. Symp. on Fault-Tolerant Computing Systems,* Tokyo, Japan, 88, pp. 246-251.

[10] J. Arlat, M. Aguera, L. Amat, Y. Crouzet, J.-C. Fabre, J.-C. Laprie, E. Martins and D. Powell, "Fault Injection for Dependability Validation — A Methodology and Some Applications", *IEEE Transactions on Software Engineering,* vol. 16, pp. 166-182, Feb. 90.

[11] M.-C. Hsueh, T. Tsai and R. Iyer, "Fault Injection Techniques and Tools", *Computer,* vol. 30, pp. 75-82, April 97.

[12] J. M. Voas, "Certifying Off-the-Shelf Software Components", Computer, vol. 31, pp. 53-59, June 1998.

[13] P. Koopman, J. Sung, C. Dingman, D. Siewiorek and T. Marz, "Comparing Operating Systems using Robustness Benchmarks", in *Proc. 16th IEEE Symp. on Reliable Distributed Systems,* Durham, NC, 1997, pp. 72-79.

[14] W. Kao, R. K. Iyer and D. Tang, "FINE: A Fault Injection and Monitoring Environment for Tracing the UNIX System Behavior under Faults", *IEEE Transactions on Software Engineering,* vol. 19, pp. 1105-1118, 1993.

[15] N. P. Kropp, P. J. Koopman and D. P. Siewiorek, "Automated Robustness Testing of Off-The-Shelf Software Components", in *Proc. of the 28th IEEE Symp. on Fault Tolerant Computing,* Munich, Germany, 1998, pp. 230-239.

[16] A. Mukhejee and D. Siewiorek, "Measuring Software Dependability by Robustness Benchmarking", *IEEE Transactions on Software Engineering,* vol. 23, pp. 366-378, 1997.

[17] Z. Segall, D. Vrsalovic, D. Siewiorek, D. Yaskin, J. Kownacki, J. Barton, D. Rancey, A. Robinson and T. Lin, "FIAT — Fault Injection-based Automated Testing Environment", in *Proc. 18th IEEE Int. Symp. on Fault-Tolerant Computing,* Tokyo, Japon, 1988, pp. 102-107.

[18] S. Han, K. G. Shin and H. A. Rosenberg, "DOCTOR: An IntegrateD SOftware Fault InjeCTiOn EnviRonment for Distributed Real-Time Systems", in *Proc. IEEE Int. Symp. Computer Performance and Dependability,* 1995, pp. 204-213.

[19] G. A. Kanawati, N. A. Kanawati and J. A. Abraham, "FERRARI: A Flexible Software-Based Fault and Error Injection System", *IEEE Trans. on Computers,* vol. 44, pp. 248-260, 1995.

[20] W.-L. Kao and R. K. Iyer, "DEFINE: A Distributed Fault Injection and Monitoring Environment", in *Fault-Tolerant Parallel and Distributed Systems,* (D. Pradhan and D. R. Avresky, Eds.), pp. 252-259, Los Alamitos, CA, USA: IEEE Press, 1995.

[21] D. R. Avresky and P. K. Tapadiya, "A Framework for Developing a Software-based Fault Injection Tool for Validation of Software Fault-Tolerant Techniques under Hardware Faults", in *Proc. 2nd ISSAT Int. Conf. on Reliability and Quality in Design,* Orlando, USA, 1995.

[22] J. Carreira, H. Madeira and J. G. Silva, Xception: A Technique for the Experimental *Evaluation of Dependability in Modern Computers,* IEEE Transaction on Software Engineering, vol. 24, pp. 125-136, 1998.

[23] Chorus systems, "Chorus/ClassiX r3 - Technical Overview", Technical Report CS/TR-96-119.8, 1996.

[24] Chorus systems, "Chorus/ClassiX r3.1b for ix86 - Product Description", Technical Report CS/TR-96-221.1, 1996.

[25] M. Rozier et al., "Overview of the CHORUS Distributed Operating Systems", Technical Report CS/TR-90-25.1, Chorus systemes, 1991.

[26] S. Landis and S. Maffeis, "Building Reliable Distributed Systems with Corba", *Theory and Practice of Object Systems, Special Issue on the Future of Corba 3,* vol. 3, pp. 59-66, 1997.

Coping with COTS

Minimalist Recovery Techniques for Single Event Effects in Spaceborne Microcontrollers

D. W. Caldwell*, D. A. Rennels*
University of California, Los Angeles, CA 90024
doug@cs.ucla.edu, rennels@cs.ucla.edu

Abstract

This paper presents a fault-tolerant design approach to allow the use of non-hardened, commodity microcontrollers as embedded computing nodes in spacecraft, where a high rate of transient errors and occasional latch ups are expected due to the space radiation environment. In order to preserve their primary advantage of high functional density, low-cost approaches were explored that leverage features of existing commercial microcontrollers. A built-in, high-speed serial port is used for voting among redundant devices and a novel wire-OR output voting scheme exploits the bidirectional controls of I/O pins. A fault-tolerant node testbed was implemented, and fault-insertion tests were conducted to test the effectiveness of the fault-tolerance techniques.

1. Introduction

Microcontrollers are highly integrated computer systems on a single low-cost commodity chip containing a processor, program memory, RAM, discrete I/O, A/D converters, serial ports, and other support functions [1,2]. They offer great potential for reducing the cost and increasing the performance of modern spacecraft, but they have not been widely used in space because of their relatively low radiation tolerance. They are susceptible to single event upsets (SEU) which are transient bit-flips, and less frequent but more destructive single event latchups (SEL) which stimulate parasitic circuits within a CMOS device causing a local short that can only be cleared by power-cycling [3,4].

The fault-intolerance approach (radiation-hardening) is costly because rad-hard chips are difficult and time-consuming to develop. Functional density must be sacrificed to the design rules of rad-hard and SEE-immune layout. Because the fabrication technologies for EPROM, program memory, and A/D converters are generally incompatible with each other in rad-hard processes, such functions are

---

* Also with the Jet Propulsion Laboratory, Pasadena, CA

often moved off-chip. Fault-tolerance techniques potentially allow a much wider choice of higher performance devices, supported by a wider range of development tools, which evolve as device families and thus incorporate the latest software development paradigms.

Microcontrollers have little or no built-in fault-tolerance features and, since they are very highly integrated, it becomes an interesting design challenge to protect the features already there (e.g., serial buses, programmable bi-directional I/O pins) while using as few on-chip resources as practical in implementing fault-tolerance. A key constraint is to minimize the amount of external support logic so that the main advantage of microcontrollers' high functional density can be maintained, otherwise it makes more sense to use a microprocessor and design custom I/O.

The architecture presented is intended to handle transient errors and some permanent faults. When viewed from a spacecraft engineering perspective, the subsystem-embedded microcontroller often has a lower permanent failure rate than its host subsystem. If some single points of failure represent a small part of the overall failure rate of the microcontroller, but covering them would significantly add to its complexity, then they may be accepted without significantly compromising the reliability of the host subsystem. Similarly, although we would like to provide uninterrupted computations, an occasional restart of a subsystem is acceptable for most of our applications. Since our fault-tolerance requirements are less stringent than many other applications and our resources are much more constrained, we trade reliability for simplicity [5].

To test the approaches described herein, an inertial measurement unit (IMU) was constructed as an example of a typical spacecraft application and integrated with the microcontroller fault-tolerance testbed.

The techniques described herein are necessarily somewhat *ad hoc* because of the limitations of off-the-shelf devices. We apply well-known fault-tolerance techniques in a different context: How much tolerance can be provided against errors induced by space radiation using redundant microcontrollers with a minimum amount of additional hardware? Most previous work is based on microprocessor designs where the basic computers can be customized by adding a significant amount of circuitry for fault-tolerance, e.g., ECC in memory and custom hardware voters [6]. We achieved substantial improvements in coverage using only an external power switch, isolation resistors, and a couple of low-density programmable chips. We attempted to choose fault-tolerance techniques that apply to a wide range of microcontrollers and to take maximum advantages of their common features, e.g., serial buses for intercommunication of messages for voting and programmable bi-directional I/O pins that can be used to provide a level of I/O protection.

We will discuss very simple techniques which use small amounts of microcontroller resources to yield substantial improvements in fault-tolerance. If one considers that these may be embedded as controllers in a dozen or more subsystems on a small power-constrained spacecraft, the resource limitations become clear.

2. Physical Architecture

The block diagram of a spacecraft subsystem (e.g., an IMU) containing a fault-tolerant set of microcontrollers is shown in Figure 1. Redundant microcontrollers are voted to create an error containment region. At the top of the figure, the subsystem interface is shown as just a source of power and communications. The I/O of multiple microcontrollers are combined and protected by I/O isolation and connected with the sensors and actuators. An External Conflict Resolver circuit may reset or power-cycle the individual microcontrollers to support recovery.

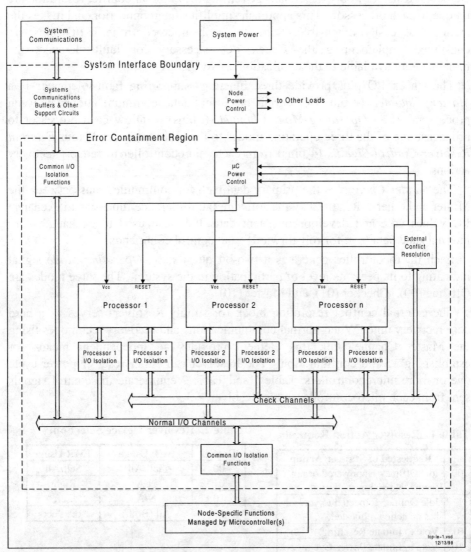

Figure 1. Physical Architecture.

During normal operation, one microcontroller is the Master of the system, while the others provide redundant computation and voting opinions as Checkers.

The Master and Checkers are loosely synchronized and execute identical application programs, periodically calling support functions which implement the fault-tolerance features. If a microcontroller disagrees with its peers, it can be commanded offline and brought back as a Checker if it can be successfully restarted. Devices are not statically assigned, so the operating mode of each device is fluid [7].

Most of the I/O pins of the multiple microcontrollers are bussed together – corresponding pins are connected to a common circuit node through isolation elements (resistors); only the signals governing the external conflict resolution are unique to each processor. This approach simplifies interconnection and makes the architecture easily extensible. Some of each microcontroller's I/O pins are consumed implementing the Check I/O necessary for fault-tolerance; the remainder are available to the application as Normal I/O.

The Check I/O pins provide three functions supporting fault-tolerance: 1) a *Master Channel* (2-pin I^{2}C serial bus) for data communications between processors, 2) an *Operating Mode Channel* (6 pins) to allow each processor to broadcast one of the three operating modes to the other two, and 3) four *External Resolver Control Signals* (4 pins) from each microcontroller to request recovery actions.

The *Master Channel* is the primary data path for communications between the Master and others. It is used by the software fault-tolerance functions to exchange I/O values vote and develop consistent data. It is also used to exchange other internal state data (e.g. for roll-forward) , and control commands.

Each microcontroller generates a two-bit quasi-static *Operating Mode* signal indicating to its peers its level of participation in the system. The three modes are Off-line (00), Checker (01), and Master (10).

The external conflict resolution block (or simply Resolver) serves as a hard core recovery unit. When normal communications and recovery techniques using the Master Channel fail, this element provides an independent means for establishing a valid configuration. The Resolver can either reset or power-cycle one or more microcontrollers. Table 1 and Table 2 enumerate the control signals sent from each microcontroller to the Resolver.

Table 1. Resolver Action Requests.

	Requested of State or Action
00	Idle Offline. Unpowered or not voting. No action requested.
11	Idle Online. Expected to vote but no action requested.
01	Vote to Initiate Resetting.
10	Vote to Initiate Power-Cycling.

Table 2. Resolver Device Selection.

DevSel	SCP Usage	TMR Usage
00	Self/All	Self/All
01	N/A	Right
10	N/A	Left
11	All (Both)	Both Peers

The Action Request bits indicate the state of the microcontroller and whether an action request is being made. When an action is requested, the Device Select bits specify the microcontroller(s) to be acted upon. An action request by a microcontroller directed at itself is immediately taken, but action requests directed at other microcontrollers must be concurred by a peer for the requested action to be taken. The "reset self" combination of Action Request and Device Select is not required since this action can be taken by any device without the aid of the Resolver. Thus, this input combination is redefined to mean "power-cycle all."

Finally, the Microcontroller Power Control block of Figure 1 allows the devices to be power-cycled by the Resolver and also provides some SEL mitigation functions. More details about the hardware may be found in [7,8,11].

3. Application Characteristics

Most microcontroller applications are structured around some real-time task which is executed frequently and periodically [9]. A "real-time frame" is initiated by a real-time interrupt (RTI) and will have many sub-tasks. In the prototypical application investigated, the R-T frame is 62.5 ms long, being initiated by a 16 Hz interrupt. A low-level I/O task samples three rate gyros at 10.8 kHz, and 220 samples are aggregated for each gyro in every frame. After data are gathered, some output results are generated; these may be outputs which will drive physical devices, telemetry data returned to a higher-level (system) application, or state data which will be used as the initial conditions of the next R-T frame.

A number of fault-tolerance processes are required to support this application processing. Before outputs are generated or propagated to the next R-T frame, they must be checked for validity to prevent error propagation. Data may also be checked at various user-defined intermediate points to limit error detection latency. The asynchronous detection of Single-Event Latchup (by external hardware) will result in a device being automatically power-cycled. The loss of any processor, such as due to a peer-commanded reset following a vote should not interrupt processing but is unavoidable in some pathological cases which result in a system restart. Finally, time at the end of the frame is reserved for communicating state data to a previously reset or power-cycled processor to rejoin the voting ensemble as an online member.

4. Fault-Tolerance Functionality Overview

Figure 2 expresses system behavior in a statechart containing four state machines. One of these, SYSTEM_STATE, represents system state as a whole; each of the n microcontrollers operates according to a very similar state machine (PROCESSOR_n_STATE). For each of the n processors, a state machine determines the operating mode of that processor. The aggregate of these operating modes results in a system state which is the mastership of the system.

Initially OFF, the system transitions to a RESET state as soon as any processor is powered. Processors automatically transition from their individual PROCESSOR_RESET states to running code. Initialization codes are executed which perform self-tests, configure I/O and start the processor fault-tolerance (PFT) functions. The first PFT function is to select one of the processors as a Master. When at least two processors are online and have agreed on a Master, the user application starts running. At user-specified locations in the application code, calls are made to PFT functions which implement the fault-detection and recovery functions.

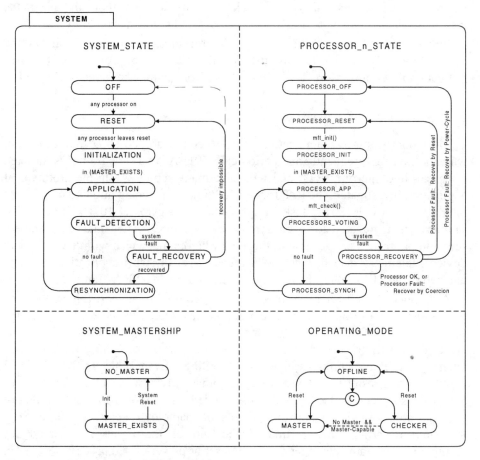

Figure 2. System-Level Statechart.

Fault-detection and isolation are primarily covered by software-implemented voting algorithms. In voting, the Master transmits a packet of data to each Checker. Since both Master and Checkers run the same code, they remain roughly synchronized. Thus, the Checker will reach its voting point at the same time as the Master and start expecting a check-packet. Each Checker computes its own check-packet, compares the received packet with its own, and reports equality (OK) or inequality. If no error is detected, the processors are resynchronized and the application continues.

If an error is identified, correct data are transmitted to the disagreeing member. If a processor does not receive an expected message (identified by a timeout), it can generate an action request to restart the expected sender. If a Checker is restarted, processing continues and the Checker is resynchronized at the next rejoin point specified by the application. If a Master is restarted, the Checkers must detect the corresponding change in the Operating Mode Channel, and have the highest numbered Checker take over as Master to prevent processing disruption. One reason that the Master may go Offline is that current-sensing hardware in the external power control can detect an SEL in the Master at any time and will then immediately power-cycle the Master to clear the latchup. Because the Master is the sole generator of some outputs (e.g., high-speed clocks), an output glitch will occur if the application waits until the next cooperative voting point to deal with the error. Thus, the system must identify this case, select a new Master, and the new Master must reconfigure its outputs to fill the void. If all the processors are restarted, they must revert to a system restart point in the application software.

5. I/O Isolation and Fault-Masking

Circuit isolation is essential in this design: (i) to prevent catastrophic shorts, and (ii) to make it possible to remove power from a module for latchup circumvention. Isolation is provided with resistors in series with the bussed I/O pins of the microcontroller as shown in Figure 3. Pull-down resistors are also employed so that the common output becomes the logical OR of the individual signals.

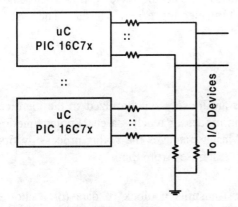

Figure 3: Circuit Isolation

Power must quickly be removed when a latchup is detected, but current from external logic signals leaking through input protection diodes can parasitically power the chip enough to sustain the latchup. In this design when power is removed, Vcc is shorted to ground, and the series resistors divide logic voltages to an acceptably low level.

In addition to the conventional ways of protecting outputs (voting outputs at the actuators or strobing data into radiation-resistant latches in the actuators immediately after a successful vote), a novel low-cost masking approach was developed to protect outputs against single-event upsets. Since the isolation circuits between microcontrollers produce a logical OR of their individual output signals, if any microcontroller produces a "one" on a bussed output line, the result will be a logic "one". A bi-directional microcontroller pin is implemented with two flip flops one which controls the data direction (input or output) and one which contains output data (one or zero). In order to output a "one," both flip-flops must be set appropriately. In order to make a "zero" farther away from a "one" than a single bit-flip, the output value can be configured as zero and the pin set as an *input* with an external pull-down resistor. In this way, it takes two bit-flips to generate an erroneous output.

Latent faults in port registers can lead to double-bit errors, and output errors can be generated if a machine fails in such a way as to output a "one" before its error is detected by its neighbors. Periodic scrubbing (including reading in and comparing output values) can be used to detect errors of this type. This, and other pathological cases associated with high speed inputs cannot be discussed here due to space limitations, but they are discussed further in [11].

6. Detection, Reconfiguration and Recovery

Fault masking only applies to output ports. In general, errors are identified and corrected through software-implemented detection, reconfiguration and recovery. The detection process begins with software voting. Following diagnosis, the system is reconfigured if necessary by taking the errant device offline (isolating it from the rest of the system) and possibly selecting a new Master. The system recovers by forcing errant devices to restart.

6.1.   Normal Operation

During normal operation, processors are loosely synchronized so the identical application code running on each voting processor reaches a checkpoint function at approximately the same time. The Master manages the voting process by first passing data to the Checkers and getting responses from them.

Voting by Exact Match – The Master transmits a block of data (or a shorter syndrome) to a Checker which has computed its own check-packet and expects one from the Master. The Checker compares the received block (or syndrome) with its own block and reports equality (OK) or inequality in an encoded status message.

Inexact Inputs – For data which are derived directly from noisy sources, such as A/D converters, an exact match is generally impossible. Here, the Master passes its value to the Checkers and, if it is within an acceptable tolerance of the value they sampled, they signal agreement and use the Master's value. Other algorithms may also be implemented. Greater accuracy can be obtained for analog values by selecting the middle value as the best or by computing an average (after discarding outliers). Details of implementing voting using the I^2C bus are described in [11].

"Meta-Measurements" – In microcontroller applications, it is common to perform simple processing on a possibly large number of samples. For example, the reported angular rate of a gyro may be the normalized average of many rate measurements. In the testbed application, three gyros are sampled at 10.8 kHz, and 220 sample values from each gyro are aggregated to form a reported angular rate. This rate is reported to the host system 16 times a second. In this case, it is completely impractical to vote each individual sample – but it is also unnecessary; an aggregated value is essentially a single measurement from an abstract input device. Since the values are simply summed and averaged, the resulting averages can be dealt with by inexact voting as described above. This is discussed in more detail in [11].

Placement of Checkpoints – The simplest approach of voting after every input may be prohibitively expensive and unnecessary. However, data which will be output to ports, intermediate results which can lead to control-flow divergence, and state variables which are "output" by one iteration of processing (e.g., a periodic calculation) and then used as input to the next iteration must all be voted. It is probably wise to simply "vote early, vote often" with only as much moderation as dictated by the computational and communication resources available.

6.2. Control Errors in Checkers

Data-only upsets are fairly benign but an upset can cause a processor control error, e.g., causing it to jump erroneously or get locked up looping on completely invalid data. A significant effect on a Checker is for it to not reach its next voting checkpoint thereby precluding the Master from exchanging data with it. Timeouts are used by the Master to diagnose this condition.

During voting, communications timeout durations are set to accommodate the maximum expected clock skew between processors and any additional delay which results from application interrupt processing (e.g., handling real-time tasks) and from differences between Master and Checker fault-tolerance functions. If a Checker fails to communicate within the allocated time, either the Checker has failed or neither Checker was expecting the Master, in which case the latter is probably in error.

In the former case, the Master can communicate with the functioning Checker and the data to be checked can be at least tested for validity (as a self-checking pair). Additionally, the Master will request that the functioning Checker participate in voting the failed Checker to the Offline state using the External Resolver.

6.3. Control Errors in the Master

Just as a Checker may get lost, so may the Master. The process for dealing with a Master is necessarily quite different because the cooperative process of asking for help cannot be effected without the control of the Master; the Checkers are on their own.

Just as the Master sets communication timeouts, so too do the Checkers. If the Master fails to contact a Checker and the Checker believes itself to be healthy, it must conclude that the Master is in error. Without waiting for some confirmation of this error, it signals to the Resolver its desire to reset the Master. If the other Checker observes the same phenomenon, it will also have voted for an external reset and the Resolver will reset the Master.

When the Master is reset or power-cycled, its Operating Mode bits will go tri-state and be pulled down to (0, 0). This transition indicates a Master-less system and must be identified by the Checkers; if any outputs are generated solely by the Master (as already described), loss of the Master must immediately be followed by the selection of a new Master and its outputs properly configured. An interrupt may be generated externally by the all-zeroes case on the Master Operating Mode signals. Microcontrollers which can generate interrupts on input port pin changes do not need such external hardware; the PIC16C73 can flag a change on any of the high-order four bits of port B with an interrupt.

When the system loses its Master, the change is detected immediately if an interrupt is used (as is necessary if there are Master-only outputs) or when the next data checking operation occurs. In both of these cases and when the system is first started, a Master must be selected.

When the processor is restarted, the initialization process first checks whether a Master is present. No action is required if one is already present; the processor remains Offline until the Master commands it to join the ensemble. If there is no Master and the device is Master-capable, it will attempt to claim membership. A potential race condition exists between Master-capable devices so an additional step reverts to Checkers those peers with lower priority than that of the highest priority Master-claimant. Once a Master has been selected, it begins transmitting its system state to Offline members and follows the data with "join" commands. If a peer is ready, it will accept the incoming state data and become a Checker when it sees the join command. An example timeline of this process is shown in Table 3. It also includes the case where a restarted checker is brought back on-line.

Note that when a Master goes offline, the system may not operate non-stop; the Mastership selection process takes a few microseconds and glitches may be observed on Master-only high-speed outputs as the responsibility for their generation changes from the old Master to the new one. Any deleterious effects of this outage must be dealt with at the application level.

Table 3. Master Selection Process Timeline.

Conditions or Event	Operating Mode		
	P0	P1	P2
Initial condition after system reset.	o	o	o
Two Master-capable processors reach Master selection and claim Mastership.	M	M	o
Second processor observes a higher priority Master (P0) and relinquishes its claim.	M	o	o
Third processor (P2) initializes; sees Master; takes no action.	M	o	o
Master (P0) transmits state data to Offline peers.	M	o	o
Master sends "join" command to peers; they do so.	M	C	C
--- Arbitrary time passes. System operates nominally. ---			
P1 is taken offline; system is unaffected.	M	o	C
--- P1 reset occurs; one real-time frame passes ---			
Master sends state data to P1, requests that it rejoin as Checker.	M	C	C
--- Arbitrary time passes. System operates nominally. ---			
P0, the Master, taken offline; system has no Master.	o	C	C
P1, a Master-capable Checker, observes the Master-less system, claims Mastership, and reconfigures its outputs as Master.	o	M	C
--- P0 reset occurs; one real-time frame passes ---			
Master sends state data to P0, requests that it rejoin as Checker.	C	M	C

6.4. Corrupted Master Channel

The most severe fault is one which renders the Master Channel inoperative. A "babbling" device may cause this but the simplest mechanism is a Checker which simply sets one of its Master Channel I/O lines to an active state thereby creating a conflict for the channel.

Although the Master Channel could be designed to preclude (with high probability) that Checkers cannot take it down, the complexity required to both preclude bad behavior but allow all devices to be Master-capable will violate any notion of minimality. Thus, it must be assumed that there is a non-negligible probability that either the Master or a Checker can make the Master Channel inoperative.

If any processor sees that the Master Channel is inoperative, it cannot know which peer is at fault so after a self-check it requests a reset of both of its peers. In reality, this condition is indistinguishable from a failed Master as seen by the Checkers. If the two correctly-functioning processors identify this condition and are the first ones to command the Resolver, the failed processor will be reset by the Resolver.

However, if the processor which caused the error has also managed to command the Resolver to reset its peers, then when the first correctly-functioning processor requests that the Resolver reset both its peers, the other correctly-functioning processor will wrongly be reset (since the Resolver would have received two votes to reset it). The one remaining good processor will then observe a device going Offline and then expect communication over the Master Channel, either transmitting as the Master or receiving as a Checker. Since this operation will fail, the good processor requests that the Resolver restart all three processors. Since this design is only intended to mitigate transient faults, the full restart would be expected to clear whatever fault initiated the entire chain.

Clearly in this worst case the system will be taken Offline for a period of time but in doing so it will not permit bad data from being propagated beyond the error-containment boundary.

6.5.   Resolver Operation

The implemented Resolver is a synchronous state machine, with the Action Requests and Device Select as its control inputs. If the selected device is "Self" or "All", the action takes place immediately. If another device is selected, two such votes are required to take action against a device. This approach allows a microcontroller which believes itself to be in error to be reset or power-cycled and it allows a single microcontroller to believe that the entire ensemble is beyond help and to restart everyone. But it does not allow any lone device to affect others except when it is included by selecting "all", thus preventing a large class of wayward behavior.

The control inputs are used to control the Resolver state machine shown in Figure 4. The [GO_xxx] conditions are derived from the control signals from each processor, but the formulae are beyond the scope of this paper. A processor may be turned off (power-cycled) either as the result of an Action Request (GO_CYCLE) or asynchronously as the result of an overcurrent (IFAULT) being detected. The substates of PROCESSOR_OFF shown with broken outlines may or may not be implemented distinctly. The ONLINE state contains the substates of MASTER and CHECKER.

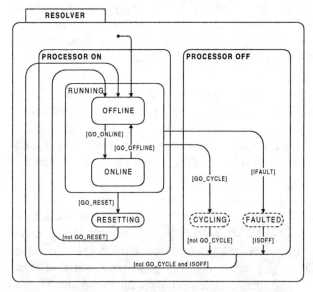

Figure 4. Statechart for Single-Processor Restart.

Figure 4 is principally comprised of two smaller state machines, one for power on/off state and one for reset state. The External Resolution - Power Cycling (ERP) state machine has only two states, Processor On and Processor Off, represented by a single register bit which controls the processor's local power switch (a totem-pole FET pair). The External Resolution - Reset (ERR) state machine similarly has only two states, Resetting and Running, with its single output bit tied directly to the microcontroller's reset pin. As is evident in Figure 4, the state of the ERR machine is irrelevant if the microcontroller is off. The three copies (one for each microcontroller) of Figure 4 are implemented in two PALs, one for three ERP machines and one for three ERR machines. The resetting state machine (ERR) outputs a reset pulse which satisfies the timing requirements of the target processor. Timing details are described in [11].

The power-cycling state machine (ERP) is similar to the ERR machine except that it awaits positive confirmation of the desired effect. By watching for the ISOFF flag which indicates that the current flowing into the microcontroller has dropped below a hardware-set threshold, a closed-loop control is implemented which obviates the need for precise control of the state machine's clock frequency.

7. The Experimental Testbed

In order to produce an outcome valuable to the spacecraft avionics community and to provide a testbed for evaluating the effectiveness of the techniques, a prototypical application was built that is representative of a typical spacecraft subsystem, specifically a 3-axis inertial measurement unit (IMU). This application is sufficiently complex to provide insights into real problems while sufficiently simple that its implementation was not overly distracting. The supporting testbed accommodates three microcontrollers to implement fault-tolerance and thus provide examples of different processor (duplex and triplex) configurations. The application example forces many I/O requirements to be addressed, including bi-level and analog voting, pulse train generation, event timing, and serial communications. The testbed and IMU application use the Microchip PIC16C76 and '77 [2]. Its functionality, while relatively limited, is sufficient to implement the chosen applications but these same limitations force a frugal approach to fault-tolerance – it would be very easy to use all the I/O pins just implementing fault-tolerance.

A block diagram of the testbed environment is shown in Figure 5.

A circuit board was constructed for the three redundant microcontrollers with a daughter board for the External Resolver. PIC in-circuit emulators were substituted for the three microcontrollers to provide ease of controlling and monitoring the processors while maintaining fidelity as to their behavior. A laptop PC was used to inject faults and monitor the state of the External Resolver. A photo of the testbed is shown in Figure 6.

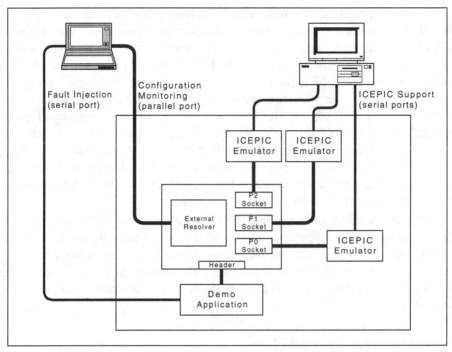

Figure 5: TMR Testbed Hardware Configuration

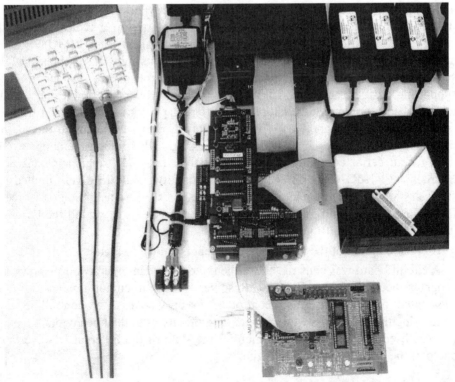

Figure 6. The Testbed

8. Fault Injection

Simulated SEUs were injected into the system and its response monitored to determine if the recovery mechanisms worked and to get insights into the coverage of the system. To inject faults, each processor of the fault-tolerant system contains an interrupt service routine (ISR), which receives messages from the asynchronous serial (RS-232) port. An external support program randomly generates and sends messages consisting of two bytes specifying the processor (1-3), byte (0-255), and bit (0-7) to upset. All such generated "strikes" are upsets consisting of flipping the state of one bit. One, two or all three processors can be the targets of this random process. During the time that faults are injected into the system, statistics are gathered to characterize the system's responses.

8.1.   Fault Response and Monitoring

Each injected fault can be viewed as an experiment that can have many possible outcomes of decreasing desirability:

1. No effect.
2. Latent effect. A fault creates a situation which will cause an error only after some other fault occurs.
3. Computing continues correctly without significant interruption. The system correctly identifies a failed device and the operational devices reset the errant one; the two good devices continue after a brief delay.
4. Computing continues correctly after an automatic retry. Recovery is effected by a system reset but the user data is unaffected; the system recovers with no data loss but a slightly higher temporal impact than in case 3.
5. System output is flagged as invalid. Computations are correct and somehow corrupted before the user sees their results, but the incorrect results are easily identifiable (e.g., using a checksum). System state is not lost.
6. Computing continues correctly after a rollback. Recovery following a system reset requires the use of previously-checkpointed user state data; the data since the last checkpoint is lost (e.g., the data taken during one real-time frame).
7. Computing continues following system re-initialization. Volatile user data is lost.
8. System outputs incorrect results. Data errors which are not easily identifiable by the user are produced.
9. Computing ceases. The system fails. It stops computing or becomes unstable (and thus useless).

The monitoring program (which is part of the fault-injection program) uses externally-visible information to identify behavior in the above categories and accumulate statistics to characterize the probability of each response. From these statistics, the effectiveness of the techniques can be determined.

The externally-visible indications of behavior which the monitor observes are: the system's Operating Mode configuration; the occurrences of hard resets; the integrity of the serial channel which communicates computational results to the monitor; and the computational results themselves.

Operating Mode Configuration Monitoring – The system Operating Mode configuration is the easiest indicator to monitor. The monitoring program samples the Operating Mode at about 430 Hz, keeping a histogram of how long the system dwelled in each mode and the number of times a mode was entered.

Reset Event Counting – The generation of a reset action by the Resolver is the best indication that a non-recoverable error took place. Because these actions are too short-lived (10 µs) to be easily monitored externally, the spare PAL socket on the Resolver daughter board was populated with a device programmed to capture the resets and hold them until the external monitor could sample and rearm it. The monitor tallies the number of times that one, two or three resets are observed during one sample time (at the 430 Hz rate).

Behavioral Model Monitoring – To trap errors which were not caught by communications software, a behavioral model of the test application was incorporated into the monitoring program. This model implements algorithms similar to the IMU application and propagates them for each data packet received. It then compares the received data with the model to determine if the application is behaving properly (i.e., according to the model). Observable system resets, and therefore interruptions in operation, are identified when the application output reverts to its initialized state. Time, rate and position errors are counted as data errors when the application output lies exceeds an allowed tolerance of the model.

8.2.   Test Runs, Results and Analysis

Exploring the significant dimensions of a complex system requires more than a single demonstration run. Approximately 80 multi-hour test runs were performed on the system, starting from the time the software became relatively stable. As would be expected, the majority of these runs resulted in discovery of a number of "interesting behaviors" which required subsequent software improvements. Many of the insights gained from this process are documented in [11] "Problems Encountered." Table 4 summarizes about 15 runs made near the end of the experimentation phase. In these tests, both TMR configurations and pairs of microcontrollers operating as self-checking pairs (SCP) were exercised.

Table 4. Summary of Test Runs.

				Errors		Coverage		Effectiveness	
Run	Cfg	Configuration Notes	Strikes	Resets	Data	Reset	Data	Reset	Data
A	SCP	no retry, 8-bit checksum	33650	2013	1	94.0%	99.994%	88.0%	99.988%
B	SCP	with retry, 8-bit checksum	59191	2540	3	95.7%	99.993%	91.4%	99.986%
C	SCP	same as B, hits only on P1	28462	1105	0	96.1%	99.996%	96.1%	99.993%
D	TMR	with retry, 8-bit checksum	30552	538	6	98.2%	99.977%	94.7%	99.931%
E	SCP	with retry, 16-bit checksum	47669	1814	0	96.2%	99.998%	92.4%	99.996%
F	TMR	with retry, 16-bit checksum	44846	762	13	98.3%	99.969%	94.9%	99.906%
G	TMR	cfg F, w/o P2 participation	16199	622	4	96.2%	99.969%	92.3%	99.907%
H	SCP	cfg E, with user checkpoint	49691	1003	3	98.0%	99.992%	96.0%	99.984%
I	SCP	cfg H, with 2x strike-rate	77673	1260	2	98.4%	99.996%	96.8%	99.992%

An estimate of the non-coverage with respect to system resets or data errors is the number of resets or data errors recorded divided by the number of faults (strikes) injected into the system. Since some of the test runs resulted in small numbers of data errors (e.g., zero), the values shown for data coverage (and effectiveness) are the mean likelihood estimates. "Effectiveness" is coverage relative to a single-device system; since the number of injected faults are spread over two or three target processors (for SCP and TMR), the number of faults injected into a single device is one half or one third as large. Thus, the effectiveness is coverage computed by dividing the number of faults (strikes) by the number of processors participating in the run.

In run "A" all internal resets (2013) result in observed Reset Errors. With subsequent runs, "retry" and "user checkpointing" were used to reduce the number of externally visible resets.

The simplest approach is to simply "retry" a voting operation after a system reset. Since many errors are due to control errors, a very low overhead improvement is to allow a resetting system to immediately retry the voting process. If state data are unaffected, the vote will succeed and the operation may continue. Obviously, if the state data were affected, the system must reinitialize. The improvement due to this approach is about a 30% reduction in system errors (case A to case B).

Instead of reinitialization, the state data may be checkpointed (by making a copy) and following a retry failure, the saved data may be used (a "rollback" recovery). This approach has higher coverage at the expense of significantly higher memory resource requirements (and consequently could not be tested in the TMR case). The improvement over retry only is an additional 50% reduction in system errors (case E to case H).

Specific details of the tests can be found in [11].

It is interesting that SCP was uniformly more robust than TMR. This is undoubtedly due to the larger effective cross section presented by TMR due its complexity. It may be that the very simple application program was dominated by the voting software. If so, more complex applications (on more sophisticated processors) might not show this disparity. However, it is apparent that there is a trade-off which must be considered lest the apparent benefit of TMR be offset by its substantially higher complexity.

9. Summary

This paper has described steps toward a generic approach to implementing cost-effective fault-tolerance augmentations of commercial microcontrollers in spacecraft control systems, focusing on the transient error recovery needed in a space radiation environment. The work explores how much fault-tolerance can be implemented in a minimal design that preserves the high functional density advantages of microcontrollers – without taking the costly step of implementing microprocessor designs with extensive supporting interface circuitry. While there has been extensive research and development of systems which provide extremely high levels of fault-tolerance, including Byzantine resilience, they are expensive custom designs which exceed the limited resources available for spaceborne applications [5].

The described techniques are simple ones that allow multiple microcontrollers to be connected in multi-processor fault-tolerant configurations. A hardware testbed and software prototype allowed experimentation with variants on a set of core architectural concepts. For the given experimental fault set, coverage with respect to propagation of bad information due to simulated single-event upsets was demonstrated to be higher than 99.99%. The highly integrated nature of microcontroller chips make it impossible to access internal variables (e.g., the processor-memory bus) for experimental fault insertion. Thus these experimental test results based on software-induced disturbances must be viewed as preliminary. Validation in a high-energy radiation test facility is needed to obtain more accurate coverage estimates and to obtain an increased level of confidence.

10. Acknowledgments

This work was sponsored by the Office of Naval Research, under grant #N00014-96-1-0837 at the University of California, Los Angeles.

11. References

[1] "8XC196Kx, 8XC196Jx, 87C196CA Microcontroller Family User's Manual." Intel Corporation, June 1995.

[2] "PIC16/17 Microcontroller Data Book." Microchip Technology, Inc. 1995/1996.

[3] A. Holmes-Siedle, L. Adams. "Handbook of Radiation Effects." Oxford Science Publications, Oxford, 1993.

[4] G. C. Messenger, M. S. Ash. "The Effects of Radiation on Electronic Systems." Second Edition. Van Nostrand Reinhold, New York, 1992.

[5] R. E. Harper, J. H. Lala, J. J. Deyst. Fault Tolerant Parallel Processors Overview. FTCS-18, pp. 252-257. 1988.

[6] T. Takano, et. al., "Fault-Tolerance Experiments of the "Hiten" Onboard Space Computer ," FTCS21, pp. 26-33, 1991.

[7] D. W. Caldwell, D. A. Rennels. "A Minimimalist Hardware Architecture for Using Commercial Microcontrollers in Space." 16th Digital Avionics Systems Conference, Irvine, CA. 28-30 Oct 1997.

[8] D. A. Rennels, D. W. Caldwell, R. Hwang, M. Mesarina. "A Fault-Tolerant Embedded Microcontroller Testbed." 1997 Pacific Rim Fault-Tolerance Conference, Taipei, Taiwan. 15-16 Dec 1997.

[9] H. Kopetz, et al. Distributed Fault-Tolerant Real-Time Systems: The MARS Approach. IEEE Micro, February 1989.

[10] S. G. Frison, J. H. Wensley. Interactive Consistency and Its Impact on TMR Systems in Dig. Int. Symp. Fault Tolerant Computing, FTCS-12, June 1982, pp. 228-233.

[11] Douglas Caldwell, "Minimalist Fault Masking, Detection and Recovery Techniques for Mitigating Single Event Effects in Non-Radiation-Hardened Microcontrollers", Ph.D. Dissertation, UCLA Computer Science Department, Los Angeles, CA, June 1998.

Building Fault-Tolerant Hardware Clocks from COTS Components

Christof Fetzer and Flaviu Cristian
Department of Computer Science & Engineering
University of California, San Diego
La Jolla, CA 92093−0114*
cfetzer@cs.ucsd.edu
http://www.cs.ucsd.edu/~cfetzer

Abstract

Clocks with a bounded drift rate are an important tool in the construction of dependable applications. However, the drift rates of clocks provided by operating systems on some computing platforms are not always bounded, e.g. due to lost interrupts or leap seconds. We show how one can build clocks with a bounded drift rate from components off-the-shelf (COTS). Our approach can be used to achieve a tight synchronization with UTC (Coordinated Universal Time) in systems with access to at least one GPS (Global Positioning System) receiver.

1 Introduction

Many dependable applications need to perform certain tasks within a given time frame. A deadline of a dependable real-time application might be classified as *soft* or *hard* according to the potential cost introduced by missing the deadline. In soft and hard real-time systems it is advantageous at the least – and in most cases even necessary – that application processes have access to clocks. Clocks can have different properties. For example, a clock RC can be *externally synchronized*, i.e. the absolute value of the difference between RC and real-time is always bounded by some known constant ϵ. A clock H can have a *bounded drift rate*, i.e. the difference between the clock and real-time can change every second at most by some known constant $\rho \ll 1$.

We call a clock with a bounded drift rate a *hardware clock*. Hardware clocks allow processes to communicate by time [5], i.e. a process can learn that certain properties hold in a distributed system by waiting until its clock has reached a certain value. For example, in a fail-safe system, communication by time might allow

*This research was supported by grants F49620-93 and F49620-96 from the Air Force Office of Scientific Research. See http://www.cs.ucsd.edu/~cfetzer/HWC

processes to switch the system to a safe state if the communication between processes is disrupted [5]. Hardware clocks are therefore an essential part of the *timed
asynchronous system model* [2].

This paper addresses the issue of how to implement hardware clocks such that
the probability that a hardware clock fails, i.e. the drift rate is not always bounded,
is negligible. To do this, we first explain why not all operating systems can provide
clocks with a bounded drift rate. Second, we show how one can use a commercial-
off-the-shelf (COTS) board to build a fault-tolerant hardware clock. Finally, we
describe how one can use this counter/timer board to achieve external synchronization with GPS time or Coordinated Universal Time (UTC).

2   Problem Statement

Operating systems maintain *real-time clocks* for application processes: real-time
clocks are more or less synchronized with real-time. Typically, one cannot assume that real-time clocks are externally synchronized, i.e. there exists no a priori
known constant ϵ such that a clock is always synchronized within ϵ of real-time.
In UNIX systems connected to the Internet, NTP [7] can synchronize these clocks
quite tightly with real-time. NTP also computes an upper bound on the current
deviation between a clock and real-time. The synchronization provided by NTP
might be sufficient for most applications. However, NTP has also some deficiencies which might prohibit its usage in mission and safety critical applications. For
example, it appears that the upper bound computed by NTP might not correct during
leap seconds and in particular, the measurement of certain time intervals might have
an unexpected large error due to a leap second. Furthermore, due to certain clock
hardware restrictions, the clock failure probability might be unacceptably high. To
explain the latter, we will review a typical implementation of a real-time clock in
an operating system kernel.

Linux sets a timer that generates an interrupt every 10ms. The kernel increments
a counter every time such a timer interrupt occurs. The real-time clock is defined
as the concatenation of the counter value and the timer value. The problem with
this approach is that when the timer generates a new interrupt before the previous
interrupt is processed, the clock loses about 10ms with respect to real-time. Is the
probability of a lost timer interrupt negligible? The answer depends on the used
hardware and software architecture and the requirements of the application.

For example, in some systems the serial interface has a higher interrupt priority
than the timer interrupt. Hence, if the serial interface keeps the processor busy, then
a timer interrupt might be lost [8]. A related problem is that some operating systems
turn off interrupts to ensure the atomic execution of certain kernel routines. If the
interrupts are turned off too long, the system might lose a timer interrupt.

Some systems might lose timer interrupts. How serious can a lost timer interrupt
be? In particular, how does a lost timer interrupt affect the drift rate of the real-time
clock? The short term stability of the timer, i.e. the maximum change of its drift
rate over a period of a few seconds (see below), is in the order of 10^{-6}. Hence, a

lost timer interrupt (100Hz interrupt frequency) might change the short term drift rate substantially. For example, for a time interval with a duration of 1 second the drift rate increases from 10^{-6} to about $\frac{10ms}{1s} = 10^{-2}$. This is not acceptable for applications that depend on a known small maximum clock drift rate.

Besides having clocks with a bounded drift rate, it is advantageous if they are also externally synchronized. To achieve external clock synchronization, the system has to have access to an external time source such as a GPS receiver. In this paper we also addresses the issue that the time information provided by an external time source might be faulty. In particular, one cannot necessarily detect that the time information are faulty, even when using local hardware clocks and multiple external time sources. Hence, one does not want to use a software PLL (phase locked loop) that synchronizes the local clock(s) unconditionally to the external time sources to be able to guarantee a bounded drift rate even when all external time sources have failed. We will show how to achieve a very tight external synchronization as long as the external time signal is correct and how to bound the drift rate of local clocks even if all external time signals suffer undetectable arbitrary failures.

3 Approach

We explain our approach in several steps. First, how to address the problem of lost timer interrupts by using concatenated counters. Second, how to calibrate hardware clocks to decrease their maximum drift rate ρ. Third, how to synchronize the drift rate of several hardware clocks. Fourth, how to synchronize the speed of the clocks with real-time using the PPS (one pulse per second) signal of a GPS receiver. Fifth, how to extend this approach to mask hardware clock failures. Finally, how to synchronize the values of the clocks with real-time.

3.1 Hardware Clocks

Currently, most COTS counter/timer PC boards, e.g. the DCC-20P from Industrial Computer Source, contain a collection of 16-bit timers. The DCC-20P has four AMD9513 timer chips. Each of these chips contains five 16-bit counters, i.e. there are a total of 20 16-bit counters on the board. The problem with using only one 16-bit timer is that it requires the usage of interrupts to maintain an overflow counter. However, one can concatenate four 16-bit counters of a timer chip to form a 64-bit counter by programming the chip appropriately.

To simplify matters, we assume that we have the following hardware support to implement a *hardware clock* (see Figure 1):

- an oscillator with a nominal frequency f_{nom}, and

- a 64-bit counter that is incremented by the ticks of the oscillator.

Note in some systems such a counter is already available on the motherboard. The frequency f_{nom} should be at least 1MHz to provide at least a microsecond resolu-

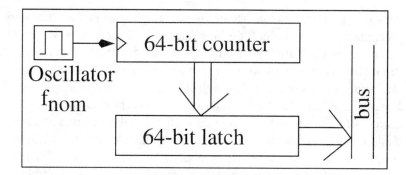

Figure 1: *A hardware clock can be implemented by an oscillator with a nominal frequency* f_{nom} *and a 64bit counter. The latch allows reading the counter atomically.*

tion. Higher frequencies are preferable to keep synchronization/drift errors low (see Section 3.5).

The advantage of having a 64-bit timer is that practically it will not wrap around. For example, even if the oscillator has a frequency of 1GHz, the counter will not wrap around for at least 583 years. Hence, there is no danger of lost timer interrupts since it is not necessary to interrupt the CPU to maintain an overflow counter.

3.2   Oscillator and Hardware Clock Model

Quartz oscillators found in workstations can be characterized as being *stable* (i.e. precise) but not very *accurate*, i.e. the frequency of an oscillator hardly changes over time, however, the frequency of the oscillator might be different from its nominal frequency. The stability of a quartz oscillator depends on the averaging time. Typically, the stability of a quartz oscillator is at least an order of magnitude better in an interval of length $[1s, 100s]$ than it is for much longer intervals like a day (see [12]).

An oscillator has some nominal frequency f_{nom}, i.e. the oscillator is supposed to oscillate with frequency f_{nom}. The average frequency per day might however be f_{avg} instead and might change slowly over time due to aging. Yet, even very inexpensive quartz oscillators age typically only between 5 ppm to 10 ppm per year. Aging has usually a logarithmic dependence on time. We assume that the maximum daily change of the average frequency of a correct oscillator can be bounded.

The frequency of an oscillator might change due to aging, temperature changes, voltage changes, vibration, radiation, and other factors. We assume that all factors that can change the frequency are combined in a constant maximum factor Δf. In particular, Δf includes the maximum daily frequency change due to aging and temperature changes. For convenience, we increase Δf by a constant in the order of 10^{-7} to account for the maximum error we make when estimating f_{avg} (see Section 3.4). The frequency f of a correct oscillator is always bounded by

$$f \in [f_{avg}(1 - \Delta f), f_{avg}(1 + \Delta f)]. \tag{1}$$

The granularity g of a hardware clock is defined as

$$g := \frac{1}{f_{nom}}, \tag{2}$$

i.e. this is the nominal unit of the LSB of the counter. For example, for a nominal frequency of 10MHz, the granularity of the clock is 100ns. The current drift rate γ of a hardware clock with a current frequency of f is defined as:

$$\gamma := \frac{f}{f_{nom}} - 1 = \frac{f - f_{nom}}{f_{nom}} \stackrel{Eq.2}{=} g(f - f_{nom}). \tag{3}$$

If needed, we will use a superscript to refer to the drift rate at a certain time, e.g. we use γ^t to denote the drift rate at time t. To explain γ, consider a frequency difference of 1Hz and a granularity of $1\mu s$, then the drift rate is 1ppm, i.e. the clock gains every second $1\mu s$ with respect to real-time.

Since we assume that the frequency f of the oscillator is bounded by $f_{avg}(1 \pm \Delta f)$ (see Equation 1) and the drift rate is defined as $g(f - f_{nom})$ (see Equation 3), we can bound the drift rate by,

$$\gamma \in [g((f_{avg} - f_{nom}) - f_{avg}\Delta f), g((f_{avg} - f_{nom}) + f_{avg}\Delta f)]. \tag{4}$$

We mentioned before that quartz oscillators are typically quite precise but not very accurate. With respect to the above equation this means that $f_{avg}\Delta f$ is typically much smaller than $f_{avg} - f_{nom}$. Usually, the drift rate caused by frequency instabilities (i.e. $gf_{avg}\Delta f$) is in the order of 10^{-6} while $g(f_{avg} - f_{nom})$ is in the order of 10^{-4}. We will show in Section 3.4 how clock calibration can decrease the maximum drift of a clock to about Δf.

Observing the behavior of oscillators, we can assume that the frequency and hence, the drift rate changes slowly over time. We introduce a *short term stability* π. We define "short term" by a constant τ which is the maximum validity period of π. In what follows, we choose a conservative and hence, somewhat arbitrary $\tau := 11s$. This is a "relative drift rate" in the following sense: given a time interval I of a length of at most some τ and any two times $s, t \in I$, the difference of the current drift rates at s and t of a correct hardware clock is at most π, i.e.

$$\forall s, t : |s - t| \leq \tau \Rightarrow |\gamma^s - \gamma^t| \leq \pi. \tag{5}$$

We use this oscillator and hardware clock model (given by Equations 1-5) to design and simulate algorithms to synchronize hardware clocks and to mask clock failures. For example, Figure 2 shows the drift rate of a simulated clock over a period of 10000s. Note that the drift rate of this clock could be reduced quite dramatically by changing the speed of the clock (see Section 3.4). The short term stability π is usually an order of magnitude smaller than the difference between the maximum drift rate and the average drift rate.

We denote the counter value of a hardware clock H at real-time t by $H(t)$. If we have to distinguish between multiple hardware clocks, we will add subscripts.

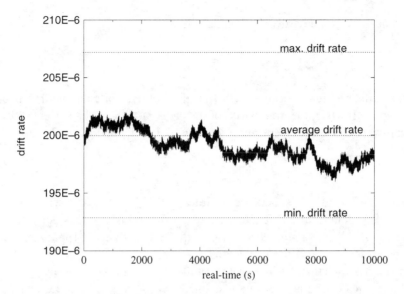

Figure 2: *Simulated drift rate of a clock over a period of 10000s with an average drift rate of* $200*10^{-6}$ *and a short term stability of* $\pi = 10^{-6}$. *The drift rate is bounded by* $(200 \pm 7)*10^{-6}$.

For example, we will use $H_i(t)$ or g_i to refer to the value and granularity of clock "i". A hardware clock is *correct*, iff all its components are correct. In particular, 1) when a read request arrives at the latch at real-time t, the current value $H(t)$ of the counter is put on the bus, 2) the frequency of the oscillator is within $f_{avg} \pm \Delta f$ of its yesterday's daily average frequency f_{avg}, and 3) the drift rate of a hardware clock changes by at most π over a period of τ. Note, one can detect and/or mask failures that occur after the clock value is put on the bus by using ECC on the bus.

3.3 Normalized Hardware Clocks

We would like for all clocks at the API level to have the same frequency and resolution: we choose a normalized frequency $f_N := 1GHz$ and hence, all clocks have a $1ns = \frac{1}{1GHz}$ resolution. For example, if one uses a hardware clock H with $f_{nom} = 1MHz$, one has to multiply the value $H(t)$ by $\frac{f_N}{f_{nom}} = 1000$ since the LSB of H is $1\mu s$ while the LSB of a normalized clock has to be $1ns$.

To normalize a hardware clock H, we want to multiply $H(t)$ by a normalization factor $\mathcal{N}$ which is defined as follows

$$\mathcal{N} := \frac{f_N}{f_{nom}}. \tag{6}$$

The normalized hardware clock H^N is defined as

$$H^N(t) := \mathcal{N}H(t) \stackrel{Eq.6}{=} \frac{f_N H(t)}{f_{nom}}. \tag{7}$$

Note that the average frequency of a normalized clock changes from f_{avg} to $\mathcal{N}f_{avg}$.

3.4 Calibrated Hardware Clocks

Section 3.2 explains that the drift rate of a hardware clock is mainly caused by the difference between its average frequency f_{avg} and its nominal frequency f_{nom} (see also Figure 2). *Clock calibration* tries to determine the average frequency of a clock. A *calibrated hardware clock* is a normalized hardware clock in which we "virtually" change the average frequency from originally $\mathcal{N}f_{avg}$ to about f_N. Conceptually, one can read a normalized hardware clock H^N and then multiply its value with an estimate of $\frac{f_N}{\mathcal{N}f_{avg}}$. Hence, the "frequency" f of the calibrated hardware clock is about

$$f \overset{Eq.1,Eq.7}{=} \frac{f_N}{\mathcal{N}f_{avg}} \mathcal{N}f_{avg}(1 \pm \Delta f) = f_N(1 \pm \Delta f). \tag{8}$$

To estimate the average frequency $\mathcal{N}f_{avg}$, one can use a reliable time service that is accessible via the Internet. For example, NIST (National Institute of Standards and Technology, US) provides several time services via the Internet. One can even use multiple different time services to be able to mask Byzantine failures of some services (see [6]).

An important requirement for accessing a remote time service is the possibility to authenticate the time server and to determine the age of the time data received from the server. In particular, the system should be able to detect if an adversary sends faked or delayed time data. For example, non-military grade GPS receivers can only use the non-authenticated GPS time signals. Hence, it is theoretically possible to send faked GPS messages that provide such GPS receivers with wrong time data. Military grade GPS receivers have access to an authenticated time signal and hence, they can detect if an adversary sends faked time data. However, an adversary might be able to delay GPS time signals by receiving the original information and broadcasting the received data after some delay.

We assume that one can access a time service via the Internet to get authenticated clock readings and use probabilistic clock reading [1] to reject delayed time information: one measures the duration between sending the request to the time service and the time the reply is received. If the measured duration is too long, one retries periodically until getting a clock reading with an error of at most a few ms. Our measurements at UCSD show that one can get a reply from a remote time server in about $40ms$. If one accepts replies within at most $40ms$, one can read remote clocks with an error of at most $20ms$. Hence, one can estimate the average drift rate of a normalized clock by (see also Equation 3)

$$\rho_{avg} := \frac{\mathcal{N}f_{avg}}{f_N} - 1 \tag{9}$$

with an error of at most $\frac{2*20ms}{24hours} \approx 4.6*10^{-7}$.

Given the measured drift rate ρ_{avg}, we can calibrate a normalized hardware clock, i.e. we change the average frequency from $\mathcal{N}f_{avg}$ to about f_N. To avoid rapid changes in the clock speed due to a new estimate of ρ_{avg}, and since the aging of a clock proceeds very slowly anyhow, one can change ρ_{avg} very slowly over time. For example, a change of at most 10^{-9} per minute should be sufficient for most clocks.

Conceptionally, clock calibration is done by multiplying the output of the normalized hardware clock by some calibration factor $\frac{f_N}{N f_{avg}} \stackrel{Eq.9}{=} \frac{1}{1+\rho_{avg}}$ (see Equation 8). However, since we update the calibration factor periodically, the calibration is actually a little more complicated. We define the calibrated and normalized hardware clock H^C as follows. Assume we want to determine the value of H^C at real-time v and we know its value $H^C(u)$ for some earlier time u. Also assume that u is the time of the most recent update of ρ_{avg} before v. We define $H^C(v)$ by

$$H^C(v) := \frac{H^N(v) - H^N(u)}{1 + \rho_{avg}} + H^C(u) \stackrel{Eq.7}{=} \frac{N(H(v) - H(u))}{1 + \rho_{avg}} + H^C(u). \quad (10)$$

We assume that there exists a time u_0 at which ρ_{avg} is measured for the first time. Typically, u_0 is some time during the initialization phase of the system. We define $H^C(u_0)) := H^N(u_0)$ to make sure that Equation 10 is well defined. An implementation of H^C might store at each update of ρ_{avg} the current value of $\frac{N}{1+\rho_{avg}}$ (and the current value of H^C) to be able to compute H^C efficiently.

One can view H^C as a hardware clock that has an oscillator with a nominal frequency of f_N and its actual frequency f is bounded by (see Equation 8)

$$f \in [f_N(1 - \Delta f), f_N(1 + \Delta f)], \quad (11)$$

The drift rate of H^C is therefore bounded by (see Equation 3),

$$\gamma \in [-\Delta f, \Delta f]. \quad (12)$$

Hence, we can define the *maximum drift rate* ρ of H^C to be

$$\rho := \Delta f. \quad (13)$$

In Figure 3 we show the drift rate of three hardware clocks before and after the calibration. The parameters of the clocks are $\rho = 7*10^{-6}$, $\pi = 10^{-6}$ and the remote clock reading error is $20ms$. While all figures are derived from a simulation, the parameters are typical for good TTL oscillators. The simulation results also match well with our measurements of the drift rate of clocks in real systems [2].

3.5   Drift Synchronization

Some timer/counter boards like the DCC-20P contain multiple counter/timer chips. We can clock these chips using separate oscillators (see Figure 4) to avoid that an oscillator failure will result in multiple hardware clock failures. We will show that having $N = 2F + 1$ hardware clocks allows us to mask at least F clock failures: we can build a fault-tolerant clock that consists of some N hardware clocks to mask at least F hardware clock failures. To simplify matters, we assume that we have an odd number N of hardware clocks, i.e. $N = 2F + 1$ for some given F. In

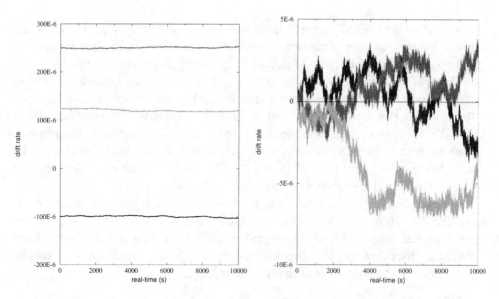

Figure 3: *The left graph shows the drift rate of three normalized hardware clocks while the right one shows the drift rates of the three calibrated clocks during the same simulated run.*

this section we address the issue of how we can synchronize the drift rates of multiple hardware clocks. We introduce this synchronization of the drift rates because it allows us later on to define a fault-tolerant hardware clock with better properties (smaller granularity ; see Section 3.8).

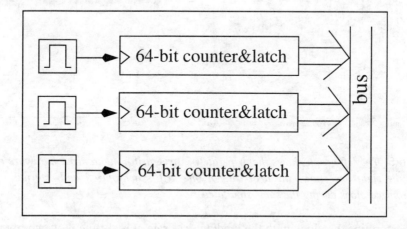

Figure 4: *Hardware support for the implementation of a fault-tolerant clock.*

Even if we calibrate and normalize all hardware clocks, these clocks can drift apart from each other by 2ρ (see right graph of Figure 3). Note that the short term stability π is typically much smaller than ρ. We show in this subsection how we can synchronize the drift rate of the N hardware clocks. We will see that as long as a majority of the underlying hardware clocks are correct, the maximum drift rate of a "drift-synchronized" correct hardware clock is still at most ρ. However, all drift-synchronized correct hardware clocks drift apart from each other by at most $\approx 2\pi$ (see left graph of Figure 5) instead of 2ρ (see right graph of Figure 3).

The drift synchronization of the normalized and calibrated hardware clocks is done periodically. Every second we update for each clock a multiplication factor ι_i. To compute ι_i, we determine the clock H_m^C that has the median drift rate (averaging period is $10s$) amongst all calibrated hardware clocks. The intuition is that if a majority of the hardware clocks are correct, we can find two correct calibrated clocks such that one has a drift rate not greater than H_m^C and the other has a drift rate not smaller than H_m^C. Hence, the drift rate of H_m^C is bounded by $\pm\rho$.

For each clock H_i^C, we define ι_i to be the measured relative drift rate between H_i^C and H_m^C. The speed of all drift-synchronized correct clocks will therefore be synchronized with the speed of the median clock. As long as a majority of the hardware clocks are correct, all correct clocks will have a maximum drift rate of $\approx \rho$ while drifting apart from each other by at most $\approx 2\pi$.

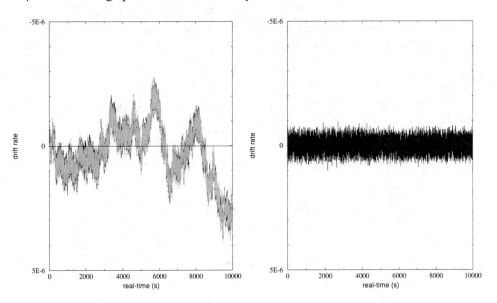

Figure 5: *The left graph shows the drift rate of* **three** *drift-synchronized hardware clocks while the right one shows the drift rate of one drift-synchronized and externally drift-synchronized clock during the same simulated run.*

To determine the clock with the median drift rate at real-time u, we compute for each clock H_i^C the *increase* (denoted by D_i) over the last ≈ 10 seconds. Assume we read the values of all calibrated clocks at some time t and u such that $u - t \approx 10s$. We define $D_i := H_i^C(u) - H_i^C(t)$ for $i \in \{1, 2, ..., N\}$. We then select the median D_m and determine the relative drift of all clocks with respect to H_m^C.

Intuitively, if all clocks would be perfectly drift (and phase) synchronized, the increase of all clocks would be the same, i.e. $D_i = D_j$ for $i, j \in \{1, 2, ..., N\}$. Hence, to synchronize the drift of the clocks, we can adjust the speed of clock H_i^C

by

$$\iota_i := \frac{D_m}{D_i} \tag{14}$$

since the increase of $\iota_i H_i^C$ is $\frac{D_m}{D_i} D_i = D_m$. Note that the phase of the oscillators of the clocks can be out of sync. Hence, even if a clock H_i^C is perfectly drift synchronized with H_m^C, the factor ι_i might be $\neq 1$ since D_m and D_i might be off by ± 2 "ticks". If f is the frequency of an oscillator, a tick happens every $\frac{1}{f}$ and a tick of an oscillator increases the hardware clock H by $\frac{1}{f_{nom}}$. Note that the normalization and calibration transforms a tick of the oscillator into an increase of H^C by $\frac{1}{f_{avg}}$. Let E denote the maximum increase per tick amongst all calibrated clocks, i.e.

$$E := \max\left\{\frac{1}{f_{avg}^1}, \dots, \frac{1}{f_{avg}^N}\right\}. \tag{15}$$

We now derive a formula for the error of our approximation of the relative drift between H_m^C and H_i^C. Let f_i be the average frequency of the calibrated clock H_i^C in interval $[t, u]$ and $\hat{\gamma}_i$ the average drift rate of H_i^C in $[t, u]$. The relative drift between clocks H_i^C and H_m^C can formally be defined as follows,

$$\rho_{i,m} := \frac{f_i}{f_m} - 1 \stackrel{Eq.3}{=} \frac{(1+\hat{\gamma}_i)f_N}{(1+\hat{\gamma}_m)f_N} - 1 = \frac{1+\hat{\gamma}_i}{1+\hat{\gamma}_m} - 1. \tag{16}$$

If processes would know $\rho_{i,m}$, we would use a factor of $\frac{1}{\rho_{i,m}+1}$ instead of ι_i to drift synchronize the clocks. However, $\rho_{i,m}$ is not known to the processes and hence, we use ι_i instead. The increase D of a calibrated clock within a time interval $[t, u]$ is

$$D = (1+\hat{\gamma})(u - t) \pm E, \tag{17}$$

where the error term $\pm E$ takes care of the "phase differences" between the oscillator and the interval start and end. Hence, we can express $\frac{1}{\iota_i}$ as follows:

$$\frac{1}{\iota_i} \stackrel{Eq.14}{=} \frac{D_i}{D_m} \stackrel{Eq.17}{=} \frac{(1+\hat{\gamma}_i)(u-t) \pm E}{(1+\hat{\gamma}_m)(u-t) \pm E} \approx \frac{(1+\hat{\gamma}_i)}{(1+\hat{\gamma}_m)} \pm \frac{2E}{u-t} \tag{18}$$

When we approximate the relative drift error $\rho_{i,m}$ by $(\frac{1}{\iota_i}-1)$, we make the following error:

$$\left(\frac{1}{\iota_i} - 1\right) - \rho_{i,m} \stackrel{Eq.18,Eq.16}{=} \pm \frac{2E}{u-t} \tag{19}$$

Synchronizing the drift rates of the calibrated clocks might raise the maximum drift rate of the clocks since 1) we might over or under estimate $\rho_{i,m}$, and 2) the speed of the underlying hardware clock might change by up to π from one measurement interval to the next. Hence, in the worst case the drift rate of the drift-synchronized clocks might be up to $\frac{2E}{10s} + \pi$ greater than ρ. We therefore define the maximum drift rate of the drift-synchronized clocks to be:

$$\rho^S := \rho + \pi + \frac{E}{5s}. \tag{20}$$

This increase is negligible as long as the average frequencies of the clocks are sufficiently high and the short term stability of clocks is substantially smaller than ρ. Note that we introduced the drift-synchronization to make use of the fact that $\pi \ll \rho$. In a situation were the increase from ρ of ρ^S is not negligible, one can trade synchronization precision for keeping the same maximum drift rate ρ. This can be done by restricting the clock speed changes such that there remains a $\pi + \frac{E}{5s}$ "drift gap" to the median clock. This gap makes sure that we never increase the drift rates of drift-synchronized clocks above ρ but we might decrease the tightness of the drift synchronization between two clocks by $2(\pi + \frac{E}{5s})$.

We define the drift-synchronized, calibrated, and normalized hardware clock $H_i^S(v)$ by:

$$H_i^S(v) := \iota_i(H_i^C(v) - H_i^C(u)) + H_i^S(u) \overset{Eq.10}{=} \frac{\iota_i \mathcal{N}_i(H_i(v) - H_i(u))}{1 + \rho_{avg}} + H_i^S(u), \quad (21)$$

where $u < v$ is the most recent time at which ι_i, $\mathcal{N}_i$, and $\rho_{avg,i}$ were updated. We set $H_i^S(u_0) := H_i^C(u_0)$ for the time u_0 at which ι_i is defined for the first time.

Even though drift-synchronization might increase the maximum drift rate a little, in the average case it reduces the drift rate of the drift-synchronized clocks in comparison to the calibrated clocks: all drift-synchronized clocks have about the same drift-rate as the current median drift rate amongst the calibrated clocks. For example, the right graph of Figure 3 shows that the maximum drift rate of three calibrated clocks (with $f_{avg} \approx 4\text{MHz}$, 8MHz, and 10MHz) is worse than $6 * 10^{-6}$ while the maximum drift rate of the drift-synchronized clocks in the same simulated run (see the left graph of Figure 5) is less than $4 * 10^{-6}$.

We define the maximum relative drift rate ρ_r (between a clock H_i^S and the median clock H_m^S) as,

$$\rho_r := \pi + \frac{E}{5s}. \quad (22)$$

Note that two correct drift-synchronized clocks can drift apart from each other by at most,

$$2\rho_r = 2(\pi + \frac{E}{5s}). \quad (23)$$

3.6 Externally Drift-Synchronized Clocks

We shall show how to reduce the drift rate of clocks even further – if we can read the current real-time with a low error. There are several alternatives to get access to real-time, e.g. one can access a time service via the Internet. GPS receivers provide a very accurate time signal in form of a "one pulse per second" (PPS) signal: the receiver generates every second a pulse and the leading edge of the pulse is synchronized with UTC (Coordinated Universal Time) within $1\mu s$. We show how one can synchronize clocks very tightly with the PPS signal.

There are several problems when synchronizing clocks with the PPS signal. The GPS satellite signals are very weak and at least the civil signals can easily be jammed. An attacker might even be able to send faked or delayed GPS signals to confuse GPS receivers. Military grade GPS receivers have access to an authenticated signal that allows the receiver to detect faked GPS messages but they might not be able to detect all delayed/replayed GPS messages. Civil GPS receivers are also still subject to the *Selected Availability* option which artificially degrades the civil GPS time information.

For safety critical applications one might not want to place too much reliance on the correctness and availability of the PPS GPS signal. Our approach uses the PPS signal to provide very tight external synchronization as long as the PPS signal is correct. If the PPS signal is corrupted, we can still guarantee that the maximum drift of the clocks is at most about $2\rho^S$ (see Equation 20).

In this subsection we show how one can use an external time signal to determine the current drift rate of the median calibrated hardware clock: this allows us to decrease the maximum drift rate to about π. However, if the external time signal is faulty (it might suffer Byzantine faults), we still make sure that the maximum drift rate of the clocks is at most $2\rho^S$ and the correct clocks are still drift-synchronized within $2\rho_r$ (see Equation 22).

3.6.1 Hardware Support   We introduced in Section 3.1 the hardware support for the implementation of a hardware clock. To be able to synchronize a clock very tightly with the PPS signals, one has to be able to determine the value of the hardware clock at the rising edge of the PPS signal. In the simplest case this can be done using a second latch (see Figure 6). On the leading edge of the PPS signal, the current value of the counter is stored in the latch. This allows a very precise measurement of the deviation between a clock and UTC.

Using commercially available counter/timer boards, one might not have access to a second latch. However, one might have access to another counter (see Figure 7). One can use this timer to count the ticks since the last PPS signal. If one can read the 64-bit counter and the 16-bit counter at about the same time, one can compute the value of the clock at the PPS signal with a very small error.

We assume that K hardware clocks are connected to a PPS signal. Constant K can assume values between 0 (i.e. no access to a PPS signal) and N (i.e. all hardware clocks are connected to a PPS signal). To distinguish between hardware clocks attached to a PPS signal and those not attached to one, we call the former *reference clocks* and the latter non reference clocks.

3.6.2 Drift Rate Measurement   The PPS signals give us the possibility to determine the drift rate of the calibrated clocks. At every PPS signal, the current hardware clock value is latched. To drift-synchronize the calibrated clocks, we read the clocks every second (see Section 3.5). This is scheduled to be done at some real-time u which is within a few ms after we expect the PPS signal. At real-time u we not only determine the increase D_i of the calibrated hardware clocks since some real-time t, where $u - t \approx 10s$ (see Section 3.5), we also try to determine the current real-time u using the K reference clocks. We can use the latched values of the reference clocks

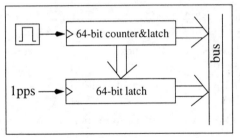 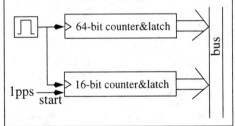

Figure 6: *Ideally, each hardware clock has an additional latch: the counter value is stored in this latch at the rising edge of the PPS signal.*

Figure 7: *The 16-bit counter starts counting on the rising edge of the PPS signal. It allows to determine the ticks since the last PPS signal. The 16-bit counter does not wrap around (non-cyclic counter) to allow the detection of overflows.*

to extrapolate the real-time u with an error of at most Λ (for a correct reference clock). Typically, $\Lambda \approx 1\mu s$ for civil GPS receivers. For each reference clock we determine the difference between the reading at u and the reading at t. Let us denote these K differences by U_i, $i \in \{1, \dots, K\}$. We expect that all U_is are approximately $10s$. To be able to mask at least $F_R := \lfloor \frac{K-1}{2} \rfloor$ reference clock/PPS failures, we determine the median U_i:

$$U_M := median\{U_i : i \in \{1, \dots, K\}\} \tag{24}$$

Note that if a majority of the reference clocks are correct, we can bound the error of U_M by Λ, i.e.

$$|U_M - u| \le \Lambda. \tag{25}$$

After determining the median difference D_m (see Section 3.5) and the approximation of $u - t$ we can determine the drift rate of the median clock H_m^C. The average drift rate $\hat{\gamma}_m$ of H_m^C in $[t, u]$ is bounded by

$$\hat{\gamma}_m \stackrel{Eq.17}{=} \frac{D_m \pm E}{u - t} - 1, \tag{26}$$

where the error term E accounts for the granularity of the clock. Let T_M denote the median reference clock value at time t. We can approximate $u - t$ by $U_M - T_M$ with an error of at most 2Λ given that a majority of the reference clocks are correct, i.e.

$$\hat{\gamma}_m = \frac{D_m \pm E}{(U_M - T_M) \pm 2\Lambda} - 1. \tag{27}$$

Hence, we can approximate $\hat{\gamma}_m$ with a maximum error of $\approx \frac{E+2\Lambda}{10s}$ when using the following synchronization factor κ:

$$\kappa := \frac{U_M - T_M}{D_M} = \frac{1}{1 + \hat{\gamma}_m} \pm \frac{E + 2\Lambda}{10s} \tag{28}$$

Since the maximum drift rate of a correct calibrated hardware clock is ρ, an implementation can make sure that the value of κ is bounded by

$$\kappa \in [\frac{1}{1-\rho}, \frac{1}{1+\rho}]. \tag{29}$$

This guarantees that one increases the maximum drift rate by at most $\pm\rho$ in case half or more of the reference clocks are faulty.

To minimize drift changes due to errors reading real-time, one might want to limit the change of κ from one round to the next. The drift rate of a correct calibrated hardware clock can change by at most π from one to the next second. Since we can switch the median clock from H_i^C in one round to H_j^C in the next round, we want to make sure that the new value of κ is at most π apart from the old values of $\kappa + \iota_j$.

Factor κ allows us to define externally drift-synchronized hardware clocks H_i^E:

$$H_i^E(v) := \kappa(H_i^S(v) - H_i^S(u)) + H_i^E(u). \tag{30}$$

As before, at real-time $u < v$ was the most recent update of κ. If a majority of the reference clocks are correct, the maximum drift rate of the clocks are bounded by

$$\rho_{min}^E \overset{Eq.28,Eq.22}{:=} \rho_r + \frac{E + 2\Lambda}{10s}. \tag{31}$$

Even when half or more of the reference clocks are faulty, we can bound the drift rate of the clocks since we bound the value of κ. In this case one can guarantee that,

$$\rho_{max}^E \overset{Eq.20,Eq.29}{:=} \rho^S + \rho. \tag{32}$$

The right graph of Figure 5 shows the simulated drift rate (averaging time 1s) of an externally drift-synchronized clock H^E base on a hardware clock with a $1\mu s$ short term stability and a reference clock reading error Λ of $1\mu s$.

3.7 Defining a Fault-Tolerant Clock FC

We shall explain how one can mask up to F hardware clock failures by combining N externally drift-synchronized clocks $H_i^E, i \in \{0, .., N-1\}$ into one fault-tolerant clock FC. We know that the drift rate of correct externally drift-synchronized clocks is at most ρ^E. Since the clocks are drift-synchronized, two correct clocks drift apart from each other by at most $2\rho_r$. This fact allows one to identify some (but not necessary all) faulty clocks. Given that a majority of the hardware clocks are correct, we can select the clock with the median drift rate to define the clock value of FC. If a majority of the clocks are faulty and their drift rate stays within $2\rho_r$ of each other, the combined clock FC might have a drift rate greater than ρ^E. Hence, one has to choose the number of hardware clocks sufficiently large such that the probability that half or more of the hardware clocks are faulty becomes negligible. For critical applications one might have to use temperature sensors and voltage sensors to detect unexpected environment conditions that might affect all oscillators (and hence, all hardware clocks), i.e. one has to detect common mode failures in case the probability of such a failure is not negligible.

The fault-tolerant clock FC is defined as follows. To calculate the value of FC at time v, we determine the clock H_i^E with the median drift rate since the time $u < v$ at which κ was updated last. The value of FC at time v is defined as:

$$FC(v) := median\{H_i^E(v) - H_i^E(u) : i \in \{1, .., N\}\} + FC(u). \qquad (33)$$

An implementation of FC therefore stores the value of FC every time κ is updated. In the following we assume that $FC(u)$ is stored in a variable $Offset$.

3.8   Properties of FC

Even if there exists only one clock H_j^E that suffers a Byzantine (i.e. an arbitrary) failure, the (short term) drift rate and granularity of FC might degrade below the quality of a correct H^E clock. In particular,

- the median clock can be faulty and can "jump", and hence, FC might jump, and

- the computation of $Offset$ might introduce a small error due to the granularity of the clocks that might increase the maximum drift rate of FC above ρ_{min}^E.

Let us quantify these two errors. We update $Offset$ about every $1s$. Each time we update $Offset$ we might introduce an error of up to E in the sense that $Offset$ might grow by $1s(1 + \rho_{min}^E) + E$ instead of at most $1s(1 + \rho_{min}^E)$, or it might grow by only $1s(1 - \rho) - E$ instead of by at least $1s(1 - \rho)$. In other words, the maximum drift rate of FC might be up to,

$$\rho_{min}^{FC} \overset{Eq.31}{:=} \rho_{min}^E + \frac{E}{1s}, \qquad \rho_{max}^{FC} \overset{Eq.32}{:=} \rho_{max}^E + \frac{E}{1s}, \qquad (34)$$

where ρ_{min}^E is only guaranteed to be valid if a majority of reference clocks are correct while ρ_{max}^E is valid even if a majority of reference clocks have failed.

To compute the "maximum jump" G of a faulty median clock (and hence, also of FC) consider the following. Two correct clocks can drift apart by at most $2s\rho_{min}^E$ before being "resynchronized" by updating $Offset$. Hence, the median clock can jump by at most

$$G := 2s\rho_{min}^E + E \qquad (35)$$

since its value is always bounded by the values of two correct clocks. Note this can also be a negative jump (if the median clock is faulty). Hence, if we compute the value of FC we have to test if there is a "negative jump" and we just increase the clock by $1ns$ instead. This is a valid approach as long as clocks cannot be read with a frequency greater than $\frac{1}{1ns}$.

3.9 External Synchronization

Even though the drift rate of FC and also the H^E clocks are very small, they can drift apart from real-time (see Figure 8). Hence, in the final step of our derivation we want to show how one can synchronize the value of a clock to real-time. The idea is that clock FC can drift apart from real-time by at most $\rho_{min}^{FC} \overset{Eq.34}{=} \rho_{min}^{E} + \frac{E}{1s}$ from real-time (when majority of reference clocks are correct). Hence, we want to define a clock EFC that changes the drift rate of FC by up to ρ_{min}^{FC} towards the current median reading of real-time. Of course, this speed change increases the drift rate of EFC to a maximum of $\rho^{EFC} := \rho_{max}^{FC} + \rho_{min}^{FC}$ in case half or more of the reference clocks are faulty. Figure 8 shows that this speed change can keep the clock within a few μs of real-time. For a more elaborate description of how to bound the external deviation please see [6].

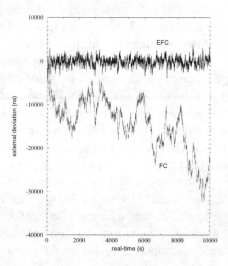

Figure 8: *Even though the drift-rate of FC is very small, FC can accumulate a substantial deviation from real-time (see lower graph of simulated run). The externally synchronized clock EFC stays within a few μs of real-time as long as a majority of the PPS signals are correct.*

4 Related Work

Verissimo, Rodrigues, and Casimiro describe in [11] a hybrid internal/external clock synchronization scheme that places a limited trust on the external time signal provided by a GPS receiver. A similar approach is described by Fetzer and Cristian in [6] that also proposes an external/internal clock synchronization algorithm for distributed systems and showed the limits on the detectability of failures of external time signals. In this paper we concentrate on how one can implement a reliable local hardware clock and how one can synchronize it with a external time signal subject to failures. If needed, one can extend this work by the approach of [6] to provide synchronization with fault-tolerant clocks of other computers (even when the external time signal is faulty).

The approach closest to the one described in this paper is the SynchUTC project of Schmid and Schossmaier [9, 10]. Their approach uses an ASIC that implements a clock that is synchronized with UTC via a GPS receiver. The ASIC allows an accurate time-stamping of network messages at send and receive time.

5 Conclusion

Clocks with a bounded drift rate are an important tool to provide communication by time between remote processes in a distributed system, even after processes become partitioned. Hence, one can use this type of communication for the reliable communication of safety critical information, e.g. to signal to processes that the system has to be switched to a fail-safe mode (see [4, 5]). However, in this paper we have explained that the drift rate of real-time clocks provided by operating systems might be severely affected by lost interrupts due to short timers and wrong interrupt priorities. Thus, these clocks might not be appropriate for mission and safety critical applications that depend on clocks with a known bounded drift rate.

This paper demonstrates that one can use COTS boards to implement fault-tolerant hardware clocks with a bounded drift rate. Of course, our approach can also be used to custom design fault-tolerant clock boards in case the reliability of available COTS boards is not sufficient for the target application. We show that $2F + 1$ hardware clocks (and not $3F + 1$ like one might expect from the lower bound for internal clock synchronization [3]) are sufficient to mask F clock failures. We cautioned that one should place only a limited trust on GPS signals since they are suseptible to delay and jamming attacks. Authenticated time servers with a request/reply pattern are more trust worthy than an one-way broadcast time service (like GPS) since one can compute the maximum reading error that enables the detection of delay attacks (and also faked messages). Thus, we use a request/reply based time service to calibrate hardware clocks.

If GPS receivers are not under attack, they provide much more accurate time information than those provided by Internet based time services. Our approach shows that one can use the GPS time information to improve the properties of the clocks as long as the information is correct while limiting the influence of faulty GPS receivers. Note that one cannot always correctly decide if an external time signal is correct or faulty [6]. Thus, one cannot completely eliminate a degradation of the local clock properties in case of faulty external clock information.

6 Appendix

Sym.	Sec.	Eq.	Meaning
D	3.5	17	increase of clock during $[t, u]$
Δf	3.2		frequency stability of a oscillator
E	3.5		maximum reading error of a calibrated clock
EFC	3.9		externally synchronized fault-tolerant clock
F	3.5	33	number of maskable hardware clock failures
FC	3.7		fault-tolerant clock
F_R	3.6.2		number of maskable reference clock failures
f_{nom}	3.2		nominal frequency of an oscillator of a hardware clock
f_{avg}	3.2		daily average frequency of an oscillator
g	3.2	2	granularity of a hardware clock
G	3.8	35	maximum granularity of fault-tolerant clock FC
E	3.5	15	maximum increase of a calibrated clock per tick
γ	3.2	3	current drift rate of a hardware clock
H_i	3.2		hardware clock i
H_i^N	3.3	7	normalized hardware clock i
H_i^C	3.4	10	calibrated clock i
H_i^S	3.5		drift-synchronized clock i
H_i^E	3.6	30	externally drift-synchronized clock i
ι_i	3.5	14	drift synchronization factor of H_i^S
K	3.6		number of hardware clocks connected to a 1PPS signal
κ	3.6.2		short term calibration factor
Λ	3.6.2		maximum external deviation of a correct reference clock
N	3.5		number of hardware clocks
$\mathcal{N}$	3.2	6	normalization factor
π	3.2		short term stability of a hardware clock
ppm			parts per million
PPS	3.6		one pulse per second
ρ	3.4	13	maximum drift rate of a calibrated clock
ρ_{avg}	3.4	9	average drift rate of a hardware clock
$\rho_{i,m}$	3.5	16	relative drift rate between H_m^C and H_m^C
ρ_{max}^E	3.6.2	32	max. drift rate of an externally drift-synchronized clock
ρ^{EFC}	3.9		maximum drift rate of EFC
ρ_{FC}	3.8	34	maximum drift rate of fault-tolerant clock FC
ρ_r	3.5	22	maximum relative drift rate of a drift-synchronized clock
ρ^S	3.5	20	maximum drift rate of a drift-synchronized clock
s, ms, ns			second, millisecond, nanosecond
t, u, v			real-time values
u_0	3.4		start time of system
U_M	3.6.2	24	clock value of median clock at u
τ	3.2		averaging period for short term drift rate

References

[1] F. Cristian. Probabilistic clock synchronization. *Distributed Computing*, 3:146–158, 1989.

[2] F. Cristian and C. Fetzer. The timed asynchronous distributed system model. *IEEE Transactions on Parallel and Distributed Systems*, Jun 1999. http://www.cs.ucsd.edu/˜cfetzer/MODEL.

[3] D. Dolev, J. Y. Halpern, and R. Strong. On the possibility and impossibility of achieving clock synchronization. *Journal of Computer and System Science*, 32(2):230–250, 1986.

[4] D. Essame, J. Arlat, and D. Powell. Padre: A protocol for asymmetric duplex redundancy. In *Proceedings of the Seventh IFIP International Working Conference on Dependable Computing for Critical Applications*, San Jose, USA, Jan 1999.

[5] C. Fetzer and F. Cristian. Fail-awareness: An approach to construct fail-safe applications. In *Proceedings of the 27th Annual International Symposium on Fault-Tolerant Computing*, Seattle, Jun 1997. http://www.cs.ucsd.edu/˜cfetzer/FAPS.

[6] C. Fetzer and F. Cristian. Integrating external and internal clock synchronization. *Journal of Real-Time Systems*, 12(2):123–171, March 1997. http://www.cs.ucsd.edu/˜cfetzer/TP.

[7] D. L. Mills. Internet time synchronization: the network time protocol. *IEEE Trans. Communications*, 39(10):1482–1493, Oct 1991.

[8] D. L. Mills. Modelling and analysis of computer network clocks. Technical Report 92-5-2, University of Delaware, Electrical Engineering Department, May 1992.

[9] U. Schmid. Synchronized utc for distributed real-time systems. *Control Engineering Practice*, pages 877–884, 1995.

[10] K. Schossmaier and D. Loy. An asic supporting external clock synchronization for distributed real-time systems. In *Proceedings of the 8th Euromicro Workshop on Real-Time Systems*, pages 277–282, L'Aquila, Italy, June 1996.

[11] P. Verissimo, L. Rodrigues, and A. Casimiro. Cesiumspray: a precise and accurate global clock service for large-scale systems. *Real-Time Systems*, 12:243–294, 1997.

[12] J. R. Vig. Introduction to quartz frequency standards. Technical Report SLCET-TR-92-1 (Rev. 1), Army Research Laboratory, Electronics and Power Sources Directorate, Fort Monmouth, NJ 07703-5601, U.S.A., Oct 1992.

Formal Methods

A methodology for proving control systems with Lustre and PVS[*][†]

S.Bensalem, P.Caspi, C.Parent-Vigouroux, C.Dumas
VERIMAG
name@imag.fr

Abstract

In this paper, we intend to show how to use the synchronous data-flow language Lustre, combined with the PVS proof system in deriving provably-correct (distributed) control programs. We hopefully illustrate, based on a railway emergency braking system example, the features of our approach — asynchronous periodic programs with nearly the same period, communicating by sampling — equational reasoning which leaves to the Lustre compiler the task of scheduling computations — no distinction between control programs and physical environments which are sampled in the same way. This allows us to provide "elementary" proofs based on difference equations instead of differential ones which require more involved PVS formalization.

1 Introduction

Control systems form an important class of critical computer systems: it is in this domain that some of the most critical applications can be found, for instance in civil aircrafts, ground transportation, nuclear power etc. Thus, a lot of activity has been devoted to ensuring and improving hardware and software reliability. Concerning software, fault avoidance has always been, beside fault tolerance, an important issue and program deductive proofs can be, in complement with other methods, a tentative answer to the problem. Proving software is a broad subject which has drawn the attention of many researchers for a long time and tools, languages, and methods become widely available for handling the problem in general. We want to address here the problem of using these tools within the context of critical control systems. This, in our opinion, requires taking into account the following features of the domain:

---

[*]This work has been partially supported by Esprit Projects SYRF and CRISYS, and INRIA action PRESYSA

[†]This paper appeared in the proceedings of the seventh Working Conference on Dependable Computing for Critical Applications (DCCA7), San Jose, January 1999.

Data-flow: Control engineers use to think (analyze, specify) of their systems in terms of data-flow. For instance, they use tools such as Matlab and MatrixX to build and simulate systems. Translating these specifications into imperative programs can be seen as a boring and error-prone task. On the contrary, it may be expected that the use of synchronous data-flow languages is likely to alleviate this task and provide for safer programs.

Distribution: Beside the fact that most control systems are distributed, there is an intrinsic factor of distribution based on the division between the system and its environment. In general for control systems, it is not possible to even express (not to speak of proving) properties of the system without taking into account its environment (closed loop systems). Thus distribution has to be carefully taken into account, and some methodology is needed for that.

Hybridity: Furthermore, this environment is in most cases continuous, modeled with differential equations, for instance, while computers have discrete time behaviors. This is an important issue that must be carefully discussed and taken into account.

1.1 Paper content

In this paper we shall try to address these issues through a toy example, consisting of an emergency brake system for railways. The data-flow aspect will be taken into account by using the Lustre [9] synchronous data-flow language for describing and programming systems and by using the PVS [18] verification system for handling proofs of Lustre programs. Distribution will be handled here by expressing *both* the control program, the environment, and communication between both within the *same* Lustre-PVS framework, thanks to the sampling and holding primitives of Lustre. This calls for some methodological precaution, consisting of carefully distinguishing between environment variables and the way they are perceived by the control program. This raises the question: since Lustre does not allow for continuous time systems, how to take into account the hybrid aspect of the example? The proposed answer is quite simple: instead of building a complex theory of continuity and mathematical analysis in PVS, we propose here to simply take care of it through a careful handling of integration errors (in the same way as engineers compute bounds on errors).

This will be presented as follows: first we shall present Lustre, PVS and the principles of a translation tool from Lustre to PVS. Then we present in Lustre the toy example and the PVS proof of its principle. Finally, we introduce the distributed nature of the example and take care of the environment.

1.2 Related issues

On the one hand, many aspects of control systems are shared with hardware systems and protocols, and a long lasting research has been devoted to them, within the verification community. However, most associated tools are based on (automatic) algorithmic methods, while control is mostly based on numerical properties which can hardly be automatically handled for reasons of complexity and decidability. For instance the Lustre language has an associated model-checker, Lesar which has been successfully applied to hardware and simple control problems [10]. However, we have checked that it cannot cope with the problems we address here.

On the other hand, deductive tools like PVS [18] and Coq [6] provide very general frameworks that need being specialized to some particular domain.

In between we find methods well adapted to sequential programming like B and VDM [1, 12]. These methods can be adapted to the problems we want to address, but there is some price to pay for it, because data-flow programming is not natural here: in [1], Abrial describes and handles a control problem, the celebrated steam boiler. Yet a large part of the control program derivation consists of sequencing the program and proving it, an operation which is for instance automatically performed by the Lustre compiler.

We also find specific proof tools adapted to reactive systems like the TLA approach [15]. This method is more general than our Lustre-PVS one, in the sense that it can handle both synchronous and asynchronous systems and could as well support the proposed methodology.

Finally, we find so-called hybrid system methods and tools. For instance a very similar problem is handled in PVS by N.Lynch and co-authors [7]. However we differ from this approach because we think continuous time is uselessly complex and can be avoided by sampling both the system and its environment. This is clearly an opinion that somewhat contradicts current research trends on hybrid systems. Yet, using computers for controlling physical systems is a long lasting activity which goes back to the early eighties [14]. According to control theory, there are two possible approaches: either design a continuous controller and then sample it, or sample the process to be controlled and design a sampled controller based on sampled control system theory. We follow here the later approach.

2 The Lustre-PVS approach

Synchronous data-flow programming has become a popular approach, for the quite obvious reason that automatic control engineers use to analyze and specify their systems in terms of signals flowing through networks of operators (block diagrams). Thus, synchronous data-flow languages allow them to directly translate their specifications into code without undertaking a manual, error prone, coding phase. Several real world achievements have been obtained in this way, among which we can cite the "fly-by-wire" system of Airbus aircrafts [4], the monitoring system of FRAMATOME nuclear plants, designed by SCHNEIDER ELECTRIC [2],

and the interlocking system of the Hong Kong subway designed by CS TRANS-
PORT. Of these examples, the last two ones have been based on the Lustre data-flow
synchronous language [9].

2.1 The Lustre language

In this presentation, we focus on semantic aspects, perhaps at the expense of
syntactic details, the more so as our main interest is in the translation to PVS.

2.1.1 Basic concepts   Basically, a Lustre program describes stream functions whose
values can be recursively defined. Those functions are given by sets of equations
defining output and local streams thanks to expressions built over input, output
and local streams, constant streams, stream primitive operators and user defined
functions:

- Constants denote constant streams; for instance `true` denotes the stream
  $[t, t, t \ldots]$

- variables denote streams,

x	x_0	x_1	x_2	...

- Usual operators operate pointwise over streams; for instance `1 + 2` is the
  stream $[3, 3, \ldots]$. Similarly,

c	t	f	t	...
x	x_0	x_1	x_2	...
y	y_0	y_1	y_2	...
if c then x else y	x_0	y_1	x_2	...

- A unit delay operator `fby` "followed-by" (actually `->pre` in Lustre) can be
  represented by the diagram:

x	x_0	x_1	x_2	...
y	y_0	y_1	y_2	...
x fby y	x_0	y_0	y_1	...

These constructs represent the core of Lustre. Complex behaviors can be easily
created using this simple language, for instance:

An integrator:

```
y = (0 fby y) + x
```

whose behavior is depicted in the diagram:

x	x_0	x_1	x_2	...
y	x_0	$x_0 + x_1$	$x_0 + x_1 + x_2$	...
0 fby y	0	x_0	$x_0 + x_1$	...

A clock divider:

```
c = true  fby (not c)
```

whose behavior is depicted in the diagram:

not c	f	t	f	$\ldots$
true fby (not c)	t	f	t	$\ldots$

These examples illustrate the use of the delay operator in building recursive stream definitions without deadlocks. The Lustre compiler performs static checks ensuring deadlock freedom.

2.1.2 Advanced concepts

Nodes: Convenient systems of equations can be saved into user-defined functions called nodes, which can be elsewhere used in expressions; for instance:

```
node integr (x : int) returns (y : int)
let
     y = (0 fby y) + x ;
tel
...
z = integr (x fby z) + u
```

Node parameters are typed and the compiler performs usual type checks. Furthermore, the compiler checks for functionality: any local and output stream of a node should have one and only one defining equation.

Multi sampling: It may be that slow and fast processes coexist in a given application. A sampling (or filtering operator) "when" allows fast processes to communicate with slower ones:

c	f	t	f	t	$\ldots$
x	x_0	x_1	x_2	x_3	$\ldots$
x when c		x_1		x_3	$\ldots$

Conversely, a holding mechanism, `current` allows slow processes to communicate with faster ones:

c	f	t	f	t	$\ldots$
x	x_0	x_1	x_2	x_3	$\ldots$
y		y_0		y_1	$\ldots$
current(c,x) y	x_0	y_0	y_0	y_1	$\ldots$

As we can see in the diagrams above, when discards its input x when the input condition c is false. Conversely, `current` fills the holes created by when with the input value y it got the last time the condition c was true, if any, and otherwise with an initializing sequence x. A free use of these primitives can yield overflow memory effects. Here also, the compiler checks for bounded memory. Those checks are called "clock calculus" and are essential in the synchronous nature of Lustre.

Assertions: Always "true" boolean expressions can be asserted for several purposes, for instance for expressing non independent input properties; for instance:

```
assert (c or (true fby c));
```

says that c will not stay "false" for more than one time unit.

2.2   Lustre in PVS

In this section, we first give a brief description of the PVS system and then we show how Lustre semantics can be specified using PVS.

2.2.1   PVS Features   PVS (Prototype Verification System) [18] is an environment for constructing specifications and verifications that has been developed at SRI International's Computer Science Laboratory. In comparison to other widely used verification systems, such as Coq [6], HOL [8] and the Boyer-Moore prover [3], the distinguishing characteristic of PVS is a coherent realization, combining within a single system:

- a highly expressive specification language which is based on higher-order logic with a parser, and an expressive type system. The type-checker checks for simple type correctness and generates proof obligations. A specification in PVS is organized in theories, which may depend on other theories via an importing mechanism. In particular, any theory may import from the set of built-in theories. A theory consists of a sequence of declarations, which provide names for types, constants, variables, axioms, and formulas. The language supports modularity and reuse by means of parameterized theories.

- an interactive proof checker consisting of a higher-level collection of inference steps (written in a strategy language) that can be used to reduce the proof goal to simpler subgoals that can be proved automatically by primitive rule steps of the prover. The primitive proof steps for constructing proofs involve efficient decision procedures for equality and linear arithmetic, automatic rewriting, and BDD-based propositional simplifications.

2.2.2   Lustre in PVS   We now focus on the specification of the Lustre constructs in PVS. In doing this, we face the problem that, as we have seen at section 2.1.1, streams can be recursively defined in Lustre programs. But, unfortunately, these "non-terminating" recursive definitions are not allowed in PVS. All definitions in PVS are total [17], and form a conservative extension. In order to guarantee these

```
lustre [t:TYPE] : THEORY

  BEGIN
  x       : VAR t
  i       : VAR nat
  c       : VAR sequence[bool]
  xs, ys : VAR sequence[t]

  const(x)(i) : t = x
  CONVERSION const

  fby(xs,ys)(i) : t = IF i=0 THEN xs(0) ELSE ys(i-1) ENDIF

  ifl(c,xs,ys)(i) : t = IF c(i) THEN xs(i) ELSE ys(i) ENDIF

  END lustre
```

Table 1: Lustre theory

conditions, a function named MEASURE is required. This function is used to show that the definition terminates, by generating a proof obligation consisting of proving that the MEASURE function decreases with each call. There exist at least two ways of overcoming this problem:

- the first solution uses a functional style and views streams as a co-inductive type [19, 16, 11],

- the second one consists simply of viewing streams as infinite sequences. In this framework, a constant stream v of type t would be translated in PVS as:

```
const(v:t) : sequence[t] = LAMBDA(i) : v
```

that is to say, the function which associates with any natural number i the value v.

2.2.3 Specification of Lustre primitives The parameterized theory lustre, displayed at table 1 implements the second solution. ifl is the extension of the current conditional over sequences. The parameter t is treated as a fixed uninterpreted type. When the theory lustre is used by another theory it must be instantiated.

The parameterized theory lustre_extend, displayed at table 2 allows us to extend pointwise operators over sequences.

The specification of current and when are more complicated than the previous ones. We need an intermediate function count : intuitively, count can be seen as a function on natural numbers which counts the number of c(i) = true for

```
lustre_extend [t1,t2:TYPE]  :  THEORY

  BEGIN

  i      : VAR nat
  xs,ys  : VAR sequence[t1]
  f      : VAR [t1->t2]
  g      : VAR [t1,t1->t2]

  map(f)(xs)(i)  :  t2 = f(xs(i))

  map2(g)(xs,ys)(i)  :  t2 = g(xs(i),ys(i))

  CONVERSION lustre_extend.map, map2

  END lustre_extend
```

Table 2: Map theories

$0 \leq i \leq n$. Furthermore, we need to restrict to clocks having an infinite number of occurrences, so as to keep infinite sequences when filtering. The corresponding theory, inspired from [5] is shown at table 3.

2.2.4 The feedback loop problem

Yet this still doesn't solve the problem of Lustre recursive stream definitions; for instance we would like to write:

```
integr( x : sequence[int] )  :  sequence[int] = y
   WHERE y =  fby(0, y) +  x
```

which is not allowed. We propose here to overcome the problem by writing instead the input/output predicate:

```
integr(x,y:sequence[real])  :  THEORY
   BEGIN

   y_ax : LEMMA y =  fby(0, y) +  x

   END integr
```

However, this is not strictly equivalent, in the sense that we may now have either several or no output sequence corresponding to one input sequence. This solution works because we only aim at translating valid Lustre programs for which the compiler has checked for functionality and deadlock-freedom.

In this context, this solution looks acceptable and then yields valuable benefits:

- it is easy to read and user-friendly: input-output predicates encapsulate equations very close to the original Lustre equations,

```
exten2_lustre [ t : TYPE] : THEORY
  BEGIN
    IMPORTING lustre, lustre_extend, bounds

    clock : TYPE = {c:sequence[bool] |  (NOT c(0)) AND
                 FORALL (n: nat):
                     EXISTS (m: nat): m >= n and c(m)}

    n          : VAR nat
    c          : VAR clock
    xs, ys     : VAR sequence[t]

    count(c) (n): recursive nat =
     IF c(n) THEN 1 ELSE 0 ENDIF +
     IF n=0 THEN 0 ELSE count(c)(n-1) ENDIF
     MEASURE n

    current (c,xs) (ys) (n) : t =
      LET m = count(c)(n)
      IN IF m = 0 THEN xs(0) ELSE ys(m-1) ENDIF

    index(c)(n) : nat = glb {m:nat | count(c)(m) >= n}

    lwhen(c,xs)(n) : t = xs(index(c)(n+1))

  END exten2_lustre
```

Table 3: Extensions

- it sometimes yields very simple proofs: for instance, the PVS proof of

```
map2(+)(const(1), const(2)) = const(3)
```

is automatic and doesn't use any induction at all.

- a disadvantage of this approach is that, while functional composition is straightforward, composing predicates requires creating intermediate variables unknown to the programmer. We are currently working on an alternative solution based on the theory of Kahn networks [13].

3   A toy railway control problem

This section demonstrates our approach using a simple but non-trivial example taken from the automatic control of a railway systems. Each train on the track has a computerized controller which periodically receives some information about its speed, given by some sensor, and the position of the train in front of it, broadcasted by some transmission device. Based on this information the controller decides whether or not to actuate an emergency brake in order to avoid colliding with the preceding train.

3.1   Specification

In this specification, all variables are Lustre variables and denote streams. Our specification is made, first, of assumptions about the physical world. For this, we consider the train 1 that is behind:

- Its acceleration, a, is, if the controller actuates the brake then -afu, where afu is the (positive) deceleration of the emergency brake, otherwise am, some unknown stream, yet not larger than a maximal acceleration constant amax:
  ```
  const afu, amax : real;
  a = if fu then -afu else am;
  assert( (afu > 0 ) and (am < amax) );
  ```
- Trains are not supposed to move backward and are assumed to be initially stopped.
  ```
  const dt :real;
  assert dt>0;
  vv = (0 fby v) + a*dt;
  v = if vv>=0 then vv else 0;
  ```
  where dt is the time period at which the system runs.

- The distance between trains 2 and 1, d, is the difference between the position of train 2, x2 and the integral of the speed of train 1 v. A positive initial distance is assumed, and train 2 does not move backward:

```
assert ((x2    >= 0) fby true)
          and x2 - (x2 fby x2) >= 0);
x = (0 fby x) + v*dt;
d = x2 - x;
```

Given this environment a specification could be:

Find a controller law for fu *such that trains never collide:* d > 0

3.2   A controller proposal

fu is a boolean stream which says whether the train has to brake or not. To synthesize it, at each time, the worst situation has to be considered: train 2 stops (its speed is 0) and train 1 has the maximal acceleration amax. If, when in this situation, the train waits the next instant for braking and this results in a collision, then it must begin braking now.

```
fu = df((x2 fby (d - v*dt)) - amax*dt*dt,
        (0 fby v) + amax*dt
      )< 0 ;
```

where df is the final distance function: df(d,v) is the distance between the current train and the preceding one that will be reached starting from distance d and speed v if the later doesn't move and if the former continuously brakes with deceleration -a:

$floor(\frac{v}{a*dt}) = u$ is the number of steps up to which the speed will get zero. Thus,

$$df(d,v) = d - \sum_{i=1}^{u}(v.dt - \sum_{j=1}^{i} a.dt^2) = d - uv.dt + \frac{u(u+1)}{2}a.dt^2$$

3.3   Controller correctness

In order to prove the controller correctness, we translate the specification into PVS. The translation is shown at table 4. Then, we prove that the two trains never collide.

```
correctness : THEOREM FORALL (n:nat): prop(n)
```

In doing this, we need the following steps:

1. speed is always positive,

    ```
    vpos : THEOREM FORALL (n:nat): v(n) >= 0
    ```

2. a positive final distance is a system invariant

    ```
    inv : THEOREM FORALL (n:nat): df(d(n),v(n)) >=0
    ```

```
train: THEORY [am,x2,v,d:sequence[real],prop:sequence[bool]]
 BEGIN
   IMPORTING lustre, lustre_extend

     a  : sequence[real]
     fu : sequence[bool]

     amax,afu,dt : real

     a_ax : AXIOM a = ifl(fu,-afu,am)

     v_ax : AXIOM v = let vv = fby(0,v) + a*dt
                      in   ifl(vv >= 0 ,vv,  0)

     x_ax : AXIOM x = fby(0,x) + v*dt

     d_ax : AXIOM d = x2 - x

     fu_ax: AXIOM fu =
         df( fby (x2, d-v*dt)- amax*dt*dt,
             fby (0,  v)+ amax*dt
           )< 0

     assert_ax : AXIOM
        afu > 0 AND am < amax AND dt > 0
           AND fby((x2  >= 0), true)
              AND x2 - fby(x2,x2) >= 0

     prop_ax : AXIOM prop = d >=0

  END train
```

Table 4: Train theory

3. as a consequence, the trains will not collide.

The proofs are mainly based on induction over naturals and on algebraic properties of equalities and inequalities. Note two important lemmas that are proved meanwhile and that will be very useful in the sequel:

- the final distance function is an increasing function of d and a decreasing function of v:

```
mondf : LEMMA
   FORALL (d1,d2,v1,v2:real):
      d1<= d2 AND v2 >=0 AND v2 <= v1
         => df(d1,v1)   <= df(d2,v2)
```

- when braking, the final distance function remains constant:

```
dminus : LEMMA
   FORALL (d,v:real): v>=0 AND a >= 0
      =>   df(d,v) = df(d-(v + a*dt)*dt, v-a*dt)
```

4   Implementation

Up to now, the proposed system is an abstract one. In order to make it realistic, we must split it into parts:

- the train, which receives from the controller an acceleration and "computes" a speed and a distance,

- the controller which reads a speed , receives a position from the train ahead, and computes an acceleration,

- and the controller of the train ahead which communicates its position.

4.1   The distributed system

4.1.1   The train   The train is merely the preceding train, but for the acceleration and control law:

```
const  dt :real;

node train(a, x2:real) returns (v, x, d:real);
var vv:real;
let
   vv = (0 fby v) + a*dt ;
   v = if vv>=0 then vv else 0;
   x = (0 fby x)  + v*dt;
   d = x2 - x;
   assert   ((x2 >= 0) fby true)
            and  (x2 - (x2 fby x2) >= 0);
tel
```

4.1.2 The train controller It performs the other computations. Yet, it does not receive the distance and has to recompute it. Thus, we shall have in the system two copies of the distance: the "real" one, computed by `train` and the computed one, computed by `controller`. Also note that the controller issues its position toward the train behind it.

```
const afu, amax: real;

node control (am, v, x2 :real) returns (a, x  :real);
var d:real; fu: bool;
let
   assert am < amax;
   x = (0 fby x) + v*dt;
   d = x2 - x;
   fu  = df((x2 fby (d - v*dt)) - amax*dt*dt,
            (0 fby v) + amax*dt
          )< 0;
   a   = if fu then -afu else am;
tel
```

4.2 Subsystem communication

Now, those subsystems need to communicate. The idea here is that both the physical world `train` and train controllers run periodically with the same period `dt` but *asynchronously* and communicate by sampling. This is realistic concerning communications between computers and corresponds to actual popular implementations in the control field: networks of periodic computers communicating by shared memory, periodic field busses, serial lines, or even radio. It may be less realistic when it comes to the relations between a computer and a physical environment. However, in many cases, it looks convenient because most often controllers need to simulate the environment, so as to take correct decisions [1]. Thus, the period of the controller has to be small enough in order to get an accurate simulation. Simulating the actual environment with the same period will then also be accurate, and the only assumption we need is the asynchronous sampling communication between them.

This can be modeled as follows: Each process p runs on its own clock `cp` . A value v issued from p is visible from outside through its past current value:

```
current(cp,v0)(v)
```

where v0 is an initial value known by everybody. When another process p′ wants to read it, it just samples it according to its own clock cp′.

Furthermore, we will need, in the proofs, to express the fact that those clocks, though independent, share the same period. This will be done thanks to an assertion stating that there cannot be more than two ticks of clock 1 between two ticks of clock 2 and conversely. Let `same_period` be that property. It can be strengthened to account for any clock drift by:

---

[1]This is the case of our controller, which has to integrate the speed for computing the distance.

```
const   dt, afu, amax : real; drinv:int;
node system(am1,am2,x3,xp3:real;c1,c2,ct:bool)
     returns (prop:bool)

var v1,v2,x1,x2,xp1,xp2,a1,a2,d1,d2:real;
let
  v1,x1,d1 = current(ct,(0,0,0))train((a1,x2)when ct);
  v2,x2,d2 = current(ct,(0,0,0))train((a2,x3)when ct);
  a1,xp1 = current(c1,(0,0))control((am1,v1,xp2) when c1);
  a2,xp2 = current(c2,(0,0))control((am2,v2,xp3) when c2);
  assert     same_period(ct,c1,drinv)
         and same_period(ct,c2,drinv)
         and same_period(c1,c2,drinv);
  assert dt > 0 and afu > 0 and amax > 0;
  prop = d1 >= 0;
tel
```

Table 5: The whole system

```
c1,c2     : VAR clock
driftinv : VAR nat;

drift_def(c1,c2,driftinv) : bool =
  FORALL (n,m :nat): m <= driftinv
     =>
  index(c1)(n+m+1)>index(c2)(count(c2)(index(c1)(n))+m)

same_period(c1,c2,driftinv) : bool =
  drift_def(c1,c2,driftinv) AND drift_def(c2,c1,driftinv)
```

Here, `driftinv` counts the number of periods needed for a clock to exceed the other one by one unit.

4.3 The whole system

The whole system is shown at table 5. It is made of the two trains and their respective controllers. Each controller has its own clock, the environment (the two trains) also has a clock, and these clocks are assumed to share the same period.

4.4 Communication abstraction

However, this system, when translated to PVS, is too large to be proved. A first step toward a proof consists of abstracting communication. For this we consider a variable `v`, computed on clock `c`, communicated to another subsystem working on clock `c'` and then re-sampled on clock `c`:

```
v' = (current(c',v) ((current(c,v) v) when c')) when c
```

Then we prove the property:

Theorem 1 (Sampling) `sampling : THEOREM`
```
(FORALL (n:nat): same_period(c,c',1)(n))
 => FORALL (n:nat):
    ((v' = v) or (v'= fby(v,v)) or (v'= fby(v,fby(v,v))))(n)
```

meaning that the value used by another process cannot be two time unit older than the value used by the process issuing it.

Now, this property has an interesting corollary, when applied to smooth signals, i.e. signals with bounded variations. This corollary is as follows:

Theorem 2 (Smooth sampling) `smooth_sampling : THEOREM`
```
(FORALL (n:nat): abst_val(v - fby(v, v))(n) < e )
   => FORALL (n:nat):  abst_val(v'- v)(n) < 2*e
```

4.5 The system revisited

When trying to apply these results to the system, we meet two obstacles:

- train speeds are not upper-bounded and, thus, train positions are not smooth. We must redesign the controller so as to enforce speed limits:
```
const vlim : real;
assert vlim > 0;
fu  = df((x2  fby (d - v*dt)) - amax*dt*dt,
         (0 fby v) + amax*dt
       )< 0
      or (0 fby v) + amax*dt > vlim;
```

- even in case of speed limits, we still cannot prove the system; this is due to the fact that the difference between the train position computed by the controller and the one "computed" by the train cannot be upper-bounded. Position computation is an integral and can be seen as a non-stable system[2]. Such a system sums up input and integration errors and two such systems (the "real" and the computed one) put in parallel, will sooner or later diverge. This is why train controllers need, from time to time to be given the actual position, for instance thanks to beacons located on the track. However, taking into account these features is complicated and goes far away from the object of the paper. We shall thus limit ourselves to assuming that each train controller always samples its position.

We can now compute :

---
[2]In fact a limit-stable system.

Speed errors: Defining

```
vlc = (current (c1,0) (v1 when c1)) when ct;
```

i.e. the image in the "train" of the speed as sampled by the controller, we can prove:

```
speed_error: LEMMA FORALL (n:nat):
  v1(n) <= vlc(n) + 2*amax*dt
```

Distance errors: Similarly, letting

```
xlc = (current (c1,0) (x1 when c1)) when ct;
```

be the image, in the "train", of the position as sampled by the controller, we can prove:

```
distance_error: LEMMA FORALL (n:nat):
  x1(n) <= xlc(n) + 2*vlim*dt
  AND
  x1(n) >= xlc(n)
```

Finally, the control program which allows us to prove the correctness property is:

```
node control (am,v,x2,x1:real)
     returns (a,xp:real);
var d:real; fu: bool;
let
  d   = x2 - x1 -2*vlim*dt;
  fu  = df((x2  fby (d - v*dt)) - 3*amax*dt*dt,
           (0 fby v) + 3*amax*dt
          )< 0
        or (0 fby v) + 3*amax*dt > vlim ;
  a   = if fu then -afu else am ;
  xp = x1 ;
tel
```

5   Conclusion

In this paper, we intended to show how to use the synchronous data-flow language Lustre, combined with the PVS proof system in deriving a proved (distributed) control program. We hopefully illustrated the features of our approach :

- asynchronous periodic programs with nearly the same period, communicating by sampling and well taken into account by Lustre,

- equational reasoning which leaves to the Lustre compiler the task of scheduling computations,

- no distinction between control programs and physical environments which are sampled in the same way. This allows us to provide "elementary" proofs based on difference equations instead of differential ones which require more involved PVS formalization.

However the approach is only partially automated: the translation tool from Lustre to PVS does not yet handle sampling and holding primitives. A new, more complete and fully functional version based on Kahn's theory [13] is in progress.

Furthermore, it can be objected that this sampling-based approach may be better adapted to numerical problem, like the one presented here, than to logical ones involving complex state machines. This will be a subject for future work.

Finally the question of whether this experiment can be extended to larger applications and other domains is left open. Let us simply note here that the chosen example is a favorable one, in the sense that it bears simple, logical specifications. This may not be the case of most control systems. For instance a specification for an aircraft controller could be "keep the aircraft within its flight domain", and this is surely a less favorable case.

Acknowledgment   The authors acknowledge Daniel Pilaud from INRIA who initiated this work, and Oder Maler from Verimag for friendly discussions on hybrid systems.

References

[1] J.-R. Abrial. *The B-Book*. Cambridge University Press, 1995.

[2] J.L. Bergerand and E. Pilaud. SAGA; a software development environment for dependability in automatic control. In *SAFECOMP'88*. Pergamon Press, 1988.

[3] R.S. Boyer and J.S.Moore. *A Computational Logic*. Academic Press, 1979.

[4] D. Brière, D. Ribot, D. Pilaud, and J.L. Camus. Methods and specification tools for Airbus on-board systems. In *Avionics Conference and Exhibition*, London, December 1994. ERA Technology.

[5] P. Caspi and N. Halbwachs. A functional model for describing and reasoning about time behaviour of computing systems. *Acta Informatica*, 22:595–627, 1986.

[6] T. Coquand and G. Huet. The calculus of construction. *Information and Computation*, 76(2), 1988.

[7] E. Doginova and N. Lynch. Safety verification fo automated platoon maneuvers: A case study. In O. Maler, editor, *Hybrid and real-Time Systems, Grenoble*, volume 1201 of *Lecture Notes in Computer Science*, pages 154–170. Springer, 1997.

[8] M. J. Gordon and T. F. Melham. *Introduction to HOL : A Theorem Proving Environment for Higher-Order Logic*. Cambridge University Press, Cambridge, UK, 1993.

[9] N. Halbwachs, P. Caspi, P. Raymond, and D. Pilaud. The synchronous dataflow programming language LUSTRE. *Proceedings of the IEEE*, 79(9):1305–1320, September 1991.

[10] N. Halbwachs, F. Lagnier, and C. Ratel. Programming and verifying real-time systems by means of the synchronous dataflow language LUSTRE. *IEEE Trans. on Software Engineering*, 18(9):785–793, September 1992. Available through anonymous ftp at `imag.fr:pub/SPECTRE/LUSTRE/PAPERS/lustre.tse.ps.gz`.

[11] U. Hensel and B. Jacobs. Coalgebraic theories of sequences in pvs. Technical Report CSI-R9708, Computer Science Institute, University of Nijmegen, 1997. available at `http://www.cs.kun.nl/˙bart/PAPERS/`.

[12] C. B. Jones. *Systematic Software Development using VDM*. Prentice Hall International, 1990.

[13] G. Kahn. The semantics of a simple language for parallel programming. In *IFIP 74*. North Holland, 1974.

[14] K.J.Åström and B.Wittenmark. *Computer Controlled Systems*. Prentice-Hall, 1984.

[15] L.Lamport. The temporal logic of actions. *ACM Trans. Prog. Lang. and Sys.*, 16(3), 1994.

[16] P.S. Miner and S.D. Johnson. Verification of an optimized fault-tolerant clock synchronization circuit. In Mary Sheeran and Satnam Singh, editors, *Designing Correct Circuits*, Electronic Workshops in Computing, Bastad, Sweden, September 1996. Springer-Verlag.

[17] N.Shankar, S.Owre, and J.Rushby. The PVS Proof Checker : A Reference Manual. march 1993.

[18] S. Owre, J. Rushby, and N. Shankar. PVS: a prototype verification system. In *11th Conf. on Automated Deduction*, volume 607 of *Lecture Notes in Computer Science*, pages 748–752. Springer Verlag, 1992.

[19] C. Paulin-Mohring. Circuits as streams in Coq, verification of a sequential multiplier. Research Report 95-16, Laboratoire de l'Informatique du Parallélisme, September 1995. Available at `http://www.ens-lyon.fr:80/LIP/lip/publis/`.

Prototyping and Formal Requirement Validation of GPRS: A Mobile Data Packet Radio Service for GSM

Laurent Andriantsiferana, Brahim Ghribi, Luigi Logrippo
Telecommunications Software Engineering Research Group,
School of Information Technology and Engineering, University of Ottawa
{andrian, bghribi, luigi}@csi.uottawa.ca

Abstract

A methodology and an experience for validating a substantial part of a mobile data standard, ETSI's General Packet Radio Service, is presented. The standard was specified in LOTOS, which provided a formal prototype for the system. Testing processes were composed with the specification, and temporal logic properties were checked. At least two major design errors were identified.

1. Introduction

The application of formal methods is becoming a crucial step in detecting design flaws and in validating the requirements of complex systems. Formal methods can be used in the specification, development and verification of systems to increase the confidence in their quality and reliability.

Formal methods have witnessed a growing interest in the past decade in the areas of prototyping, simulation, and validation of informal requirements. They are increasingly used as means to build confidence in designs. LOTOS [1][2] is a formal specification language that is well suited for telecommunication systems and has been used extensively in the past few years for a wide variety of applications. Concepts from CSP, CCS, and data algebras have been combined in LOTOS, making it suitable for specifying protocols and services.

This paper describes our experience in using LOTOS to formally specify a subset of the General Packet Radio Service (GPRS) and the validation tools and techniques used. We have focused in this project on the service description stage 1 and stage 2 proposed by ETSI for GPRS. This work has faced many challenges mainly because of the following reasons:

- GPRS is a standard under design, hence it is still evolving.
- GPRS incorporates several features and while it includes some already known protocols, it also introduces some new ones.
- GPRS is a packet-switched mobile system. This implies complexity due to location management issues and packet delivery.

- The analysis of complex systems, such as GPRS, is constrained by the well-known problem of combinatorial state explosion.

We start by describing the approach used to capture the informal requirements and their translation into a formal specification. We then provide an overview of the GPRS system and give a background on the main LOTOS operators. We provide some details related to the LOTOS specification of GPRS before we focus on the validation activities. Finally we present the properties we have checked and we discuss in detail two design problems that we found.

2. From requirements to formal specification

Standards documents combine a mixture of text, tables, and visual notations such as *Message Sequence Charts* (MSCs) [3]. An iterative process is usually needed to go from the informal requirements to a high-level abstract and formal representation (formal specification). The evolving nature of standards, and the multitude of styles and notations used to describe them, add complexity to the process. One must not forget that standards tend to be quite unstable at their early stages and for this reason, the specification should be flexible enough to accommodate changes. Figure 1 illustrates the steps we used in this process. In the first step, *requirements capture*, we identify the *architectural requirements* which specify the various objects, processes, or entities of the system and their inter-relations and interfaces. We also extract the *behavioural requirements* which define the expected behaviour of the system. In the second step, *requirements synthesis,* we translate these captured requirements into a formal representation in LOTOS. The iterative nature of this process may reveal incompleteness, ambiguities, and inconsistencies in the specification. We can revisit the captured requirements and the original draft documents for several iterations (step 3).

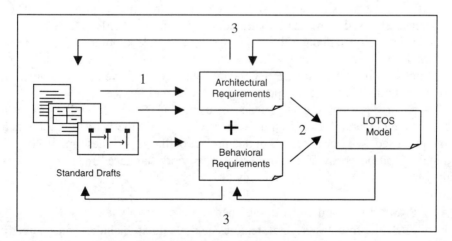

Figure 1. Requirements capture and modeling

Since it is executable, a LOTOS specification can be considered as a *model* or *prototype* of the system and can serve several purposes:

- It can be formally validated with respect to several properties.
- It can be used for system simulation.
- It can be used to generate scenarios (also called use cases) and test cases.
- It can be used as a guide for implementation.

We focus in this paper on the specification and validation steps of the requirements which are to be discussed later. Work related to the translation of informal requirements into a LOTOS specification can be found in [4].

3. Overview of GPRS

GSM (Global System for Mobile communications) [5] is a European standard for cellular communications developed by ETSI (European Telecommunications Standards Institute). GPRS is a set of new GSM bearer services that provide packet mode transmission within the GSM network and inter-works with external packet data networks [6]. GSM is a full digital system and is still an evolving standard that spans beyond telephony and circuit switched services. GPRS is a major activity in the phase 2+ of the GSM standard.

GPRS service subscribers will be able to send and receive data in a end-to-end packet transfer mode. GPRS Services are divided into two categories: Point-to-Point (PTP) and Point-to-Multipoint (PTM) services. Possible PTP services include data base access and information retrieval, the Internet, messaging and conversational services from user to user, credit card validation, etc. Examples of PTM services include unidirectional distribution of information such as news and weather reports. They also include conferencing services between multiple users.

3.1 Architecture of the GPRS network

GPRS introduces a new functional element to the GSM network (Figure 2): GSN (GPRS Support Node) which can be either a Serving-GSN (SGSN) or a Gateway-GSN (GGSN). This addition is necessary for the GSM network in order to support packet switched data services. We give below a summary of the main components of the GPRS network and their functions:

SGSN: responsibilities include maintaining the logical link with the Mobile Station (MS), forwarding incoming packets from the MS to the appropriate network nodes and vice versa, and authenticating access to GPRS services. Only one SGSN serves the MS in its service area.

GGSN: provides the interface to external Packet Data Networks (PDNs) and forwards packets destined for the MS to the SGSN that is serving it.

HLR: the Home Location Register is a database that contains subscriber's information. The subscriber's service profile and location information are stored in the HLR.

VLR: the Visitor Location Register is a database that stores temporary information for visiting subscribers.

MSC: the Mobile Switching Center is in charge of the telephony switching functions and authenticates access to circuit-switched services.

BTS: the Base Transceiver Station handles radio transmission and reception devices, including the antennas, and also all the radio interface signal processing.

BSC: the Base Station Controller manages the radio resources and controls handovers between cells. Several BTSs can be managed by one BSC.

Several interfaces have been introduced in GPRS to define entity-to-entity interactions. For instance, the *Gb* interface is required between the BSC and the SGSN. Two GSNs communicate through a *Gn* interface, and the SGSN communicates through the *Gr* interface with the HLR to send queries and to receive subscriber information. The *Gi* interface which connects a GGSN to a PDN was left open in the standard to accommodate implementation preferences while the Gs interface between the SGSN and the MSC/VLR was left optional.

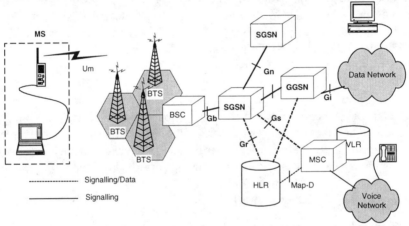

Figure 2. GPRS network architecture

The GPRS network is divided into several service areas assigned to different SGSNs. Each service area is composed of several Routeing Areas (RAs) which in turn form sets of cells.

3.2 Accessing the GPRS network

A MS can connect to the GPRS network by performing an *attach* procedure. The outcome is the establishment of a logical link between the MS and the SGSN and a mobility management context is created. Once this link is established, the MS can request to activate one or more Packet Data Protocol (PDP) contexts which specify the Packet Data Networks (PDNs) that it wants to connect to. In other words, it asks the SGSN to create routeing paths to the appropriate GGSNs. Once the PDP contexts are activated, the MS can send and receive data in an end-to-end packet transfer mode.

3.3 Mobility management states

The MS is defined to have three possible states: *Idle*, *Ready*, and *Standby* depending on the level of functionality it requires (Figure 3).

Idle State: a MS in this state is not traceable and can only receive multicast transmissions. The MS keeps track of cell changes locally. The MS needs to perform the *attach* procedure to connect to the GPRS network and become reachable.

Ready State: data is sent or received in this state and PDP contexts may also be activated and deactivated. Mobility management in this state happens at the cell level; the MS updates the SGSN when it changes cell. The MS may request a *detach* procedure in which case it moves to *Idle*. A timer monitors the *Ready* state and upon its expiry, the MS goes to the *Standby* state.

Standby State: a MS which has been inactive for a period of time is put in *Standby* state. The MS keeps track of the cell changes locally and informs the SGSN of RA changes only. It is possible in this state for the MS to activate PDP contexts establishing routeing contexts for data transmissions and receptions. The MS may wish to terminate the connection by requesting a GPRS *detach* procedure in which case it returns to *Idle*. A *Standby* timer also monitors the MS activity and causes it to go to *Idle* upon expiry.

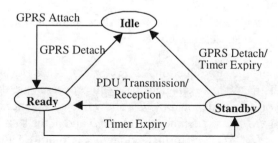

Figure 3. Mobility management state model

3.4 Location management in GPRS

Location management is the means by which the GPRS network keeps track of the MS position. Specific location management procedures are required depending on the current mobility management state of the MS. Since in GPRS the network is divided into smaller SGSN service areas containing several RAs, the term routeing update is used to refer to the location management procedures for GPRS. Geographically speaking, there are two types of procedures: *intra-SGSN* routeing update when the MS switches RAs within the same SGSN service area and *inter-SGSN* update to reflect a change of the SGSN service area.

4. LOTOS background

It is not possible in this paper to give a meaningful overview of the language LOTOS. Below, we list the main operators, however we realize that only readers familiar with the language will be able to follow the examples of the LOTOS code.

A LOTOS specification describes a system via a hierarchy of process definitions. A process performs internal unobservable actions, and interacts with its environment (other processes) via interaction points called *gates*. A process can combine actions and behaviour expressions by means of operators as follows:

a; B: the *action prefix* operator ";" means that an action or a gate **a** precedes the behaviour **B**.

B_1 [] B_2: the *choice* operator means that the process will behave as B_1 or as B_2 exclusively.

B_1 || B_2: the *full synchronization parallelism* operator means that B_1 and B_2 must synchronize on every action they offer.

B_1 ||| B_2: the *interleaving* operator expresses parallelism between B_1 and B_2 when no synchronization is required.

B_1 |[$g_1,g_2,...g_n$]| B_2: the *selective parallel* operator expresses parallelism between B_1 and B_2 when synchronization is only required on gates $g_1, g_2,...g_n$.

B_1 [> B_2: the *disable* operator means that any time during the execution of B1, B_2 can take over, thus terminating B_1.

B_1 >> B_2: the *enable* operator means that B_2 can be activated only after B_1 terminates its execution successfully.

As mentioned in the introduction, LOTOS combines ideas from several preexisting formalisms. Value exchanges between processes are defined similarly to CSP [7]. Value offers are denoted by "!", and value acceptances are denoted by "?". For example, *g ! 3 ? y: int* denotes offering a 3 and at the same time accepting a value for *y* at gate *g*. LOTOS formal semantics is mainly based on CCS [8]. Hence LOTOS operators have a number of algebraic properties, and also have executable semantics based on inference rules. Being executable, a LOTOS specification provides a formal prototype, or model, of its object system. A number of LOTOS execution tools exist, and the ones used in this project are documented in Refs. [9][10][11][12].

5. Formal specification of GPRS

5.1 Scope of the specification

5.1.1 Logical functions. Several groupings of logical functions have been defined for GPRS. Our specification covers the following functions:

- *Network access control*
  Registration: the association of a mobile to PDPs and addresses within the network.

- **Logical Link Management**
  Logical link establishment: occurs when the MS attaches to the GPRS network.
  Logical link maintenance: controls the status and state changes of the logical link
  Logical link release: this function de-associates the MS-SGSN logical link.
- **Packet Routeing and Transfer**
  Routeing: determines the network node to which a message should be forwarded.
  Encapsulation: adds address and control information to PDUs for packet routeing.
  Tunneling: transfers encapsulated PDUs between two end-points in the network.
- **Mobility Management**
  Location management: a set of functions responsible for keeping track of the mobile station.

5.1.2 Protocol layers. A layered protocol structure is adopted for the transmission and signalling planes. The functions we specified are supported by several layers (shaded layers in Figure 4). The SNDCP (SubNetwork Dependent Convergence Protocol) serves as a mapping of the characteristics of IP/X.25 to the underlying network. Mobility management functionality is supported by the GMM (GPRS Mobility Management) and SM (Session Management) layers. The LLC (Logical Link Control) layer provides a logical link between the MS and the SGSN and manages reliable transmission while at the same time supporting point-to-point and point-to-multipoint addressing. The RLC (Radio Link Control), MAC (Medium Access Control), and GSM RF (Radio Frequency) layers control the radio link, the allocation of physical channels and radio frequency. LLC PDUs between the MS and the SGSN are relayed at the BSS. The BSSGP (Base Station System GPRS Protocol) layer handles routeing and QoS between the BSS (Base Station System) and the SGSN. The GTP (GPRS Tunneling Protocol) is the basis for tunneling signalling and user PDUS between the SGSN and GGSN. The remaining layers are already well known and defined protocols.

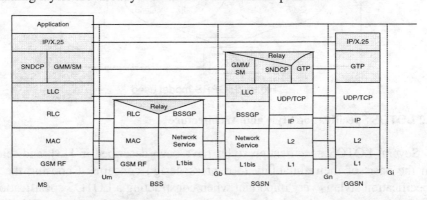

Figure 4. GPRS signalling and transmission planes from MS to GGSN

5.1.3 Model used and assumptions. We assume in our specification that the radio interface details such as the allocation of channels is somehow accomplished successfully. Since we are concerned mainly with the GPRS entities, we are more interested in the establishment of a logical link between the MS and the SGSN than in the medium used. For this reason, we chose to abstract from the details related to the radio interface in order to simplify the prototype and to focus on pure GPRS functionality. Functions related to the BTS and BSC are outside the scope of our specification. In our model shown in (Figure 5), we chose to adopt the following assumptions:

- The GPRS network is composed of four RAs. One RA is composed of two cells.
- There are one SGSN and one MSC/VLR for each pair of RAs.
- There is one HLR in the network.
- Two GGSNs serve as connections to the external networks. Both SGSNs can connect to either of them.

In a mobile network, the most interesting functions are usually related to mobility management (how to keep track of the mobile). In GPRS, complex location management occurs when the mobile switches SGSNs. By using this model, we are guaranteed to address this scenario and all the logical functions outlined above.

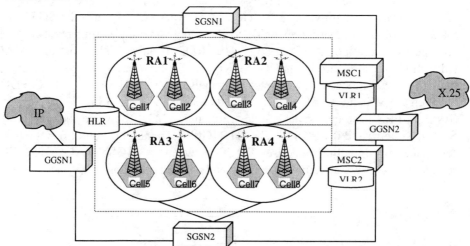

Figure 5. GPRS model used

5.2 LOTOS Specification Style and Architecture

Several LOTOS specification styles have been described in [13], and selected on the basis of their suitability to express design concerns. Choosing the right specification style is very important when constructing a LOTOS specification. In our work, we used the *resource-oriented* style, because it supports modularity and parallel structures. The term *resources* here refers to system entities with well defined interfaces to other entities. This choice is natural because it eases the mapping of a system's architecture into a LOTOS specification. System's components (resources) are described as LOTOS *processes* composed in parallel and interacting through *gates*. Other styles were used to specify detailed behaviour. The behaviour of the GPRS network entities (processes) is a collection of alternative sequences of interactions that depend on the mobility management states. The *state-oriented* style was a perfect choice to specify the behaviour of the individual processes. In some instances, the *monolithic* style was applied because events were presented as ordered collections of alternative sequences of interactions in branching time.

The GPRS system is seen as a LOTOS process interacting with the environment through the external gates *ms* and *ext_net*. These gates provide, respectively, the means to the user to initiate and simulate transactions of the mobile station and the external networks. They will be of particular use during the validation phase. By refining the GPRS process, we decompose it into three processes (Figure 6):

- **The_MS**: a set of interleaved Idle Mobile Stations (MS). The gate *Um_Gb* joins the *Um* and the *Gb* interfaces and carries messages between the MS and the SGSN. We needed this gate since we abstract from the radio link details.
- **GPRSNetwork**: an encapsulated process that is mapped to our geographical model described in Figure 5. In addition to the *Um_Gb* gate, messages are carried to and from the external networks via the *Gi* gate.
- **The_ExternalNetworks**: a set of external networks interleaving. An external network process is parameterized by a network type (IP or X.25) and communicates through the *Gi* and *ext_net* gates.

Due to the length of the specification, we will limit our explanation to the general structure of the GPRS network specification and give a high level description of the SGSN process.

The top level structure of the GPRS specification in LOTOS is shown in Figure 7. From the environment point of view, any message exchange occurring within the GPRS system is internal and cannot be observed. Only events that take place at gates *ms* and *ext_net* are observable. This explains the use of the *hide* operator within the GPRs process. The gates *Um_Gb*, *Gi*, *STmeout*, and *RTimeout* are therefore hidden to reflect their internal nature. The three processes *The_MS*, *GPRS_Network*, and *ExternalNetworks* run in parallel but have to synchronize on certain gates in order to communicate. This is expressed in LOTOS by using the selective parallel composition operator |[..]|.

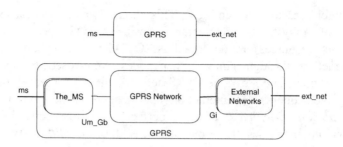

Figure 6. High-level specification architecture

We also need to add the two special gates *STimeout* and *RTimeout* to provide a mechanism for the SGSN and the MS to synchronize on *Standby* and *Ready* timers expiry, but explicit timing constraints are not modeled.

```
specification GPRS_Spec[ms,ext_net]:noexit
    (*Data type definitions omitted*)
    behaviour
    GPRS[ms,ext_net]
    where
        process GPRS[ms,ext_net]:noexit:=
            hide Um_Gb,Gi,STimeout,RTimeout in
            ( The_MS[ms,Um_Gb,STimeout,RTimeout]
                I[Um_Gb,STimeout,RTimeout]I
              GPRSNetwork[Um_Gb,Gi,STimeout,RTimeout]
                )
                I[Gi]I
              ExternalNetworks[ext_net,Gi]
        endproc (* GPRS *)
endspec (*GPRS_Spec*)
```
Figure 7. Top-level LOTOS specification of GPRS

It is easy to map our GPRS model of the GPRS network into a LOTOS process (Figure 8).

```
process GPRSNetwork[Um_Gb,Gi,STimeout,RTimeout]:noexit:=

    hide Gr,map_d,Gs,Gn,inter_sgsn in

        (* Some initilialization *)
        (*One HLR synchronized with two MSC/VLRs interleaving*)
        (HLR[Gr,map_d](InitSet,InitPDPSet)
         I[map_d]I
        (MSC_VLR[Gs,map_d](VLR(1),{} of MscVlrAssSet,0)
         III
        MSC_VLR[Gs,map_d](VLR(2),{} of MscVlrAssSet,0) ))
         I[Gr,Gs]I
        (SGSN[Um_Gb,Gr,Gn,Gs,inter_sgsn,STimeout,RTimeout](SGSN(1),LA(1))
         I[inter_sgsn]I     (*Two SGSNs synchronized*)
        SGSN[Um_Gb,Gr,Gn,Gs,inter_sgsn,STimeout,RTimeout](SGSN(2),LA(2)) )
         I[Gn]I             (*Two GGSNs interleaving*)
        (GGSN[Gi, Gn](GGSN(1))
         III
        GGSN[Gi, Gn](GGSN(2)) )

    endproc (* GPRSNetwork *)
```
Figure 8. Specification of the GPRS network process

By using the appropriate parallel operators, we can compose the various entities (processes) so that they reflect the architectural requirements. For instance, the GGSNs do not need to mutually synchronize on any action and therefore we use the interleaving operator (|||) to express their unsynchronized parallelism. On the other hand, they must interact with the SGSNs through the *Gn* interface. The selective parallel composition operator is appropriate in this case.

The SGSN process consists of several instances of *SGSNHandlers* synchronized with a process *SGSNManageLLC*. Data structures used for routeing and mobility management purposes are handled by process *SGSNContextsDBase*. A handler has been defined for each functionality performed by the SGSN such as handling mobile requests to attach to the network or routeing update requests. The handlers are interleaved, but since the *detach request* may occur at any time, the process *SGSNHandleDetach* has been composed with the disable operator ([>). By doing so, when a mobile user wishes to detach from the network, the request can disrupt the execution of the other handlers. Figure 9 illustrates the SGSN process architecture.

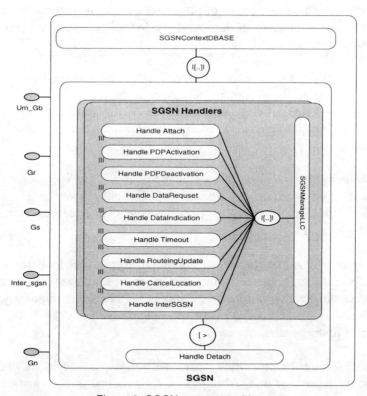

Figure 9. SGSN process architecture

6. Validation of the specification

Our methodology for the validation of the specification combines concepts of testing and model checking. We mean by testing the process of composing the specification in parallel with a test process which will force the specification through certain desired scenarios. This is done because it is impossible to execute all behaviour paths and different testing processes can be chosen to select the scenarios of interest. It is then possible to execute other validation activities such as model checking on the limited behaviour model narrowed by the test scenarios.

The steps involved in our validation methodology (Figure 10) are the following:

1. *Requirements capture and synthesis*: this step was described in Section 2 and its outcome is a formal specification of the requirements. In our case, this formal specification is expressed in LOTOS.

2. *Test definition:* we start by identifying the test objectives and then we derive the corresponding test scenarios. These scenarios will serve as a guide to the formal specification to perform specific execution sequences.

3. *Formulation*: some requirements can be expressed by means of a logical specification. The result is a set of properties that can be viewed as a partial correctness specification. In our work, we formulate several properties of the system using temporal logic.

4. *Composition:* the test scenarios derived in step 2 are composed with the formal specification to obtain test specifications. While the formal specification defines all the possible sequences of execution of the system, the test specifications are restricted to those sequences that are related to the test scenarios.

5. *Behaviour tree generation:* all possible paths in the test specifications are executed up to a certain depth yielding behaviour trees. These trees are graphical models representing the possible execution sequences dictated by the test scenarios.

6. *Test exploration*: all sequences of execution in the behaviour tree should normally be conformant to the test scenarios. However, erroneous sequences can be present indicating faulty behaviour. Most commonly, they show a situation where a specification deadlocks with a tester. In this step, we aim at finding such sequences.

7. *Model checking*: the properties formulated in temporal logic are checked against the behaviour trees of step 5. A formula that is not satisfied may reveal an erroneous behaviour. This step complements the test exploration activities because it addresses specific properties rather than scenarios.

8. *Analysis:* the tests and model checking results are then explored to identify the causes of the discovered problems. This step involves extraction of faulty traces of execution, and the generation of the corresponding MSCs for inspection.

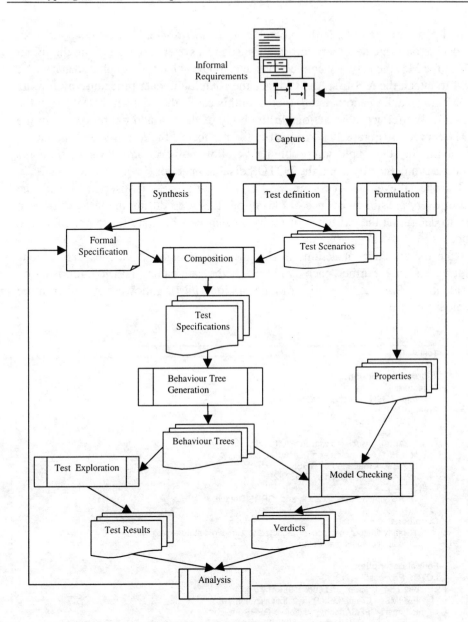

Figure 10. Validation methodology

6.1 Test definition

A test scenario describes possible behaviour sequences of the system and may reflect several interacting GPRS functions. We express these tests in terms of LOTOS processes. This approach follows the definition of *Testing Equivalence* [14]: tests are exercised by specifying a test process and synchronizing it with the behaviour under test. Our tests are characterized by two parts: an informal part consisting of their objective, a set of preambles and conditions, and a body reflecting the desired sequences of events. The LOTOS process represents the formal part. For example, in the preamble of the *intra-SGSN routeing update* test, we decide on some necessary information such as system configuration, the initial cell of the MS, the network connections, etc. To be able to test such a scenario, we need to attach the MS first, then trigger the routeing update procedure by forcing the MS to switch to another cell (cell 3 in this case), then detach the MS from the network. We reflect these actions in the body of the test and express them in the LOTOS process (Figure 11). We restrict the number of the *Ready* state timeouts to 1 to avoid the state explosion problem. We allow however *Standby* state timeouts to occur at any time by using the LOTOS disable operator ([>).

The special event "success" in the LOTOS test process is inserted to mark the end of every possible sequence of execution. It is used during the test exploration step to determine the existence of faulty sequences which are those not ending in "success".

Note the structure of actions in this process. Because it is a test, all actions offer values only. Further, each action offers the gate name first (*ms*), followed by an identifier that identifies the mobile station (*imsi*), followed by on or more parameter values.

```
Test 4_1

Informal Description
Objective:
    Intra-SGSN Routeing Update
Preamble:
    1 MS with IMSI(1)
    MS in Cell 1
    NSAPI(0) associated with PDPAd(1), IP
    NSAPI(1) associated with PDPAd(1), X.25
    IP network managed by GGSN(1)
    X25 network managed by GGSN(2)
Body:
    GPRS Attach , Select Cell 3, and  GPRS Detach

Conditions:
    1 Ready timeout may occur (restricted to 1 to avoid state explosion)
    StandBy timeouts may occur

Formal Description
LOTOS Process:
process TS4_1[ms,ext_net,success]:exit:=
  let imsi:IMSI = CreateIMSI(1) in  (* Intitialization*)
     ms ! imsi ! GPRSAttach; (* Initiate a GPRS Attach *)
        (ms ! imsi ! cellSelection ! Cell(3); (* Move to Cell 3 triggering intra-SGSN RA update *)
        ms !imsi ! RoutingUpdateAcc;
        ms ! imsi ! GPRSDetach;   (* Initiate a Detach *)
        ms ! imsi ! DetachAcc;
        success;
        exit)
        [>
        (ms ! imsi ! TimerExpAcc; (* Timeouts are possible *)
          success;
          exit )
  endproc
```

Figure 11. Test definition example

4 test suites were identified for our system with a total of 35 tests. The test suites are organized as follows:

Suite 1 (3 tests): Attach and detach procedures.

Suite 2 (8 tests): PDP context activation and deactivation procedures.
Suite 3 (13 tests): Data delivery (from MS to external network and vice versa).
Suite 4 (11 tests): Routeing update procedures and data delivery.

6.2 Composition

To compose a test process with the GPRS specification, we explored two different LOTOS tools. We first used LOLA [10] which performs the composition automatically. However, for some test processes containing interleaved sequences, LOLA was unable to handle the composition. We then resorted to RTL [12] to overcome this problem. The generation of the test specifications is done manually by synchronizing the test process and the GPRS specification using the LOTOS selective parallel operator (|[..]|).

6.3 Behaviour tree generation

The result of the execution of all paths of a LOTOS formal specification is a graphical model or representation describing the complete behaviour of the system it represents. This representation is called a Labeled Transition System (LTS) [8][15]. An LTS intuitively encodes the operational behaviour of a process. It contains the set of states the process may enter, and the set of actions the process may perform at each state. An LTS is a state transition machine where each edge is labeled by a LOTOS action.

For systems with infinite behaviour, a complete LTS cannot be generated. This problem is usually solved by specifying limits for the execution such as a maximum number of actions for each path. Another serious drawback is related to the well-known state explosion problem. In our system, the state explosion problem is due to two main reasons:

- Several processes run in an interleaved manner causing the number of possible actions and global states to increase very rapidly with time.
- The GPRS standard describes timers to monitor the mobility management state transitions. Timeouts are expressed in our system as events that can occur at any time. This multiplies further the number of actions and states to be explored.

We made some restrictions as to the number of timeouts allowed depending on the complexity of the tests to keep the state space tractable. Also, since we do not generate the LTS from the formal specification but rather from its composition with the tests, the size of our LTSs is controllable because they include only actions dictated by the test scenarios.

We used the RTL tool [12] to translate the LOTOS test specifications into LTSs. We then reduce the resulting LTSs with respect to some equivalence relations [15] using the Aldebaran tool [16].

6.4 Test exploration

A test is successful if all execution sequences of its composition with the behaviour terminate normally. We have seen (Figure 11) that the "success" event is inserted at the end of the test processes to indicate a successful termination. The presence of an execution sequence in the LTS that does not end with the "success" event indicates the possibility of a deadlock situation. Our task is then to find out if such abnormal terminations exist in the LTS.

In testing theory [14], the composition of a formal specification with a test leads to one of the following test results:

- *Must pass*: all the possible executions terminate successfully.
- *May pass*: some executions terminate successfully.
- *Reject*: none of the executions terminate successfully.

All the failing tests in our suites had a *May pass* result. This implied the existence of some abnormal sequences. To be able to inspect such sequences, we needed to extract them from the LTS. We used the Exhibitor tool of the CADP toolbox [10] for this purpose. Given an LTS, Exhibitor is capable of finding paths with certain given characteristics.

6.5 Model checking

Starting from the captured requirements, we identified a set of correctness properties (over twenty) to verify against our GPRS specification. To formulate these properties, we used a variation of the propositional μ-calculus [17] interpreted over the actions of the LTS. μ-calculus is sufficiently powerful to express safety and liveness properties. The formulas expressing the properties are therefore a combination of μ-calculus syntax and LOTOS actions. We used the model checker of the CADP toolbox [10] to accomplish this step.

6.5.1 Examples of correctness properties. We do not present the syntax and semantics of μ-calculus here, and we only show one property expressed in its precise syntax. We list in natural language a subset of the properties verified to give an idea of the type of properties we addressed.

1. *When in Standby, the MS is not allowed to move to Idle unless a detach or Standby timer timeout occur.*

   Formulation: to express this property, we need to check that for every path in the LTS starting with a *Standby* state action "*state !IMSI1 !STANDBY*", an *Idle* state action "*state !IMSI1 !IDLE*" is observed only after a confirmation of detach "*ms !IMSI1 !DetachAcc*" or a timer expiry "*ms !IMSI1 !TimerExpAcc*".

```
ALL (
    ["state !IMSI1 !STANDBY"]
    SU (["state !IMSI1 !IDLE"]F)
      (<"ms !IMSI1 !DetachAcc">T or <"ms !IMSI1 !TimerExpAcc">T)
      )
```

2. *Data transfers (PTP) to and from the MS are not possible during Idle.*
3. *After a successful attach to the network, it should be possible to detach.*
4. *The MS cannot receive or send PTP data in Standby.*
5. *A PDP context shall be activated before the MS can be paged, or can send, or receive data.*
6. *During an inter-SGSN routeing update, the new SGSN should request the MS context from the old SGSN.*

6.6 Analysis and results

Whether we use testing processes or model checking, the difficult task remains to find the causes of the abnormal sequences or failing properties. In case of testing, inspecting the traces of execution can be tedious and time consuming. Model checking on the other hand requires an elaborate diagnostics system to explain why a property was not satisfied by the system. To facilitate our task, we relied heavily on automatic generation of MSCs from traces of executions. Faulty sequences could then be inspected visually in a more efficient way. MSCs are also generated for correct sequences of execution and compared with the original MSCs defined in the standard documents. Alternative solutions to a specific scenario can be provided in this way. Figure 12 shows an example MSC that was generated for a successful *attach* procedure. We chose to show this simple MSC because it is impossible to provide a more complex trace of execution without compromising its readability.

Several specification problems were detected using our validation techniques. The two main ones are described below:

1. *Mobility Management state conflicts*: these problems are due to timer expiry during the reception of data destined to the MS by the SGSN. The SGSN and the MS have to agree on the mobility management states. In our analysis, we identified a case where the SGSN and the MS engaged in a conflict. While the MS switched to *Standby*, the SGSN was still in the *Ready* state. Packets arriving to the SGSN could not be forwarded properly to the MS. This problem was addressed in later versions of the standard by adding recovery mechanisms from inconsistent mobility management states in the MS and the SGSN.

2. *Routeing updates and data delivery conflicts*: these conflicts occur when incoming packets destined to the MS arrive at the SGSN during a routeing update procedure. During an intra-SGSN update, the SGSN needs to forward the data to the new RA. On the other hand, the old SGSN needs to forward the data to the new SGSN during an inter-SGSN update. When a routeing update procedure is in progress, the data gets lost. This issue was addressed later in

the standard by adding a buffering mechanism that allows the SGSN to hold the data until it completes successfully the routeing update procedure, and then forward it to the right destination.

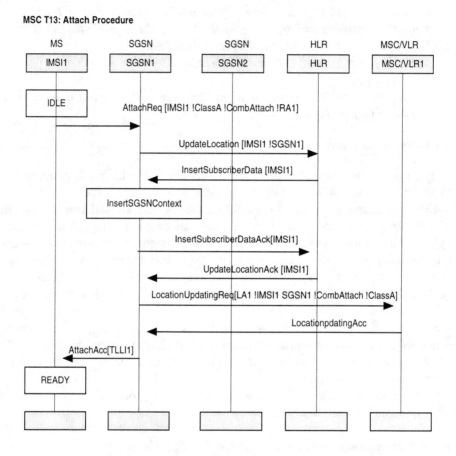

Figure 12. Successful attach procedure (MSC)

7. Conclusion

In the mobile data communication area, market forces oblige standard committees to develop new standards rapidly. These standards include complex protocols that should be checked for correctness before they are implemented, otherwise problems will result, leading to high development costs, customer dissatisfaction or even the failure of major systems that use the standards.

In this paper, we have presented an experience in the use of formal methods for the verification of crucial properties of a forthcoming standard. Although the methods used are based on existing ideas, the application to this complex system has required a lot of ingenuity, from developing a suitable formal model for the system, which was continuously being modified, to making the tools work towards our goals.

At least two significant design errors were found. Each one of them, if not addressed, would have led to faulty functioning of the system, possibly involving loss of data or of connectivity to the mobile user.

This experience confirms the usefulness of formal methods in the design of dependable critical systems.

Acknowledgment

This research was funded by grants of Motorola Canada, and of the Natural Sciences and Engineering Research Council of Canada. We would like to thank Bernard Stepien for his early contribution to this project, and the members of the LOTOS group for their helpful comments and discussions.

References

1. ISO, Information Processing Systems, Open Systems Interconnection, *LOTOS* – A Formal Description Technique Based on the Temporal Ordering of Observational Behaviou*r*, IS 8807 (E. Brinksma, ed.), 1988.
2. L. Logrippo, M. Faci, M. Haj-Hussein. An Introduction to LOTOS: Learning by Examples. Computer Networks and ISDN System, 23 (1992), 325-342. (errata in 25 (1992) 99-100).
3. ITU, Recommendation Z. 120: Message Sequence Charts (MSC), Geneva (1996).
4. L. Logrippo and R. Tuok. Formal Specification and Use Case Generation for a Mobile Telephony System. Computer Networks and ISDN Systems, 30 (1998), 1045-1063.
5. M. Mouly and M. B. Pautet. The GSM System for Mobile Communications, Palaiseau, France, 1992.
6. ETSI, Digital cellular telecommunications system (Phase 2+): General Packet Radio Service, GSM 02.60 Service Description Stage 1, version 5.1.0, October 1997 and GSM 03.60 Service Description Stage 2, version 5.2.0, December 1997.
7. C.A.R Hoare. Communicating Sequential Processes. Prentice-Hall, 1985.
8. R. Milner, A Calculus of Communicating Systems, Lecture Notes in Computer Science, Vol.92, Springer-Verlag, 1980.
9. B. Ghribi. And L. Logrippo. A Validation Environment for LOTOS. In: Danthine, A., and Leduc, G. (eds.) Protocol Specification, Testing, and Verification, XIII (Proc. of the 13th International Symposium on Protocol Specification, Testing, and Verification, organized by IFIP WG 6.1, Liège) North-Holland, 1993, 93-108.
10. J.-C. Fernandez, H. Garavel, A. Kerbrat, R. Mateescu, L. Mounier, and M. Sighireanu. CADP (CÆSAR/ALDEBARAN Development Package): a Protocol validation and Verification Toolbox. In Rajeev Alur and Thomas A. Henzinger, editors, Proceedings of CAV'96 (New Brunswick, New Jersey, USA), Vol. 1102 of LNCS, pages 437-440. Springer Verlag, August 1996.
11. J. Quemada, A. Fernandez, and J. A. Mañas. LOLA: Design and verification of Protocols using LOTOS. In IBERIAN Conference on Data Communications, Lisbon, May 1987.
12. J. P. Courtiat and R.C. de Oliveira. Reachability Analysis of RT-LOTOS Specifications. In Proc. 8th Int. Conf. On Formal Description Techniques (*FORTE'95*), Montreal, Canada, October 1995, 101-108.
13. C. A Vissers, G. Scollo, M van Sinderen, and E. Brinksma. Specification styles in distributed systems design and verification. Theoretical Computer Science, 89 (1991), 179-206.
14. R. de Nicola and M. Hennessy. Testing Equivalences for Processes. Theoretical Computer Science, 34(1,2):83-133, Nov 1984.
15. R. Milner. Communication and Concurrency. Prentice-Hall, 1989.
16. J. C. Fernandez, A. Kerbrat, and L. Mounier. Symbolic Equivalence Checking.In C. Courcoubetis, editor, Proceedings of CAV'93 (Heraklion, Greece), Vol. 697 of LNCS. Springer Verlag, June 1993.

17. D. Kozen. Results on the propositional mu-calculus. Theoretical Computer Science, 27:333-354, 1983.

Glossary

BTS	Base Transceiver Station
BSC	Base Station Controller
EIR	Equipment Identity Register
ETSI	European Telecommunication Standards Institute
GGSN	Gateway GPRS Support Node
GMM/SM	GPRS Mobility Management and Session Management
GPRS	General Packet Radio Service
GSM	Global System for Mobile communications
GSN	GPRS Support Node
GTP	GPRS Tunneling Protocol
HLR	Home Location Register
IMSI	International Mobile Subscriber Id
IP	Internet Protocol
LLC	Logical Link Control
MAC	Medium Access Control
MS	Mobile Station
MSC	Message Switching Center
NSAPI	Network Service Access Point Identifier
PDN	Packet Data Network
PDP	Packet Data Protocol
PDU	Protocol Data Unit
PTP	Point-to-Point
PTM	Point-to-Multipoint
RA	Routeing Area
RLC	Radio Link Control
SGSN	Serving GPRS Support Node
SNDCP	SubNetwork Dependent Convergence Protocol
TID	Tunnel Identifier
TLLI	Temporary Logical Link Identity
VLR	Visitor Location Register

Formal Description and Validation for an Integrity Policy Supporting Multiple Levels of Criticality

A. Fantechi [1], S. Gnesi [2], L. Semini [1]

1. Dipartimento di Sistemi e Informatica, Università di Firenze
e-mail: {fantechi,semini}@dsi.unifi.it
2. Istituto di Elaborazione dell'Informazione, C.N.R., Pisa
e-mail: gnesi@iei.pi.cnr.it

Abstract

Formal methods are increasingly used to validate the design of software and hardware components of safety critical systems. In particular, formal validation is needed for those mechanisms which support the overall dependability of the systems.

Inside the GUARDS project, a novel integrity mechanism has been proposed to implement the Multiple Levels of Criticality model within an object–oriented framework.

In this paper we present the application of model checking techniques to the formal validation of this integrity level mechanism.

1 Introduction

The need for a rigorous validation of the safety critical systems often contrasts with their large dimensions. However, rarely all the components of a large system have the same degree of criticality, and the question naturally arising is whether or not the whole system has to be validated with the same care.

A solution is not to make any distinction, and to treat all the components as critical ones. In fact, the failures that could occur in a non critical and less verified component might be propagated by the interaction with a critical one. Another solution is to isolate critical components, but complete isolation is not always possible because of the inevitable cooperation among the various parts of the system.

A compromise among the high cost of the first solution, and the non-effectiveness of the second one, is defined by an *integrity policy* [1, 4, 10, 25]: it is not needed to validate all the components with the same effort, but only those which accomplish a critical task and those which provide data to these task–critical components.

An integrity policy assigns a level of criticality to each component of an application. The highest the level is, the more critical the component. Thus, the components with high level of criticality are those which need a rigorous validation.

Then, the policy states the communication patterns among pairs of components, depending on the respective criticality levels.

We consider in this paper the integrity policy [25] recently defined within the GUARDS (Generic Upgradable Architecture for Real–time Dependable Systems) European project. This project addresses the development of architectures, methods, techniques, and tools to support the design, the implementation and validation of critical systems [26].

In GUARDS, the *Multiple Levels of Criticality* model characterizes the integrity policy adopted, in an object–oriented framework. The Multiple Levels of Criticality model is realized through the definition and implementation of a suitable mechanism. This mechanism becomes itself a critical component of the GUARDS architecture, which needs a proper validation effort.

In this paper we propose a formal validation of the GUARDS multi–level integrity mechanism, exploiting the model–checking approach supported by the JACK (*Just Another Concurrency Kit*) verification environment [6], following the methodology already adopted in GUARDS for other fault–tolerant mechanisms [3].

To this purpose we have provided a process algebra specification of the mechanism, from which a finite state model of its behavior has been derived following an operational approach. Validation is carried out automatically by expressing some desired properties of the mechanism as temporal logic formulae, and by checking their satisfiability over the mechanism model.

2 Background

2.1 The CCS/MEIJE process algebra

Process algebras [18, 20] are recognized as a convenient means for describing sequential or concurrent interacting systems at different levels of abstraction. They rely on a small set of basic operators, which correspond to primitive notions of concurrent systems, and on one or more notions of behavioral equivalence or preorder. The operators are used to build complex specifications from more elementary ones. The behavioral equivalences are used to study the relationships between descriptions of the same system at different levels of abstraction (e.g., specification and implementation).

The process algebra we use is CCS/MEIJE [8]. In CCS/MEIJE a system consists of a set of communicating processes. Each process executes input and output actions, and synchronizes with other processes to carry out its activities. The CCS/MEIJE syntax is based on a set of labels *Act* of atomic action names. Such names represent output actions if they are terminated by "!", or input ones if they are terminated by "?" (let $a \in Act$, $a!$ and $a?$ are the output and input actions, respectively). Moreover, τ denotes the special action not belonging to *Act*, representing the unobservable action (to model internal process communications). We assume $Act_\tau = Act \cup \{\tau\}$.

The subset of the CCS–MEIJE operators we use follows:

$a:P$	Action prefix	Action a is performed, and then process P is executed. Action a is in Act_τ
$P+Q$	Nondeterministic choice	Alternative choice between the behavior of process P and that of process Q
$P \parallel Q$	Parallel composition	Interleaved executions of processes P and Q. The two processes synchronize on complementary input and output actions (i.e. actions with the same name but a different suffix)
$P \setminus a$	Action restriction	The action a can only be performed within a synchronization

The usual semantic models of process algebras are Labeled Transition Systems (LTSs) which describe the behavior of a process in terms of states, and labeled transitions, which relate states. An LTS is a 4-tuple $\mathcal{A} = (Q, q_0, Act_\tau, \rightarrow)$, where: Q is a finite set of states; q_0 is the initial state; Act is a finite set of observable actions and τ is the unobservable action; $\rightarrow \subseteq Q \times Act_\tau \times Q$ is the transition relation.

We provide the structural operational semantics of the above CCS/MEIJE operators, in terms of LTSs [20].

$$a:P \qquad a:P \xrightarrow{a} P$$

$$P+Q \qquad \frac{P \xrightarrow{a} P'}{P+Q \xrightarrow{a} P'} \qquad \frac{Q \xrightarrow{a} Q'}{P+Q \xrightarrow{a} Q'}$$

$$P \parallel Q \qquad \frac{P \xrightarrow{a} P'}{P \parallel Q \xrightarrow{a} P' \parallel Q} \qquad \frac{Q \xrightarrow{a} Q'}{P \parallel Q \xrightarrow{a} P \parallel Q'} \qquad \frac{P \xrightarrow{a?} P', Q \xrightarrow{a!} Q'}{P \parallel Q \xrightarrow{\tau} P' \parallel Q'}$$

$$P \setminus a \qquad \frac{P \xrightarrow{b} P'}{P \setminus a \xrightarrow{b} P' \setminus a} \, b \neq a$$

2.2 The ACTL temporal logic

Modal and temporal logics have been proposed [17, 15, 14] to provide a more abstract specification of reactive systems than process algebras, since they are more appropriate for describing system properties rather than system behaviors.

We now introduce the branching time temporal logic ACTL [14], which is the action based version of CTL [15]. ACTL is well suited to describe the behavior of a system in terms of the actions it performs at its working time. In fact, ACTL embeds the idea of "evolution in time by actions" and is suitable for describing the various possible temporal sequences of actions that characterize a system behavior.

The syntax of ACTL is given by the following grammar, where ϕ denotes a state property:

$$\phi ::= true \mid \sim\phi \mid \phi \, \& \, \phi' \mid [a]\phi \mid AG\,\phi \mid A[\phi\{\mu\}U\{\mu'\}\phi'] \mid E[\phi\{\mu\}U\{\mu'\}\phi']$$

In the above rules a is an action in Act_τ, and μ is an action formula defined by:

$$\mu ::= true \mid a \mid \mu \wedge \mu \mid \sim\mu \qquad \text{for } a \in Act$$

In the following, we will often use μ as a shorthand for "an action satisfying μ".

Labelled transition systems are the interpretation domains of ACTL formulae. We provide here an informal description of the semantics of ACTL operators. The formal semantics is given in [14].

Any state satisfies $true$. A state satisfies $\sim\phi$ if and only if it does not satisfy ϕ; it satisfies $\phi \; \& \; \phi'$ if and only if it satisfies both ϕ and ϕ'. A state satisfies $[a]\phi$ if for all next states reachable with a, ϕ is true. The meaning of $AG\,\phi$ is that ϕ is true now and *always* in the future.

A state P satisfies $A[\phi\{\mu\}U\{\mu'\}\phi']$ if and only if in each path exiting from P, μ' will be eventually executed. It is also required ϕ' to hold after μ', and all the intermediate states to satisfy ϕ. Finally, before μ' only μ or τ actions can be executed. The formula $E[\phi\{\mu\}U\{\mu'\}\phi']$ has the same meaning, except that it requires one path exiting from P, and not all of them, to satisfy the given constraint. A useful formula is $A[\phi\{true\}U\{\mu'\}\phi']$ where the first action formula is true, this means that any action can be executed before μ'.

Some derived operators can be defined: $\phi \mid \phi'$ stands for $\sim(\sim\phi \; \& \; \sim\phi')$; $<a>\phi$ stands for $\sim[a]\sim\phi$; finally, $EF\,\phi$ stands for $\sim AG \sim\phi$ (this is the *eventually* operator, whose meaning is that ϕ will be true sometime in the future).

In the following picture we exemplify the truth of some formulae on some models.

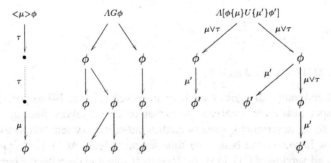

Example. The ACTL logic may express *safety* and *liveness* properties in terms of the actions a system can perform. Safety properties claim that nothing bad happens; i.e., that there is no path in the LTS in which a given action sequence occurs. Liveness properties claim that something good eventually happens; i.e., that there exists a path in the LTS in which a given action sequence occurs. In this setting, for example, the formula:

$$AG[a]A[true\{false\}U\{b\}true]$$

means that, in all paths of the LTS, any action a is immediately followed by an action b. The formula well characterizes safety requirements. On the other hand, a typical ACTL formula stating a liveness property is, for example:

$$EF < b > true$$

which means that on some path of the LTS, action b will eventually be executed.

Logic can be used in the study of concurrent systems following two different approaches: the model–theoretical approach and the proof–theoretical one. Each of these approaches has advantages and drawbacks. The model–theoretical approach is almost intuitive. It works on a finite state representation of the behavior of a system. Verification is usually carried out by expressing a desired property of the system as a logic formula and by automatically checking the satisfiability of the formula over the model of the system by model checking algorithms [11].

The proof–theoretical approach is in general less intuitive than the previous one; in this approach the system state is modeled in terms of set–theoretical structures on which invariants are defined, while operations on the state are modeled by specifying their pre- and post–conditions in terms of the system state. Properties are described by invariants, which must be proved to hold through the system execution, by means of theorem proving.

The proof–theoretical approach can overcome some of the drawbacks of the model–theoretical one, expecially those related to state explosion problems when dealing with real systems.

In the case of the ACTL logic the model–theoretical approach has been chosen and a linear–time model checker, AMC, has been defined, which verifies the satisfiability of ACTL formulae on Labelled Transition Systems [13].

2.3   The JACK environment

The JACK environment[1] combines different specification and verification tools, independently developed at different academic sites (I.E.I.- C.N.R. and the University of Rome in Italy, and INRIA in France). Within JACK, a user can choose from several verification tools by means of a user–friendly graphic interface, and can create a general system for managing any tool that has an input or output based on the FC2 file format, used by JACK for representing LTSs [7]. In this format, an LTS is defined by means of a set of tables that keep the information about state names, arc labels, and transition relations between states. FC2 makes it possible to exchange LTSs between JACK tools. Moreover, tools can easily be added to the JACK system, thus extending its potential.

Some of the tools in JACK allow a process specification to be built. This can be done both by entering a specification in a textual form [19], or by drawing graphically the LTS that describes the behavior of the process. Moreover, JACK allows, by using sophisticated graphical procedures, a specification to be built as a network of processes [24]. Other tools provide different verification strategies ranging from

---

[1]Detailed information about JACK is available at http://rep1.iei.pi.cnr.it/projects/JACK. At the same address, there is a downloadable version of the JACK package.

behavioral equivalence proofs [5] to logical verifications. ACTL can be used to describe temporal properties and *model checking* can be performed, by using AMC, to check whether a LTS, model of a system, satisfies the properties.

JACK has been successfully tested on several case studies. In [22], the formal specification and the verification of some liveness and safety properties of a hydroelectric plant were presented. In [12], JACK was used to formally specify the hardware components of a buffer system, and to verify the correctness of the specification with respect to some safety requirements. Finally, the JACK environment has been applied in the validation of an interlocking safety critical system developed by Ansaldo Trasporti [2].

3 The Multiple Levels of Criticality model

The Multiple Levels of Criticality model presented in [25] defines an Object Oriented integrity policy. The framework of their work is the definition of a programming paradigm for safety–critical systems in which it is possible to assign a level of confidence (integrity level) to each object of an application. These integrity levels distinguish components with respect to their criticality: a critical component needs to have an high level of confidence, while a non-critical one can have a low level. The integrity levels are used to guide the validation process: low integrity level components will need a smaller validation effort. The mechanism implementing the model consists of a run–time system guaranteeing that the cooperation among different components does not affect the overall confidence of the application, i.e that a non-critical component does not corrupt a critical one.

The policy presented in [25] is based on the following concepts:

- Each object O is assigned an integrity level $il(O)$, ranging from 0, the lowest, to 3, the highest.

- The communication model is based on the notion of service invocation and message–passing. Each message is assigned the integrity level of the object which sent it.

- *Single Level Objects* (SLO) are objects whose integrity level is fixed.

- *Multiple Level Objects* (MLO) are objects whose integrity level can be dynamically modified. A MLO of level 3 is allowed to receive data from an object of level 3, but also from an object of level 2 (or 1, or 0), in which case its level is decreased to 2 (1,0, resp.).

- A set of rules is given, describing all the possible communication patterns among pairs of components, depending on the respective criticality levels.

There is a third kind of objects, the *Validation Objects*, which are used to extract reliable data from low level objects. An example of Validation Objects is the one that uses a redundant number of objects as source for the data. From the point of view of the integrity policy, the Validation Objects are SLO, since they provide information at a fixed level of integrity.

4   Description of a MLO via a process algebra

Process algebras describe the behaviours of a system as a sequence of elementary actions, where each action is seen as a state transformer. Our claim is that process algebras are particularly suited to model the multi–level integrity policy. In fact, the policy definition abstracts on the functionality of the objects, and the relevant events we need to describe are the object invocations (the actions) which may change the object integrity level (the state).

Moreover, with reference to validation, the process algebra description has a low complexity, and the generation of the model to be checked does not suffer the state explosion problem.

In this section we present a formal description of the integrity policy introduced in [25] using the CCS/MEIJE process algebra. In particular, we concentrate on a Multi Level Object (MLO).

A MLO is assigned three integrity levels:

maxil which represents the maximum integrity level that the MLO can reach. It is also called the *intrinsic level* of the MLO. This is a statically defined value which does not change at execution time.

minil which represents the minimum value the integrity level of the MLO can reach while interacting with other objects. Differently from *maxil* this is not a stat-ically defined value: every time the MLO is invoked, with a read, a write, or a read–write request, a value to *minil* can be assigned, and this value can change (only to increase) during the computation to serve the request. More-over, *minil* is local to an invocation and no memory of its value is kept after the answer. You can think that a new instance of MLO is created every time the object is invoked, and that the instance takes, at activation time, a value for *minil*.

il is the current integrity level. Every time the MLO is invoked, *il* takes a given value. During the computation to serve the invocation, *il* can then assume any value among *maxil* and *minil*, according to the rules in [25]. As for *minil*, *il* is local to the invocation and no memory of its value is kept between distinguished invocations.

As in [25], any number of concurrent invocations of an object is allowed. For the sake of validation via model checking, we rather need to model the MLO's behaviour via a finite state machine and thus we need to limit the number of possible concurrent invocations to a bound quantity. However, this limitation occurs also in the actual implementation of the policy. Let a MLO A be serving n invocations concurrently, then its behaviour can be seen as that of:

$$\underbrace{A \parallel \ldots \parallel A}_{n \ times}$$

4.1 Notation

Before describing the behaviour of a MLO, we need to introduce some notation. In the following,

$$MLO_x$$

will denote a Multiple Level Object with the statically defined *maxil* value $= x$. With

$$SAT\_REQ_{x,y,z}$$

we represent a MLO which is satisfying an invocation. At this point the MLO is characterized by the three values *minil, il,* and *maxil* considered equal to x, y, and z, respectively. We recall that, when satisfying an invocation, the MLO can change its integrity level, depending on the integrity level of other objects it communicates with during the computation. When the request has been satisfied, the MLO forgets the *minil* and *il* values and keeps only its intrinsic integrity level (*maxil*). This is possible under the hypothesis that also the functional part of the object keeps no memory of previous invocations.

$$read\_request_y$$

will denote a read request of level y. This means that the invocation was issued either by a SLO with y as *il* or by a MLO with y as *minil*. We also attach a level to the answers as in:

$$answer_x$$

Value x can be the current *il* of the object which is answering, or -1: $answer_{-1}$ means something like: "I cannot answer", we use this notation for uniformity purposes. Then, with

$$write\_request_x$$

we denote a write request issued by an object with x as *il*. We call x the level of the write request. Finally, with

$$read\_write\_request_{x,y}$$

we denote a read–write request issued either by a MLO with x as *minil* and y as *il* or by a SLO with $il = x = y$.

4.2 Behaviour of MLO_x

We now give the formal definition of a MLO with *maxil* = x. We only consider the integrity policy and nothing is said on the objects functionalities and on their implementation.

We first consider the case of reception of a read request.

$$MLO_x = \quad read\_request_y? \text{ (case } y \leq x) \ : \ SAT\_REQ_{y,x,x} \qquad\qquad +$$
$$read\_request_y? \text{ (case } y > x) \ : \ answer_{-1}! \ : \ MLO_x \qquad +$$

(behaviour when a write or read–write request are received)

When a read request of level y is received and $y \leq x$, then the MLO makes the needed computation to serve the request taking y as *minil* value, and x, its *maxil* value, as value for *il*.

On the contrary, a read request of level greater than x cannot be considered, since the MLO has not the needed integrity level to supply an answer.

To satisfy a request, a MLO can:

- provide the answer to the caller. In this case the MLO has ended its duty. The answer carries the current integrity level of the MLO: this is needed if the invoking object is another MLO that might need to update its *il*; (1)

- send a write request to another object and continue; (2)

- send a read request, wait for the answer and eventually continue. Continuation depends on the level of the answer received, if this is too low[2], then the computation is stopped, and a "I cannot answer your request" message is sent; (3)(4)(5)

- send a read–write request. (6)(7)(8)

---

[2]Actually, in the object model adopted by [25], either the read request is not accepted, or the integrity policy guarantees that the answer received has the appropriate integrity level. This means that the only possible low level answer received here is $answer_{-1}$. On the contrary, if the more general ICP communication model is considered, it is not possible to guarantee that if a read request is accepted, then the answer will have the right integrity level. Our description, exploiting -1 as a possible level of an answer, permits to uniformly treat the two models.

$SAT\_REQ_{min,il,max} =$

$\qquad answer_{il}! \ : \ MLO_{max}$ $+$ (1)

$\qquad write\_request_{il}! \ : \ SAT\_REQ_{min,il,max}$ $+$ (2)

$\qquad read\_request_{min}! \ : \ ($

$\qquad\qquad answer_x?(\text{case } x < min) \ : \ answer_{-1}! \ : \ MLO_{max} +$ (3)

$\qquad\qquad answer_x?(\text{case } min \le x \le il) \ : \ SAT\_REQ_{min,x,max} +$ (4)

$\qquad\qquad answer_x?(\text{case } x \ge il) : SAT\_REQ_{min,il,max})$ $+$ (5)

$\qquad read\_write\_request_{min,il}! \ : \ ($

$\qquad\qquad answer_x?(\text{case } x < min) \ : \ answer_{-1}! \ : \ MLO_{max} +$ (6)

$\qquad\qquad answer_x?(\text{case } min \le x \le il) \ : \ SAT\_REQ_{min,x,max} +$ (7)

$\qquad\qquad answer_x?(\text{case } x \ge il) : SAT\_REQ_{min,il,max})$ (8)

This description permits the MLO to indefinitely continue trying to satisfy the request, without ever sending an answer back. This happens if steps (1), (3), or (6) are never taken. In particular, step number (1), which is the normal loop exit, is taken or not depending on the object functional behaviour, and it is correct that, if no integrity level violation occurs (in this case step (3) or (6) are taken), the overall behaviour of the object depends only on its functional description.

We now consider the case of reception of a write or read–write request and complete the description of the MLO behaviour.

$MLO_x =$

$\qquad$ *(behaviour when a read request is received)* $+$

$\qquad write\_request_y?(\text{ case } y \le x) \ : \ COMPUTE_{0,y,x} \ : \ MLO_x$ $+$

$\qquad write\_request_y?(\text{ case } y > x) \ : \ COMPUTE_{0,x,x} \ : \ MLO_x$ $+$

$\qquad read\_write\_request_{y,z}?(\text{ case } y \le z \le x) \ : \ SAT\_RW\_REQ_{y,z,x}$ $+$

$\qquad read\_write\_request_{y,z}?(\text{ case } y \le x \le z) \ : \ SAT\_RW\_REQ_{y,x,x}$ $+$

$\qquad read\_write\_request_{y,z}?(\text{ case } y > x) \ : \ answer_{-1}! \ : \ MLO_x$

When a write request is received, the MLO takes 0 as *minil* (zero is a default value, according to [25]), and the minimum among x (its *maxil*) and y (the level of the request) as *il*. A computation can then be performed, but no answer is due.

A read–write request is dealt with as the composition of a read and a write ones, and we will not dwell on this description.

5   Validation of MLO properties

According to the integrity policy, data of a low integrity level cannot flow to an higher integrity level (unless through a Validation Object, which is the only kind of objects authorized to break this rule).

This property should hold in any situation, in particular within any complex schema of interaction among objects. Since the most complex schemata can be reduced to combinations of nested invocations of objects and concurrent invocations of objects, we address these two interaction patterns as validation cases.

Moreover, actual validation by model–checking requires non-parametric finite state models, derived by particular instances of the general formalization.

Therefore, in the sequel we will define particular instances of the considered validation cases, which will be shown to be representative enough to be generalized. We will use this instances to prove a set of temporal logic formulae expressing the integrity property sketched above, for the addressed validation cases.

We first deal with the properties of a single MLO, and then address the interaction patterns among MLO's: nested and concurrent invocations.

Using the tools of the JACK environment, we are able to:

- Generate the complete models of the considered interaction patterns.

- Visualize the models (or an abstracted view of them), as shown in Figures 1 and 2.

- Check the satisfiability of some interesting properties of the policy on the generated models.

5.1 Properties of a MLO_2

Assume a system to be composed only of object A_2, which is a MLO with *maxil* 2. Using JACK we have proved that A_2 cannot provide answers of level 3, nor serve read requests of level 3, i.e., that it satisfies the following ACTL properties.

$$\sim EF \langle A_2\_answer_3! \rangle \, true$$

$$AG \, [A_2\_read\_request_3?] \, A \, [true \, \{false\} \, U \, \{A_2\_answer_{-1}!\} \, true]$$

Here and in the following messages are labelled: requests carry the name of the object which is invoked to serve the request, answers take the name of the answering object.

5.2 Nested invocations

Since we need to work on a finite state model, we need to consider the instances of the nested invocations pattern. We take into account here the case in which a MLO of a given level, in response to a read–request, invokes, again by means of a read–request, another MLO of a lower integrity level. This is indeed the most complex case. All the other combinations (SLO vs. MLO, read–request vs. write–request or read/write–request, different levels of integrity) can be reduced to this one: anyway, a separate validation by model–checking of these other cases can be done following what presented here.

Assume a system to be defined as the combination of the two objects:

A_2 which is a MLO with *maxil* 2

B_0 which is a MLO with *maxil* 0

We model a possible behaviour of this system as the parallel composition $A_2 \parallel B_0$. Let a read request $read\_request_1$ be received by A_2 (This means that the request was either sent by a MLO with $minil = 1$ or by a SLO with $il = 1$). We assume that the functional description of A_2 imposes that, to serve a request, a further read request must be sent to B_0. Let's see the various steps of this computation:

1. at the beginning we have: $A_2 \parallel B_0$;
2. A_2 receives $read\_request_1$;
3. the request is accepted, since $request\_level = 1 \le maxil(A_2) = 2$;
4. we now have: $SAT\_REQ_{1,2,2} \parallel B_0$;
5. a $read\_request_1$ is sent from A_2 to B_0;
6. the request cannot be accepted since:

$$minil(SAT\_REQ_{1,2,2}) = request\_level = 1 > maxil(B_0) = 0$$

7. we thus now have: $(A_2$ waiting for an answer$) \parallel answer_{-1} : B_0$ where "A_2 waiting for an answer" is equivalent to:

$$answer_{-1}? : answer_{-1}! : A_2 +$$
$$answer_0? : answer_{-1}! : A_2 +$$
$$answer_1? : SAT\_REQ_{1,1,2} +$$
$$answer_2? : SAT\_REQ_{1,2,2} +$$
$$answer_3? : SAT\_REQ_{1,2,2}$$

8. $answer_{-1}$ is sent from B_0 to A_2;
9. we thus have: $answer_{-1}! : A_2 \parallel B_0$;
10. $answer_{-1}$ is sent from A_2 to acknowledge that it cannot satisfy the request it was trying to serve;
11. we end back in the initial configuration: $A_2 \parallel B_0$

We formally list the transitions:

$A_2 \parallel B_0$

$\xrightarrow{read\_request_1?} SAT\_REQ_{1,2,2} \parallel B_0$

$\xrightarrow{\tau} \underbrace{\ldots + answer_{-1}? : answer_{-1}! : A_2 + \ldots}_{A_2 \ waiting \ for \ an \ answer} \parallel answer_{-1}! : B_0$

$\xrightarrow{\tau} answer_{-1}! : A_2 \parallel B_0$

$\xrightarrow{answer_{-1}!} A_2 \parallel B_0$

5.2.1 Properties in case of nested invocations

We prove that in a situation as in section 5.2 ($A_2 \parallel B_0$), the following holds:

$$AG\,[A_2\_read\_request_1?]\,A\,[true\,\{false\}\,U\,\{A_2\_answer_{-1}\}\,true] \qquad\qquad \text{(F1)}$$

i.e. if A_2 receives $read\_request_1$, then the unique next visible transition is $answer_{-1}$.

Actually, this is true or false depending on the implementation of the functional part of A_2. We isolate object A_2. After receiving a read request of level 1, i.e. after performing action $A_2\_read\_request_1?$, A_2 can: answer back, send a further read request to B_0, or perform other actions, as expressed by the following formula.

$$AG[A_2\_read\_request_1?]A[true\,\{false\}\,U$$
$$\{A_2\_answer_2! \mid B_0\_read\_request_1! \mid write\_request_2! \mid read\_write\_request_{1,2}!\}\,true]$$

We proved that this is true. We can now make a commitment on the A_2's behaviour, and assert that a read–request of level 1 is always served by sending a read–request to B_0:

$$AG\,[A_2\_read\_request_1?]\,A\,[true\,\{false\}\,U\,\{B_0\_read\_request_1!\}\,true]$$

Then, we isolated object B_0, and showed that:

$$AG\,[B_0\_read\_request_1?]\,A\,[true\,\{false\}\,U\,\{B_0\_answer_{-1}!\}true]$$

Finally, we proved that after receiving an answer of level -1, i.e. after performing action $B_0\_answer_{-1}?$, A_2 can only send a negative answer:

$$AG\,[B_0\_answer_{-1}?]\,A\,[true\,\{false\}\,U\,\{A_2\_answer_{-1}!\}\,true]$$

Then, combining these formulae, we can derive that the system composed of A_2 and B_0 satisfies (F1).

5.2.2 Generalization of the results

It is easy to see that we can obtain an equivalent model (modulo the name of the actions) if instead of A_2, B_0, and $read\_request_1$, we use A_i and B_j, and $read\_request_k$, for any i, j, k such that $i \geq k > j$. Consequently, if we rename the checked formulae accordingly, the result of model–checking will not change.

Since the proved properties guarantee that data do not flow from a given level of integrity to an higher level of integrity through a pair of nested invocations, we can conclude, by transitivity, that data do not flow from a given level of integrity to an higher one, through any number of nested invocations either.

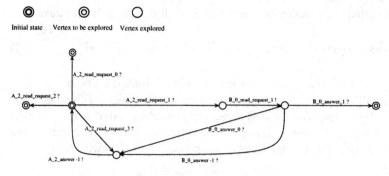

Figure 1: Nested Invocations.

5.3 Concurrent invocations

Let us consider now the case of concurrent invocations of the same object; the two parallel invocations will be modelled as two parallel processes.

Assume A_2 is a MLO with *maxil* 2, which can manage two invocations concurrently. We see what happens if the MLO receives a read request of level 1 and then a write request of level 0 and show that the latter does not influence the answer to the former.

1. at the beginning we have $A_2 \parallel A_2$;
2. a $read\_request_1$ is received;
3. the request is accepted, since $1 \leq maxil(A_2)$:
4. we now have $SAT\_REQ_{1,2,2} \parallel A_2$;
5. a $write\_request_0$ is received;
6. the request is accepted unconditionally;
7. we then have: $SAT\_REQ_{1,2,2} \parallel COMPUTE_{0,0,2}$;
8. $answer_2$ is sent back;
9. we are in situation $A_2 \parallel COMPUTE_{0,0,2}$;
10. the computation started by the write request ends, and we are back to the initial situation $A_2 \parallel A_2$.

5.3.1 Properties in case of concurrent invocations

We have considered and MLO with *maxil* 2 (call it A_2), that provides answers of level 2 to any read requests of level 1, i.e. an MLO satisfying:

$$AG \, [A_2\_read\_request_1?] \, A \, [true \, \{true\} \, U \, \{A_2\_answer_2!\} \, true] \qquad \text{(F2)}$$

and we have proved that the parallel composition $A_2 \| A_2$ satisfies both F2 and:

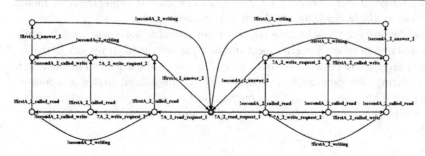

Figure 2: Concurrent Invocations.

$$AG\,[A_2\_read\_request_1?]\,E\,[true\,\{\sim A_2\_answer_y!\}\,U\,\{A_2\_write\_request_0?\}\,true]$$

where $A_2\_answer_y!$ stays for
$$A_2\_answer_{-1}!|A_2\_answer_0!\ldots$$

this means that a write request of level 0, which decreases the MLO integrity level, can be accepted while a read request is being served, without influencing it: the two requests are dealt with independently by the two instances of A_2.

A second proof on this example has been done, showing that when one of the copies of A_2 accepts a request, then it cannot accept other requests before answering to the first one. Exploiting JACK, we proved:

$$AG\,[firstA_2\_called\_read!]$$
$$A\,[true\,\{\sim firstA_2\_called\_read!\,\&\,\sim firstA_2\_called\_write!\}$$
$$U\,\{firstA_2\_answer_y!\}\,true]$$

where $firstA_2\_answer_y!$ stays for
$$firstA_2\_answer_{-1}!|firstA_2\_answer_0!\ldots$$

Labels *first* and *second* are introduced to distinguish the actions of the two objects. We assume that each of the two copies of object A_2 sends an acknowledgement after having received a request. The acknowledgement to a read request can be $firstA_2\_called\_read!$ or $secondA_2\_called\_read!$, depending on which A_2 copy accepted the request.

Conclusions

We presented the application of a model–checking approach to validate the multi–level integrity mechanism of GUARDS. A formal description of the mechanism has been provided, in CCS style, and a set of properties have been formally stated in the

ACTL temporal logic. Property satisfaction was proved exploiting the AMC model checker, available inside the JACK verification environment.

Validation by model–checking requires non-parametric finite state models, while our description of the integrity mechanism is parametric (with respect to the integrity levels). We have considered a pair of instances of the general modelization (considering two representative models of object invocation: nested and concurrent), we have based the validation on these instances, and generalized the results to objects with different integrity levels and to situations with many interacting objects.

Acknowledgements

This work was supported by the ESPRIT project GUARDS (Generic Upgradable Architecture for Real-time Dependable Systems).

References

[1] Bell, D.E., LaPadula, L.J., "Security Computer Systems: Mathematical foundations and model", Technical Report M74-244, MITRE Corp., Bedford, Mass., 1974.

[2] Bernardeschi, C., Fantechi, A., Gnesi, S., Larosa, S., Mongardi, G., Romano, D.,"A Formal Verification Environment for Railway Signaling System Design", in Formal Methods in System Design 12, 139-161, 1998.

[3] Bernardeschi, C., Fantechi, A., Gnesi, S., Santone, A., "Automated verification of fault tolerance mechanisms", 3rd International Workshop on Formal Methods for Industrial Critical Systems (FMICS'98), CWI, Amsterdam, May 1998.

[4] Biba, K., "Integrity Considerations for Secure Computer Systems", Tech. Rep. ESD-TR 76-372, MITRE Co., April 1997.

[5] Bouali, A., De Simone, R., "Symbolic bisimulation minimization," in Proceedings Fourth Workshop on Computer-Aided Verification, Lecture Notes in Computer Science 663, Springer-Verlag, 1992, pp. 96-108

[6] Bouali, A., Gnesi, S., Larosa, S., "The integration Project for the JACK Environment". Bulletin of the EATCS, 54, October 1994, pp. 207–223.

[7] Bouali, A., Ressouche, A., Roy, V., De Simone, R., "The FC2TOOLS set," in Proceedings Workshop on Computer-Aided Verification, Lecture Notes in Computer Science 1102, Springer-Verlag, 1996.

[8] Boudol, G., "Notes on Algebraic Calculi of Processes," Notes on Algebraic Calculi of Processes, NATO ASI Series F13, 1985.

[9] Boyer, R.S., Moore, J.S., "A Computational Logic", ACM Monograph Series, Academic Press, 1979.

[10] Clark, D.D., Wilson, D.R., "Comparison of Commercial and Military Computer Security Policies", IEEE Symp. on Security and Privacy, Oakland, CA, pp. 184-194, IEEE Computer Society Press, 1987.

[11] Clarke, E.M., Emerson, E.A., Sistla, A.P., "Automatic Verification of Finite–State Concurrent Systems Using Temporal Logic Specification," ACM Transaction on Programming Languages and Systems, 8 (2), April 1986, pp. 244–263.

[12] De Nicola, R., Fantechi, A., Gnesi, S., Ristori, G., "Verifying Hardware Components within JACK," in Proceedings of CHARME '95, Lecture Notes in Computer Science 987, Springer-Verlag, 1995, pp. 246–260.

[13] De Nicola, R., Fantechi, A., Gnesi, S., Ristori, G., "An action–based framework for verifying logical and behavioural properties of concurrent systems". Computer Networks, Vol. 25 No. 7, 1993, pp. 761 – 778.

[14] De Nicola, R., Vaandrager, F.W., "Action versus State based Logics for Transition Systems," in Proceedings Ecole de Printemps on Semantics of Concurrency, Lecture Notes in Computer Science 469, Springer-Verlag, 1990, pp. 407–419.

[15] Emerson, E.A., Halpern, J.Y., "Sometimes and Not Never Revisited: on Branching Time versus Linear Time Temporal Logic," Journal of ACM, 33 (1), January 1986, pp. 151–178.

[16] Ferro, G., "AMC: ACTL Model Checker. Reference Manual," IEI-Internal Report, B4-47 December 1994.

[17] Hennessy, M., Milner, R., "Algebraic Laws for Nondeterminism and Concurrency," Journal of ACM, 32, January 1985, pp. 137–161.

[18] Hoare, C.A.R., "Communicating Sequential Processes", Prentice Hall Int., London, 1985.

[19] Madelaine, E. and Vergamini, D., "AUTO: A Verification tool for Distributed Systems using Reduction of Finite Automata Networks," Formal Description Techniques, II (S.T Vuong, ed.), 1990, pp.61-66.

[20] Milner, R., "Communication and Concurrency," Prentice Hall,1989.

[21] Park, D., "Concurrency and Automata on Infinite Sequences," in Proceedings Fifth GI Conference, Lecture Notes in Computer Science 104, Springer-Verlag, 1981, pp. 167–183.

[22] Pugliese, R., Tronci, E., "Automatic Verification of a Hydroelectric Power Plant" in Proceedings FME'96 Industrial Benefit and Advances in Formal Methods, Lecture Notes in Computer Science 1051, 1996, pp. 425–444.

[23] Pnueli, A., "Linear and Branching Structures in the Semantics and Logic of Reactive Systems," in Proceedings of 12th ICALP, Lecture Notes in Computer Science 194, 1985.

[24] Roy, V., De Simone, R., "AUTO and Autograph," in Proceedings Workshop on Computer Aided Verification, Lecture Notes in Computer Science 531, Springer-Verlag, 1990, pp. 65-75.

[25] Totel, E., Blanquart, J.P., Deswarte, Y., Powell, D., "Supporting Multiple Levels of Criticality", in Proceedings 28th Int. Symp. on Fault-Tolerant Computing (FTCS-28), (Munich, Germany), IEEE Computer Society Press, June 1988.

[26] Wellings, A., Beus-Dukic, L., Burns, A., Powell, D., "Genericity and Upgradability in Ultra-Dependable Real-Time Architectures". Work in Progress Proceedings, Real-Time Systems Symp., Washington D.C., pp.15-18, IEEE Computer Society Press, December 1996

Distributed Systems

Proteus: A Flexible Infrastructure to Implement Adaptive Fault Tolerance in AQuA [1]

Chetan Sabnis, Michel Cukier, Jennifer Ren,
Paul Rubel, and William H. Sanders

David E. Bakken and David A. Karr

Center for Reliable and High-Performance Computing
Coordinated Science Laboratory and
Department of Electrical and Computer Engineering
University of Illinois at Urbana-Champaign
Urbana, Illinois 61801
{sabnis, cukier, ren, rubel, whs}@crhc.uiuc.edu

BBN Technologies
Cambridge, Massachusetts 02138
{dbakken, dkarr}@bbn.com

Abstract

Building dependable distributed systems from commercial off-the-shelf components is of growing practical importance. For both cost and production reasons, there is interest in approaches and architectures that facilitate building such systems. The AQuA architecture is one such approach; its goal is to provide adaptive fault tolerance to CORBA applications by replicating objects, providing a high-level method for applications to specify their desired dependability, and providing a dependability manager that attempts to reconfigure a system at runtime so that dependability requests are satisfied. This paper describes how dependability is provided in AQuA. In particular, we describe Proteus, the part of AQuA that dynamically manages replicated distributed objects to make them dependable. Given a dependability request, Proteus chooses a fault tolerance approach and reconfigures the system to try to meet the request. The infrastructure of Proteus is described in this paper, along with its use in implementing active replication and a simple dependability policy.

1. Introduction

Providing fault tolerance to distributed applications is a challenging and important goal. In many applications, the cost of a custom hardware solution is prohibitive. Even if custom hardware is used, the flexibility that software can provide makes it a natural choice for implementing a significant portion of the fault tolerance of dependable distributed systems. Furthermore, when the dependability requirements change during the execution of an application, the fault tolerance approach must be *adaptive* in the sense that the mechanisms used to provide fault tolerance may change at runtime. Together, these requirements argue for a software solution that can reconfigure a system based both on the levels of dependability desired by a distributed system during its execution and on the faults that occur.

---

[1] This research has been supported by DARPA Contracts F30602-96-C-0315 and F30602-97-C-0276.

The AQuA architecture [Cuk98] provides a flexible approach for building dependable, distributed, object-oriented systems that support adaptation due to both faults and changes in an application's dependability requirements. Its goal is to provide a simple high-level way for applications to specify the level of dependability they desire and the type of faults that should be tolerated. A dependability manager configures the system, based on notification of faults that occur and dependability requests from applications, in order to try to achieve a requested level of dependability. It is important to note that the architecture is extensible: it does not prescribe that a particular replication or group communication policy must be used, but instead provides a framework for implementing multiple advisor policies, replication policies, voting policies, and communication protocols.

In order to provide a simple way for application objects to specify the level of dependability they desire, the AQuA architecture uses the *Quality Objects* (QuO) [Zin97, Loy98] framework to process and invoke dependability requests. QuO allows distributed applications to specify quality of service (QoS) requirements at the application level using the notion of a "contract," which specifies actions to be taken based on the state of the distributed system and desired application requirements. The QuO framework provides an environment in which a programmer can specify regions of operation in terms of high-level QoS measures, and translates these measures into specific requests to *Proteus*. QuO also provides ways for multiple QoS properties to be integrated, as well as ways for an application to adapt above the ORB without involving the application, but these topics are beyond the scope of the paper.

Proteus provides fault tolerance in AQuA by dynamically managing replicated distributed objects to make them dependable. It does this by configuring the system in response to faults and changes in desired dependability levels. The choice of how to provide fault tolerance involves choosing the types of faults to tolerate, the styles of replication to use, the types of voting to use, the degrees of replication to use, and the location of the replicas, among other factors. The replication protocols in Proteus assume the existence of an underlying group communication system that provides reliable multicast, total ordering, and virtual synchrony. For our implementation, we have used the *Maestro/Ensemble* [Hay98, Vay98] group communication system. Communication between all architecture components is done using *gateways*, which translate CORBA object invocations into messages that are transmitted via Ensemble, and contain mechanisms to implement a chosen fault tolerance scheme.

This paper describes the detailed design and implementation of Proteus, and shows how Proteus provides a flexible infrastructure for implementing multiple advisor policies, multiple replication protocols, multiple voter types, and multiple group communication schemes. Particular choices among these alternatives depend on the number and type of faults an application wishes to tolerate (crash, value, and time), the performance expected, and the type of communication style (*e.g.*, synchronous vs. asynchronous) desired at the application level. Based on instructions from QuO, these choices can be made during the execution of a distributed application, and hence provide fault tolerance that adapts depending on the needs of one or more applications.

Other researchers have also seen the importance of making CORBA objects reliable. In particular, other approaches that use group communication include Electra [Maf95, Maf97], Eternal [Nar97], Maestro [Vay98], OpenDREAMS [Fel96], and ROMANCE [Rod93]. For a comparison of these approaches with AQuA, see [Cuk98].

The remainder of this paper is organized as follows. Section 2 provides an overview of Proteus, describing how its dependability manager, object factories, and gateways aim to provide a desired level of dependability. Section 3 details the functioning of Proteus's dependability manager and object factories, describing their general architecture and the current policies. Section 4 then describes the gateways, focusing on how voting and replication protocols are built on top of group communication. Details of our current implementation of active replication are given in Section 5. Finally, Section 6 presents a discussion of research directions that we are currently pursuing.

2. Proteus Overview

The organization of Proteus is shown in Figure 1. Proteus makes remote objects dependable by using 1) a replicated dependability manager to make decisions regarding reconfigurations and coordinate changes in system configurations, 2) object factories to kill and start objects and provide information to the dependability manager regarding a host, and 3) gateways that implement particular voting and replication schemes. An interface to the QuO runtime is provided to allow the application to specify the level of dependability.

The *Proteus dependability manager* is composed of two parts: an *advisor,* which makes decisions regarding reconfiguration based on reported faults and dependability requests from QuO, and a *protocol coordinator,* which, together with the gateways implements, the chosen fault tolerance approach. Depending on the choices made by the advisor, Proteus can tolerate and recover from crash failures, time faults, and value faults in application objects and the QuO runtime. Note that we do not aim to tolerate Byzantine faults, value faults in the gateway, or faults in the group communication system itself. If tolerance of more complex fault types is required, one could substitute a more secure group communication protocol (e.g., [Kih98, Rei95]) for Ensemble within the AQuA architecture.

Object factories are used to kill and start replicated applications, depending on decisions made by the dependability manager, and to provide information regarding the host to the dependability manager.

Gateways provide two functions. First, they provide a standard CORBA interface to applications. CORBA provides application developers with a standard interface to build distributed object-oriented applications, but does not provide a simple approach to allow applications to be fault-tolerant. The gateway provides a standard CORBA interface by translating between process-level communication, as supported by Ensemble, and IIOP messages, which are understood by Object Request Brokers (ORBs) in CORBA. In this way, CORBA-based distributed applications written for the AQuA architecture can use standard, commercially available ORBs. In addition to providing basic reliable communication services for application objects and the QuO runtime, the gateway also provides fault tolerance using different *voters* and *replication protocols*. These services are located in the *gateway handlers*. Both active and passive replication of "AQuA objects" can be supported. *AQuA objects* are the basic units of replication in the AQuA architecture. Each one consists of a gateway, an "application" object, and a QuO runtime, if QuO is being used to manage the desires of the application object. In this context, the *application object* can be part of the distributed application itself, or part of the AQuA architecture that uses the services of a gateway (such as the dependability manager and the object factories). The architecture of the gateway will be described in Section 4.

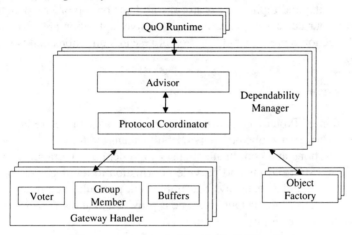

Figure 1: Proteus Architecture

3. Dependability Manager and Object Factories

This section describes Proteus's protocol coordinator, advisor, and object factories. The functional interface between the dependability manager and the gateways, the object factories, and the QuO runtimes is shown in Figure 2 and described in this section. The internal structure of the dependability manager is also described. In Figure 2, arrows are labeled with method calls, using the convention that the arrow indicates the direction of the method invocation.

3.1. Protocol Coordinator

The protocol coordinator is used to communicate with QuO, object factories, and application gateways. The role of the protocol coordinator is to carry out the decisions of the advisor in a consistent way. The protocol coordinator contains the algorithms necessary to execute the decisions and to order the different executions. The particular coordination algorithm used depends on which replication types and fault tolerance mechanisms are supported in a given implementation of the AQuA architecture, but the interface to other AQuA architecture components remains the same in all cases.

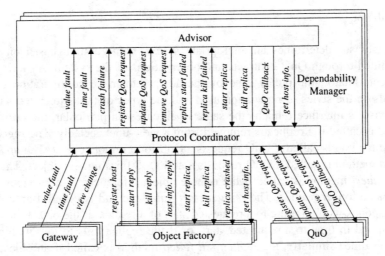

Figure 2: Protocol Coordinator and Advisor Methods

Specifically, the protocol coordinator's CORBA interface consists of several methods. The *view change* method is called by application gateways to report Maestro/Ensemble view changes. Given view change information, the protocol coordinator determines whether the view change is the result of a crash failure, a configuration change requested by Proteus, or both. The *value/time fault* method is called by application gateways if a value/time fault is reported by a gateway. This information is then passed to the advisor for processing. The *register host* method is called by an object factory to register itself. The *start reply*, *kill reply*, and *host information reply* methods are called by an object factory to report, respectively, the status of a request made to start an application, the status of a request made to kill an application, and information (e.g., the host load) concerning the host. The *register QoS request* method is called by the QuO runtime or an application object to provide a dependability request to the manager. The *update QoS request* method substitutes a new QoS request for one that was previously registered. Finally, the *remove QoS request* method eliminates a previously registered QoS request without replacing it with a new request.

The protocol coordinator also has methods that are called by the advisor. In the current implementation of the dependability manager, the four methods within the protocol coordinator used by the advisor are *start replica*, *kill replica*, *QuO callback*, and *get host information*. Upon an invocation of the first two methods by the advisor, the protocol coordinator calls *start replica* or *kill replica* on the correct object factory. The protocol coordinator uses timers to limit the time spent waiting for notification of the result of a configuration change request. In particular, the advisor is notified of a start failure if a factory response to a start request, or the view change expected from starting a replica, does not arrive within a specified amount of time. The *QuO callback* method is used to service a request from the advisor to issue a callback to the QuO runtime. Finally, the *get host information* method is called to request information concerning the host.

3.2. Advisor

The advisor determines an appropriate system configuration based on requests transmitted through QuO contracts and observations of the system. As with the protocol coordinator, the policy used by the advisor to make configuration decisions depends on the styles of replication used and the types of faults tolerated. However, the advisor's interface remains the same in all cases. In particular, the *crash failure* method is called if a replica is removed from a view unexpectedly. The *register QoS request* method is called if QuO requests a QoS for a remote object. The *update QoS request* method is called if QuO requests a new QoS for a remote object. The *remove QoS request* method is called if the remote object referenced in a previous QoS request is no longer needed. The *replica start failed* method is called if an object factory responds with a failure to a requested start of a replica, if the object factory does not respond in time to a requested start, or if the replica fails to join its replication group in time. Similarly, the *replica kill failed* method is called if an object factory replies with a failure to a requested kill of a replica. Finally, the *value/time fault* method is called if a value/time fault notification is received by the protocol coordinator.

A simple policy was developed to support crash failures. In this policy, when the *crash failure* method is invoked, the advisor chooses to start a replica on the least-loaded host in the system that does not have a replica of the same application already running. When a *replica start failed* method is invoked, the advisor applies the same policy as for the *crash failure* method, except that the method will not choose the host where the replica start failed.

The policy currently implemented also supports adaptation based on dependability requests from QuO. In particular, the *register QoS request* and *update QoS request* methods define the QoS in terms of the minimum number of crash failures to tolerate (n). If no replicas of the application are running, the advisor decides to start $n + 1$ new replicas on the least-loaded hosts. If replicas are already running, then the advisor may decide to start additional replicas (on the least-loaded hosts) or kill existing replicas (on the most-loaded hosts) so that $n + 1$ replicas are running. If more than one application requests a QoS for a remote object, the advisor chooses to maintain the maximum $n + 1$ replicas among the applications. Finally, the *remove QoS request* indicates to the advisor that it may kill all replicas of a remote object unless the QoS for the object is also requested by another application. In that case, the advisor chooses to maintain the maximum $n + 1$ replicas to support the remaining applications.

If a *crash failure, replica start failed, register QoS request,* or *update QoS request* call results in an inability to meet QoS requirements, a callback is made to QuO. In particular, a call to *crash failure* will result in a QuO callback if all available hosts have an application replica running. A call to *replica start failed* will result in a QuO callback if all available hosts, except for the host where the start failed, have an application replica running. Finally, a call to *register QoS request* or *update QoS request* will result in a QuO callback if the specified minimum number of faults to tolerate is greater than or equal to the number of hosts in the system. This object-based approach to making decisions allows for flexibility in devising advisor policies. In particular, it is possible to program and study more complicated policies without changing the mechanism by which they are executed in the protocol coordinator.

3.3. Object Factory

The functions of object factories, one of which runs on each host in a system, are to start processes, to kill processes, and to provide information about the host. The object factory is not replicated, but since it does not contain state that needs to be preserved between failures, it can be restarted after a host failure so that the host can again be used to support AQuA objects.

When a factory is started, it reads in a file that is specific to its host. This file indicates which applications a factory can start. The factory then registers itself with the dependability manager by calling the *register host* method. The dependability manager then knows that the factory's host is available to start replicas. After receiving a reply from the dependability manager, the factory is ready to start and kill processes.

When the dependability manager sends a *start replica* request to the factory, the factory attempts to start the specified application. If an exception is generated while the application is starting, a start failure is reported. If no exception is generated, the factory adds the application to a list of running applications, and a successful start is reported to the advisor.

A request from the dependability manager to kill an application (*kill replica* method) is handled in the same manner. If an exception is generated during an attempt to kill the application, a kill failure is reported. If no exception is generated, the factory removes the application from the list of running applications and a successful kill is reported.

The dependability manager also notifies the factory, through the *replica crashed* method, if a replica on the factory's host fails. This is done so that the factory has the correct state of its host. This method simply removes the crashed replica from the list of running remote objects.

The factory is also responsible for providing information to the dependability manager about its host. In the current implementation of the factory, the factory periodically sends the load of its host to the dependability manager through the *host information reply* method. The dependability manager uses this information to decide how to assign replicas to hosts. The dependability manager can also request this information at other times by using the *get host information* method.

4. Gateway Overview

The AQuA gateway has several functions: translating between object- (IIOP) and process-level (Ensemble) communication, providing an infrastructure for implementing various replication and voting schemes, and detecting and reporting faults to the dependability manager. This section first describes the physical structure of the gateway, and then describes the group structure used to support Proteus's replication schemes.

4.1. Architecture Overview

The AQuA gateway is implemented as a process, and is one part of an AQuA object. It intercepts IIOP (Internet Inter-ORB Protocol) messages generated from a CORBA object and transmits them, using the Maestro/Ensemble group communication system, to other gateways. As can be seen in Figure 3, the gateway consists of an IIOP encoder/decoder, a dispatcher, handlers, and an interface to Maestro/Ensemble. Figure 3 shows a high-level view of the gateway architecture, and its interface to the application and QuO runtime processes.

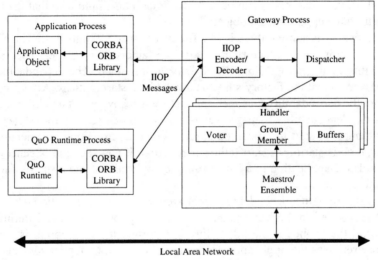

Figure 3: Gateway Architecture

The *IIOP encoder/decoder* is used to interface with a CORBA object. When an IIOP stream is intercepted by the IIOP decoder, it removes the IIOP header and passes the message to the dispatcher, which delivers it according to the protocols in Section 5. The gateway has an incoming and an outgoing queue of messages from the encoder/decoder for use by the dispatcher, which separates the IIOP encoder/decoder from the gateway mechanisms that deal with the messages once they are delivered. The encoder reads messages from the incoming queue, packs the information into an IIOP message, and sends the message to the CORBA application.

The *dispatcher* interfaces with the IIOP encoder/decoder and provides a set of functional features for delivering messages. The dispatcher's main function is to wrap extra information around an IIOP message dequeued from the outgoing queue and deliver the message to the correct handler, which takes care of sending and receiving messages. This wrapped message is called a "gateway message." The dispatcher also stores the wrappers of requests it receives from handlers. This is done so that the wrapper of an IIOP request can be reassigned to the IIOP reply when the reply is dequeued from the decoder.

Gateway messages encapsulate IIOP messages that will ultimately be delivered to some ORB, and have a header, which contains information used by replication schemes to process and deliver messages correctly. Specifically, a header contains *SenderReplicationGroup, ReceiverReplicationGroup, SequenceNumber, Opcode,* and *Endian* fields. Replication and connection groups will be described in the next subsection, but it is important to note here that the terms "sender" and "receiver" as used here refer to the sender and receiver of the CORBA *request* that is made, regardless of the sender or receiver of the message during a particular transmission. The sequence number is determined by the sending and receiving replication groups (unique when tagged with both group names), and the opcode is used to distinguish the message's purpose at a given step in the communication scheme. The "endianess" of the message is also stored, and is used by the destination ORB.

Handlers are responsible for sending and receiving messages. A handler is created in the gateway for each pair of replicated objects that wish to communicate. Currently, three types of handlers are supported in the gateway: the active replication handler, the dependability manager handler, and the factory handler. Different handler types are used depending on the type of group the object is communicating in.

Each gateway handler maintains certain state information to ensure correct the delivery of messages. In particular, the gateway keeps track of the last request sent (*ConnectionGroup.LastSent*), the last request delivered (*ConnectionGroup.LastDeliveredRequest*), the last reply delivered (*ConnectionGroup.LastDeliveredReply*), the last request multicast (*ConnectionGroup.LastMulticastRequest*), and the last reply multicast (*ConnectionGroup.LastMulticastReply*). Each gateway handler also contains buffers that hold messages whose status is not yet known, a *point to point buffer*, a *reply buffer*, and a *total order buffer*, to permit recovery from failures.

4.2. Group Structure

A key part of Proteus's design is the way it uses group communication. A simple approach would be to put all objects that need to communicate in one group, so that all messages would be totally ordered with respect to each other and view changes. While this approach would work for small systems, it scales poorly, and would not be practical for systems with a large number of hosts. To avoid these scalability problems, we have devised a scheme that uses multiple small groups of multiple types.

The group structure used in Proteus was introduced in [Cuk98]; we briefly review it here in order to describe how the communication schemes that we have implemented use this group structure. Four types of groups are used in Proteus: "replication groups," "connection groups," "point-to-point groups," and the "Proteus Communication Service (PCS) group."

A *replication group* is composed of one or more replicas of an AQuA application object. A replication group has one object that is designated as its leader, and may perform special functions, depending on the replication algorithm being implemented. Each object in the group has the capacity to become the object group leader, and a protocol is provided to make sure that a new leader is elected when the current leader fails. To maintain a group, Maestro/Ensemble uses protocols that use group leaders. For implementation simplicity, the object whose gateway process is the Ensemble group leader is designated the leader of the replication group. This allows Proteus to use the Ensemble leader election service to elect a new leader if the object leader fails.

A *connection group* is a group consisting of the members of two replication groups that wish to communicate. A message is multicast within a connection group in order to send a message from one replication group to another replication group. A connection group can define different communication schemes. The replication group sending the message must communicate according to the communication scheme specified by the connection group. For each message, the sending replication group chooses which communication scheme to use based on which connection group a message is destined for.

Reliable multicast to the dependability manager is achieved using the *Proteus Communication Service (PCS) group*. The PCS group consists of all the dependability manager replicas in the system. The PCS group also has transient members. These transient members are factory, AQuA application, or QuO objects that want to multicast messages to the dependability manager replicas. Through the PCS group, AQuA applications provide notification of view changes; QuO makes requests for QoS; and factories respond to start and kill commands and provide host load updates. After a multicast to the PCS group, the transient member will leave the group.

Finally, *point-to-point groups* are used to send messages from a dependability manager to a factory.

5. Active Replication Scheme

Multiple communication schemes can be developed, using the above group structure, depending on the communication style (e.g., synchronous, asynchronous), the replication type (e.g., active, passive), and the voter type. An active replication scheme using the *leader pass first* voter policy to send messages has been implemented. This section will describe the structure of this scheme, the algorithms to implement it, and how faults are tolerated using these algorithms.

5.1. Groups in Active Replication

We first review the steps taken to make a remote CORBA call (request/reply) when active replication is used [Cuk98]. Let $O_{i,k}$ be replica k of replication group i, and let object $O_{i,0}$ be the leader of the group. Suppose that replication group i is the sender group and group j the receiver group. To send a request to the object replicas $O_{j,k}$, as shown in Figure 4, all objects $O_{i,k}$ first use reliable point-to-point communication to send the request to $O_{i,0}$. Object replicas $O_{i,k}$ also keep a copy of the request in case it needs to be resent (step 1 in Figure 4). The leader then multicasts the request in the connection group. The objects $O_{i,k}$ use the multicast to signal that they can delete their local copy of the request. The objects $O_{j,k}$ store the multicast on a list of pending rebroadcasts (step 2). Since there can be multiple replication groups, in order to maintain total ordering of all messages within the replication group, $O_{j,0}$ multicasts the message again in the replication group j. The objects $O_{j,k}$ use the multicast as a signal that they can deliver the message and delete the previously stored copy from the connection group multicast (step 3). After processing the request, all objects $O_{j,k}$ send the result through a point-to-point communication to $O_{j,0}$ (step 4). The same set of steps used to transmit the request is then used to communicate the reply from replication group j to group i. Steps (5) and (6), which are responsible for transmitting the reply, are similar to steps (2) and (1) respectively.

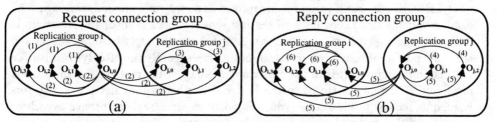

Figure 4: Communication Scheme

5.2. Active Replication Algorithms

The active replication scheme must both 1) deliver requests and replies correctly, and 2) correctly react when the number of replicas in a replication group changes. The active replication communication algorithms are used to correctly communicate CORBA requests and replies between replicated objects using the replication and connection groups that have stable group membership. When the group membership changes, view change algorithms are used to report the change of membership to the dependability manager and, if a new member is added, correctly initialize the new object with the correct state.

5.2.1. Active Replication Communication Algorithms

The algorithms that run in the active replication handler are described in this section. To illustrate their use, we will describe the algorithms in the order in which they would be executed (on various nodes) as a single request/reply is processed, using the "step" nomenclature introduced earlier in this section. More specifically, recall that each message contains an opcode to specify the communication step the message is in. The relationship between opcodes and communication steps is shown in Table 1. By following these steps, we illustrate the algorithms that implement the active replication scheme.

Step	Opcode	Step	Opcode
1	FORWARD_REQUEST_TO_LEADER	4	FORWARD_REPLY_TO_LEADER
2	CONNECTION_GROUP_REQUEST	5	CONNECTION_GROUP_REPLY
3	REPLICATION_GROUP_REQUEST	6	REPLICATION_GROUP_REPLY

Table 1. Communication Step and its Opcode

Step 1: The first step of the communication scheme consists of sending a request to the replication group leader. This is done in two phases. First, each replica on the sender side receives a remote object request, via a CORBA IIOP message to the gateway, that is processed by the IIOP decoder and dispatcher. Note that these requests may not come at the same time, but they will come in the same order (since we assume application objects behave in a deterministic way and receive all external requests in the same order). After processing, the dispatcher calls **SendRequest** (Figure 5). Each message is then tagged with the opcode FORWARD_REQUEST-_TO_LEADER, so that it is not misinterpreted as a reply to a previous message. The handler variable that keeps track of the last sent sequence number for the group is then set to the sequence number of the message. Next, the reply buffer is checked to see if a reply has already been received for this message. **RemoveReplyFromBuffer** will return the reply if it is in the buffer and a NULL if the reply to this message is not found. The reply is stored in the buffer if another replica has previously forwarded its request to the leader (which is possible, since replicas behave asynchronously) and this replica has already received the reply. If the reply is present, it is delivered to the handler, which in turn calls the IIOP encoder that delivers the message to the application (**DeliverReplyToApp**). If the reply is not contained in the reply buffer, the sequence number is checked to see if the request should be sent to the leader. The message should be sent to the leader if a copy of it has not already been multicast in the connection group (this would occur if another replica in the replication group has forwarded the request to the leader, who then multicasted it to the connection group). If the request should be sent to the leader, it is placed in a point-to-point buffer (so that it can be resent if a failure occurs), and is sent to the leader using a Maestro point-to-point send (**SendToLeader**).

SendRequest(message *request*)
   request.opcode := FORWARD_REQUEST_TO_LEADER
   ConnectionGroup.LastSent := *request.SequenceNumber*
   reply := **RemoveReplyFromReplyBuffer**(*request*)
   if (*reply* ≠ NULL) **DeliverReplyToApp**(*reply*)
   else if (*ConnectionGroup.LastMulticastRequest* < *request.SequenceNumber*)
      addToPtPBuffer(*request*)
      SendToLeader(*request*)

SendReply(message *reply*)
   reply.opcode := FORWARD_REPLY_TO_LEADER
   if (*ConnectionGroup.LastMulticastReply* < *reply.SequenceNumber*)
      addToPtPBuffer(*reply*)
      SendToLeader(*reply*)

Figure 5: **SendRequest** and **SendReply** Algorithms

The second phase begins when the leader receives the request from Ensemble and calls **ReceiveSendToLeader** (Figure 6). As seen in Figure 4, the message sent to the leader can be either a request or a reply, as denoted by the opcode FORWARD-_REQUEST_TO_LEADER or FORWARD_REPLY_TO_LEADER. At this step the message is a request. Non-leaders receiving this message do nothing. The voter then processes the message in the way defined by the communication scheme. The currently implemented voter applies the *leader pass first* policy, and thus returns the message passed to it, unless it has already been multicast (which is determined by the sequence number of the message). Since the message is a request, the opcode is changed from FORWARD_REQUEST_TO_LEADER to CONNECTION-_GROUP_REQUEST. The message is then checked to see whether it should be multicast to the connection group. The *ConnectionGroup.LastMulticastRequest* variable is used to determine this, and keeps the leader from multicasting duplicate requests that it may receive. (A duplicate request may be received if a view change occurs and a replica's point-to-point buffer is not empty). If the request is not a duplicate, it is multicast in the connection group through the **MulticastToConnectionGroup** call, which uses the Maestro multicast facility. Finally, the handler's last multicast request variable is set to the message's sequence number (since the Maestro multicast, as we have used it, does not send the message to the sender of the multicast).

Step 2: The second step of the communication scheme begins with the **MulticastToConnectionGroup** call. When a multicast message is received by a connection group member, Ensemble calls **ReceiveConnectionGroupMulticast** (Figure 6). Since each member of the connection group receives the multicast, **ReceiveConnectionGroupMulticast** needs to determine whether the received multicast is a request or reply message, and whether the original request came from a replica in the same replication group as the receiver, or a different replication group.

To distinguish among these cases, the method first checks the opcode of the message to see whether it is a request or a reply. A message received in step 2 will have the opcode CONNECTION_GROUP_REQUEST, marking it as a request multicast by the group leader. The method then checks to see if the receiver of the message is a member of the group specified by the sender replication group field. If it is, then the message may have been buffered by this group member so that it could be resent in case of failure, but since the multicasts are reliable, all other recipients of the message have now also received it. The receiver can thus safely remove this message from its point-to-point buffer, if it is there. The last multicast request variable in the handler is then set to the sequence number of this message, for future reference.

Second, the method checks whether the receiver replication group field of the message is the message receiver's replication group. If this is the case, the opcode (CONNECTION_GROUP_REQUEST) is changed to REPLICATION_GROUP_-REQUEST (initiating step 3). The message is then saved in the total order buffer to permit recovery in case of a replica failure. Then, if this replica is the leader, it multicasts the message to the members of the replication group through the **MulticastToMyReplicationGroup** call, again using the Maestro multicast facility.

Step 3: The third step of the communication scheme begins with the **MultcastToMyReplicationGroup** call. When a multicast message sent via this call is received by a replication group member, Ensemble calls **ReceiveReplicationGroupMulticast** (Figure 6). In this step, the opcode is REPLICATION_GROUP_REQUEST, so the first block of code in this method is executed. First, the sequence number of the received message is checked (against the last delivered request) to be sure that this message has not already been delivered. This could happen if a leader crashed after sending a multicast, but before the replication group members received it. If this is the case, the message is ignored. Otherwise, the request is delivered to the application after processing by the dispatcher and IIOP encoder using **DeliverRequest**. In either case, the message is removed from the handler's total order buffer, since the message has now been delivered to all replication group members. Finally, the handler's last delivered request variable is set to the message's sequence number.

ReceiveSendToLeader(message *m*)
  message *MessageToMulticast := Voter*.**Process**(*m*)
  if (*Leader* and (*MessageToMulticast* ≠ NULL))
    if (*MessageToMulticast.opcode* = FORWARD_REQUEST_TO_LEADER)
     MessageToMulticast.opcode := CONNECTION_GROUP_REQUEST
     if (*ConnectionGroup.LastMulticastRequest* < *MessageToMulticast.SequenceNumber*)
      MulticastToConnectionGroup(*MessageToMulticast*)
      ConnectionGroup.LastMulticastRequest := MessageToMulticast.SequenceNumber
    if (*MessageToMulticast.opcode* = FORWARD_REPLY_TO_LEADER)
     MessageToMulticast.opcode := CONNECTION_GROUP_REPLY
     if (*ConnectionGroup.LastMulticastReply* < *MessageToMulticast.SequenceNumber*)
      MulticastToConnectionGroup(*MessageToMulticast*)
      ConnectionGroup.LastMulticastReply := MessageToMulticast.SequenceNumber

ReceiveConnectionGroupMulticast(message *m*)
  if (*m.opcode* = CONNECTION_GROUP_REQUEST)
    if (*m.SenderReplicationGroup* = *myReplicationGroup*)
     RemoveFromPtPBuffer(*m*)
     ConnectionGroup.LastMulticastRequest := m.SequenceNumber
    if (*m.ReceiverReplicationGroup* = *myReplicationGroup*)
     m.opcode := REPLICATION_GROUP_REQUEST
     AddToTotalOrderBuffer(*m*)
     if (*Leader*) **MulticastToMyReplicationGroup**(*m*)
  if (*m.opcode* = CONNECTION_GROUP_REPLY)
    if (*m.ReceiverReplicationGroup* = *myReplicationGroup*)
     RemoveFromPtPBuffer(*m*)
     ConnectionGroup.LastMulticastReply := m.SequenceNumber
    if (*m.SenderReplicationGroup* = *myReplicationGroup*)
     m.opcode = REPLICATION_GROUP_REPLY
     AddToTotalOrderBuffer(*m*)
     if (*Leader*) **MulticastToMyReplicationGroup**(*m*)

ReceiveReplicationGroupMulticast(message *m*)
  if (*m.opcode* = REPLICATION_GROUP_REQUEST)
    if (*m.SequenceNumber* > *ConnectionGroup.LastDeliveredRequest*)
     DeliverRequest(*m*)
     RemoveFromTotalOrderBuffer(*m*)
     ConnectionGroup.LastDeliveredRequest := m.SequenceNumber
  if (*m.opcode* = REPLICATION_GROUP_REPLY)
    if (*m.SequenceNumber* > *ConnectionGroup.LastDeliveredRequest*)
     if (*ConnnectionGroup.LastSent* ≥ *m.SequenceNumber*) **DeliverReplyToApp**(*m*)
     else **AddToReplyBuffer**(*m*)
     RemoveFromTotalOrderBuffer(*m*)
     ConnectionGroup.LastDeliveredReply := m.SequenceNumber

Figure 6: **ReceiveSendToLeader, ReceiveConnectionGroupMulticast,** and
ReceiveReplicationGroupMulticast Algorithms

Step 4: Each application object in the receiving replication group processes the request and generates a reply independently. When a reply is ready, the application object generates a standard CORBA reply message and delivers it to the IIOP decoder of its associated gateway. When the gateway receives the message, it decodes it, uses the dispatcher to recover its header (saved when the request was delivered by the dispatcher), and calls the handler's **SendReply** method to send the reply to the replication group leader. Before the message is sent, its opcode is set to FORWARD-_REPLY_TO_LEADER. The message is only sent if the handler's *Connection-Group.LastSentReply* variable indicates that the reply has not yet been processed by the leader. If the message is sent, it is also added to the point-to-point buffer, so it can be re-sent in case the leader of the replication group fails. There is no need to check for a reply in the reply buffer, as was done in **SendRequest**, since there are no messages dependent on receiving this message. The message is sent to the leader using the **SendToLeader** call, which uses the Maestro point-to-point send. The leader calls **ReceiveSendToLeader** when it receives the message. This method was described in step 1; processing is identical in this step, except that the message's opcode is changed from FORWARD_REPLY_TO_LEADER to CONNECTION_GROUP_-REPLY, and the handler's *ConnectionGroup.LastMulticastReply* variable is updated.

Step 5: Step five consists of an execution of the **MulticastToConnectionGroup** method by the leader of the receiver replication group and an execution of the **ReceiveConnectionGroupMulticast** method by all members of the connection group. These calls execute like those described in step 2, except that the opcode of the message (CONNECTION_GROUP_REPLY) now indicates that it is a reply, so a member of the sending group will set its last multicast reply (not request) variable, and a member of the receiving group will change the message opcode to REPLICATION-_GROUP_REPLY (initiating step 6) before buffering or multicasting it to the replication group.

Step 6: Finally, the **MulticastToMyReplicationGroup** and **ReceiveReplicationGroupMulticast** methods are performed by the leader of the requesting replication group and the members of the requesting replication group, respectively. These execute like those described in step 3, except that the opcode is REPLICATION-_GROUP_REPLY, and the handling of the messages in **ReceiveReplicationGroupMulticast** is more complicated. As before, if the message has already been delivered (this time, compare the sequence number to the last delivered reply), it is ignored. Then, if the corresponding request message has not yet been generated by the application, the message is placed in the reply buffer to be held until the replica produces the corresponding request. Otherwise, the message is delivered to the application (after processing by the dispatcher and IIOP encoder) using **DeliverReplyToApp**. As in step 3, the message is removed from the total order buffer, but this time the last delivered reply variable is set. Completion of these steps results in the delivery of the reply to all members of the requesting replication group.

5.2.2. View Change Algorithms

When the membership of a group changes, a view change occurs. Replication group view changes signal changes that must be accounted for to maintain the correct replication group state and structure. A replication group view change will occur if a new member joins the replication group, a member crashes, or a member is killed by an object factory. When a new member enters a replication group, a state transfer is needed to set the new member's state to a state that is correct, with respect to the other replicas in its replication group. The state transfer is implemented with the help of Maestro state transfer calls. The state transfer occurs as part of Maestro view change processing, so it is atomic with respect to the processing of other messages in the group.

More specifically, Maestro initiates a state transfer when a new member joins a group by calling the **GetState** method (Figure 7) of the handler of an existing group member. This method collects the state information needed by the new replica in a "transfer message." The transfer message holds the state information needed to construct a new replica and is passed to the new replica specified by a requestor. The transfer message consists of three parts: the connection group state, the replication group state, and the application object state. The connection and replication group state (as defined in Section 4.1) is added to the transfer message using the **AddConnectionGroupState** and **AddBufferState** methods, respectively. The application object state is added to the transfer message using the **AddApplicationState** method. To get the state of the application, **AddApplicationState** executes a **GetApplicationState** method on the associated application object. This method, which must be implemented by the application object, packages up the needed state so that it can be placed in the transfer message and, ultimately, delivered to the new application object.

Once the transfer message is received by Maestro in the new replica, the replica calls the new replica handler's **SetState** method (Figure 7) to set the state of the replica to that prescribed by the transfer message. More specifically, the state of the new replica's handler is set via the **SetConnectionGroupState** and **SetApplicationState** calls. The state of the new application object is set by invoking the **SetApplicationState** method on the new application object. This method, implemented by the application object, unpacks the message to obtain the state information needed to set the new application object state to that obtained from an existing replica. Once the new member is integrated into the group, Maestro invokes each group member's **ViewChange** method, to notify each replication group member's handler that a view change has occurred.

The first step of **ViewChange** (Figure 7) is executed only if the view has changed because the (old) leader left the replication group. The existence of a new leader is determined via a call to method **NewLeader**. If the group has a new leader, all messages in each group member's handler's point-to-point buffer need to be sent to the (new) leader, since the buffer contains messages that were sent to the leader, but not yet multicast to the connection group. Likewise, the leader multicasts all messages in its total order buffer to its replication group, since these are messages that were received by the replication group from an associated connection group, but not yet successfully multicast by the leader to the group. Finally, the leader informs the dependability manager of the membership of the changed group, using the PCS group structure described in Section 4.2.

```
GetState( Requestor r )
    TransferMessage t
    AddConnectionGroupState( t )
    AddBufferState( t )
    AddApplicationState( t )

SetState( TransferMessage t )
    SetConnectionGroupState( t )
    SetBufferState( t )
    SetApplicationState( t )

ViewChange( view newView )
    if ( NewLeader() )
        for each message  m in PtPBuffer
            SendToLeader( m )
        if ( Leader )
            for each message  m in TotalOrderBuffer
                MulticastToReplicationGroup( m )
        if ( Leader ) SendToPCSGroup( newView )
```

Figure 7: **GetState**, **SetState**, and **ViewChange** Algorithms

5.3. Dependability Manager Communication

Algorithms also exist for communication from the gateways, QuO runtime, and object factories to the dependability manager (via the PCS group), and from the dependability manager to a factory (via point-to-point groups). These algorithms are much simpler than those for active replication, since reliable multicasts between multiple groups are not needed. The details of these algorithms can be found in [Sab98]; they are omitted here due to space limitations.

5.4. Algorithm's Response to Faults

We now show how crash failures are tolerated using these algorithms. In particular, we consider all the points at which a crash can occur, for both the leader and non-leader replicas, in both the sender and receiver replication groups. Tolerating failures of non-leader replicas is simple using the Proteus group structure, since no message retransmission is necessary. In particular, a replica can crash before or after a multicast message is delivered. If a non-leader replica crashes after a multicast is delivered, there is no need to retransmit the message, because the message was delivered to all the correct replicas. If a non-leader replica crashes after the multicast is sent, but before it is delivered, there is no need to retransmit the message, because Maestro/Ensemble will deliver the multicast to all of the non-failed replicas. The other cases in which a non-leader replica can crash (before and after sending a point-to-point message) also require no action from other replicas.

If the leader of the sender replication group crashes before **ReceiveSend-ToLeader** was complete, the message transmission process is restarted by using **ViewChange** once the replication group has gone through a view change and elected a new leader. In that case, **SendToLeader** is performed again. Specifically, the replicas in the sender replication group, having kept a copy of the message in the point-to-point buffer, resend the message to the new leader of the sender replication group. The new leader then multicasts each message in the connection group via **Receive-SendToLeader** and the message transmission process is resumed. If the original leader crashes immediately after sending the multicast, a new leader may be elected before the multicast is delivered. This case uses the same sequence calls as above. The new leader will also multicast the message, and this second multicast will be ignored by the members of the connection group. If the leader crashes in other stages of the communication scheme, no message retransmission is necessary, since the sender replication group leader is not responsible for message transmission in these stages.

If the leader of the receiver replication group crashes before **ReceiveConnectionGroupMulticast** is complete, the message transmission process is performed via **ViewChange** once the replication group has gone through a view change and elected a new leader. The new leader, having stored a copy of the message from the connection group multicast in total order buffer, multicasts the message in the receiver replication group via **MulticastToReplicationGroup**. If the old leader crashes immediately after sending the multicast in the receiver replication group, a new leader may be elected before the multicast is delivered. In that case, the same sequence calls are used. The new leader will multicast the message in the receiver replication group, and this second multicast of the message will be ignored by the members of the replication group. If the leader crashes in other stages of the communication scheme, no message retransmission is necessary, since the receiver replication group leader is not responsible for message transmission in these stages.

6. Results and Conclusions

This paper has described Proteus, a flexible infrastructure for providing adaptive fault tolerance to CORBA applications. Our design permits an application to change the level of dependability that it requires, including the type of faults that should be tolerated dynamically during its execution. In order to make this possible, we have designed Proteus in a modular way, developing a scalable group structure, and a set of communication algorithms that preserve needed communication properties during intergroup communication. Gateways were designed that make use of this group structure, and support multiple communication schemes through the use of different handlers. In addition, the gateways provide the translation facilities needed to convert IIOP messages, understood by standard CORBA ORBs, into a series of group communication multicasts, to achieve reliable communication between replicated CORBA objects. Furthermore, the gateways were designed to be configurable during the execution of an application, accepting requests from the dependability manager to use particular handlers and detect particular fault types. Finally, we designed a dependability manager that makes decisions on how to configure a system based both on high-level, application-driven requests for particular levels of dependability, and on faults and failures that occur. In addition, the dependability manager provides a protocol coordinator that carries out the decisions of the advisor by starting, killing, and reconfiguring object replicas as needed.

Our first implementation of Proteus is complete, and has been successfully tested on several applications (see [Sab98], for details). In each case, the application was first developed as a standard (non-fault-tolerant) distributed CORBA application, and then ported to the AQuA architecture with almost no effort. In fact, the only changes to the applications that were needed were the addition of a **SetApplicationState** and a **GetApplicationState** method to each object that was to be replicated. The implementation has fully functioning versions of all Proteus components, including a dependability manager with advisor and protocol coordinator, object factories that can start and kill replicas and report load information to the manager, and a gateway with several types of handlers that support the active replication and PCS communication schemes.

The implementation includes support for crash failures, an advisor policy that permits changing the degree of replication and placement of replicas during execution based on the dependability desires of an application, and a standard CORBA interface to distributed applications. In addition, a graphical user interface for the dependability manager and object factories was developed to allow the functioning of Proteus to be monitored as it responds to dependability requests from applications and faults that occur. A user can monitor changes in membership that occur in replication and connection groups and in assignment of objects to hosts. This interface was extremely helpful in developing the active replication and PCS communication schemes, and in observing the results of fault injection experiments we used to validate the implementation.

While the current implementation of Proteus can provide significant dependability enhancement for standard CORBA applications, much more can be done. In particular, we are currently implementing voters in gateways to support detection of value faults, and are developing an advisor policy that can determine how to treat such faults. We are also implementing the handlers necessary to replicate the dependability manger, which was not replicated in our original implementation, and to support passive replication.

Acknowledgment

We would like to acknowledge the other members of the AQuA team, namely Mark Berman, David Henke, Jessica Pistole, and Rick Schantz, for many constructive discussions.

References

[Cuk98] M. Cukier, J. Ren, C. Sabnis, D. Henke, J. Pistole, W. H. Sanders, D. E. Bakken, M. E. Berman, D. A. Karr, R. E. Schantz, "AQuA: An Adaptive Architecture that Provides Dependable Distributed Objects," Proc. of the 17th IEEE Symposium on Reliable Distributed Systems, pp. 245-253, West Lafayette, IN, USA, October 1998.

[Fel96] P. Felber, B. Garbinato, R. Guerraoui, "The Design of a CORBA Group Communication Service," Proc. of the 15th IEEE Symposium on Reliable Distributed Systems, pp. 150-159, Niagara on the Lake, Ontario, Canada, October 1996.

[Hay98] M. G. Hayden, "The Ensemble System," Ph.D. thesis, Cornell University, 1998.

[Kih98] K. P. Kihlstrom, L. E. Moser and P. M. Melliar-Smith, "The SecureRing Protocols for Securing Group Communication," Proc. of the IEEE 31st Annual Hawaii International Conference on System Sciences, vol. 3, pp. 317-326, Kona, Hawaii, January 1998.

[Lan97] S. Landis, S. Maffeis, "Building Reliable Distributed Systems with CORBA," in *Theory and Practice of Object Systems*, vol. 3, no. 1, 1997, pp. 31-43.

[Loy98] J. P. Loyall, R. E. Schantz, J. A. Zinky, D. E. Bakken, "Specifying and Measuring Quality of Service in Distributed Object Systems," in Proc. of ISORC'98, Kyoto, Japan, April 1998.

[Maf95] S. Maffeis, "Run-Time Support for Object-Oriented Distributed Programming," Ph.D thesis, University of Zurich, 1995.

[Maf97] S. Maffeis, "Piranha: A CORBA Tool for High Availability," *IEEE Computer*, vol. 30, no. 4, 1997, pp. 59-66.

[Nar97] P. Narasimhan, L. E. Moser, P. M. Melliar-Smith, "Replica Consistency of CORBA Objects in Partitionable Distributed Systems," *Distributed Systems Engineering*, vol. 4, no. 3, September 1997, pp. 139-150.

[Rei95] M. K. Reiter. "The Rampart Toolkit for Building High-Integrity Services," *Theory and Practice in Distributed Systems* (Lecture Notes in Computer Science 938), pp. 99-110, Springer-Verlag, 1995.

[Rod93] L. Rodrigues, P. Verissimo, "Replicated Object Management using Group Technology," Proc. of the Fourth Workshop on Future Trends of Distributed Computing Systems, pp. 54-61, Lisboa, Portugal, September 1993.

[Sab98] C. Sabnis, "Proteus: A Software Infrastructure Providing Dependability for CORBA Applications," M.S. thesis, University of Illinois, Urbana, IL, 1998.

[Vay98] A. Vaysburd, K. P. Birman, "The Maestro Approach to Building Reliable Interoperable Distributed Applications with Multiple Execution Styles," *Theory and Practice of Object Systems*, vol. 4, no. 2, 1998.

[Zin97] J. A. Zinky , D. E. Bakken, R. E. Schantz, "Architectural Support for Quality of Service for CORBA Objects," *Theory and Practice of Object Systems*, vol. 3, no. 1, April 1997, pp. 55-73.

Improving Performance of Atomic Broadcast Protocols Using the Newsmonger Technique

Shivakant Mishra
Department of Computer Science
University of Wyoming, P.O. Box 3682
Laramie, WY 82071-3682.
mishra@cs.uwyo.edu

Sudha M. Kuntur
MINC Incorporated
6755 Earl Dr.
Colorado Springs, CO 80918.
sudhak@minc.com

Abstract

We propose a new technique, called the newsmonger technique, that can be applied to a large number of atomic broadcast protocols and results in improving their performance. We provide an extensive experimental evaluation of this technique by incorporating it in two existing atomic broadcast protocols, and measuring the resulting performance improvement by varying five different operating parameters: group size, interarrival time between update arrivals, communication failure probability, maximum silence period, and update arrival pattern. This evaluation shows that this techniques can decrease the average stability time of an atomic broadcast protocol by as much as 80%, without significantly affecting any other performance indices.

1 Introduction

Group communication services have been successfully used to construct applications with high availability, dependability, and real-time responsiveness requirements [4, 13, 17, 15, 5, 3, 9, 1, 16]. An *atomic broadcast protocol* is a part of a group communication service that group members use to disseminate service state updates to all group members [4, 3, 9, 1]. This protocol is a system-level protocol. As a result, its performance is one of the most important factor in determining the performance of an application built using this protocol. Improving the performance of an atomic broadcast protocol is the subject of this paper.

We proposed a technique called the newsmonger technique in the context of the pinwheel protocols in [8]. This technique significantly improved the performance of pinwheel protocols [8]. Informally, the newsmonger technique comprises of a token circulated among group members along a logical ring from time to time. During circulation, this token gathers some vital information about the replicated service state from different group members, and conveys some vital information to the group members. This information is used by group members to stabilize service state updates and detect communication failures.

In this paper, we show that the newsmonger technique is a general technique that can be applied to a large number of existing atomic broadcast protocols, and will result in significantly improving the performance of these protocols under certain operating conditions. The pinwheel protocol, in which we first used the newsmonger technique belongs to the token-based atomic broadcast protocol category [7]. To show that the newsmonger technique can be applied to atomic broadcast protocols that belong to other categories, we have incorporated it in two different atomic broadcast protocols that belong to the sequencer-based atomic broadcast protocol category (see [7] for a classification of atomic broadcast protocols).

The newsmonger technique is described in detail in Section 3 and the two atomic broadcast protocols are briefly described in Section 4. We have simulated two versions of these two atomic broadcast protocols: one with the newsmonger technique incorporated in them, and the other, without the newsmonger technique incorporated in them. To study the effect of the newsmonger technique, we measured the performance of the two versions of the two protocols by varying five operating parameters: group size, update arrival rate, update arrival pattern, communication failure frequency, and maximum silence period. The performance indices measured are average stability time and the average number of messages exchanged per update broadcast. A comparison of the performance from the two versions shows that the newsmonger technique significantly improves the average stability time without significantly affecting the other performance indices under low update arrival rates or high communication failure frequency. We describe this simulation, present the performance measured, and provide a comparison in Section 5. Finally, we conclude the paper in Section 6.

2   Assumptions

The newsmonger technique is applicable to the set of atomic broadcast protocols that are designed for an asynchronous distributed computing environment. Communication is assumed to be via a datagram service that has omission/performance failure semantics: messages can get lost or be late, but corruption of their contents is unlikely [5, 12]. In this paper, we assume a constant group membership, i.e., no process crash and join events occur. The reason for this assumption is that process crash and join events are handled by a membership protocol and the newsmonger technique is specifically designed for atomic broadcast protocols.

To simplify the discussion, we assume that an atomic broadcast protocol uses two kinds of messages: *proposal messages* and *order messages*. A group member sends a proposal message to disseminate one or more updates to all

group members. This message is uniquely identified by a *proposal id*. Specific
group members associate unique global sequence numbers to each update being
broadcast, and use order messages to convey these global sequence numbers
to all group members. Updates are delivered by group members in the order
of the global sequence numbers associated with them. All sequencer-based
atomic broadcast protocols have these two kinds of messages.

In this paper, we are interested in two performance indices that are significantly affected by the newsmonger technique: average broadcast stability
time and average number of messages needed to broadcast an update. The
broadcast stability time of an update is the duration between the moment
a broadcast server receives that update to be broadcast and the moment all
broadcast servers learn that the update is *stable*. An update becomes stable at
a group member when the member learns that the update has been received
by all group members. The *number of messages* needed to broadcast an update includes all messages sent by different group members to complete the
broadcast of the update.

3   Newsmonger Technique

The newsmonger technique comprises of a token, called the newsmonger,
circulated among group members along a logical ring from time to time. During circulation, this token gathers some vital information about the replicated
service state from different group members, and conveys some vital information to the group members. This information is used by group members to
stabilize service state updates and detect communication failures.

The goal of the newsmonger technique is to reduce the update stability times
and the time to detect communication failures when update arrival rate is low.
In all the atomic broadcast protocols, stability of an update u is established
at a group member when it receives some messages that were broadcast by
group members after receiving the proposal message carrying u. Essentially,
the messages that are broadcast later include information about the receipt
of u. This information aids a group member in establishing the stability of
u. So, if the update arrival rate is low, these later messages will be broadcast
after a larger time interval, and so, the group members will receive stability
information after a larger time interval. As a result, the time to establish the
stability of updates will be quite large (see [6] for some examples). Similarly, in
the atomic broadcast protocols that use negative acknowledgement technique
to detect communication failures, the time to detect a communication failure
depends on when some of the following messages are sent. This is because a
group member detects the loss of a message only after receiving a message that
was sent later. When update arrival rate is low, the group members have to
wait longer to receive these following messages, and hence, the time to detect
message losses is large.

The main idea behind the newsmonger technique is that the newsmonger is circulated among group members when there is low system activity. The newsmonger first gathers the information needed to establish the stability of updates and to detect communication failures from the group members, and then conveys this information to the group members. In particular, the newsmonger is generated by an *a priori* agreed-upon group member called the newsmonger owner. The newsmonger owner sends a newsmonger message to its next neighbor in the cyclic order when it does not receive a new broadcast update, either from a local client or from some other member, for *msp* (maximum silence period) units of time. Once generated, the newsmonger circulates for two rounds among group members. On receiving a newsmonger message in the first round, a member first updates the contents of the newsmonger from its local state, and then forwards the newsmonger to the next member in the cyclic order. On receiving a newsmonger message in the second round, a member retrieves the information stored in the message and uses it to detect lost messages and establish update stability. It then forwards the newsmonger message to the next group member.

3.1 Detailed Description

A newsmonger message consists of three variables:

1. hp:[0,N-1] $\rightarrow$ Integer; $hp[r]$ is the highest proposal sent by group member r and N is the number of members in the group,

2. hd: Integer; hd is the highest global sequence number, and

3. $mhdo$: Integer; $mhdo$ is the minimum of the highest delivered global sequence number of all members.

The purpose of hp is to let group members detect missing proposals. When the newsmonger is generated, the newsmonger owner initializes each hp entry according to the proposals it has received. On receiving a newsmonger message in the first round, a group member p modifies an entry $hp[s]$, if p has received a proposal sent by s with proposal number greater than $hp[s]$. It detects a proposal message loss, if the highest proposal sent by s that p has received is less than $hp[s]$.

The purpose of hd is to let group members detect missing ordering messages. The newsmonger owner initializes this variable to the highest global sequence number it has seen so far. On receiving a newsmonger message in the first round, a group member p modifies hd if the highest global sequence number it has seen so far is greater than hd. It detects an ordering message loss, if hd is greater than the highest global sequence number it has seen so far.

Finally, the purpose of $mhdo$ is to let group members establish update stability. The newsmonger owner initializes this variable to its highest delivered global sequence number. On receiving a newsmonger message in the first round, a group member p modifies $mhdo$ to its highest delivered global sequence number, if its highest delivered global sequence number is smaller than *mhdo*. After the completion of one round, *mhdo* satisfies the inequality $mhdo \leq min\{hdo(p) \mid p \in [0,\text{N-1}]\}$, where $hdo(p)$ is the highest delivered global sequence number at group member p. This implies that all updates with global sequence number less than or equal to *mhdo* have been delivered by all group members, i.e. all these updates are stable. So, when a group member receives a newsmonger message in the second round, it stabilizes all updates with global sequence number less than or equal to *mhdo*.

3.2 Loss of newsmonger

Since atomic broadcast protocols operate in a computing environment where communication failures may occur, we need a mechanism to recover from the loss of a newsmonger message. Although a newsmonger resembles a token in a token-based protocol, it plays a very different role. While a token in a token-based protocol is used for implementing mutual exclusion in real time, a newsmonger is simply used to convey some information about the replicated system state to the group members. In particular, while the presence of zero or multiple tokens in a token-based protocol would be fatal for the system, the presence of zero or multiple newsmongers in the system does not affect the correctness or progress of the atomic broadcast protocol. So, we use a very simple strategy to recover from the loss of a newsmonger. This may result in zero or multiple newsmongers in the system for a limited period of time.

Each new newsmonger generated by the newsmonger owner is stamped with a monotonically increasing version number. A group member does not relay a newsmonger to its next neighbor, if it has already relayed a newsmonger with a higher version number. After generating a newsmonger, the newsmonger owner expects to receive the newsmonger after one round with in $N \times \delta$ time units, where δ is a one-way timeout delay. If the newsmonger owner does not receive the newsmonger with in this time interval, it generates a new newsmonger with a higher version number.

3.3 Effects of the Newsmonger Technique

The newsmonger technique affects the protocol performance by conveying replicated system state information to the group members when there is low protocol activity. The average stability time is improved by using the newsmonger technique, because this technique enables group members to acquire stability information faster. On the other hand, by circulating additional messages (the newsmonger messages), this technique also increases the average number of messages exchanged per update broadcast. Our goal is to find the operating conditions under which the newsmonger technique substantially improves the stability time without affecting the average number of messages in any significant way.

3.4 Maximum Silence Period

Maximum silence period (msp) is an important parameter in the news-monger technique. It determines how much this technique affects the average stability time and the average number of messages exchanged per update broadcast. Recall that if the newsmonger owner does not receive a new update in msp units of time, it generates a newsmonger, which then circulates for two rounds. So, if msp is small, the newsmonger owner will generate a new newsmonger more often. While this will result in decreasing the average stability time, it will also substantially increase the average number of messages exchanged per update broadcast. On the other hand, if msp is very large, the newsmonger owner will generate a new newsmonger at a very slow rate. This will reduce the increase in average number of messages exchanged per update broadcast. However, if the newsmongers are generated at a very slow rate, the decrease in the average stability time will be minimal. So, an important issue in using the newsmonger technique is to find an optimal value of msp that will result in a significant improvement in the average stability time with minimal effect on the average number of messages exchanged per update broadcast. Such an optimal value will typically depend on some of the operating parameters such as group size and update arrival rate. Finding such an optimal value of msp is one of the issues addressed in this paper.

4 Overview of Atomic Multicast Protocols

4.1 Positive Acknowledgement Protocol

This protocol, the PA protocol, was described in [6]. It is a sequencer-based atomic broadcast protocol. In this protocol, a sender s initiates the multicast of an update u by sending a proposal message containing u and a local sequence number l to the sequencer. If the sequencer has received all earlier proposal messages sent by s, it attaches a global sequence number n to this update and sends messages (u,n) to every group member. If the sequencer has not received some proposal message sent earlier by s, it stores (u,l) in a local buffer until all earlier proposal messages have been received and then globally orders all the updates consistently with their origination order at s. Upon receipt of (u,n), each member sends a positive acknowledgement for n to the sequencer. Message losses are detected by timeouts, and result in message re-transmissions; the timeout is set to four times the average message communication delay in our experiment. Updates are delivered at members in the order imposed by the sequence numbers attached by the sequencer. Concurrency is allowed among group members as well as among multiple multicast requests at a single member.

Update stability is determined as follows. Group members piggyback on their messages to the sequencer the sequence number ld of the last update they have delivered. The sequencer records them in an array with one entry

per member and piggybacks the minimum sequencer number ld_all stored in
the array on all messages it sends to group members. Thus, an update u with
sequence number n is stable at a group member, if the piggybacked stability
number received by the member is at least n.

4.2 Negative Acknowledgement Protocol

This protocol, the NA protocol, is based on ideas similar to those used in the
Isis ABCAST protocol [3]. Unlike the Isis ABCAST protocol, that makes use
of a reliable causal order broadcast protocol (CBCAST) to exchange messages,
the NA protocol is implemented directly on top of an unreliable datagram
protocol such as UDP. This protocol is also a sequencer-based atomic broadcast
protocol. In this protocol, a sender s initiates the multicast of an update u by
sending a proposal message (s,u,l) to all group members; l is a local sequence
number. If the sequencer has received all proposal messages sent earlier by s,
it assigns a global sequence number n to this update and sends an ordering
message (s,l,n) to every group member. Group members deliver updates in
the order imposed by global sequence numbers assigned by the sequencer. A
member detects a message loss when it receives a message out of order, i.e.,
when it receives a proposal message (s,u,l), but hasn't received a proposal
message sent by s with local sequence number less than l, or when it receives
an ordering message (s,l,n), but hasn't received either an ordering message
with global sequence number less than n or a proposal message sent by s
with local sequence number less than or equal to l. In case a message loss
is detected, a member sends a retransmission request for that message to the
sender of the missing message. On receiving a retransmission request from a
member r, a member q retransmits the requested message to r. The sequencer
orders updates consistently with the order in which they were sent by a sender.

Update stability is determined as follows. Group members piggyback the
global sequence number of of the last update they have delivered on all messages they send. Based on this piggybacked information, each member maintains an array $hdgn$ (highest delivered global sequence number) with one entry
for each member q, that records the highest global sequence number of the updates that q has delivered. An update u is stable at a member q, if the global
sequence number assigned to u is less than or equal to the minimum number
in its $hdgn$ array.

5 Evaluation

5.1 Simulation Environment

We make use of *discrete event simulation* [11] to simulate the two atomic
broadcast protocols. The assumptions made in this simulation are described
in detail in [6], and can be summarized as follows. Communication delays
between group members are assumed to follow the distribution shown in Figure

5.1[1], which was experimentally obtained in the Computer Science Department of the University of Wyoming; the mean value of the communication delay was 1.29 ms (millisecond), minimum observed delay was 0.6 ms, and 99% of the observed delays were less than 6.35 ms. We assumed that the CPU time needed to process a message is negligible. This processing time is typically a few microseconds, which is negligible when compared to the communication delays that are of the order of thousands of microseconds (i.e. milliseconds). Hence, by considering only the communication delay as the time to send and process a message provides a fairly accurate result.

We have used this simulation model, with the same set of assumptions, in several earlier projects [6, 8, 10]. One of the protocols we simulated in this simulation model was the Pinwheel atomic multicast protocol [8], which we also implemented on a network of Sun IPCs connected by a 10 Mb/sec Ethernet. The performance measured from this implementation matched fairly well with that measured from the simulation. This indicates that this simulation model is reasonable, and predicts fairly accurate performance.

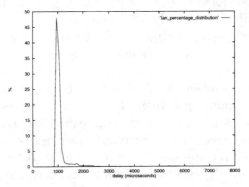

Figure 1: Communication Delay Distribution

5.2 Operating Parameters

Performance of an atomic broadcast protocol depends significantly on the operating conditions under which the protocol runs [6]. In our simulation environment, we considered five operating parameters: *group size, interarrival time between update arrivals, communication failure probability, maximum silence period,* and *update arrival pattern.* Performance of the two atomic broadcast protocols was measured by varying the values of these five operating parameters. Group size was varied between 2 and 10. Interarrival time between update arrivals was assumed to be negative exponential with mean expected value $1/\lambda$. $1/\lambda$ was varied between 3 and 300 milliseconds. Three communication failure probabilities were used: 0% (no failures), 0.1%, and 1%. In

---

[1]The communication delay distribution used in these experiments is different from the one used in [6].

cases where a protocol used the newsmonger technique, the performance was measured by varying the maximum silence period from 25 milliseconds to 300 milliseconds.

Update arrival pattern depends on the semantics of the application using the group communication service. We considered three update arrival patterns: *uniform, one active,* and *bursty.* In the uniform update arrival pattern, $1/\lambda$ is same at all group members, and it remains same throughout a simulation run. In other words, each group member initiates update broadcasts at a constant average rate and this rate is same at all members. In the one-active update arrival pattern, $1/\lambda$ is very small at one member (active member) and very large at all other members. In other words, one member initiates update broadcasts at a very fast rate, while all other members initiate update broadcasts at a very slow rate. We considered two versions of this arrival pattern: one in which the sequencer of the group is the active member, and the second in which a member other than the sequencer is the active member. In the bursty update arrival pattern, $1/\lambda$ alternates at a group member between small periods of very small value of $1/\lambda$ and large periods of very large value of $1/\lambda$ over the duration of a simulation run. In other words, a group member remains quiet (initiates update broadcast at a very slow rate) most of the time. However, it initiates update broadcasts at a very fast rate intermittantly for short periods.

5.3 Performance Overview

We simulated two versions of the two atomic multicast protocols: one without the newsmonger technique and the other with newsmonger technique. We executed both of these versions for more than 300 times, each time with a different combination of the five operating parameters. This resulted in more than 2,000 runs. In all these simulation runs, we simulated the sending of ten thousand updates. Here, we report only those results that are relevant in determining the effects of the newsmonger technique. Specifically, we report the percentage decrease in the average stability time and the percentage increase in the average number of messages exchanged per update broadcast due to the newsmonger technique for various operating parameters.

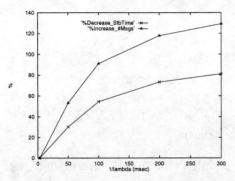

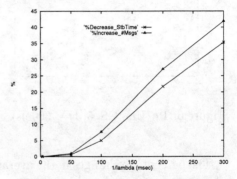

Figure 2: PA(Uni, GS: 2, MSP: 50ms)   Figure 3: PA(Uni, GS: 5, MSP: 50ms)

5.4   Performance of PA

5.4.1   Uniform Arrival Pattern   The percentage changes in the average stability time and the average number of messages per update broadcast as a function of $1/\lambda$ are shown in Figures 2, 3, and 4 for group sizes 2, 5, and 10 respectively. The maximum silence period was 50 ms. An important observation we make here is that the decrease in average stability time and the increase in average number of messages increase with increase in $1/\lambda$. Similar behavior was observed for other values of maximum silence period. The reason for this is as follows. Because stability of an update in PA is established when the sequencer sends a following message, the stability time in PA increases with increase in $1/\lambda$ (See [6] for a detailed explanation). As $1/\lambda$ increases, the newsmonger circulates more often due to large silence periods in the system. Each time the newsmonger circulates, it results in a further decrease in stability time and a further increase in the number of messages.

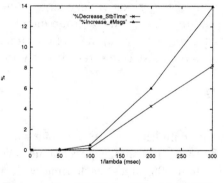

Figure 4: PA(Uni, GS: 10, MSP: 50ms)

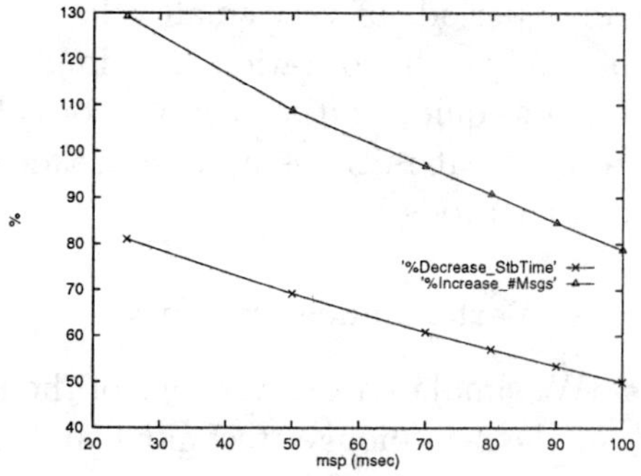

Figure 5: PA(Uni, GS: 2, $1/\lambda$: 300ms)

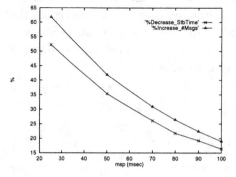
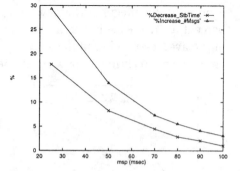

Figure 6: PA(Uni, GS: 5, $1/\lambda$: 300ms)

Figure 7: PA(Uni, GS: 10, $1/\lambda$: 300ms)

The percentage changes in the average stability time and the average number of messages per update broadcast as a function of *msp* are shown in Figures

5, 6, and 7 for group sizes 2, 5, and 10 respectively. $1/\lambda$ in all these runs was 300 ms. The main observation we make from these figures is that the decrease in stability time and the increase in number of messages decreases with increase in *msp*. The reason for this is as follows. As *msp* increases, the rate of newsmonger circulation decreases, which in turn results in a decrease in the decrease in stability time and a decrease in the increase in number of messages. Another important observation we make from Figures 2 through 7 is that the decrease in stability time and the increase in number of messages decreases with increase in group size. The reason for this is as follows. As group size increases, the newsmonger owner receives proposals at a faster rate (for a given $1/\lambda$). As a result, the length of silence periods in the system is smaller. This results in a slower rate of newsmonger circulation, thus resulting in a decrease in the decrease in stability time and a decrease in the increase in the number of messages.

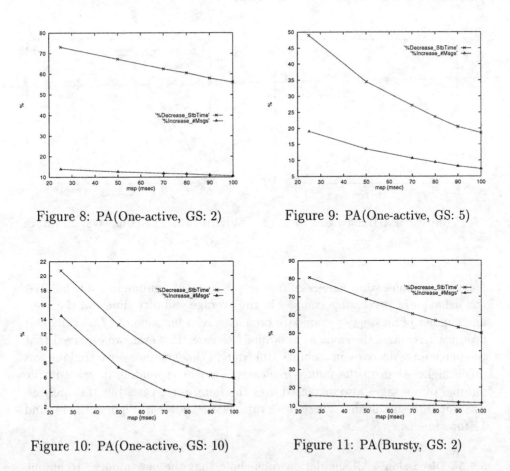

Figure 8: PA(One-active, GS: 2)   Figure 9: PA(One-active, GS: 5)

Figure 10: PA(One-active, GS: 10)   Figure 11: PA(Bursty, GS: 2)

5.4.2 One-Active Arrival Pattern In these experiments, $1/\lambda$ was set to 5 msec at the active member and 300 msec at all other members. Figures 8,

9, and 10 show the percentage variation in average stability time and average number of messages as a function of *msp* for group sizes 2, 5, and 10 respectively. There are two main observations. First, the decrease in stability time and the increase in number of messages decreases with increase in *msp*. Second, the decrease in stability time and the increase in number of messages decreases with increase in group size. Both of these observation are similar to the ones we made in case of uniform arrival pattern, and the reasons for these behaviors are same as those in case of uniform arrival pattern.

5.4.3 Bursty Arrival Pattern   Figures 11 and 12 show the percentage variation in average stability time and average number of messages as a function of *msp* for group sizes 2 and 10 respectively. Once again we observe a similar behavior when *msp* or group size increases as that in uniform or bursty arrival patterns. The reasons again are the same.

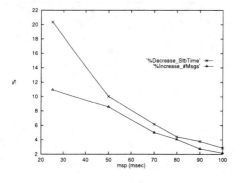

Figure 12: PA(Bursty, GS: 10)

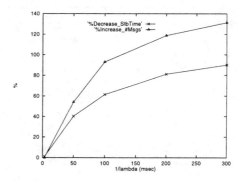

Figure 13: PA(Uni, GS: 2, MSP: 50ms)

5.4.4 Communication Failures   In the presence of communication failures, the behavior of percentage changes in the average stability time and the average number of messages per update broadcast as a function of $1/\lambda$, or *msp*, or group size remains the same as in failure-free case. However, we observed that the percentage decrease in stability time due to the newsmonger technique was much higher than in the failure-free case. The corresponding increase in the number of messages also increased over the failure-free case, but this increase was not very significant. These observations are shown in Figures 13, 14, and 15 for some cases.

5.4.5 Discussion   All simulation runs show that the newsmonger technique results in decreasing the average stability time in PA. However, at the same time, this technique also increases the average number of messages exchanged per update broadcast. Based on the simulation results, we notice that when the

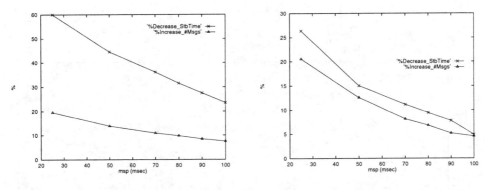

Figure 14: PA(One-active, GS: 5)   Figure 15: PA(Bursty, GS: 10)

update arrival pattern is uniform, the increase in number of messages is always significantly high. While the decrease in update stability time may be as large as 75% in some cases, the increase in number of messages is more than 100% for those cases. In the presence of communication failures, the improvement in stability time is very significant (more than 80% in some cases). However, the increase in number of messages still remains very high (50-60%). Thus, even though the newsmonger technique improves the stability times significantly in the positive acknowledgement protocol under uniform arrival pattern, we do not recommend using this technique. This is because of the significant increase in the number of messages exchanged due to the newsmonger technique.

The real benefit of the newsmonger technique in a positive acknowledgement protocol comes when the update arrival pattern is non-uniform, such as one-active or bursty. For these arrival patterns, the decrease in stability time is very significant, as high as 75%, while the increase in number of messages is very low (less than 12%). These benefits improve further when there are communication failures. Thus, our conclusion is that a newsmonger technique is useful in a positive acknowledgement protocol when the update arrival pattern is non-uniform, such as one-active or bursty.

Another observation of Figures 8 through 12 shows that as *msp* gets smaller, the decrease in stability time increases significantly without affecting the increase in the number of messages in any significant way. Thus, when the update arrival pattern is non-uniform in a positive acknowledgement protocol, a choice of small *msp* is more useful. In our experiments, the smallest *msp* chosen was 25 msec, and that is certainly the best choice of *msp* among the ones we used for maximizing improvement in a positive acknowledgement protocol performance.

5.5 Performance of NA

5.5.1 Uniform Arrival Pattern
The percentage changes in the average stability time and the average number of messages per update broadcast as a

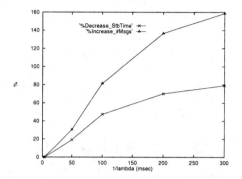

Figure 16: NA(Uni, GS: 2, MSP: 50ms)

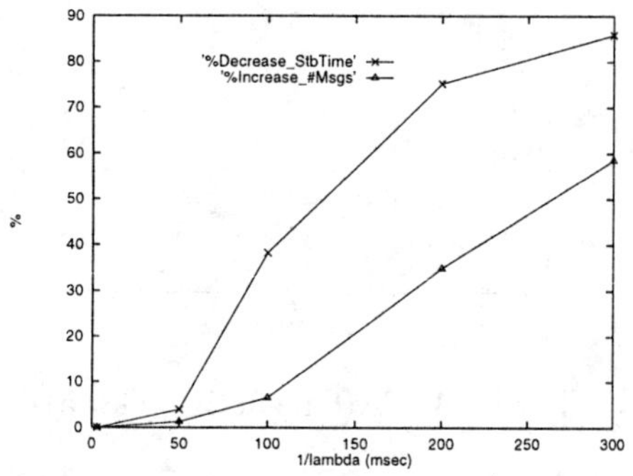

Figure 17: NA(Uni, GS: 5, MSP: 50ms)

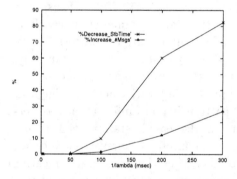

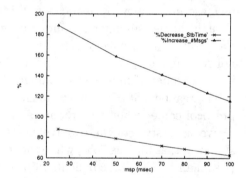

Figure 18: NA(Uni, GS: 10, MSP: 50ms)

Figure 19: NA(Uni, GS: 2, $1/\lambda$: 300ms)

function of $1/\lambda$ are shown in Figures 16, 17, and 18 for group sizes 2, 5, and 10 respectively. The maximum silence period was 50 ms. An important observation we make here is that the decrease in average stability time and the increase in average number of messages increase with increase in $1/\lambda$. Similar behavior was observed for other values of maximum silence period. Note that this behavior was also observed in the positive acknowledgement protocol. The reason for this is as follows. Stability of an update in NA is established when the group members send a message after receiving the update. Since the time taken by group members to send their message depends on $1/\lambda$, the stability time increases with increase in $1/\lambda$ (See [6] for a detailed explanation). As $1/\lambda$ increases, the newsmonger circulates more often due to large silence periods in the system. Each time the newsmonger circulates, it results in a further decrease in stability time and a further increase in the number of messages.

The percentage changes in the average stability time and the average number
of messages per update broadcast as a function of *msp* are shown in Figures
19, 20, and 21 for group sizes 2, 5, and 10 respectively. $1/\lambda$ in all these runs
was 300 ms. The main observation we make from these figures is that the
decrease in stability time and the increase in number of messages decreases
with increase in *msp*. The reason for the is as follows. As *msp* increases, the
rate of newsmonger circulation decreases, which in turn results in a decrease
in the decrease in stability time and a decrease in the increase in number of
messages. Another important observation we make from Figures 16 through 21
is that the decrease in stability time and the increase in number of messages
decreases with increase in group size. The reason for this is as follows. As
group size increases, the newsmonger owner receives proposals at a faster rate
(for a given $1/\lambda$). This results in the length of silence periods in the system
being smaller. As a result, the newsmonger circulates at a slower rate, thus
resulting in a decrease in the decrease in stability time and a decrease in the
increase in the number of messages.

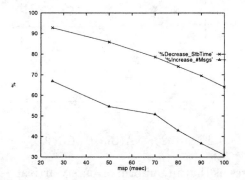 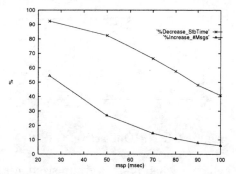

Figure 20: NA(Uni, GS: 5, $1/\lambda$: 300ms)   Figure 21: NA(Uni, GS: 10, $1/\lambda$: 300ms)

5.5.2 One-Active Arrival Pattern Figures 22, 23, and 24 show the percentage variation in average stability time and average number of messages as a
function of *msp* for group sizes 2, 5, and 10 respectively. There are two main
observations. First, the decrease in stability time and the increase in number
of messages decreases with increase in *msp*. Second, the decrease in stability
time and the increase in number of messages decreases with increase in group
size. Both of these observation are similar to the ones we made in case of
uniform arrival pattern, and the reasons for these behaviors are same as those
in case of uniform arrival pattern.

5.5.3 Bursty Arrival Pattern Figures 25 and 26 show the percentage variation in average stability time and average number of messages as a function
of *msp* for group sizes 2 and 10 respectively. Once again we observe a similar

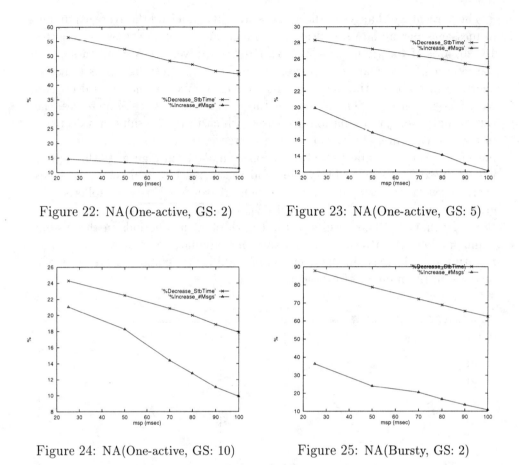

Figure 22: NA(One-active, GS: 2)   Figure 23: NA(One-active, GS: 5)

Figure 24: NA(One-active, GS: 10)   Figure 25: NA(Bursty, GS: 2)

behavior when *msp* or group size increases as that in uniform or bursty arrival patterns. The reasons again are same.

5.5.4 Communication Failures In the presence of communication failures, the behavior of percentage changes in the average stability time and the average number of messages per update broadcast as a function of $1/\lambda$, *msp*, or group size remains the same as in failure-free case. However, we observed that the percentage decrease in stability time due to the newsmonger technique was much higher than in the failure-free case. The corresponding increase in the number of messages also increased over the failure-free case, but this increase was not very significant. These observations are shown in Figures 27, 28, and 29 for some cases.

5.5.5 Discussion Once again, all simulation runs show that the newsmonger technique results in decreasing the average stability time in NA. However, at the same time, this technique also increases the average number of messages exchanged per update broadcast. When the update arrival pattern is uniform,

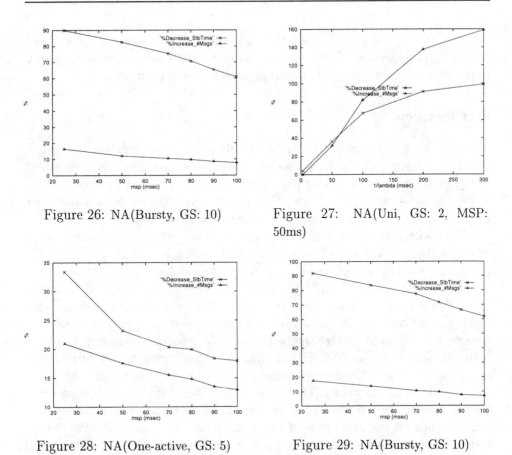

Figure 26: NA(Bursty, GS: 10)

Figure 27: NA(Uni, GS: 2, MSP: 50ms)

Figure 28: NA(One-active, GS: 5)

Figure 29: NA(Bursty, GS: 10)

the benefits of the newsmonger technique depend on the group size. When group size is small, the newsmonger technique is not useful. In these cases, the increase in number of messages is significant (See Figures 16 and 19). However, when the group size is large, the newsmonger technique is useful. As seen in Figures 18, 20, and 21, the newsmonger technique improves the stability time significantly, without affecting the number of messages in any significant way. In the presence of communication failures, the benefits of the newsmonger technique are even higher for larger group sizes.

The benefits of the newsmonger technique in a negative acknowledgement protocol are very significant when the update arrival pattern is non-uniform, such as one-active or bursty. For these arrival patterns, the decrease in stability time is very significant, as high as 70%, while the increase in number of messages is very low (less than 10%). These benefits improve further when there are communication failures.

Figures 22 through 26 show that as *msp* gets smaller, the decrease in stability time increases significantly without affecting the increase in the number of messages in any significant way. Thus, when the update arrival pattern is non-uniform in a negative acknowledgement protocol, a choice of small *msp* is more useful. In our experiments, the smallest msp chosen was 25 msec, and that is certainly the best choice of msp among the ones we used for maximizing improvement in a negative acknowledgement protocol performance.

6 Discussion

Performance of an atomic broadcast protocol is one of the most important factor in determining the performance of an application built using a group communication service. In this paper, we have proposed a general technique, called the newsmonger technique, that can be applied to a large number of atomic broadcast protocols and improves their performance.

We have provided an extensive evaluation of this technique in terms of its effect on the performance of sequencer-based atomic broadcast protocols. In particular, we have considered five operating parameters: group size, interarrival time between update arrivals, communication failure probability, maximum silence period, and update arrival pattern. The effect of the newsmonger technique depends on the values of these parameters, and so, they must be chosen carefully to maximize the benefits of the newsmonger technique.

In any actual setting where an application is built using an atomic broadcast protocol, two of the five operating parameters mentioned above are typically well-known in advance. These are group size and update arrival pattern. Group size is based on the degree of replication used and update arrival pattern depends on the semantics of the application. For example, the update arrival pattern is bursty in a video conferencing application [14], while it is one-active in a brokerage and trading application [2].

The usefulness of the newsmonger technique depends on these two parameters. This technique is very useful when the update arrival pattern is non-uniform (bursty or one-active) in both the positive and the negative-acknowledgement protocols. In these cases, the newsmonger technique improves the average stability times substantially (more than 80% in some cases) with minimal increase in the average number of messages exchanged per update broadcast. The performance improvement becomes even better when there are communication failures or when msp is small. When the update arrival pattern is uniform, this technique is useful only in negative acknowledgement protocol when the group size is large. In positive-acknowledgement protocol or in negative acknowledgement protocol with small group size, the newsmonger technique is not useful. Table 1 summarizes this conclusion.

An important feature of the newsmonger technique is that it can easily be switched off in a protocol when it is not useful. To do so, the newsmonger owner simply stops sending newsmonger messages. Since the operating conditions on which the usefulness of the newsmonger technique depends (update arrival pattern and group size) are typically well-known in advance, it is straight-forward to determine when to switch on or switch off this technique.

The amount of improvement in the broadcast protocol performance due to

Protocol	Update Arrival Pattern		
	Uniform	One Active	Bursty
PA	Not useful	Useful Small msp	Useful Small msp
NA	Useful for group size > 5	Useful Small msp	Useful Small msp

Table 1: Usefulness of the newsmonger technique

the newsmonger technique depends on interarrival time between update arrivals, msp, group size, and communication failure probability. While the interarrival time between update arrivals, group size, and communication failure probability are determined by the system in which the application is implemented, msp is a parameter of the newsmonger technique that can be adjusted to maximize the improvement in the protocol performance. In the experiments we performed, a low value of msp generally resulted in a greater performance improvement, particularly when the update arrival pattern was non-uniform.

In all our experiments, we fixed the value of msp in advance. While this did result in performance improvement, we believe that the performance can further be improved if we change the value of msp dynamically during protocol execution. When interarrival time between updates is large, the system experiences large silence periods. As a result, the newsmonger rotates many times in one such silence period of the system. While the first few of these rotations do result in performance improvement, the later rotations only result in increasing the average number of messages. So, it would be useful to dynamically increase msp as the system silence period prolongs. We are currently testing this dynamic variation in msp.

References

[1] Y. Amir, L. Moser, P. Melliar-Smith, D. Agarwal, and P. Ciarfella. The totem single-ring ordering and membership protocol. *ACM Transactions on Computing Systems*, 13(4):311–342, 1995.

[2] K. Birman. The process group approach to reliable distributed computing. *Communications of the ACM*, 9(12):36–53, Dec 1993.

[3] K. Birman, A. Schiper, and P. Stephenson. Lightweight causal and atomic group multicast. *ACM Transactions on Computer Systems*, 9(3):272–314, Aug 1991.

[4] J. Chang and N. Maxemchuk. Reliable broadcast protocols. *ACM Transactions on Computer Systems*, 2(3):251–273, Aug 1984.

[5] F. Cristian. Understanding fault-tolerant distributed systems. *Communications of ACM*, 34(2):56–78, Feb 1991.

[6] F. Cristian, R. de Beijer, and S. Mishra.   A performance comparison of asynchronous atomic broadcast protocols. *Distributed Systems Engineering*, 1(4):177–201, Jun 1994.

[7] F. Cristian and C. Fetzer.   Probabilistic internal clock synchronization.   In *Proceedings of the 13th Symposium on Reliable Distributed Systems*, Data Point, CA, Oct 1994.

[8] F. Cristian, S. Mishra, and G. Alvarez. High-performance asynchronous atomic broadcast. *Distributed Systems Engineering*, 4(2):109–128, Jun 1997.

[9] S. Mishra, L. Peterson, and R. Schlichting.   Consul: A communication substrate for fault-tolerant distributed programs. *Distributed Systems Engineering*, 1(2):87–103, Dec 1993.

[10] S. Mishra and L. Wu.   Flow control in high performance atomic multicast services. In *Proceedings of the 11th Annual International Symposium on High Performance Computing*, pages 295–306, Winnipeg, Canada, Jul 1997.

[11] M. K. Molloy. *Fundamentals of Performance Modelling*. Macmillan Publishing Co., NewYork, NY, 1989.

[12] D. Powell. Failure mode assumptions and assumption coverage. In *Proceedings of the 22nd Symposium on Fault-Tolerant Computing*, pages 386–395, Boston, MA, Jul 1992.

[13] D. Powell, D. Seaton, G. Bonn, P. Verissimo, and F. Waeselynk. The Delta-4 approach to dependability in open distributed computing systems. In *Proceedings of the Eighteenth Symposium on Fault-Tolerant Computing*, Tokyo, Jun 1988.

[14] S. Ramanathan, V. Rangan, and H. Vin.   Optical communication architectures for multimedia conferencing in distributed systems. In *Proceedings of the 12th International Conference on Distributed Computing Systems*, pages 46–53, Yokohama, Japan, Jun 1992.

[15] F. Schneider.   Implementing fault-tolerant services using the state machine approach: A tutorial. *ACM Computing Surveys*, 22(4):299–319, Dec 1990.

[16] R. van Renesse, K. Birman, and S. Maffeis. Horus: A flexible group communication system. *Communication of the ACM*, 39(4):76–83, Apr 1996.

[17] P. Verissimo and J. Marques.   Reliable broadcast for fault-tolerance on local computer networks. In *Proceedings of the Ninth Symposium on Reliable Distributed Systems*, pages 54–63, Huntsville, AL, Oct 1990.

Time-Triggered Architecture

The Transparent Implementation of Fault Tolerance in the Time-Triggered Architecture

Hermann Kopetz and Dietmar Millinger
Technische Universität Wien, Austria
{hk,dietmar}@vmars.tuwien.ac.at

Abstract

The time-triggered architecture (TTA) is a novel architecture for the implementation of fault-tolerant distributed hard real-time systems. The TTA is interface driven, i.e., the different subsystems are encapsulated between interfaces that are fully specified in the value domain and in the time domain at design time. In this paper we introduce a new interface that hides all services that are required for the implementation of fault tolerance from the host processors that perform the application functions. Since this new interface corresponds syntactically and semantically to the existing communication interface of the time-triggered protocol (TTP) controller, existing software can be ported to a fault-tolerant configuration with minimal modifications.

1. Introduction

The ever-improving price/performance ratio of highly integrated *systems on a chip* (SOC) opens many new application domains for the embedded system technology. In the future, according to Randel and Ringland [13], the embedded system market will be one of the important growth markets for microelectronics technology. It is already planned to apply embedded computer systems in safety-critical mass-market products, such as the braking system or steering system of an automobile. In these applications the delivery of a timely and dependable service, even in the presence of faults, is of utmost concern. One technique to achieve the requested dependability is the use of a system architecture that provides generic support for the implementation of active redundancy. Ideally, the fault-tolerance functions should be encapsulated in a dedicated autonomous layer, which provides its services across an interface that is identical to the service interface of a non-fault-tolerant system. At the end, such a fault-tolerance layer could be implemented in silicon. The huge market potential of the automotive market (tens of millions of systems each year) makes it economical attractive to develop a generic VLSI solution that encapsulates the fault-tolerance functions in hardware and simplifies the system software and application software.

At present, we do not know of COTS architectures for safety critical real-time systems that encapsulate the fault-tolerant services in a separate hardware layer. The research projects "Fault-Tolerant Parallel Processor --FTPP" [3], "Multicomputer Architecture for Fault-Tolerance --MAFT" [5] try to isolate the fault-tolerance mechanisms from the application software functions. The projects Spring [14] and the project "Maintainable Real-Time System MARS" [7] intertwine the fault-tolerance functions with the operating system functions, or with the application functions. Even the AIMs architecture [2] that is developed jointly between Boeing and Honeywell for the aerospace industry is solving most of the fault-tolerance functions at the operating system level.

Ideally, the replication of components for the achievement of fault-tolerance should have no effect on the application software. Otherwise, the increased software complexity required for the implementation of fault tolerance at the application software level, can entail additional design errors in the application software that can have a negative effect on the overall system dependability.

The Time-Triggered Architecture (TTA), designed for the implementation of high-dependability distributed real-time applications, is characterized by small and well-specified interfaces between the communication system and the host computers within the nodes, the CNIs (Communication Network Interface). These precise interface specifications, both in the temporal domain and in the value domain, make it possible to decompose a large system in nearly autonomous subsystems that can be developed independently. Since the properties of the interfaces are not modified during system integration, the TTA is composable and supports the constructive integration of large real-time systems.

It is the objective of this paper to show how the services that are needed for the implementation of fault tolerance can be hidden transparently behind this CNI of the TTA. A new layer of the architecture, the Fault-Tolerant-Unit Layer, provides all services that are required for the implementation of fault tolerance without changing the fundamental structure and semantics of the CNI.

This paper is organized as follows. Section 2 describes the Time-Triggered Architecture from the structural and behavioral point of view. Section 3 introduces the Communication Network Interface. Section 4 informs about the fault-tolerance mechanisms of the Time-Triggered Architecture. In Section 5, the core section of this paper, the services of the newly introduced fault-tolerance layer are presented. The paper closes with comments on the implementation in Section 6.

2. The Time-Triggered Architecture

The Time-Triggered Architecture (TTA) is an architecture for distributed real-time systems that are intended for high-dependability applications [6]. In the TTA all control actions (e.g., the sending of messages, the activation of tasks) are triggered by the progression of a globally synchronized fault-tolerant time base.

A large TTA system is decomposed into a set of subsystems called *clusters*. Each cluster realizes a particular application function. An example for clusters in the automotive context is a cluster for body electronics and a cluster for vehicle dynamics control. A gateway node that is a member of both clusters can implement a data-sharing channel between these two clusters [10]. In the following section, we first describe the structure of a TTA system and then focus on its behavior.

2.1 Structure of the TTA

A *cluster* is a distributed computer system consisting of a set of nodes that are interconnected by a serial channel. In order to accomplish system functions that cannot be realized on a single node, e.g., the tight coordination of the engine, the steering, and the brakes in the four wheels, the nodes exchange messages via the serial communication channel.

A *node* of the distributed system consists of three major subsystems, the *host computer*, the *communication controller (CC)*, and the *process I/O subsystem* to interface with the signals of the sensors and actuators in the environment (Figure 1). These three subsystems are connected by two interfaces: the *communication network interface* (CNI) between the host computer and the communication controller, and the *controlled object interface* (COI) between the host computer and the process I/O subsystem.

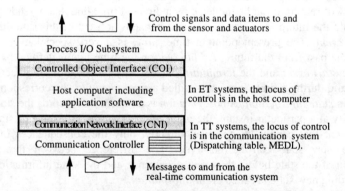

Figure 1: Structure of a Node.

The host computer of the node contains a CPU, memory, a local real-time clock, an operating system and the application software. The host computer receives its input data via the CNI and COI and delivers its output data to the CNI and COI. The purpose of the host computer is to execute the computational tasks of the real-time application within the given deadlines.

The *communication system* is formed by the communication channel and the entirety of all communication controllers in the nodes of a cluster. The purpose of the communication system is to carry messages from the sender node to one or more receiver nodes in the same cluster within given time constraints. A message carries a statement about attributes of significant state variables (e.g., speed, torque) at a particular point in real-time or about the occurrence of an event. A message is an *atomic unit* consisting of three parts:

(i)   the name of the state variable or of the event,
(ii)   the observed value of the state variable $v(t)$, and
(iii)   the time t of observation of the state variable or of the event

If a message does not contain the observation time, it is sometimes assumed that the time of arrival of the message at the receiver can be taken as the observation time. In this case the latency jitter, i.e., the difference between the maximum and the minimum protocol execution time, determines the error in the temporal domain.

A time-triggered communication controller contains a dispatching table in its local memory, the Message Descriptor List (MEDL), that determines at what points in time a particular message is sent or is expected to arrive. An event-triggered communication controller does not need such a dispatching table, because the transmission of a message is triggered by a send command from the host (see Figure 1).

2.2 Behavior of the TTA

To understand the behavior of the time-triggered architecture, it is necessary to explain the differences between event-based and state-based systems. We start with the definition of the basic notions *event* and *state*.

The flow of real time can be modeled by a directed time line that extends from the past into the future. Any occurrence that happens at a cut of this time line is called an *event*. The present point in time, *now,* is a very special event that separates the past from the future. An *interval* on the time line is defined by two events, the *start event* and the *terminating event*. Any property of an object that remains valid during a finite interval is called a *state attribute*, the corresponding information *state information*. An *observation* is an event that records the state of an RT entity at a particular instant, the *point of observation*. A change of state is thus an event that cannot be observed directly, only the consequences of the event, the new state can be observed. The difference between the state information of the state before the event occurrence and the state information of the succeeding new state is called *event information*.

A message is called an *event message* if it is sent immediately after the occurrence of an event and contains in its data field the event information. A message is called a *state message* if it is sent periodically at *a priori* known time points and contains in its data field the state information about the observed state. The following Table 1 depicts the differences between state messages and event messages.

Characteristic	Event Message	State Message
Example of message contents	"Valve has closed by 5 degrees"	"Valve stands at 60 degrees"
Contents of data field	event information	state information with limited temporal validity.
Instant of sending	After event occurrence	Periodically at *a priori* known points in time.
Temporal control	Interrupt caused by event occurrence	sampling, caused by the progression of time
Idempotence [6]	no	yes
Handling at receiver	queued and consumed on reading	new version replaces previous version, not consumed on reading
Semantics at receiver	Exactly once	At least once
Consequences of message loss	Loss of state synchronization between sender and receiver	Unavailability of current state information for a sampling interval.
Typical communication protocol	Positive Acknowledgment or Retransmission (PAR)	Unidirectional datagram
Typical communication topology	Point to point	Multicast
Load on communication system	Depends on number of event occurrences	Constant

Table 1: **Differences between event messages and state messages.**

There are a number of intermediate message forms between state and event messages. For example it is possible--and in many instances useful--to pack the state information about the new state into an event message that is only sent after the occurrence of a state change. An extensive discussion about all these intermediate forms is contained in [6] p.32.

A communication system that is designed for the transmission of event messages is called an *event-triggered (ET) communication system*. In an ET system, the signaling of significant events from the environment to the computer system is realized by the well-known interrupt mechanism, which brings the occurrence of a significant event to the attention of the CPU.

A communication system that is designed for the transmission of state messages is called a *time-triggered (TT) communication system*. An example of a protocol for a time-triggered communication system is the Time-Triggered Protocol (TTP). There is only one interrupt in each node of a distributed TT system, the programmable clock interrupt, which partitions the continuum of time into the sequence of equally spaced granules.

2.3 Services of the Time-Triggered Protocol TTP/C

The Time-Triggered Protocol (TTP/C) is a TDMA (time-division multiple access) based protocol organized into a set of rounds. Each node is allowed to send a message in each round. The most important services of TTP/C that are provided across the CNI are:

(i)   Autonomous time-triggered communication controlled by the controller internal Message Descriptor List (MEDL)

(ii)   Distributed fault-tolerant clock synchronization [8]

(iii)   Consistent membership service informing each node about which node has been operational in the last TDMA round.

The available discrete component TTP controller contains a special device, a bus guardian with its own clock, that assures that even if the controller is faulty it cannot monopolize the bus by sending babbling idiot messages.

3. The Communication Network Interface

The most important interface in a time-triggered architecture is the communication network interface (CNI) between the TTP/C communication controller and the host processor. Nodes communicate by the exchange of *state messages* across the CNI. Since a state message looses its temporal validity as time progresses (see Table 1), the information producers must periodically update the contents of the CNI. A new version of a state message overwrites the previous version, there is no queuing of messages in the CNI. The TTP/C CNI is implemented in a dual-ported RAM (DPRAM) where the TTP controller delivers/fetches the data from one side and the host CPU from the other side. In addition to the state data, the CNI contains a set of status and control words to inform the node about the operation of the protocol.

3.1 Structure of the CNI

The CNI consists of the following four sections:

(i)   The status fields contain status information about the protocol operation. The most important status fields are the time field and the membership field. The membership field in the CNI provides an accurate and consistent view about which nodes of the cluster are operational and which nodes are non-operational.

(ii)   The control fields enable the host to exert some influence on the operation of the TTP controller. For example, it can be controlled when the controller is to start its operation and which types of time-interrupts should be raised by the controller across the CNI. Control actions that can have an effect on the operation of the protocol in general can be blocked by setting corresponding bits in the MEDL. An important control field is the rate correction field for external clock synchronization.

(iii)   The message area contains the data that are delivered by the controller to the CNI and that are fetched from the CNI. There is a status field associated with every message that informs the host about the reception status of the message.

3.2 Obligations of the communication system

TTP is a regular TDMA based protocol where the following information about the controller operation is known *a priori* to all communicating partners:

(i)   The absolute points in time and the update intervals, correct within the precision of the clock synchronization, when a message is delivered to the CNI and when a message is fetched from the CNI by the TTP controller.

(ii)   The duration of the interval between fetching a message from the sending CNI and delivering the information to the receiving CNI. At the CNI this interval is exactly one transmission slot plus the fetch/update intervals. At the FTU CNI, this interval is configurable.

(iii)   The maximum latency of the membership information.

(iv)   The meaning and the lengths of the messages that are transmitted at a certain point of time. It is therefore not required to carry the name of a message in the message. The sending and receiving controller translate the CNI addresses into these *a priori* known time points and vice versa by making use of the information stored in the MEDL.

The implementation of the communication system must meet these obligations or otherwise fail in the fail-silent mode. The implementation of fail-silence in the temporal domain is in the responsibility of the communication controller. For this purpose a special device, the bus guardian, monitors the operation of the controller and shuts the controller down in case it observes a fail-silence violation of the controller.

3.3 Obligations of the host computer

The host system obligations are concerned with the constraints under which the host system may access the information in the CNI. The host system is not allowed to access the CNI during the *a priori* known intervals when the controller accesses the CNI. The non-blocking-write (NBW) protocol can detect such an access violation by the host. In case the host is the reader, the host can retry the operation at another time (when the controller is not writing). In case the host writes while the controller reads information from the CNI, a fatal error is indicated by the controller.

4. Fault tolerance in the TTA

The TTA can mask internal physical faults [11] by the replication of components and the duplication of the communication channels.

4.1 Fault model

In a properly configured TTA system there may not be a single element, the failure of which can cause the loss of an important system service. This implies that all significant system elements must be replicated. In a number of safety-critical applications, this "no-single-point-of-failure" requirement is demanded by the certification authorities.

At the system level, it is assumed that the nodes are fail-silent, i.e., they either produce correct messages at the correct time or produce detectable incorrect messages at the correct time or produce no messages at all. A detectable incorrect message is discarded at the receiver and is thus mapped into the case where no message is produced. The implementation must assure that this fault model is maintained in reality with a sufficiently high probability.

Fail-silence in the temporal domain is achieved by the design of the TTP communication controller. The transmission pattern of a TTP system is regular; it is known *a priori* when a node is expected to send a message. Hence, it is possible to monitor the temporally correct operation of the communication controller by an independent monitor, called a *bus guardian*. The bus guardian grants write access the communication channel only during the send-time interval in the TDMA communication pattern assigned to that node [15].

Fail-silence in the value domain is in the responsibility of the host computer. For this purpose, a special high-error-detection-coverage (HEDC) mode has been designed and tested by fault-injection experiments [4]. In the HEDC mode an end-to-end CRC field that is generated and tested at the level of the communicating application tasks is concatenated to each application message.

4.2 Active replication of nodes

In the TTA, fault tolerance is achieved by the active replication of the fail-silent nodes and by the duplication of the communication channels. We call a fail-silent node a smallest replaceable unit (SRU) and a unit that is formed by a number of replicated SRUs in order to mask failures, a fault-tolerant unit (FTU). There are different FTU configurations possible (Figure 2). SRUs that are fail-silent can be used to build fail-silent active redundant FTUs (FSAR). In case SRUs are not fail-silent in the value domain, but are guaranteed to be fail consistent in the value domain, these SRUs can be used to form triple modular redundant FTUs (TMR).

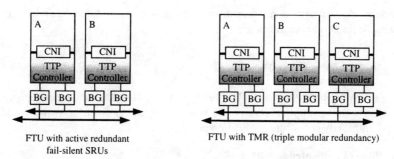

FTU with active redundant fail-silent SRUs

FTU with TMR (triple modular redundancy)

Figure 2: Different FTU configurations.

A prerequisite for the active replication of SRUs is *replica determinism* of the host computers [12].

4.3 The FTU CNI

In a fault-tolerant configuration, many administrative services must be provided by the architecture, e.g., the elimination of redundant messages, the detection of failures that are masked by the redundancy, or support for the reintegration of repaired components. In the proposed architecture, these services are compressed in a dedicated layer of the communication system, the fault-tolerance-unit (FTU) layer.

The FTU layer is sandwiched between two CNIs, the SRU CNI and FTU CNI (Figure 3). From the point of view of the host computer, these two CNIs are identical, having the same structure and fields with the same meaning, as far as the application software is concerned.

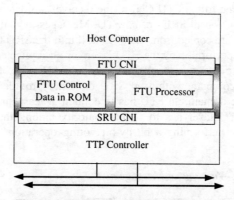

Figure 3: Placement of the FTU Layer

At the SRU CNI, the interval between the sending of a message from one SRU and the receipt of this message at the other SRUs is exactly one slot. At the FTU CNI, this interval is increased since replicated messages are sent by the replicated nodes of an FTU. The duration of this interval is determined during the system design and depends on the level of replication and the assumptions about common mode transient communication faults that can mutilate both messages on the replicated communications.

5. Functions of the FTU Layer

It is the main purpose of the FTU layer to hide all fault-tolerance mechanisms in the TTA from the application in order to simplify the application software and to keep complexity out of the application code.

5.1 Handling of replicated messages

A host that waits for an application message transmitted by an FTU receives multiple instances of the message in its SRU CNI, since every replicated node of an FTU transmits a *version* of the message. It is the task of the FTU layer to reduce this plurality of message versions and to deliver a single correct message into the FTU CNI. First, the FTU layer has to wait until all message versions transmitted by the replicated SRUs have arrived. This absolute interval in time is called the *instability interval* of an FTU CNI message (see Figure 4). Corrupted message versions that are the result of transmission errors are detected by the CRC check in the TTP controller and are discarded. The FTU layer has to select one of the correctly received message versions from the SRU CNI and copy it into the FTU CNI. For messages that contain a high error detection coverage end-to-end CRC (HEDC messages), the HEDC check must be positive before the message is delivered at the FTU CNI. The messages are delivered to the FTU CNI at the same *a priori* determined time point in all SRUs that form an FTU.

The exact time points when a message is fetched from the FTU CNI of the sender and is delivered to the FTU CNI of the receiver are determined at design time and are identical for all SRUs of an FTU. Messages, which are transmitted by a host of an FTU, are copied from the FTU CNI into the SRU CNI by the FTU layer. This action is performed by the FTU layers of all replicated FTU nodes at the same point in time to ensure the identical temporal behavior of all replicas.

In case the host computer within an SRU does not provide the fail-silence property in the value domain, an FTU has to contain at least three SRUs (TMR FTU). The TMR-FTU layer has to find a majority among the three arriving message versions by performing a bit-by-bit voting operation on the received versions.

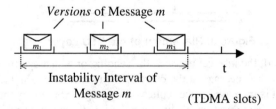

Figure 4: Instability Interval of FTU Message *m*

5.2 FTU membership

The membership service of TTP provides at the SRU CNI information about which SRUs have been operational during the last TDMA round. Duplicated SRUs of an FTU have duplicated entries in this SRU membership information. To hide the replication of SRUs from the application, the node membership in the SRU CNI must be merged into a single FTU membership at the FTU CNI.

The fusion of the SRU membership into an FTU membership value takes place at a particular point in time. This point in time when the fusion of the SRU membership into the FTU membership takes place determines the semantics of the FTU membership values. An FTU membership value with well-defined semantics can be established if the membership value of an FTU is merged from the SRU membership immediately after every instability interval of the FTU. This FTU membership information indicates the operational state of the complete FTU during the defined delivery interval of an FTU message.

The merging operation of the FTU membership is different for FSAR and TMR FTUs. For FSAR FTUs the FTU membership is generated using a logical *OR* operation. If at least one SRU membership of the replicated SRUs of the FTU is set then the FTU membership is set. For TMR FTUs, at least two of the three SRUs must be alive for an operational FTU, otherwise the TMR FTU membership is cleared.

The membership information at the SRU CNI is extended by *null-frame information* that indicates completely empty TDMA slots for the nodes of a cluster. This null-frame information is merged to an FTU null-frame information by the FTU layer following the same rules as for the SRU membership.

5.3 External clock synchronization

The external clock synchronization is a TTP service, which is required to synchronize a TTP cluster consistently with an external time reference [8]. For external clock synchronization, the a common mode clock drift must be enforced on all SRU clocks of the cluster in order that the cluster time comes closer the external time. The SRU CNI contains a control register for this common-mode clock-drift correction.

A time-gateway SRU periodically compares a selected tick of the cluster time with the corresponding tick of an external time reference and calculates the required drift value for the cluster. The time-gateway copies this drift clock values into its local FTU CNI, and the FTU layer distributes the values to the local FTU layers of all SRUs. All receiving FTU layers write the received correction values into the appropriate control register of the SRU CNI. The host of the SRU is not aware of this resynchronization activity, since no clock ticks are added or lost, only the duration of a granule is slightly extended or reduced to bring the local clock into agreement with the external clock.

5.4 Diagnosis

In a properly configured TTA cluster many transient and permanent faults are masked by the provided redundancy and are not visible at the FTU CNI. In order to detect these faults and to be able to restore the required level of redundancy, a special diagnosis service must be implemented within the FTU layer. This service is based on the diagnosis information provided by TTP and displayed in the status fields of the TTP controller in the SRU CNI. Some of this diagnosis information must be exchanged among the SRUs (within the FTU CNI) to arrive at a consistent view of the diagnosed state of a cluster. For example, it is not possible for a single SRU to determine whether a complete communication channel has failed without exchanging the local diagnosis information --loss of one input channel-- with the other SRUs of the cluster.

The diagnosis service maintains failure counters to determine whether a transient fault appears repeatedly at a particular node.

The FTU layer can be configured to transmit the diagnosis information over the TTP communication network for remote diagnosis. Either diagnosis information can be sent during normal application execution, if there is communication bandwidth reserved, or otherwise during a dedicated maintenance mode, which is entered for diagnosis and maintenance purposes.

5.5 Startup and ground state recovery

The tasks in the host computer of an SRU perform periodic computations, which fetch input messages from the FTU CNI, carry out the intended data transformation, and generate output messages to the FTU CNI. Some of these tasks may contain an internal state, *h-state* (history state), that is read as input data before a computation and updated after the computation has finished. We call the union of the h-states of all tasks of a host between the termination of all computational tasks and the start of the recurrent set of computational tasks the *ground state* of the SRU. In the ground state, there is no task active in an SRU [1] (see Figure 5).

During this interval of inactivity at the host the ground-state messages are exchanged between the SRUs of an FTU

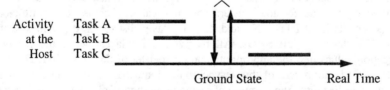

Figure 5: Ground State of a Host

On startup and after the reintegration of a repaired SRU it must be ensured that the ground states are identical in all SRUs of an FTU. The ground state of the host is contained in two special state messages of the FTU CNI. The *input ground state* message contains the ground state that is used by the next set of computational activities in the host. The *output ground state* message contains the ground state that is generated by a set of computational activities. The FTU layer of an SRU must send the output ground state to the FTU layers of the other SRUs of the FTU and must generate a new input ground state before the next set of computations begins again (i.e. during the inactivity interval). In a TMR configuration, this input ground state is the result of a majority vote on the ground state of the three replicas.

During a cold start, the FTU layer must provide the same cold-start ground state to all hosts of the FTU.

6. Implementation concerns

In the present implementation of the TTA, the FTU layer is implemented within the operating system that is executed in the host computers. This has the following two disadvantages

(i)   The task of the FTU layer and the application tasks within the host compete for the same CPU. Both sets of tasks have to observe hard real-time deadlines. Consequently, the scheduling problem for this single CPU is utterly complex.

(ii)   The FTU layer software is not contained within its own error-containment region. A fault in the application software can effect the proper operation of the FTU layer. The intermingling of the FTU layer software with the application software leads to unnecessary complexity at the host computer.

As an intermediate result this implementation has shown that the execution of the FTU layer tasks require considerable less processing time than the execution of the TTP protocol.

In future implementations we plan to develop a hardware architecture where the FTU layer has its own computational resource and where the temporal firewall [9] of the FTU CNI is not compromised by unjustified resource sharing.

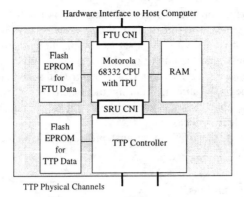

Figure 6: Architecture of a TTP Controller with an integrated FTU Layer

Figure 6 depicts the hardware architecture of a TTP controller with an integrated FTU layer. The FTU CPU executes all tasks that are assigned to the FTU layer. The required information is stored in the FTU data file. After we have gained practical experience with such an architecture, we will try to integrate the FTU layer functionality within a new version of a TTP controller chip.

7. Conclusion

The introduction of a new interface, the FTU CNI, between the basic TTP/C controller communication network interface, the SRU CNI, and the host computer of a node makes room for an autonomous fault-tolerance layer where all functions that are needed for the implementation of fault tolerance can be concentrated. Since the SRU CNI and the FTU CNI have identical structure and semantics, as seen from the view of the application software in the host, the introduction of fault-tolerance is transparent to the host software. In the future, it is planned to implement the FTU layer in hardware and thus provide generic hardware support for the implementation of fault tolerance in the time-triggered architecture.

Acknowledgment

This work has been supported in part by ESPRIT OMI project TTA, by Brite Euram project X-by-Wire and by the ESPRIT LTR project DEVA.

References

[1] Ahuja, M., A. D. Kshemkalyani, et al. (1990). A Basic Unit of Computation in a Distributed System. *10th IEEE Distributed Computer Systems Conference*, IEEE Press. pp. 12-19.

[2] ARINC (1997). Avionics Application Software Standard Interface. ARINC Annapolis.

[3] Harper, R. E., J. H. Lala, et al. (1988). Fault-Tolerant Parallel Processor Architecture Overview. *Proc. FTCS 18*, IEEE Press. pp. 252-257.

[4] Karlsson, J., P. Folkesson, et al. (1995). Integration and Comparison of Three Physical Fault Injection Techniques. *Predictably Dependable Computing Systems* B. Randell, J. L. Laprie, H. Kopetz and B. Littlewood Eds. Heidelberg. Springer Verlag. pp. 309-327.

[5] Kiekhafer, R. M., C. J. Walter, et al. (1988). The MAFT Architecture for Distributed Fault Tolerance. *IEEE Trans. on Computers*. Vol. **37**. pp. 398-405.

[6] Kopetz, H. (1997). *Real-Time Systems, Design Principles for Distributed Embedded Applications; ISBN: 0-7923-9894-7*. Boston. Kluwer Academic Publishers.

[7] Kopetz, H., A. Damm, et al. (1989). Distributed Fault-Tolerant Real-Time Systems: The MARS Approach. *IEEE Micro*. Vol. **9**. pp. 25-40.

[8] Kopetz, H., R. Hexel, et al. (1996). A Synchronization Strategy for a TTP/C Controller, SAE paper 960120. S. International. *Application of Multiplexing Technology SP 1137*, Detroit. SAE Press, Warrendale. pp. 19-27.

[9] Kopetz, H. and R. Nossal (1997). Temporal Firewalls in Large Distributed Real-Time Systems. *Proceedings of IEEE Workshop on Future Trends in Distributed Computing*, Tunis, Tunesia. IEEE Press. pp. 310-315.

[10] Kopetz, H. and T. Thurner (1998). TTP--A new approach to solving the interoperability problem of independently developed ECUs. *SAE Congress 1998*, Detroit, USA. SAE Press 981107. pp. 1-7.

[11] Laprie, J. C. Eds. (1992). Dependability: Basic Concepts and Terminology - in English, French, German, German and Japanese. Dependable Computing and Fault Tolerance. Vienna, Austria. Springer-Verlag.

[12] Poledna, S., Fault-Tolerant Real-Time Systems: The Problem of Replica Determinism, Kluwer Academic Publishers, 1995

[13] Randell, B., G. Ringland, et al. Ed. (1994). Software 2000: A View of the Future of Software. Brussels. ESPRIT.

[14] Stankovic, J. A. and K. Ramamritham (1991). The Spring Kernel: A new Paradigm for Real-Time Systems. *IEEE Software*. Vol. **8**. pp. 62-72.

[15] Temple, C. (1998). Avoiding the Babbling-Idiot Failure in a Time-Triggered Communication System. *Fault Tolerant Comp. Symp. FTCS 28*, Munich, Germany. IEEE Press. pp. 218-227.

Formal Verification for Time-Triggered Clock Synchronization*

Holger Pfeifer, Detlef Schwier, Friedrich W. von Henke
Universität Ulm
Fakultät für Informatik
D-89069 Ulm

{pfeifer,schwier,vhenke}@informatik.uni-ulm.de

Abstract

Distributed dependable real-time systems crucially depend on fault-tolerant clock synchronization. This paper reports on the formal analysis of the clock synchronization service provided as an integral feature by the Time-Triggered Protocol (TTP), a communication protocol particularly suitable for safety-critical control applications, such as in automotive "by-wire" systems. We describe the formal model extracted from the TTP specification and its formal verification, using the PVS system. Verification of the central clock synchronization properties is achieved by linking the TTP model of the synchronization algorithm to a generic derivation of the properties from abstract assumptions, essentially establishing the TTP algorithm as a concrete instance of the generic one by verifying that it satisfies the abstract assumptions. We also show how the TTP algorithm provides the clock synchronization that is required by a previously proposed general framework for verifying time-triggered algorithms.

1 Introduction

Distributed dependable real-time systems crucially depend on fault-tolerant clock synchronization. This is particularly true in distributed architectures in which processes (or nodes) perform their actions according to a pre-determined, static schedule, i.e. triggered by the progress of time. Such "time-triggered architectures" are commonly proposed or used in safety-critical applications, such as automotive control functions [5, 7]. Obviously, clock synchronization is a central element of a time-triggered architecture for it to function properly: it is essential that the clocks of all processes be kept sufficiently close together and that the synchronization be able to tolerate faults to a limited extent.

---

*This work has been partially supported by the European Commission under the ESPRIT OMI project 23396 "Time-Triggered Architecture (TTA)".

The main purpose of this paper is to present a formal analysis of the clock synchronization algorithm embedded in a specific time-triggered context, the "Time-Triggered Protocol" (TTP) [8, 9]. TTP is the core of the communication level of the Time-Triggered Architecture, an architecture that has been developed and evaluated in two recent European projects: "Time-Triggered Architecture" (Esprit OMI program) and "X-by-Wire" (Brite EuRam program). The Time-Triggered Architecture is intended to be employed in connection with devices controlling safety-critical electronic systems without mechanical backup, so-called "by-wire"systems, e. g. for steering, braking, or suspension control [17]. Hence, high trust must be placed in its correct functioning. It has been argued that the kind of reliability required in such situations cannot be achieved without a careful formal analysis of the mechanisms and algorithms involved [2].

In the Time-Triggered Protocol, several distinct services, such as clock synchronization, group membership or redundancy management, are integrated. Among these services, clock synchronization is the most basic since for achieving the required real-time properties the other services rely on its providing a time basis common to all processors. It is for this reason that clock synchronization has been chosen as the starting point for a formal analysis of TTP. The different services provided by TTP are so tightly integrated that for the formal analysis it is first necessary to extract a clock synchronization algorithm from the integrated protocol by abstracting from those features that are irrelevant for synchronization. Furthermore, the existing description of TTP [8] is "structured English" that has to undergo a process of formalization to obtain a formal specification. The resulting formal model can then be subjected to a rigorous mathematical analysis.

Distributed fault-tolerant algorithms like those for clock synchronization are inherently difficult to reason about. However, it has been observed (first by F. Schneider [18]) that the correctness arguments, i. e. the verification of the essential properties, for many synchronization algorithms are quite similar and can be derived from rather general assumptions. In our verification of TTP clock synchronization we make use of this observation and of our own formalization of the generic derivation in PVS [19]. However, the existing PVS model could not directly be used for TTP, since the synchronization algorithm of TTP differs from other algorithms in various ways: First, there are no special synchronization messages that provide the reading of a node's clock to other nodes; instead, the delay in the arrival of incoming messages is used to estimate the value of the sender's clock. Second, TTP provides a means to collect timing information only from selected nodes; this feature is intended for ignoring clock values of nodes that are known to have oscillators of inferior quality. Finally, the estimated readings of only four clocks are used for the calculation of a correction term of a node's clock, even if the cluster consists of more than four nodes. Because of these peculiarities of TTP the generic PVS model for verifying clock synchronization algorithms had to be generalized. The main effort for proving the correctness of the TTP synchronization algorithm is then to establish a mapping from the specification of the TTP algorithm to the notions that are used in the generic verification. The formal development has been carried out using the PVS system [13]; in this way, we have obtained a complete and mechanically checked formal verification of the TTP algorithm.

To put our development into a larger context, we also link it to previous work by J. Rushby (using PVS) on a general framework for verifying time-triggered algorithms; specifically, we show how the TTP algorithm provides the clock synchronization that is required by that framework. The link is facilitated by our structuring of specifications in such a manner that they "fit" the framework seamlessly. This is similar to the demonstration by Di Vito and Butler [3] that the treatment of the interactive convergence algorithm presented in [16] satisfies the synchronization requirements of the Reliable Computing Platform.

The remainder of this paper is structured as follows. The next sections give an overview of the Time-Triggered Protocol to the extent needed for this paper and describe the extraction of the clock synchronization algorithm. The formal verification presented in Section 4 consists of two parts: the first part summarizes the generic arguments, the assumptions on which they are based, and the adaptation of the generic model required for TTP; in the second part, we show, by way of example, how our formal model of TTP clock synchronization satisfies the assumptions. A subsequent section discusses the embedding into the verification framework for time-triggered algorithms. The concluding section summarizes the presented work and gives an outlook of ongoing and planned extensions.

2 Clock synchronization in the Time-Triggered Protocol

The distinguishing characteristic of time-triggered systems is that all system activities are initiated by the progress of time. From an abstract point of view, the TTP protocol operates cyclically. Each node is supplied with a clock and a static schedule, the *message descriptor list (MEDL)*. The schedule determines when certain actions have to be performed, in particular when messages of a certain type are to be sent by a particular node. The message descriptor list contains an entry which determines at which clock time a particular slot begins.

The MEDL contains global information common to all nodes in the cluster about the communication structure, such as the duration of a given slot or the identity of the sending node. As the intended system behavior is thus known to all nodes, important information can be obtained indirectly from the messages. For example, explicit acknowledgments need not be sent since a receiving node can determine that a message is missing immediately after the anticipated arrival time has passed. Similarly, from the successful reception of a message is a sufficient condition for the sending node to be considered active.

The nodes communicate via a replicated broadcast bus. Access to this bus is determined by a time-division multiple access (TDMA) schema which is pre-compiled into the schedule. Every node thus owns certain slots, in which it is allowed to send messages on the bus. A complete cycle during which every node has had access to the bus once is called a *TDMA round*. After a TDMA round is completed, the same temporal access pattern is repeated again. The length of the message descriptor list reflects the number of different TDMA rounds and determines the duration of the so-called *cluster cycle* which, as the name suggests, is repeated over and over again.

In each slot, one of the nodes of a cluster sends a frame on each of the two channels of the bus, whereas the other nodes listen on the bus for incoming messages for a certain period of time, the *receive window*. According to certain aspects of the received message, such as content, arrival time, etc., each node then changes its internal state at some point in time before the next slot begins. Each slot is conceptually divided into two phases: during the first, the *communication phase*, the current sender is broadcasting a message via the bus; in the second, in the *computation phase*, each node changes its internal state depending on the current state and the received message. In TTP, these phases roughly correspond, respectively, to the receive window, the time frame within which nodes expect messages to arrive, and to the inter-frame gap, during which is silence on the bus.

Obviously, the clocks of the nodes must be synchronized tightly enough for them to agree on the current slot and to scan the bus at appropriate times for messages to arrive. To prevent a faulty node from speaking out of turn, the bus interface is controlled by a "bus guardian" that has independent knowledge and gives access to the bus only at appropriate times. Each node is supplied with a *physical clock* that is typically implemented by a discrete counter. The counter is incremented periodically, triggered by a crystal oscillator. As these oscillators do not resonate with a perfectly constant frequency, the clocks drift apart from real time. It is the task of clock synchronization algorithms to repeatedly compute an adjustment of a node's physical clock in order to keep it in agreement with the other nodes' clocks. The adjusted physical clock is what is used by a node during operation and it is commonly called a node's *local clock*.

The general way clock synchronization algorithms operate is to gather estimates of the readings of other nodes' clocks to estimate an adjustment for the local clock. Since every node knows beforehand at which time certain messages will be sent the difference between the time a message is expected to be received by a node and the actual arrival time can be used to calculate the deviation between the sender's and the receiver's clock. In this way, no special synchronization messages are needed in TTP. The time measurements are stored on a push-down stack of depth four with the most recent one on top. Thus, older values get discarded after a while. In general, there are more than four nodes in a cluster and hence not every node contributes to the calculation of a new correction term for a node's local clock. This approach is feasible under the hypothesis that at most one of the values on the stack may be faulty in some sense, i. e. does not represent a proper clock reading.

TTP allows messages from nodes with clocks of minor quality to be excluded from the calculation of adjustments in order to improve the precision of the synchronization. This is accomplished by selecting the messages according to a *SYF* flag (for *synchronization frame*) in the message descriptor list. If this flag is not set in the MEDL for the current slot, the obtained time difference value is not stored on the stack.

In some slots, after the communication, the adjustment term is calculated from the time values on the stack. The slots in which this is to occur are marked in the message descriptor list by a special flag named *CS* (for *clock synchronization*). TTP uses the Fault-Tolerant Average Algorithm (FTA) [10] to calculate the adjustment: The largest and the smallest value are discarded and the average of the remaining two is used as the new adjustment term.

To summarize, the TTP clock synchronization algorithm that is executed by each node individually can informally be described as follows: In every slot, perform the following steps:

1. Determine the difference between expected and observed arrival time for the incoming message.

2. If a valid message has been received and the SYF flag is set in the message descriptor list for the current slot, then push the measured time difference value onto the stack; otherwise discard it.

3. If the CS flag is set in the message descriptor list for the current slot, calculate a new correction term using the four values held on the stack and adjust the local clock accordingly.

Obviously, there are certain constraints on how the SYF and CS flags can be set in the message descriptor list for the various slots. First of all, the flags must be equally set in the message descriptor lists of all nodes. Moreover, the SYF flag must be set frequently enough in order to collect sufficiently many new time difference values. As the TTP algorithm is designed to tolerate one arbitrary (Byzantine) fault in every TDMA round, there must be at least four slots in every TDMA round with the SYF flag set.

3 Formal model for the TTP synchronization algorithm

This section describes a formal specification of the TTP clock synchronization algorithm that has been developed from an informal description of the TTP protocol [8]. Since in TTP many different services are tightly integrated the first step towards a formal model is to abstract from those features that are not relevant for clock synchronization in order to make the mechanical analysis feasible at all. In particular, the internal state of a node which in the TTP implementation comprises quite a number of registers for various purposes has been reduced in the model to contain only a few components. More precisely, the internal state of a node is modeled as a record consisting of the following elements:

- a counter *current_slot* which records the number of the current slot,

- a stack *timediffs* of depth four for storing the time difference values,

- two registers *current_correction* and *total_correction* that contain the value of
  the most recently calculated clock adjustment and the sum of all adjustments
  calculated so far, respectively.

In addition we assume another stack, also of depth four, to record the slots in
which the corresponding entries of the stack of time values have been obtained. This
stack is not a component of the TTP data structure, but it is needed for verifying the
synchronization algorithm.

We use the PVS notation of projection functions to denote the components of
the state record; thus *timediffs(s)*, for example, denotes the stack of time difference
values of state *s*.

Initially, the slot counter, the adjustment values, and the entries of the stack of
time difference values are all set to zero; the stack of slot numbers is initialized with
negative values in order to distinguish them from proper slot numbers; the latter are
represented by natural numbers. The function *initialstate* maps every node to its
initial state.

Usually two views of time are distinguished: real time is given by some external
frame of reference while clock time is a node's local approximation provided by
the physical clock. Real time is taken as ranging over the real numbers, and integer
values are used to model clock time. We adopt the convention of using lower-case
variables, such as t or t_p^i to denote real-time entities whereas clock-time quantities
will be denoted by upper-case identifiers. In our formalization the physical clock
of a node p is modeled by a function PC_p which maps real time to clock time; thus,
$PC_p(t)$ denotes the reading of p's physical clock at real time t. The rate at which a
physical clock may drift apart from real time is assumed to be bounded by a small
positive quantity.

The reading of the local clock of a node p in some given state s at real time t is
obtained by adding the adjustment adj_s to the reading of the node's physical clock
PC.

$$adj_s = current\_correction(s) + total\_correction(s)$$
$$LC_p^s(t) = PC_p(t) + adj_s$$

In order to describe the state of a node at particular clock times we introduce a
function *schedule(r)* which denotes the clock time at which a given slot r starts.
The schedule is not directly available in TTP, but there is an entry for the duration
of each slot r in the message descriptor list; this is formally captured by the function *duration*. Given a clock time constant *system_start_time* which is assumed to
initially show up on every node's local clock, it is a simple matter to define *schedule*
by recursively summing up the duration of the slots:

$$schedule(r) = \begin{cases} system\_start\_time & \text{if } r = 0 \\ schedule(r-1) + duration(r-1) & \text{if } r > 0 \end{cases}$$

The state of a node p at a certain clock time T is given by a function *ttss* (for
time-triggered system state). The definitions involving *ttss* are adapted from work
by Rushby [15]. By the start of the first slot, p is in its initial state:

$$ttss(p)(schedule(0)) = initialstate(p)$$

Let *comm_duration*(*r*) denote the duration of the communication phase of a slot *r*, during which a node *p* waits for a message to arrive. Within the communication phase the internal state of *p* remains unchanged:

$$ttss(p)(T) = ttss(p)(schedule(r))$$
$$\text{for } schedule(r) \le T \le schedule(r) + comm\_duration(r)$$

At some point during the computation phase node *p* is changing its internal state depending on its current state and the message it has received. This behavior is described by a state transition function *trans* such that *trans*(*p*, *m*)(*s*) denotes the next state of a node *p* that has received message *m* in state *s*. The state of *p* is unspecified during the computation phase; all that is said is that by the beginning of the next slot *schedule*(*r* + 1) node *p* has changed into a new state.

$$ttss(p)(schedule(r+1)) = trans(p, ttin(p, T))(ttss(p)(T))$$
$$\text{where } T = schedule(r) + comm\_duration(r)$$

Here, the function *ttin*(*p*, *T*) models the message *p* receives at clock time *T*. As the contents of the message is irrelevant as far as clock synchronization is concerned (only the arrival times of messages are of importance) we need not to be too specific about the reception of messages and leave *ttin* uninterpreted. For our purpose it is sufficient to assume a set *Message* of messages with a distinguished element *null* to model the case when a node has not received any message.

So far we have described the general behavior of a node in a time-triggered system. What remains is to model the state transitions that a node performs in each slot, i. e. the state transition function *trans*. This function formalizes the clock synchronization algorithm that has informally been described in the previous section. From the synchronization point of view there are two sorts of slots: "ordinary" ones in which only message delays are measured, and slots in which a new correction term is calculated. Accordingly, the definition of the state transition function *trans* is divided into two parts: the first is described by the function *do_slot*(*p*, *m*, *s*) which is evaluated in every slot and gathers the time difference values and stores them on the stack. The second function, *update*(*p*, *s*), computes new values for the correction terms. The latter function is only evaluated if in the current slot the clock synchronization algorithm is to be executed, i. e. when the CS flag is set in the message descriptor list for the current slot.

$$trans(p, m)(s) = update(p, do\_slot(p, m, s))$$

The deviation of the arrival time of a message is measured by a hardware mechanism that is captured by the function *get_time_diff*(*p*, *m*, *s*) in the formal model. Time difference values are only stored on the stack if the received message is *valid*. This is the case, e. g. if, among other things, it has been received within the receive window. In particular, *null* denoting that no message has been received is not valid. We use a predicate *new_timediff_available?*(p, m, s) to model whether a time difference is available for being stored on p's stack. In this case, function *do_slot*(p, m, s) pushes the current time difference value onto the stack; in addition, the current slot number is pushed onto the second stack to record the origin of each time measurement. Finally, the slot counter is increased.

$$do\_slot(p, m, s) = s', \text{ where}$$
$$current\_slot(s') \quad := \quad current\_slot(s) + 1$$
$$\text{and if } new\_timediff\_available?(p, m, s) \text{ then:}$$
$$timediffs(s') \quad := \quad push(get\_time\_diff(p, m, s), timediffs(s))$$
$$slots(s') \quad := \quad push(current\_slot(s), slots(s))$$

If the clock synchronization algorithm is to be executed in the current slot the function *update* updates the values of the correction terms according to the result of the fault-tolerant average algorithm. The latter is specified by the function *calculate_correction* that takes the stack of time difference values as its argument. The predicate *syncround?* is true if the *CS* flag is set in the message descriptor list for the current slot.

$$update(p, s) = \begin{cases} s' & \text{if } syncround?(current\_slot(s)) \\ s & \text{otherwise} \end{cases}$$
$$\text{where} \quad current\_correction(s') \quad := \quad calculate\_correction(timediffs(s))$$
$$total\_correction(s') \quad := \quad current\_correction(s)$$
$$\quad + total\_correction(s)$$

4   Verification of the TTP synchronization algorithm

Clock synchronization algorithms do not only have the task of keeping the clocks of a cluster of nodes tightly together. As with distributed algorithms in general, clock synchronization is usually required to work also in the presence of faults. Algorithms differ in the number and kind of faults they are designed to tolerate. The TTP algorithm, for example, is able to handle one asymmetric (Byzantine) fault in each TDMA round, i. e., as long as at most one fault occurs in any consecutive n slots, where n is the length of a TDMA round, the algorithm is able to maintain the clocks synchronized.

The required fault-tolerance of an algorithm makes it inherently difficult to reason about it, since careful attention has to be drawn to faults and failed components. Schneider [18] has observed, however, that the correctness arguments of so-called *averaging algorithms* are quite similar. This class of algorithms is described using a *convergence function*. Schneider stated several rather general assumptions on the convergence function and showed that they are sufficient to prove the correctness of the algorithm. Subsequently, Shankar used the EHDM system to mechanically verify Schneider's proof [20, 21] and Miner [12], and more recently Schwier and v. Henke [19] have further improved the constraints and the organization of the proof itself, respectively.

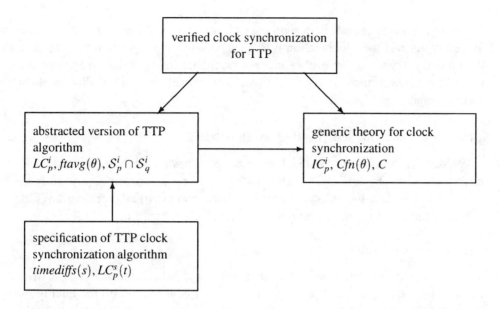

Figure 1: Structure of the TTP instance of the generic theory for clock synchronization.

By following this general two-step approach to clock synchronization we can make use of existing PVS formalizations of the generic synchronization proof. This reduces the reasoning effort required to complete the proof compared to a verification directly from the low-level specification presented in Section 3. The argument for the correctness of the synchronization is first derived from a set of generic assumptions that are independent from a particular algorithm. The second step is then to show that the assumptions on which the clock synchronization proof is based are indeed satisfied by the concrete TTP algorithm.

For the verification of the TTP clock synchronization we utilize a variant of our own formalization of the generic derivation in PVS [19]. This formalization is similar to Miner's development [12] in EHDM, a predecessor of the PVS verification system, with the organization of the various PVS theories and proofs being improved to also incorporate non-averaging algorithms. The existing formalization, however, had to be generalized in order to accommodate it to the particular needs of TTP. This generalization involved the modification of the signatures of some of the parameters, in particular that of the convergence function.

The remainder of this section first briefly summarizes the generic model for verifying clock synchronization algorithms. It is, however, beyond the scope of this paper to restate in detail the proof of the synchronization property and all of the assumptions this proof is based on. Instead, we take one of the central conditions on the convergence function as an example and describe the generalization that was necessary to capture the peculiarities of the TTP algorithm. Then we explain how the generic model is used to yield a correctness proof for the TTP synchronization algorithm. The major task in deriving a TTP instance of the generic theory is to gradually abstract the specification of the synchronization algorithm presented in the previous section to the level of the generic model and to define an appropriate translation between those two abstractions. The overall structure of this development is depicted in Figure 1.

4.1 Generic model for verifying clock synchronization

A clock synchronization protocol implements a *virtual clock*[1] by repeatedly adjusting a node's physical clock. The task of the synchronization algorithm is to bound the *skew*, i. e. the absolute difference between the virtual clock readings of any two (non-faulty) nodes p and q by a small value δ at any time t:

$$| VC_p(t) - VC_q(t) | \leq \delta$$

This property is commonly called *agreement* and relates the readings of two clocks. The other important property, *accuracy*, is concerned with the quality of the approximation to real time by a clock; this is, however, not discussed in this paper.

The proof of this property is generally accomplished through mathematical induction on the number of synchronization intervals. The induction hypothesis states that at the beginning of each interval, the skew between any two clocks is bounded by some value $\delta_S < \delta$. Then it is shown that during the next interval, when the clock readings drift apart, the skew does not exceed δ. Finally one has to prove that the application of the convergence function brings the clocks together again within δ_S. The latter step is the harder one, since the former rather imposes certain constraints on the maximum precision that can be achieved given concrete values for the drift rate ρ of the clocks and the length of a synchronization interval.

To facilitate the induction proof several additional concepts and notations have proven useful, in particular the abstract notion of *interval clocks*. Instead of repeatedly applying adjustments to a local clock one could also think of a node starting a new clock each time the synchronization algorithm has been executed. These clocks are indexed by the number of the synchronization interval i and are denoted $IC_p^i(t)$. The value of p's interval clock in the ith synchronization interval is obtained by adding the ith adjustment to the reading of p's physical clock:

$$IC_p^i(t) = PC_p(t) + adj_p^i$$

These interval clocks are then put together to form the node's virtual clock: in the ith synchronization interval p's virtual clock corresponds to the ith interval clock:

$$VC_p(t) = IC_p^i(t), \text{ for } t_p^i \leq t < t_p^{i+1}$$

Here, t_p^i denotes the begin of the ith synchronization interval. The way the adjustments to a node's physical clock are computed is abstractly captured by the

---

[1] In the description of the TTP algorithm the virtual clocks have been called *local clocks*.

concept of a *convergence function Cfn*. The convergence function takes an array Θ_p^i of readings of the clocks of some or all other nodes to calculate a corrected clock reading for p. The value $\Theta_p^i(q)$ is p's estimate of q's clock reading at time t_p^i. The adjustment to p's physical clock is then given by the difference of its physical clock and the result of the convergence function; initially it is taken to be 0:

$$adj_p^0 = 0$$
$$adj_p^{i+1} = Cfn(p, \Theta_p^{i+1}) - PC_p(t_p^{i+1})$$

Schneider has stated several conditions that are necessary to complete the proof of the bounded skew property. Some of them, e. g. those concerning the interrelationships among the various quantities introduced, are of minor importance in that they can be derived more easily for concrete algorithms. The most important of the conditions are concerned with the behavior of the convergence function that a clock synchronization algorithm exploits. The usefulness of these conditions is for the most part due to its isolation of purely mathematical properties from other concepts such as, e. g., failed nodes. We consider one of them, called *precision enhancement*, in more detail.

The property *precision enhancement* is used to bound the skew between two clocks immediately after the application of the convergence function. The actual bound depends on the skews between the value in the array of estimated clock readings. Given two such arrays γ and θ used by two nodes p and q, respectively, precision enhancement states that the absolute values of the convergence function applied by p and q, respectively, do not differ by more than a quantity $\Pi(X, Y)$, provided that corresponding entries in γ and θ differ by no more than X and the values in γ and θ, respectively, fall within a range Y. Furthermore, it is required that $\Pi(X, Y) < Y$ for the precision to be truly enhanced.

There is a bound $\Pi(X, Y)$ such that
  if for all $l \in C: |\gamma(l) - \theta(l)| \le X$
    and for all $l, m \in C: |\gamma(l) - \gamma(m)| \le Y$ and $|\theta(l) - \theta(m)| \le Y$
  then $|Cfn(p, \gamma) - Cfn(q, \theta)| \le \Pi(X, Y)$

This formalization of the precision enhancement property is taken from Schwier and v. Henke's work [19], except for some minor notational differences. Note the use of the set C: in previous presentations of this property the convergence function is assumed to use an array, θ say, of N clock readings, where N is the number of nodes. The preconditions of precision enhancement are required to be satisfied by at least $N - F$ of these readings, with F being the number of faults to be tolerated by the algorithm; this set of readings is denoted by C. For the algorithm to tolerate any arbitrary (Byzantine) fault it is crucial that N is at least $3F + 1$ (cf. [4]). This ensures that the sets of readings used in the convergence function by two nodes overlap.

The intended interpretation of C is the set of readings from non-faulty clocks. This view is due to the implicit assumption that the array of clock readings is a mapping from nodes to clock time values. However, as we show, this is not necessarily required. Moreover, the TTP algorithm does not allow for such an interpretation of the array of readings. Of course one could use the senders of the messages that lead to the time difference values on a node's stack as the domain of θ but the problem arises with the interpretation of faulty readings: in the TTP protocol the reception of a valid message at a node q is a sufficient condition for q to consider the sender of the message to be correct. Thus, a new time difference value will only be stored on the stack if being received from a non-faulty node and communication faults result in the lack of such a new value. Therefore the problem with the readings is not that they come from some faulty node but rather that some of them might remain on the stack for "too long" if they do not get pushed out by new values. Thus these old values may not represent accurate estimates of the remote clock readings; in the worst case they haven't been even gathered in the most recent synchronization interval.

For the verification of the TTP algorithm it was therefore necessary to generalize the treatment of the array of clock readings and the actual form of the generic assumptions that involve the convergence function. In particular, we allow the domain of the array of clock readings to be any set of size N with different nodes possibly having different sets and we define C to be the intersection of the respective sets of two nodes that is required to contain at least $N - F$ elements for any two nodes.

The two other of Schneider's constraints on the convergence function, called *accuracy preservation* and *translation invariance*, are affected by this generalization, too. They are, however, omitted in this presentation. For a detailed explanation of these and the other conditions we refer to Schneider [18] and Miner [12]; a complete generic derivation of the synchronization property from these conditions is given by Schneider [18] and Shankar [20].

4.2 Deriving abstract properties of the protocol

While the formal model of TTP is describing the clock synchronization algorithm on the level of slots, the generic verification is based on the notation of synchronization intervals. In order to exploit the generic proof of clock synchronization for the TTP algorithm the concrete model of TTP has to be abstracted to the level of the concepts used in the generic model. This means in particular that the definition of the local clocks and the calculation of the adjustments needs to be in terms of interval clocks and a convergence function.

A first step towards this goal is to derive from the slot-based description of local clocks an interval-based one. Obviously the adjustment adj_s is only changed if the synchronization algorithm is executed in the current slot. The slots in which this is to occur are marked in the message descriptor list with the CS flag set. Given a function *syncround* such that *syncround*(i) yields the number of the slot in which the CS flag is set for the ith time we can define the ith adjustment of p, denoted adj_p^i, as the adjustment adj_s given in p's state after the synchronization algorithm has been invoked for the ith time. Similarly, an interval-based description of the local clock, denoted LC_p^i, is defined:

$$
\begin{aligned}
adj_p^i &= adj_p^s \\
LC_p^i(t) &= LC_p^s(t)
\end{aligned}
$$

$$
\text{where } s = \begin{cases} initialstate(p) & \text{if } i = 0 \\ ttss(p)(schedule(syncround(i) + 1)) & \text{if } i > 0 \end{cases}
$$

It is easy to see that the following equation holds for $LC_p^i(t)$:

$$
LC_p^i(t) = PC_p(t) + adj_p^i
$$

In previous work on clock synchronization clocks are also sometimes expressed in terms of functions mapping clock time to real time [11, 12, 16]. Some of our definitions and proofs are more naturally described this way and we therefore introduce the inverse mapping pc_p of p's physical clock; $pc_p(T)$ denote the earliest real time that p's physical clock reads T. Thus, we can define an inverse mapping of LC_p^i as

$$
lc_p^i(T) = pc_p(T - adj_p^i)
$$

In order to cast LC_p^i into the form used in the definition of the interval clock IC_p^i several additional notations have to be introduced. First, we define the real time instant t_p^i at which p invokes the synchronization algorithm for the ith time by means of lc_p^i. Here, the clock time *scheduled_synctime(i)* denotes some instant in the computation phase of the ith synchronization slot at which the synchronization algorithm is executed.

$$
t_p^i = \begin{cases} lc_p^0(system\_start\_time) & \text{if } i = 0 \\ lc_p^{i-1}(scheduled\_synctime(i)) & \text{if } i > 0 \end{cases}
$$

The next step is to formulate the adjustments adj_p^i in terms of a convergence function. First, the array of clock readings Θ_p^i has to be defined. As described above, each node p maintains a stack of time difference values. These values are used to calculate an estimate of the reading of a remote clock by adding the time difference to the value of p's local clock at time t_p^i. As explained in the previous subsection, the array of readings can not be modeled by a function mapping nodes to clock readings. Under certain conditions it can even occur that there are two values from the same sender on the stack[2]. Therefore it is not the sender of a message but the slot number in which the message was sent that is the domain of the function Θ_p^i. The slot numbers are recorded separately on a additional stack. Note again that this stack is only an abstract concept that is used for the verification but is not implemented in the protocol.

We use S_p^i to denote the set of slot numbers that are contained on p's stack in the ith synchronization interval. Moreover, idx_p^i is a mapping that yields for every slot number s the index on p's stack at which s is stored. The elements of the stack are denoted *stack.0* (top) to *stack.3* (bottom). The array of clock readings Θ_p^i is then

---

[2]This might be the case in a cluster of four nodes when a communication fault occurs in the last TDMA-round before the synchronization.

modeled as a function mapping the values of the stack of slots to the corresponding entries of the stack of time difference values:

$$S_p^i = \{s : \mathbb{N} \mid s = stack.0 \lor s = stack.1 \lor s = stack.2 \lor s = stack.3\}$$
$$\Theta_p^i = \lambda s \in S_p^i . LC_p^{i-1}(t_p^i) + stack.idx_p^i(s)$$
$$\text{where} \quad stack = timediffs(ttss(p)(schedule(syncround(i) + 1)))$$

TTP uses the fault-tolerant average algorithm [10] to calculate the adjustments. In general, the algorithm takes N clock readings among which up to F readings might be faulty in some sense. The readings are sorted and the F largest and the F smallest values are discarded. The algorithm then returns the average of the remaining $N - 2 * F$ readings as its result. In the case of TTP, each node has $N = 4$ readings to calculate the adjustment and it is assumed that at most one of them does not represent a proper time difference value, i. e. $F = 1$.

The formalization of the fault-tolerant average algorithm *ftavg* assumes a function for sorting an array of readings θ that can be used to find the second largest and second smallest element, denoted $\theta_{(1)}$ and $\theta_{(2)}$, respectively.

$$ftavg(\theta) = \left\lfloor \frac{\theta_{(1)} + \theta_{(2)}}{2} \right\rfloor$$

$$Cfn(p, \Theta_p^i) = ftavg(\Theta_p^i)$$

Now we have collected all the ingredients to define the interval clocks IC_p^i:

$$adj_p^i = \begin{cases} 0 & \text{if } i = 0 \\ Cfn(p, \Theta_p^i) - PC_p(t_p^i) & \text{if } i > 0 \end{cases}$$
$$IC_p^i(t) = PC_p(t) + adj_p^i$$

Despite the various additional notations the interval clocks are nothing but an abstracted version of the local clocks introduced in the previous section. In fact, one can prove the following theorem that relates interval clocks to local clocks:

For all p, i, and t: $IC_p^i(t) = LC_p^i(t)$

For the rest of this section we briefly sketch the derivation of the precision enhancement property described in the previous subsection for the TTP convergence function *Cfn*. The formalized proof follows closely the one presented by Miner [12] for the fault-tolerant midpoint algorithm which coincides with the TTP algorithm since only two values are used for averaging. For both of these convergence functions, the bound $\Pi(X, Y)$ is given by

$$\Pi(X, Y) = \left\lceil X + \frac{Y}{2} \right\rceil$$

The crucial step in the proof of precision enhancement is to show that for any two nodes there is at least one good reading in the range of values that are selected for the computation of the average by those nodes; this is more formally stated in the following lemma:

> Given two arrays of readings θ and γ, there exists a $l \in C$ such that
> $$\gamma(l) \leq \gamma_{(1)} \text{ and } \theta_{(2)} \leq \theta(l)$$

For the TTP instance we define C as the intersection of the domains S_p^i and S_q^i of the two readings θ and γ, respectively. In order to accomplish the proof of this lemma, C has to contain at least $N - F$ elements and N must be greater or equal $3F + 1$. While the latter constraint is trivially true for TTP as N equals 4 and F is 1, the former requires more effort to be validated. In the concrete TTP instance this constraint requires us to show that the intersection of the slot numbers on the stacks of any two nodes p and q contains at least 3 elements. The derivation of this property can informally be described as follows:

Case 1: The messages that are sent in the last four slots immediately before the invocation of the synchronization algorithm are received correctly by both p and q.

Hence, both nodes have the same slot numbers on their stacks and thus the size of C is 4.

Case 2: A fault occurred in the last four slots immediately before the invocation of the synchronization algorithm.

In this case, one of the two nodes has received a valid message, while the other has not. In TTP it is assumed that at most one such fault occurs in any n consecutive slots where n is the length of a TDMA round. For the TTP algorithm to tolerate a Byzantine fault n must be greater or equal 4. If less than 4 nodes are left in the network, the Byzantine requirement is waived for TTP [8]. In the case of a fault one of the two nodes stores a new time difference value and the corresponding slot number, x say, on its stacks while the other does not. At this time, C would contain 3 elements. The size of the set of common slots can be further decreased only if another fault occurs before the "bad" value x is pushed out of the stack, that is, within the next three slots. This is, however, contrary to the hypothesis that faults occur at least 4 slots apart. Hence, any two given nodes have at least three time difference values from the same set of slots on their stacks at the time the synchronization algorithm is executed.

The formal verification of this property in PVS turned out to be quite challenging, especially because the additional feature of discarding correct messages from some nodes according to the *SYF* flag had to be taken into account, too. This required some subtle reasoning about the cardinality of various sets of slot numbers. The complete PVS formalization contains quite a number of the definitions and proved formulas of which only the fewest can be described in this paper. A detailed description of the overall proof of clock synchronization for TTP together with the PVS specification files can be found in a forthcoming technical report [14].

5   Integration into a general framework for time-triggered systems

As in the context of general program verification it is a natural approach to verify the various aspects of fault-tolerant algorithms at different levels of abstraction that capture the essence of the property under concern. Following this idea of a hierarchical treatment J. Rushby has presented a framework for a systematic formal verification of time-triggered implementations of round-based algorithms [15].

The algorithm is first specified as a functional program – a form that is best suited for a formal and mechanical analysis since at this level the proofs are generally accomplished by (more or less) simple inductions. Then the functional program is transformed into an untimed synchronous system. Although this transformation can be carried out systematically to some some extent [1, 15], the correctness of this step must be accomplished separately. The last step is then to refine the untimed system into a time-triggered implementation. The correctness of the latter step can be verified independently of the algorithm concerned. Thus, provided care is taken with respect to fault modes, properties and the correctness of the algorithm directly carry over from the untimed system to the time-triggered implementation.

For the proof of the correctness of this latter transformation it is required, however, that the clocks of the nodes in the cluster are synchronized. The state of a node p in the untimed synchronous system model after a given number r of rounds is specified by a function $run(r)$ that applies the state transition function $trans$ to the current state of p by recursing on r. While in the untimed system all nodes proceed in discrete steps one has to find a certain instant where the nodes of the time-triggered system all are in the same round in order to relate the global state of the time-triggered system to the one of the untimed model. Rushby defines the *global start time* of a round r, denoted $gs(r)$, to be the real time when the slowest clock begins this round and proves by establishing a simulation relationship that for all rounds the states of the two systems correspond:

$$ttss(p)(VC_p(gs(r))) = run(r)(p)$$

Synchronization of the clocks is now required to ensure that faster clocks do not drift too far that some other node would have already started its computation phase (and possibly changed its state).

In order to provide the necessary synchronization we have incorporated our development for the TTP clock synchronization into Rushby's model. This required some re-organization of the PVS theories, but the overall structure of the proofs needed not to be changed. Figure 2 shows the structure of the extended model. The two boxes on the top represent a fault-tolerant algorithm specified as a functional program and expressed in an untimed synchronous system, respectively. The dashed arrow between these boxes indicates that the relationship between these two representations of the algorithm must be established by a separate correctness proof. The box at the bottom stands for the time-triggered implementation of the algorithm that can generically be shown to be a refinement of the untimed system, hence the use of a solid arrow here.

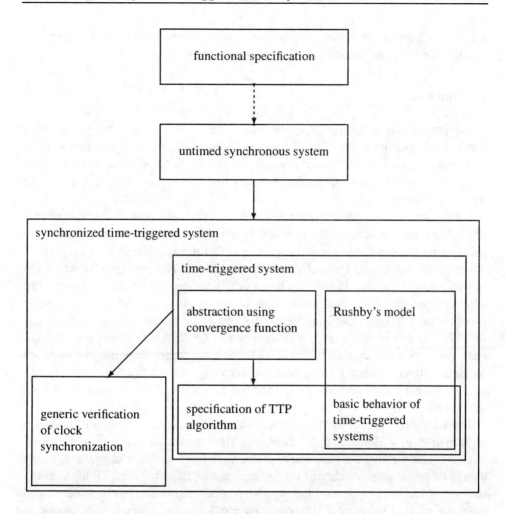

Figure 2: Structure of the general model for verifying time-triggered algorithms extended by the proof of clock synchronization.

Linking the clock synchronization proof to this general framework gives more structure to the formal model of time-triggered systems, illustrated by the box at the bottom: the right-hand side of it represents what is our adaption of Rushby's PVS theory. Some of definitions concerning the description of the basic behavior of time-triggered systems have been separated out to be used in the specification of the clock synchronization algorithm of TTP, cf. Sect. 3 . The derivation of abstract properties of the algorithm together with the remaining definitions of Rushby's model form the time-triggered implementation of the TTP clock synchronization algorithm that makes use of the generic derivation to verify the synchronization property.

In this framework it is now possible to specify other services of the TTP protocol such as group membership on the level of untimed synchronous systems (cf. [6]). This more abstract level is justified by the existence of synchronized clocks. Linking the clock synchronization proof to this level of abstraction thus makes the inter-relationship between various protocol services more explicit.

6 Conclusion

We have presented the formal verification of the clock synchronization algorithm that is implemented in the Time-Triggered Protocol (TTP). We have developed a formal model of TTP in the verification systems PVS. In order to make the mechanical analysis feasible the model abstracts from all features that are not relevant for clock synchronization.

For the actual verification, major emphasis has been given to making use of previous work on formally verifying clock synchronization algorithms. This led to splitting up the proof into a generic part in which the synchronization property is proved based on several abstract assumptions, and a TTP-specific part in which the specification of the algorithm is shown to satisfy those assumptions. This two-step approach reduced the overall verification effort, even though the existing generic proofs needed to be adapted and generalized to accommodate the particular needs of TTP. The specification and verification system PVS that has been used as mechanical proof assistant directly supports such an approach: theorems can be based on assumptions, and when using concrete instances of those theorems PVS serves as a book keeper that requires proofs for the concrete values to satisfy all the assumptions.

For the generic part of the verification with PVS we used a variant of the theory of Schwier and v. Henke [19] for averaging algorithms; for TTP we had to generalize some of the abstract parameters of the model and related assumptions. In the course of proving the validity of the generic assumptions for the TTP algorithm a major task has been to abstract the algorithm specification that has been developed from the existing informal TTP specification to a level at which it is expressed in terms of the concepts that are used in the generic proofs. In contrast to previous work on clock synchronization, the fault hypothesis of TTP would not be captured appropriately if faults were directly related to certain nodes. Instead of considering faulty nodes, it was therefore necessary to reason about whether or not a fault occurred in a given slot; this made it quite challenging to verify that at the times of synchronization all the nodes have readings that originate from a sufficiently large common set of slots.

The verified clock synchronization theory has been linked to Rushby's general approach to verifying time-triggered algorithms [15]. This framework assumes clocks to be synchronized; we have shown how the clock synchronization of TTP can be integrated, within a common PVS context, with the framework to provide the assumed service. This allows other protocol services to be analyzed at the level of untimed synchronous systems, rather than at the level of their time-triggered implementation, without losing the completeness in the chain of formal argumentation.

Future work will be concerned with extending the formal model to include other aspects and services of TTP. Currently, we are examining how the correctness proof for a group membership protocol similar to the one of TTP [6] can be adapted to the actual TTP algorithm. Moreover, the general framework could be expanded to capture initialization and re-integration of nodes.

References

[1] W. Bevier and W. Young. The Design and Proof of Correctness of a Fault-Tolerant Circuit. In J. Meyer and R. Schlichting, editors, *Dependable Computing for Critical Applications*, volume 6 of *Dependable Computing and Fault-Tolerant Systems*, pages 243–260. Springer-Verlag, 1991.

[2] R. W. Butler and G. B. Finelli. The Infeasibility of Quantifying the Reliability of Life-Critical Real-Time Software. *IEEE Trans. on Software Engineering*, 19(1):3–12, Jan. 1993.

[3] B. Di Vito and R. Butler. Formal Techniques for Synchronized Fault-Tolerant Systems. In *Dependable Computing for Critical Applications – 3*, Dependable Computing and Fault-Tolerant Systems, pages 279–306. pringer Verlag, 1992.

[4] D. Dolev, J. Halpern, and H. Strong. On the Possibility and Impossibility of Achieving Clock Synchronization. *Journal of Computer and System Sciences*, 36(2):230–250, April 1986.

[5] G. Heiner and T. Thurner. Time-Triggered Architecture for Safety-Related Distributed Real-Time Systems in Transportation Systems. In *Proc. 28th International Symposium on Fault-Tolerant Computing (FTCS '98)*. IEEE Computer Society, 1998.

[6] S. Katz, P. Lincoln, and J. Rushby. Low-Overhead Time-Triggered Group Membership. In Marios Mavronicolas and Philippas Tsigas, editors, *11th International Workshop on Distributed Algorithms (WDAG '97)*, volume 1320 of *Lecture Notes in Computer Science*, pages 155–169. Springer Verlag, September 1997.

[7] H. Kopetz. The Time-Triggered Approach to Real-Time System Design. In B. Randell, J.-C. Laprie, H. Kopetz, and B. Littlewood, editors, *Predictably Dependable Computing Systems*. Springer, 1995.

[8] H. Kopetz. Specification of the Basic TTP/C Protocol. Internal project document, not publicly available, 1998.

[9] H. Kopetz and G. Grünsteidl. TTP – A Time Triggered Protocol for Fault-Tolerant Real-Time Systems. *IEEE Computer*, 27(1):14–23, January 1994.

[10] H. Kopetz and W. Ochsenreiter. Clock Synchronization in Distributed Real-Time Systems. *IEEE Trans. Computers*, 36(8):933–940, August 1987.

[11] L. Lamport and P. M. Melliar-Smith. Synchronizing Clocks in the Presence of Faults. *JACM*, 32(1):52–78, Jan. 1985.

[12] P. S. Miner. Verification of Fault-Tolerant Clock Synchronization Systems. NASA Technical Paper 3349, NASA Langley Research Center, January 1994.

[13] S. Owre, J. Rushby, N. Shankar, and F. von Henke. Formal Verification for Fault-Tolerant Architectures: Prolegomena to the Design of PVS. *IEEE Trans. on Software Engineering*, 21(2):107–125, February 1995.

[14] H. Pfeifer, D. Schwier, and F. W. von Henke. Mechanical Verification of the TTP/C Clock Synchronization Algorithm. Ulmer Informatik Berichte, Universität Ulm, 1999. Forthcoming; will be available at http://www.informatik.uni-ulm.de/ki/PVS/papers.html.

[15] J. Rushby. Systematic Formal Verification for Fault-Tolerant Time-Triggered Algorithms. In M. Dal Cin, C. Meadows, and W. H. Sanders, editors, *Dependable Computing for Critical Applications – 6*, pages 203–222. IEEE Computer Society, March 1997.

[16] J. Rushby and F. von Henke. Formal Verification of Algorithms for Critical Systems. *IEEE Trans. on Software Engineering*, 19(1):13–23, January 1993.

[17] C. Scheidler, G. Heiner, R. Sasse, E. Fuchs, H. Kopetz, and C. Temple. Time-Triggered Architecture. In Jean-Yves Roger, Brian Stanford-Smith, and Paul T. Kidd, editors, *Advances in Information Technologies: The Business Challenge. Proceedings of EMMSEC'97 - European Multimedia, Microprocessor Systems and Electronic Commerce*. IOS Press, 1997.

[18] F. B. Schneider. Understanding Protocols for Byzantine Clock Synchronization. Technical Report 87-859, Cornell University, Aug. 1987.

[19] D. Schwier and F. W. von Henke. Mechanical Verification of Clock Synchronization Algorithms. In Anders P. Ravn and Hans Rischel, editors, *Formal Techniques in Real-Time and Fault-Tolerant Systems*, number 1486 in LNCS, pages 262–271. Springer, September 1998.

[20] N. Shankar. Mechanical Verification of a Schematic Byzantine Clock Synchronization Algorithm. Technical Report CR-4386, NASA, 1991.

[21] N. Shankar. Mechanical Verification of a Generalized Protocol for Byzantine Fault-Tolerant Clock Synchronization. In J. Vytopil, editor, *Formal Techniques in Real-Time and Fault-Tolerant Systems*, volume 571 of *Lecture Notes in Computer Science*, pages 217–236. Springer-Verlag, January 1992.

Fault Tolerance and Safety

PADRE : A Protocol for Asymmetric Duplex REdundancy

D. Essamé, J. Arlat, D. Powell
LAAS-CNRS, 7 avenue du colonel Roche, 31077 Toulouse cedex 4, France
{essame, arlat, dpowell}@laas.fr

Abstract

Safety and availability are issues of major importance in many critical systems. Ensuring simultaneously both attributes is sometimes difficult. Indeed, the introduction of redundancy to increase the overall system availability can lead to safety problems that would not otherwise exist. In this paper, we present a protocol for duplex redundancy management in critical systems that aims to increase the system availability without jeopardizing its safety. An application to a fully-automated train control system is described.

1 Introduction

Fault-tolerant computing systems are increasingly used to meet the stringent dependability requirements of automatic train control systems that, besides safety, extend to availability and to maintainability. Indeed, improvement of quality of service, continuity of service and cost-effective exploitation are adding new challenges to railway system designers beyond the underlying safety concerns. The introduction of redundant components is a necessary condition for increasing the overall system availability with respect to physical component failures. Here, we consider redundancy based on replicated *fail-safe* components. We formally investigate the conditions under which the safety properties of fail-safe components are preserved when they are replicated. We focus our analysis on duplicated fail-safe units interconnected with other such duplex systems by means of a local area network.

Given some safety constraints, we show that inconsistency of replicated units can lead to safety degradation even if each replicated component (taken individually) satisfies the given safety constraints. One way to circumvent such a problem is to avoid inconsistency by using, for example, an atomic broadcast protocol which ensures that replicated components agree on a consistent computational state. Unfortunately, such protocols rely on strong assumptions that cannot be satisfied with a sufficiently high confidence to meet the safety requirements of highly critical applications. Indeed, such a solution requires a perfectly reliable network ensuring bounded inter-process communication times.

Given that one cannot ensure that such strong assumptions will hold all the time in the real system, we propose a technique to tolerate state inconsistency. This technique consists in detecting potential inconsistencies and switching the system to a configuration that does not compromise safety in case of a real inconsistency. *PADRE* (Protocol for Asymmetric Duplex REdundancy) is an implementation of this technique for duplex redundancy, using the timed asynchronous system model [1]. We have chosen the timed asynchronous model because this model relies on realistic assumptions. Furthermore, our target systems (railway systems) have at least one safe state into which they can be switched at any point in time. This allows us to use the fail-awareness paradigm [2] to build a fail-safe protocol.

The rest of this paper is structured as follows. In *Section 2*, we state the problem by showing how state inconsistency can lead to safety degradation of replicated components even when each component is fail-safe. In *Section 3*, we present the system model. We formally investigate, in *Section 4*, the conditions under which the safety properties are preserved. In particular, we present a technique based on detection of potential inconsistencies and switching the duplex controller to a configuration where it does not impair safety in case of a real inconsistency. In *Section 5*, we present PADRE, which is a protocol that implements this technique using the timed asynchronous system model. Finally, *Section 6* concludes the paper.

2   Problem statement

The ability to build large complex systems from independently verified components is necessary for building affordable safe systems. For a critical system, it is important to guarantee that safety properties or *safety constraints* (*Sc*) of individual components are preserved in a system composed from those components. Given a set of n fail-safe redundant units u_1, u_2, ..., u_n which satisfy individually a safety constraint *Sc* and a system composed of u_1, u_2, ..., u_n, the main problem we address in this paper is the preservation of *Sc* in that composite system. We consider the special case where $n = 2$.

In this section, we show by means of an example that state inconsistency between redundant units can lead to violation of *Sc*.

2.1 Formalism and notations

In this sub-section, we define the formalism and notations that will be used in the rest of this paper. In particular, we formally define safety constraints by using temporal logic.

Here we consider a linear temporal logic, based on the set of real-time values Ω, with three temporal operators:

□ — meaning "*now and forever*",

◊ — meaning "*now or sometime in the future*",

$◊_d$ — meaning "*now or within bounded delay d in the future*".

Given a formula A then $□A$, $◊A$, and $◊_d A$ are also formulas. We use:

⊢ A to express that the formula A is a theorem, i.e., it is always true.

We now use this linear temporal logic to express safety constraints of a critical system processing a *critical transaction* defined as a sequence of actions which, if executed incorrectly, can lead to a catastrophic failure.

Given a critical transaction c_t and a unit u, we denote by h the predicate such that $h(c_t, u)$ is true if the unit u is executing the critical transaction c_t and false if not. We define a safety constraint with respect to a critical transaction c_t by means of two predicates L and R on the state S_u of a unit u as follows:

$$(h(c_t, u) \wedge L(S_u)) \Rightarrow □(h(c_t, u) \wedge R(S_u))$$

Such a formula expresses that, while executing the critical transaction c_t, if the state S_u of unit u becomes such that the predicate L holds then it must be the case that predicate R holds, and that S_u can only evolve in a way that allows the predicate R to continue to hold. We say that such a formula is a property of a unit u iff this formula is a theorem for that unit:

$$⊢ (h(c_t, u) \wedge L(S_u)) \Rightarrow □(h(c_t, u) \wedge R(S_u))$$

2.2 State inconsistency

The introduction of redundancy can lead to safety problems that would not otherwise exist. We illustrate this problem by means of an example. We consider a fully-automated train control system made up of a set of *section controllers*, each in charge of a section of railway track (Fig. 1). Control of a train is handed over from one controller to the next when the train is located in an *inter-section lock*. In such a system, one of the critical transactions to be handled is automatic train driving, which is carried out by assigning each train a "target". A target is the point up to which a train may proceed, e.g., the next station, the next intersection lock, the track block before the next train, etc. The section controller must ensure that there is no obstacle, e.g., another train, between the current position of the train and the assigned target.

One way to achieve such a requirement is to ensure that trains' positions are known precisely by the section controllers. The following strategy can be used. To enter into a new section, a train must be identified by the controller of that section while the train is in the lock. If the train is successfully identified, the train is registered in the *monitoring list* of the controller. This monitoring list allows the controller to periodically poll the trains under its control to check their positions.

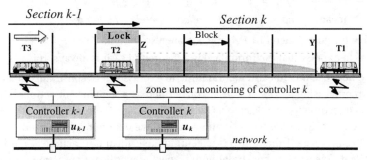

Fig. 1: Intersection handover with simplex controllers

Let us denote by *drive* the critical transaction of automatic driving. Let us consider the predicates $PROCEED_{Ti,Y}$ and $FREE_{Ti,Y}$ such that: $PROCEED_{Ti,Y}(Su_k)$ is true if the state of unit u_k allows the train Ti to proceed to the target Y and false otherwise; $FREE_{Ti,Y}(Su_k)$ is true if according to the state of unit u_k the track is free between the current position of the train Ti and the target Y and false otherwise. By using the previous formalism, one can define a safety constraint for the critical transaction *drive* with the following formula:

$$(h(drive,u_k) \wedge PROCEED_{Ti,Y}(Su_k)) \Rightarrow \Box(h(drive,u_k) \wedge FREE_{Ti,Y}(Su_k))$$

This formula means that, while unit u_k is executing drive ($h(drive, u_k)$ is true) then to authorize train Ti to proceed to Y ($PROCEED_{Ti,Y}(Su_k)$ is true), it must be the case that unit u_k perceives the track to be free between the train Ti and the target Y ($FREE_{Ti,Y}(Su_k)$ is true). Note that $PROCEED_{Ti,Y}(Su_k)$ cannot be true if u_k has not registered Ti (a controller cannot assign a target to a train it does not know), but this does not violate the safety constraint (without a new target, train Ti will stop at its previous target, in this case, point Z).

Let us consider now that the controller of section k is made up of two units u_{k1} and u_{k2} in primary/secondary configuration and with unit u_{k1} as the primary. Consider a handover scenario where, due to transmission errors, the primary unit

u_{k1} identifies and registers the train $T2$ at time t and assigns it the target Y, while the secondary unit u_{k2} does not register the train $T2$ (Fig. 1).

Now assume that unit u_{k1} fails at some time $t' > t$ while the train $T2$ is advancing to the target Y, so u_{k2} becomes the primary unit of the duplex controller (Fig. 2).

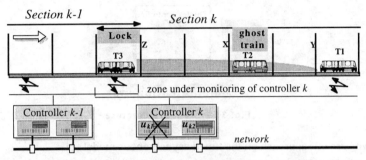

Fig. 2: Intersection handover with duplex controllers

Since u_{k2} has not registered the train $T2$, this train has become a "ghost train". Indeed, when the train $T3$ reaches the lock, it is identified by the unit u_{k2} which assigns it the target Y instead of X (Fig. 2). Of course, according to u_{k2}'s computational state there is no train between the current position of train $T3$ and the target Y ($FREE_{T3,Y}(Su_{k2}) = true$) so unit u_{k2} satisfies the safety constraint. However this will not prevent the train $T3$ from crashing into the train $T2$ if it attempts to reach its target Y. Such a situation cannot happen in absence of replication. Indeed, if the section controller consists of only a single unit and if this unit fails to register train $T2$ then, as stated earlier, train $T2$ would be forced to stop at its previous target Z instead of being authorized to enter section k.

To circumvent such a problem, one approach would be to re-specify the application, by taking into account the fact that the section controller is made up of two units. Before issuing a critical output (such as allowing a train to enter a new section), the lists of trains monitored by each unit could be compared to check that they are consistent. Unfortunately, such an *ad hoc* solution introduces redundancy-related considerations at the application level. This makes the application programs very expensive to build, to verify and to maintain. To avoid this, we propose a redundancy management mechanism (PADRE) that frees the application programmer from such complications.

3   System model

We consider distributed real-time systems for critical applications with networked controllers made up of two fail-safe units The units can communicate with each other and with remote units by messages sent over a network (Fig. 3).

Fig. 3: System architecture

We base our approach on the timed asynchronous model [1].

First, the network is very reliable, but not enough for human lives to depend on it. Thus, from a safety viewpoint, we must assume that the network can lose or delay messages. However, message integrity is ensured by error-detecting codes. In the terminology of [3], messages sent over the network have omission/performance failure semantics.

Second, the units use a cyclic real-time executive such that it can be guaranteed that a message accepted by an operational unit will be processed in a bounded time interval or the unit will halt[1].

Third, although the local clocks of units are not synchronized, every unit checks the rate of drift of its local clock with respect to real-time and switches itself off if the drift exceeds a predefined bound[2]. Consequently, the local clock of an operational unit has a bounded rate of drift from real-time.

3.1   Local hardware clock

All processes that run on a unit can access the unit's hardware clock. Given a hardware local clock H, we denote by $H(t)$ the value displayed by H at real time t. We denote by Ω the set of real time values. Let ρ be the constant maximum drift rate that bounds the drift rate of a correct clock with $\rho \ll 1$. We assume that the clock granularity is negligible with respect to any useful time interval. In fact, we assume that a correct hardware local clock H satisfies the following relation:

$$\forall\ t_1, t_2 \in \Omega \qquad (t_2 - t_1)(1 - \rho) \le H(t_2) - H(t_1) \le (t_1 - t_2)(1 + \rho)$$

---

[1] Note that this is a stronger condition than that imposed by the process management service of [1].
[2] This requires the local clock to be self-checking; see [4, pp 94-97] for a rudimentary technique.

3.2 The datagram service

The datagram service provides primitives for transmitting unicast and broadcast messages. The datagram service can delay or lose messages but provides the following properties:

- *Validity:* if the datagram service delivers a message m to a process p at time t and identifies a process q as m's sender, then q has indeed sent m at some earlier time $s < t$.
- *No-duplication:* each message has a unique sender and is delivered at a destination process at most once.

We denote by $td(m)$ the transmission delay of a message m.

We assume that any message sent between two remote processes p and q has a transmission delay that is at least δ_{min} : $\forall m, td(m) \geq \delta_{min}$.

Messages can experience arbitrary transmission delays. However, we define a one-way time-out delay δ, such that: a message m whose transmission delay is at most δ, i.e., $td(m) \leq \delta$, is called *timely* otherwise, the message is *late.* The constant δ is closely related to the availability of services built using the timed asynchronous model. So, δ must be chosen such that most messages are delivered within δ time units (Fig. 4).

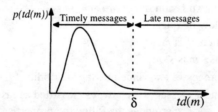

Fig. 4: Timely and late datagram messages

3.3 Δ-F-subsets and stable-subsets

Given a time interval and two processes p and q, we say that p and q are *F-connected* in that time interval, iff *i)* p and q are timely (their scheduling delays are bounded), *ii)* all but at most F messages sent between p and q are timely in that time interval (delivered within δ time units). When $F = 0$ we shall simply say that p and q are *connected.*

Given a constant Δ such that $\Delta > \delta$, a process p is Δ-*disconnected* from a process q in a given time interval, iff any message m that is delivered to p during that time interval from q has a transmission delay greater than Δ time units.

We say that a non empty subset of processes S is a $\Delta\text{-}F\text{-}subset$ in an interval $[s,\ t]$ iff all processes in S are F-connected in $[s,\ t]$ and processes in S are Δ-disconnected from all other processes. The notion of $\Delta\text{-}F\text{-}subset$ was introduced in [1][3].

We say that a non empty subset of processes S is a *stable-subset* in an interval $[s,\ t]$ iff S is a $\Delta\text{-}0\text{-}subset$ in $[s,\ t]$. The notion of stable-subset is very useful when using the timed asynchronous system model. Indeed, a stable subset has the same behavior as that defined by the synchronous system model. This allows problems such as consensus to be specifiable in the timed asynchronous system model, but with respect to stable-subsets. Such specifications rely on a *progress assumption* [5] that states that the system is infinitely often "stable": there exists some constant η such that for any time s, there exists a time $t \geq s$ and a majority of processes SS such that SS forms a stable-subset in $[t,\ t+\eta]$.

3.4 The fail-aware datagram service

The basic datagram service presented in Section 3.2 can delay messages. However, since such late messages can impair safety, we require a fail-aware datagram service similar to the one described in [6].

Given a constant Δ, the fail-aware datagram service computes an upper bound $ub(m)$ on the real transmission delay of each m and classifies m as *fast* or *slow* according to the following rule:

if $ub(m) < \Delta$ **then** m is *fast*
       else m is *slow.*

In particular, if processes exchange message periodically, the constant Δ can be chosen such that timely messages are always classified as fast messages. Then, the fail-aware datagram service provides the following properties:

- *Validity:* if the fail-aware datagram service delivers a message m to a process p at time t and identifies a process q as m's sender, then q has indeed sent m at some earlier time $s < t$.
- *No-duplication:* each message has a unique sender and is delivered at a destination process at most once.
- *Fail-awareness:* each message classified as a *fast* message has experienced a real transmission delay of at most Δ time units.

$$\forall m\ (m\ \text{is}\ \textit{fast}) \Rightarrow (td(m) < \Delta)$$

---

[3]In [1], the term $\Delta\text{-}F\text{-}partition$ was used. We have chosen the term $\Delta\text{-}F\text{-}subset$ to avoid misunderstanding with the mathematical meaning of a partition as a set of disjoint subsets.

- *Timeliness*: there exists a constant τ such that if two processes p and q exchange messages at least every τ time units then, if p and q are connected in an interval $[s - \delta, s + \tau]$, each timely message sent in $[s, s + \tau]$ must be classified as a *fast* message.

For more details on how to compute the upper bound $ub(m)$ and how to choose the constant Δ such that the Fail-awareness property and the Timeliness property always hold, the reader should refer to [6].

The fail-aware datagram service is fundamental for our redundancy management mechanism. Indeed, this service is used to detect when the communication system has suffered a performance failure. In addition, our mechanism uses the same fail-awareness philosophy to deliver messages to the application layer.

4 Safety properties preservation in a duplex controller

We have shown in Section 2.2 that state inconsistency can impair safety. One solution to handle this problem could have been to avoid state inconsistency by having units agree before accepting new inputs. Unfortunately, it has been shown that two units cannot achieve agreement if messages between them can be lost (e.g., see the two generals' problem in [7]). Here, we present an alternative solution that allows the safety constraints to be guaranteed by tolerating state inconsistency. The key idea of our approach is to detect potential state inconsistencies and to switch the duplex controller to a configuration which allows the safety constraints to hold in case of a real inconsistency. To achieve that, we use an *asymmetric coordination* of replicated units. The asymmetric coordination of replicated units consists of letting one unit, called the *Primary*, have a dominating role with respect to the other unit. The Primary can take unilateral decisions (such as the order in which the inputs must be accepted). The Primary can impose its choice on the other unit without resorting to a consensus protocol. Asymmetric coordination is particularly attractive when it is impossible to have a majority agreement, as in the case of a duplex controller. However, one can only use this technique if the Primary cannot send erroneous messages, which is the case here since all units are fail-safe.

4.1 Mode of operation of a fail safe-unit

To achieve the asymmetric coordination of a duplex controller, we define four modes of operation for each fail-safe unit: *primary*, *standby*, *quarantine* and *failed* (Fig. 5). When the unit is in the quarantine or failed modes, it is said to be *non-*

operational or *safe*, and cannot deliver outputs to the environment. A unit in the primary or standby modes is said to be *operational*.

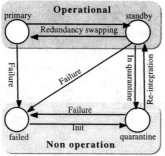

Fig. 5: Modes of operation of a fail safe unit

A unit is in the *primary* mode when it is the current Primary. A unit in the standby or the quarantine modes is called the Secondary. The current Secondary can be in the *standby* mode only if its state is consistent with the current Primary's state. Otherwise, it is in the *quarantine* mode. The quarantine mode is an intermediate mode that is introduced for safety purposes: the Secondary is put in quarantine when its state might be inconsistent with the Primary's state. Toward this goal, we can state the following objective for safe operation: *The protocol that manages the redundant pair of units must either ensure that their states are kept consistent or else force the Secondary into the quarantine mode.*

The quarantine mode allows a configuration of the duplex controller (one unit in the primary mode and the other unit in the quarantine mode) which does not impair safety. Indeed, when the Secondary unit is in quarantine, it is non-operational, so it cannot carry out any interaction with the environment (thus avoiding actions that could be in conflict with safety actions carried out by the Primary unit), nor can it be switched to the primary mode (thus avoiding the sort of situation described in Section 2.2).

We call *nominal configuration*, the configuration where one unit is in the primary mode and the other unit is in the standby mode. We call *safe configuration*, the configuration where one unit is in the primary mode while the other unit is in quarantine. In the nominal configuration, availability is ensured even a unit fails. In the safe configuration, fault-tolerance is sacrificed temporally so as to ensure safety. In that configuration, availability is only ensured if the current Primary does not fail. However, in both configurations, safety is always ensured. In the safe configuration, a recovery procedure allows the Secondary unit to reinitialize its state from the Primary unit, allowing the duplex controller to revert to the nominal configuration.

In the next two subsections, we give some safety-related and availability-related properties of the redundancy management mechanism.

4.2   Safety-related properties

We call *history* of unit u at time t, denoted $H(u,t)$, the string of events that unit u has accepted since its initialization up until time t, ordered following the time of taking them into account. Given two units i and j, we say that $H(i,t)$ is a *prefix* of $H(j,t)$ (denoted $H(i,t) \text{ p } H(j,t)$) iff $H(i,t)$ is a segment of $H(j,t)$ and $inf(H(i,t)) = inf(H(j,t))$ where $inf(H(i,t))$ denotes the first element of $H(i,t)$.

Let $S_u(t)$ be the state of a unit u at time t and $E_u(t)$ its mode, with $E_u(t) \in \{primary, standby, quarantine, failed\}$. Here we define three properties that are needed to guarantee a safe behavior of a redundant pair of fail-safe units u_1 and u_2. Given i and j, such that $i,j \in \{u_1,u_2\}$, $i \neq j$, then the following properties are required[4] :

UP: *Unique Primary:* both units cannot be in the primary mode simultaneously:

   $\vdash (E_i = primary) \Rightarrow (E_j \neq primary)$

MQ: *Quarantine:* the Secondary unit must leave the standby mode within a bounded delay Q if its state is inconsistent with the Primary's state and it cannot return to the standby mode while its state is inconsistent:

   $\vdash (E_i = primary) \wedge (S_i \neq S_j) \Rightarrow \Diamond_Q \Box ((S_i \neq S_j) \Rightarrow (E_j \neq standby))$

PH: *Prefix of History:* the history of the Primary unit must always be a prefix of the history of the Secondary unit:

   $\vdash (E_i = primary) \wedge (E_j = standby) \Rightarrow (H(i) \text{ p } (H(j))$

The *UP* property prohibits the possibility of having two Primary units. This is for safety, since we must have only one Primary at any given instant. The *MQ* property reflects the need to ensure that the Secondary unit cannot be maintained in the standby mode if its state is inconsistent with the Primary's state. However, inconsistency is authorized for a bounded duration (operator $\Diamond_Q$) at the end of which the Secondary unit must leave the standby mode. The Secondary unit cannot come back to the standby mode while its state is still inconsistent (operator $\Box$). The *PH* property ensures that the Secondary unit is aware of all events that have been taken into account by the Primary. In particular, this property ensures that the computation carried out by the Secondary unit cannot be late with respect to that of the Primary unit. This is a very useful property when redundancy switching occurs. Indeed, it ensures that the Secondary unit has

---

[4] The temporal logic notation allows all properties to be stated without explicit time parameters.

at least the same knowledge of the controlled process as the Primary unit. So, since both units are fail-safe, if the Primary unit leaves the controlled process in a non-dangerous state then the Secondary unit, when becoming Primary will maintain the controlled process in a non-dangerous state.

Moreover, property *PH* guarantees that the Secondary unit cannot revert to the standby mode without recovering its history from the Primary unit. Indeed, let us suppose that unit *i* is in the primary mode ($E_i = primary$) and that unit *j* does not recover its history from unit *i*, i.e: $\neg(H(i) \text{ p } (H(j))$, we have:

(1) $\vdash (E_i = primary)$; (hypothesis: unit *i* is in the primary mode)

(2) $\vdash \neg(H(i) \text{ p } (H(j))$; (hypothesis: unit *j* does not recover its history from unit *i*)

(3) $\vdash (E_i = primary) \wedge (E_j = standby) \Rightarrow (H(i) \text{ p } (H(j))$; property *PH*

(4) $\vdash \neg(H(i) \text{ p } (H(j)) \Rightarrow \neg((E_i = primary) \wedge (E_j = standby))$; contraposition of (3)

(5) $\vdash \neg(E_i = primary) \vee \neg(E_j = standby)$; modus ponens on (2) and (4)

(6) $\vdash (E_i = primary) \Rightarrow \neg(E_j = standby)$; rewriting of (5) and definition of $\Rightarrow$

(7) $\vdash \neg(E_j = standby)$; modus ponens on (1) and (6); or equivalently:

(8) $\vdash E_j \neq standby$; unit *j* cannot be in the standby mode ■.

This result can be summarized by the following relation:

$$\vdash (E_i = primary) \wedge \neg(H(i) \text{ p } (H(j)) \Rightarrow (E_j \neq standby).$$

In conclusion, property *PH* imposes the implementation of a recovery mechanism that allows the Secondary unit to recover its history from the Primary unit. It has been shown formally in [8] that properties *UP*, *MQ* and *PH* are sufficient to ensure preservation of the safety constraints of redundant fail-safe units in a duplex controller.

4.3 Availability-related properties

While a unit is in the quarantine mode, it cannot deliver outputs to the controlled process. Moreover, it is unable to replace the other unit should the latter fail. Consequently, to provide availability, the protocol must attempt to maintain the Secondary in the standby mode or to bring it back to that mode when it has been put into quarantine.

To ensure availability, two progress properties must therefore be respected, but only in the absence of failures:

AG: *Agreement*: there exists a constant τ such that, in absence of failures, every message accepted by one unit at time *t* must have been accepted by the other unit within the interval $[t - \omega, t + \omega]$

LQ: *Limited Quarantine*: in absence of failures, a unit in the quarantine mode must eventually switch back to the standby mode.

Property AG prevents useless solutions in which the unit in the standby mode immediately switches to the quarantine mode. Property LQ prevents the trivial solution in which one unit always remains in the quarantine mode. For safety, there is no obligation to achieve consistency or to maintain both units operational since those are availability requirements. However, there is an obligation to put and keep the Secondary unit in quarantine whenever its state is inconsistent with the Primary's state.

5 PADRE

In this section, we present a redundancy management protocol called PADRE (Protocol for Asymmetric Duplex REdundancy) which ensures the properties UP, MQ, PH, AG and LQ. The protocol is implemented by means of two protocol entities (one in each unit) which intercept all messages addressed to the application layer (Fig. 6). The protocol attempts to deliver all messages to the application layer of both units. If a transmission error should occur that prevents the message from being delivered to the application layer of both units, then a state inconsistency can occur. In this case, the protocol must ensure that property MQ holds by forcing the Secondary unit to switch to the quarantine mode.

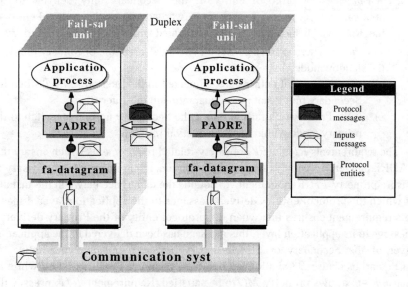

Fig. 6: Padre

5.1   Specifications

PADRE uses the fail-aware paradigm to ensure safety. The protocol relies on a fail-aware datagram service and satisfies the following requirements:

R1:   *Validity:* if PADRE delivers a message m to an application process p at time t and identifies a process q as m's sender, then q has indeed sent m at some earlier time $s < t$.

R2:   *No-duplication:* each message has a unique sender and is delivered at a destination process at most once.

R3:   *Fail-awareness:* there exist two constants ω and Q such that, if the protocol entity of the Primary unit receives a message m at time t, and the Secondary unit is in the standby mode, then:

    a)   either the protocol entity of the Primary delivers m to its application layer at time t_1 ($t_1 > t$) with a *true* indicator if m has been delivered to the application layer of the Secondary within the interval $[t - \omega, t]$.

    b)   or the protocol entity of the Primary delivers m to its application layer at time t_1 (with $t_1 > t + Q$) with a *false* indicator and the Secondary is put into quarantine, if it does not fail, at the latest at time $t + Q$.

R4:   *Asymmetry:* the protocol entity of the Secondary only delivers to the application layer messages that are forwarded to it by the protocol entity of the Primary. All such messages are delivered with their indicator set to *true*.

R5:   *Timeliness:* There exists a constant I such that when the Secondary unit is in the standby mode:

    a)   if both protocol entities are connected in the interval $[t, t + I]$, then the Secondary unit is not put in quarantine in this interval;

    b)   if the Primary unit fails at time t, the Secondary unit must switch to the primary mode within the time interval $[t, t + I]$.

The requirements *R1* and *R2* are safety-related requirements which ensure that PADRE delivers only real messages. Furthermore, requirement *R1* is necessary to ensure property *PH*. Requirement *R3* bounds the difference between the instants at which the protocol entities deliver messages to the application layer. Indeed, this requirement ensures that when the protocol entity of the Primary delivers a message to its application layer, this message has been delivered to the application layer of the Secondary or the Secondary has been put into quarantine. In particular, its clause *R3-a)* allows properties *AP* and *PH* to be satisfied while its clause *R3-b)* allows property *MQ* to be satisfied. Requirement *R4* expresses the asymmetric behavior of the protocol. An indicator set to *true* tells the application entity (should it wish to know) that the duplex pair is still capable of tolerating a fault. Requirement *R5* ensures that the duplex controller remains available in the absence of communication failures.

Property *UP* concerns the designation of the Primary unit. To fulfil this, it would have been desirable to use a software mechanism such as a leader election protocol. Therefore, considering the fault assumptions of our system model (unbounded communication delay and messages can be lost), this would require a third unit to allow a majority decision. The principle used would then be as follows: a unit of the duplex computer which wishes to become the Primary must obtain the support of that third unit, knowing that the latter can only support one unit at a time, and this support is of limited duration and has to be renewed periodically. Such an extension to redundancy levels greater than two is described in [8].

However, such an approach is contrary to the principle of autonomous duplex controllers. Therefore, the property *UP* is handled by hardware using a *bi-stable safety relay* which ensures that only one unit can be in the primary state at once.

In conclusion, the requirements *R1* through *R5*, together with the bi-stable safety relay, allow satisfaction of the properties *UP*, *MQ*, *PH* and *AP*. The property *LQ* is taken into account by the Secondary recovery mechanism, which will be described later.

5.2 Description

We successively describe the nominal and safe configurations.

Nominal configuration: in this configuration, both units are operational. So, safety is the key issue. The main idea is to attempt to ensure state consistency through broadcasting inputs to both units atomically. If atomicity cannot be ensured, the Secondary unit is put into quarantine, to ensure safety property *MQ*. The principle used is the following (Fig. 7):

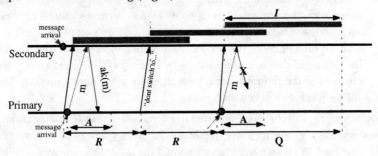

Fig. 7: PADRE principle

a) Primary

- Send, every R time units, a message to the Secondary "*Don't switch to quarantine*" and set the quarantine time out delay Q (the quarantine time-out delay is the time-out delay such that if the Primary stops sending "Don't switch to quarantine" messages at time t then the Secondary will leave the standby mode at the latest by time $t + Q$).

- Each time an input message is received from a remote controller, forward this message to the Secondary, set a *wait time-out* delay of A time units and wait for an acknowledgement:
  - if the acknowledgement is received before the *wait* time-out expires, accept the message;
  - if the *wait* time-out expires then start operating autonomously:
    - stop sending "*Don't switch to quarantine*" messages,
    - stop forwarding input messages to the Secondary,
    - accept the pending message(s) after the quarantine time-out delay Q expires.

- If the Primary fails, the safety relay will switch the current Secondary to the primary mode.

b) Secondary

- Wait for the periodic "*Don't switch to quarantine*" message. When receiving such a message, set a *stay-alive time-out* delay I (Fig. 7). If no such message is received before the stay-alive time-out expires, then switch to the quarantine mode.

- Each time an input message is received directly from a remote controller, forward this message to the Primary (when the Primary receives this message, it behaves as previously).

- Each time an input message is received from the Primary, send an acknowledgement to the Primary and accept the message. (Note that the message can be accepted immediately by the Secondary since the Primary has seen the same message, so the latter will either accept the message in a bounded time or cause the Secondary to switch to the quarantine mode.)

- The failure of the Secondary has no immediate effect. The Primary will be informed of the failure when it next attempts to forward a message since it will not receive an acknowledgement.

Safe configuration in this configuration, the Secondary unit is in quarantine. So, the key issue is availability since, while the Secondary unit is in quarantine, it is not in a position to replace the Primary should the latter fail. For availability, the state of the Secondary has to be made consistent with that of the Primary so that it can revert to its backup role. This is achieved by executing a protocol that copies the state of the Primary to the Secondary. We use the recursive state recovery protocol of [9]. In this protocol, the state is divided into "chunks" that can be transferred in a single message. A tagging mechanism is used to identify chunks that have been modified since they have been transferred. The transfer of chunks continues recursively until there are no newly-tagged chunks. The last chunk is identified as such by the Primary. The Secondary must remain in quarantine until state transfer has been successfully completed. The protocol can be summarized as follows:

a) Primary

- Transfer state to Secondary. When the last state transfer message has been sent to the Secondary[5]:
    - resume forwarding input messages, instead of delivering them directly to the application,
    - resume sending "*Don't switch to quarantine*" messages.

b) Secondary

- Wait for last state transfer message and switch to the standby mode.

For improved availability, messages and message acknowledgements can be repeated.

5.3   Choice of the quarantine time-out delay Q

Due to space restriction, we cannot give the expressions of all PADRE's parameters (A, R, I, ω and Q). However, since the quarantine time-out delay is a key parameter of PADRE, here we give the relationship that must be satisfied when choosing this delay.

To establish this relation, we consider the scenario illustrated by Fig. 8, where the Primary unit sends a "*Don't switch to quarantine*" message at time t_1 and this message is received by the Secondary unit at time t_2.

---

[5] Note that it is not necessary for the Primary to wait for the acknowledgment of the last chunk to resume forwarding input messages. If the last chunk is lost, then the Secondary will not switch to the standby mode and so will not acknowledge messages forwarded to it by the Primary, which will cause the latter to resume autonomous operation.

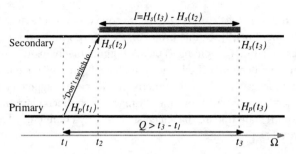

Fig. 8: The quarantine time-out delay Q

By definition, the "*Don't switch to quarantine*" message allows the Secondary unit to stay in the standby mode until time t_3 such that $I = H_s(t_3) - H_s(t_2)$ where I is the stay-alive time-out delay and H_s the clock of the Secondary unit. So that the Primary can be sure that the Secondary unit has put itself into quarantine, it is required that: $H_p(t_3) \leq H_p(t_1) + Q$ or equivalently: $Q \geq H_p(t_3) - H_p(t_1)$.

We have:

$$t_3 - t_1 = (t_3 - t_2) + (t_2 - t_1) \tag{1}$$

Since clocks of both units have bounded drift rate ($\rho \ll 1$), one can write:

$$H_p(t_3) - H_p(t_1) \leq (t_3 - t_1)(1+\rho) \tag{2}$$

and:

$$(t_3 - t_2) \leq (H_s(t_3) - H_s(t_2))(1+\rho) = I(1+\rho) \tag{3}$$

We use the fail-aware datagram service to transmit the "*Don't switch to quarantine*" messages and throw away all slow messages. This guarantees that the Secondary cannot use a message with a transfer delay greater than Δ to refresh its stay-alive time-out delay. So, one can write:

$$t_2 - t_1 \leq \Delta \tag{4}$$

Substituting (3) and (4) into (1) we obtain:

$$t_3 - t_1 \leq \Delta + I(1+\rho) \tag{5}$$

It follows from (2) and (5):

$$H_p(t_3) - H_p(t_1) \leq \Delta\,(1+\rho) + I(1+2\rho) \tag{6}$$

So, to ensure that the Secondary unit has put itself in quarantine knowing that the Primary unit has stopped sending "Don't switch to quarantine" messages, one must have:

$$Q \geq \Delta(1+\rho) + I(1+2\rho)$$

This use of time-out to communicate knowledge without explicit message passing is the "communication by time" paradigm of [1, 5].

5.4   Application of PADRE

PADRE has been applied to the fully automated train control system with networked duplex controllers considered in Section 2.2. We have shown that, in such a system, the inconsistency of lists of monitored trains maintained by each unit of a section controller can compromise safety. We illustrate in this subsection how PADRE can be used to circumvent such a problem without re-specifying the application. Indeed, PADRE allows transparent re-use of an application program designed for a non-redundant section controller.

Each replicated unit has a PADRE protocol entity which intercepts all messages that are addressed to the application modules of the unit. PADRE's protocol entity works as follows. When a message such as *"Train T2 is entering in section k"* is addressed to an application module, this message is intercepted by the protocol entity, which applies the protocol we have previously described. Let us suppose that the Primary unit of *section controller k* receives the message *"Train T2 is entering in section k"* (see Fig. 1). Its protocol entity will intercept this message and forward a copy to the protocol entity of the Secondary unit and set a timeout delay. If the protocol entity of the Secondary receives that copy, it sends an acknowledgment to the protocol entity of the Primary and delivers the message to the Secondary's application module. If the protocol entity of the Primary unit receives the acknowledgment before the timeout delay expires, it delivers the message to the Primary's application module. Otherwise, it stops refreshing the Secondary unit and waits Q time units since its last "Don't switch to quarantine" message before delivering the message to the Primary's application module.

This principle ensures that when the Secondary unit is not in quarantine, it is always aware of all events that have been taken into account by the Primary unit. This ensures safe operation of the duplex controller without changing the application modules.

6   Conclusion

In order to tolerate state inconsistency in a duplex fail-safe controller, we have presented a technique that consists in detecting potential inconsistencies and switching the duplex controller to a configuration where it does not impair safety in case of a real inconsistency.

Using the timed asynchronous model and the fail-awareness paradigm, we have developed a protocol which implements this technique. The key idea of the protocol is to try to keep both units consistent by attempting to agree on input messages; however, if this agreement fails, the protocol switches the duplex controller to a configuration ensuring safe operation.

This protocol has been applied to a fully-automated train control system made up of duplex controllers. This protocol provides a design paradigm enabling a substantial reduction in the cost of designing and validating critical systems.

Acknowledgments

This work was partially financed by Matra Transport International. The authors would particularly like to thank Philippe Forin and Benoît Fumery of Matra Transport International, for their stimulating inputs to this work. The authors also wish to express their sincere thanks to the anonymous reviewers for their valuable comments and suggestions.

7   References

[1]   F. Cristian and C. Fetzer, "The Timed Asynchronous Distributed System Model", in *28th Int. Symp. on Fault-Tolerant Computing (FTCS-28)*, (Munich, Germany), pp.140-149, IEEE Computer Society Press, 1998.

[2]   C. Fetzer and F. Cristian, "Using Fail-Awareness to Design Adaptive Real-Time Applications", in *National Aerospace and Electronics Conference*, (Dayton, Ohio, USA), pp.101-115, IEEE Computer Society Press, July 14 -18 1997.

[3]   F. Cristian, "Understanding Fault-Tolerant Distributed Systems", *Comm. ACM*, 34 (2), pp.56-78, 1991.

[4]   J. Wakerly, *Error Detecting Codes, Self-Checking Circuits and Applications*, Elsevier North-Holland, New York, 1978.

[5]   C. Fetzer and F. Cristian, "On the Possibility of Consensus in Asynchronous Systems", in *Pacific Rim Int. Symp. on Fault-Tolerant Systems*, (Newport Beach, CA), 1995.

[6]   C. Fetzer and F. Cristian, "A Fail-Aware Datagram Service", in *2nd Annual Worshop on Fault-Tolerant Parallel and Distributed Systems*, (Geneva, Switzerland), IEEE Computer Society Press, April 1997.

[7]   J. Gray, "Notes on Database Operating Systems", in *Operating Systems: An Advanced Course*, (R. Bayer, R. M. Graham and G. Seegmuller, Eds.), Lecture Notes in Computer Science, pp.393-481, Springer-Verlag, Berlin, 1978.

[8]   D. Essamé, *"Fault Tolerance in Critical Systems: Application to Automatic Subway Control"*, Doctoral Thesis, National Polytechnic Institute of Toulouse, LAAS-CNRS, Report N '98414, November 1998 (in French).

[9]   A. Bondavalli, F.-D. Giandomenico, F. Grandoni, D. Powell and C. Rabejac, "State Restoration in a COTS-Based N-Modular Architecture", in *1st IEEE Int. Symp. on Object-oriented Real-time Distributed Computing (ISORC'98)*, (Kyoto, Japan), pp.1-16, IEEE Computer Society, April 20-22 1998.

Experimental Validation of High-Speed Fault-Tolerant Systems Using Physical Fault Injection[1]

R. J. Martínez[1], P. J. Gil[2], G. Martín[1], C. Pérez[3], J.J. Serrano[2]

[1]Instituto de Robótica	[2]Dpto D.I.S.C.A.	[3]Dpto. de Informática
Universitat de València	U. Politécnica de Valencia	y Electrónica
Rafael.Martinez@uv.es	pgil@disca.upv.es	Universitat de València
Gregorio.Martin@uv.es	juanjo@disca.upv.es	Carlos.Perez@uv.es

Abstract

This paper introduces a new methodology for validation of dependable systems based on physical fault injection. The approach defines the elements of the injection environment and the requirements that are necessary to control the injection process with fine granularity, allowing for the elimination of glitches and not valid experiments and therefore making the validation process more accurate. We also show the main features of a high-speed pin level fault injection tool, AFIT (Advanced Fault Injection Tool), that incorporates most of the requirements necessary for the application of this methodology. As a practical case study we have validated FASST, a fault tolerant multiprocessor system composed of several fail-silent processor modules. The dependability of the system has been shown, including the influence of the error detection levels in the coverage and latency of the error.

Keywords: Physical fault injection, dependability validation, coverage, fail-silent module.

1. Introduction

When validating Fault Tolerant Systems (FTS's), the main objective must be to demonstrate that the behavior of the system conforms to its specifications. This process is an essential prerequisite to know how well the system will tolerate faults; it also quantifies some of the parameters that allow comparisons with other systems [1][4].

---

[1] This work has been partially supported by the ESPRIT Project contract P5212 and by the CICYT contract TAP96-1090-C04-01.

This process is not an easy task since it mostly covers aspects related to the overall design, prototyping and test of the analyzed system. Initially, the fault-tolerant algorithms and mechanisms (FTAMs) included in the system have to be identified and then quantified in order to know how well these mechanisms tolerate faults. This process is called experimental validation [2][3].

Experimental validation can be done in many stages of the system life cycle. In the design phase dependability measures can be obtained by simulating the system. However, when a prototype or the real system is available, the measurement elements can be set up in order to wait for incoming errors and then register the behavior of the system. Since fault rates of integrated circuits, systems and even software are quite low, this method is very time-intensive, becoming impractical. It is more efficient to stimulate the appearance of faults in the system (using physical or software implemented fault injection) and measure its consequences. The most important physical fault injection techniques are: heavy ion radiation [6], electromagnetic interference (EMI) [7], laser fault injection [8], scan chain-based fault injection [9] and pin level fault injection [4][5][12].

When validating a system by means of an experimental technique, especially if pin level fault injection is used, we have to care for errors derived from the measurement procedures and also for those that the measurement equipment induces over the system. If we also take into account that nowadays FTS'S are becoming very complex and fast, we soon realize the necessity of injecting faults of very short duration and the importance of the dismissal of the invalid experiments obtained during the injection campaign. These issues are studied in depth in this paper, in which are explained a new methodology that must be followed in order to obtain accuracy results in the injection campaign, the design of a high speed pin level fault injector and a practical case study of the validation of a prototype that shows the use of the methodology.

This paper first describes the methodology, establishing directions for fault injection, data acquisition and data processing procedures in order to make accurate fault injection campaigns. Section 3 describes the design of a high-speed physical fault injector named AFIT (Advanced Fault Injection Tool) [5] that solves the problems found when injecting faults in modern FTS'S [10]. In section 4 the validation of FASST (Fault Tolerant Architecture with Stable Storage Technology) [20], a fault tolerant, shared memory, multiprocessor system [16][18][19] is shown. In this section we have analyzed the latencies and coverages of error detection and recovery, in order to demonstrate the fail-silent assumptions made in the design of the processor modules. Finally, Section 5 shows the conclusions.

2. Fault injection methodology

While physical fault injection has some drawbacks (as it has been shown above), it is together with software implemented fault injection, a technique that evaluates prototypes or the real hardware. We propose the use of a new methodology, based on physical fault injection, suitable for the evaluation of high-speed processor systems. Applying this methodology we will be able to detect and discard the invalid experiments and, consequently, the goodness of the results derived from the injection will be increased.

2.1. Fault injection

One of the prerequisites of this methodology is the existence of a high-speed injection subsystem capable of perturbing the system with transient or intermittent faults of very short duration (tens of nanoseconds) at a high rate of injection. This subsystem must be capable of being programmed off-line for performing unattended experiments and should also provide an output signal to reset the system under evaluation. This signal has to drive the system to an initial state, providing the same conditions for every experiment in order to achieve the statistical correctness of the acquired data. Furthermore the injector should provide some way of signaling the beginning of the experiment and the detection of the effective error derived from the fault injection. A log file should be generated in order to account for the experiment number, injection point and kind and duration of the fault.

2.2. Data acquisition

Validation of a fault-tolerant system is intended for studying the coverages and latencies of the complex FTAMs it includes. When a single fault is injected, it is desirable to measure its influence over the whole system, since these mechanisms, in order to get maximum fault detection coverages, work in parallel.

To achieve this, for every mechanism we need to reproduce the initial conditions, inject the same fault and observe its behavior. However this practice has two drawbacks. First is very time-consuming. Second, due to the inherent complexity of the system workload and influence of the I/O subsystem, the exact conditions for each experiment are hard to guarantee. In consequence, data acquisition must be done in parallel, including several test probes that capture all the events that take place for all the FTAMs we want to evaluate.

If we inject faults at high rates, it is obvious that we also need measurement equipment capable of observing the system at these rates or higher. According to the maximum estimated latency of the fault detection mechanisms, we will therefore have to capture data at every clock cycle, in the interval starting at the time of detection of the effective error and ending when the error is no longer considered detected (maximum latency elapsed). The enormous amount of data collected can be stored, in the best of the cases, in the memory of the acquisition instrument for a single experiment. However, due to the unattended operation of the injection campaign, the readouts for multiple events must be accumulated, making this practice impossible. The solution is the use of a technique called *event triggering*, that consist in acquiring a single word of data only when changes of state in the selected signals are detected. A lot of memory space will be saved and therefore high-sampling rates for the entire campaign will be able to be used.

It is also required to incorporate in every step the time elapsed from the beginning of the injection, which will allow later calculating the latencies of the events. For example, in order to calculate the error detection coverage and latency, only the initial time and the error detection time for every experiment must be reported.

In addition, it is clear that the number of invalid experiments will be increased with speed. This is mainly produced by the induced capacitance of the probes, which can cause delays in the signals and introduce noise. Therefore it is essential to define a way for capturing data that will allow us later to discard not only the invalid experiments but also the erroneous measurements of the injection campaign. The idea is based on defining different triggers to make data acquisition that depend on the evolution of the injected fault. Every injection experiment follows a behavior pattern according to the state machine defined in Figure 1. Notice for example that if the injection has not been activated yet, or if the error is not effective, it is not possible to detect an error; or for example that the automaton will never enter the state of system recovery until the error has been detected. The sampling technique should take into account this state machine so that transitions will be enabled depending on the current state. When a transition takes place, a single acquisition and a timestamp must be done.

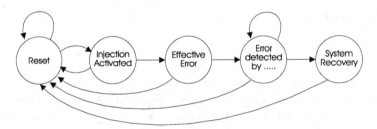

Figure 1: Evolution of the events in a experiment

2.3. Data processing

Once the injection campaign has been completed, it is necessary to process the readouts in order to calculate the most important dependability parameters of the system. The previous issues are moot if some technique to discard invalid data is not used. The simplest technique is to filter data in order to suppress glitches.

The timestamp of the acquisition instrument can be inspected to detect near coincident events that take place in the same signal. It is straightforward to eliminate the entries where a signal changes state twice and the others remain invariable for a defined short interval of time.

Once the glitches have been deleted, in addition the invalid experiments have to be eliminated. We can define the set of valid injected experiments, based on the automaton of Figure 1, as the set of every possible sequence of events (steps in the state machine) that start in the reset state and return to this state after visiting one of the rest of states. Next the readouts must be parsed and if the current experiment does not belong to the valid set of experiments we assume that an observation error has occurred and discard it. It is quite important to define a long reset time at the beginning of every experiment, since this drives the automaton to its initial state, and therefore is the basis for the parser synchronization.

The parser can also extract in parallel the timing information from the log, in order to calculate both the error detection and system recovery latencies for every valid experiment. In a simple example we can apply the following rules:

Error detection latency = Error detected timestamp − Effective error timestamp
System recovery latency = System recovery timestamp − Error detection timestamp

These values must be initialized to zero at the beginning. If the latency is still zero, this means not detection or not recovery, being straightforward to calculate the observed coverages, i.e. the percentages of error detection and recovery.

3. AFIT (Advanced Fault Injection Tool)

The first step to apply the methodology is the availability of the equipment that fulfills the requirements seen before. We have designed a new high-speed physical fault injector at the pin level that uses the forcing technique [4] for this purpose. New packaging technologies make quite difficult to include sockets in the FTS's boards, making the fault insertion technique inapplicable.

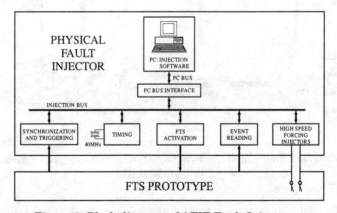

Figure 2: Block diagram of AFIT Fault Injector

AFIT injects faults at a frequency of 40 MHz, which is a considerable improvement over other fault injectors: MESSALINE [4] injects faults in signals up to 10 MHz and in [12] we can see that RIFLE injects faults in a system based on a 68000 processor running at 4 MHz. In order to achieve these high frequencies, we have carefully designed and terminated the input and output probes of the injector, taking care of reducing the capacitive effect they produce on the system

As shown in Figure 2, the injector [5] is split into five main modules: Synchronisation and Triggering module, Timing module, Fault Tolerant System

(FTS) Activation module, Event Reading module and High Speed Forcing Injectors module. All of these modules are connected through an Injection Bus to an IBM-compatible Personal Computer (PC). The PC Bus Interface block is a secondary module that connects the Injection Bus to the PC through an ISA bus interface. The rest of this section describes the main modules of the injection tool.

1. *Synchronisation and Triggering*: This module determines the beginning of the injection experiment. It is composed of two internal blocks, the Triggering Word Comparator and the Programmable Delay Generator, as Figure 3a depicts. After a Triggering Word (*TW*) has been programmed, and the injection has been enabled with the signal *IE*, this module samples some of the FTS signals (address, data or control signals) in order to determinate its Internal State (*IS*). When *IS* matches the programmed *TW*, and after a programmed delay, the second block of this module generates the Injection Triggering signal (*IT*), that activates the Timing module, which controls the fault injection. The programmed delay can be zero. In order to start the injection after the FTS has reached a stable state, several Reset Out (RESOUT) signals from the FTS have been added as inputs to this block.

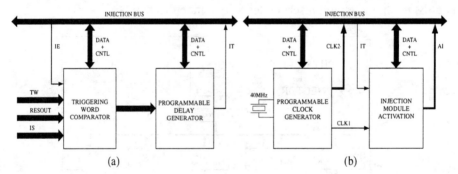

Figure 3: Block diagram of the Synchronisation and Triggering module (a), and Timing module (b)

2. *Timing*: This module (see Figure 3b) generates the clock frequencies used by the injector. These frequencies are programmable up to a maximum, currently 40 MHz. Furthermore, it provides the Activation of the Injection signals (AI) that activate the High Speed Forcing Injectors. The shapes of AI signals depend on the number of faults to inject, and on whether each fault is transient, intermittent, or permanent.

3. *FTS Activation*: The main function of this module is to prepare the FTS for each injection experiment, initialising it and activating its inputs with a predetermined Activation Vector AV. This module consists of two blocks (see Figure 4a): The Programmable Reset Generator activates several Reset Input (RESIN) signals of the FTS. The active level of each signal is programmable. These signals are used to initialise all the circuits of the

FTS. The other module, called Activation Module, programs several other activation signals (OAS) of the FTS prototype in order to set them to a predefined initial state

4. *Event Reading*: This determines the response of the FTS after the fault has been injected. This is done by measuring, using an internal counter and a trace memory based on FIFOs (see Figure 4b), the different elapsed times from the activation of IT, to the final recovery. Variations of the ERRV (Error Vector) signal, which characterise the response of the FTS after the fault, are stored in the State FIFO, and the value of the 24 bit counter, which indicates the time elapsed since the activation of IT, is stored in the Timing FIFO. The blocks Previous State Latch and New State Detector activate the Write enable of the FIFOs if any change in ERRV has occurred. If the counter overflows, the value of ERRV and the time associated are also written in the FIFOs. In this way, both fast and slow events in the ERRV signals can be managed, since this module acts as a transitional logic analyser.

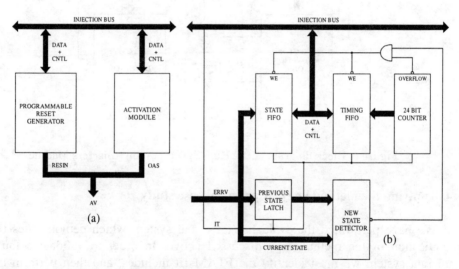

Figure 4: Block diagram of the Activation module (a) and
Event Reading module (b).

Observing the ERRV signals requires special input probes to connect this module with the FTS, since the frequency of these signals can be up to 40MHz. These probes are based in a frequency compensated voltage divider, which divides by 10 the observed signal, reducing by 10 the parasitic capacitance induced to each ERRV signal. This solution is very common in the design of input probes for oscilloscopes and logic analyzers.

5. *High Speed Forcing Injectors*: They physically inject the faults into the FTS. When the injectors receive the AI signals, the Injector Activation Logic (see Figure 5) sets one of the gates of the transistors – the one on the top injects type "1" faults and the one on the bottom injects type "0" faults.

The transistor selected injects the fault in the FTS through the lines IOUT (Injection Outputs). In order to obtain a very low delay in the injection of the faults, the injectors have been built with very low gate capacitance MOSFETs. Furthermore, a special termination circuit that loads each FTS signal only with a capacitance of about 8 pF has been implemented in each IOUT probe.

The other internal block, called Effective Error Detector, sets the MEE (Memory of Effective Error) only if the IOUT signal has forced the pin selected in the FTS. In other case, the error has not been effective, and this signal is not set. This means that the experiment is not successful, because for example, we try to inject a "1" in a pin that is already set to "1". The MEE signal can be read by the PC and is also one of the ERRV signals.

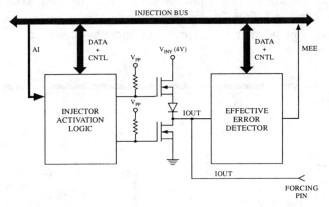

Figure 5: Block diagram of the High Speed Forcing Injectors Module

4. Applying the methodology: A practical case study

We have performed the evaluation of a real system which demonstrates the application of the methodology discussed above. In order to validate a fault-tolerant system we must identify the FTAMs it includes, and then perform the injection campaign according to these elements. First the prototype will be described, and then will be shown how the methodology has been applied.

4.1. System description

The system elected was FASST, a fault-tolerant multiprocessor system composed by several fail-silent processor modules. The FASST prototype is made of two DPUs (Data Processing Units), a stable memory module and a channel for I/O computations. Each module is a Futurebus+ Profile B compliant device [17].

When a DPU fails, in case of error detection, the processor is immediately halted and the module is disconnected [15], in order to prevent it from corrupting the rest of the system. Eventually the other modules will detect the module failure and will start the reconfiguration and recovery tasks, allowing the graceful degradation of the system.

The key to achieve fault tolerance are the processor modules, which include complex levels of fault tolerance mechanisms (see Figure 6) to ensure low error detection latencies and a high error detection coverage [11][13].

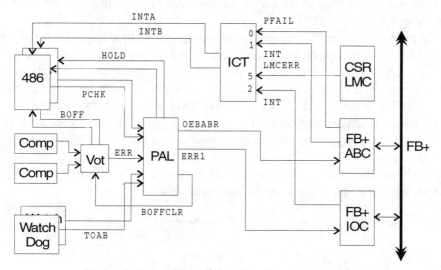

Figure 6: Error detection mechanisms in the DPUs

The module has been designed using a dual architecture. The board incorporates two Intel 486DX2-66 processors running in lock-step. Both processors execute the same instructions with identical data and most signals are compared at every clock cycle in order to detect errors. In the event of an error it is assumed to be a transient condition and the processor activity is stopped for 16 cycles. After this, the last cycle is restarted to recover the transient fault. If the error is reproduced again the module is disconnected from the system bus. In addition to this mechanism, inverted logic is used to build pairs of comparators that perform the same function. In consequence, the main checker receives information regarding processor errors in a duplicate complementary code that allows the detection of comparator errors.

The two data buses are also protected with parity and a pair of watchdog timers has been included to detect errors that affect the normal instruction flow of the processor.

Any evaluation of FASST dependability must recognize that it strongly depends on the existence of fail-silent processor modules [14] and on rollback recovery capabilities of the operative modules through the use of a stable storage system [16][18].

4.2. The injection environment

FASST validation was made using pin level fault injection. In this system, since every processor signal is compared against its pair at every clock cycle, a minimal skew in these signals will cause comparison errors. It also incorporates a complex hierarchy of fault detection mechanisms where high-speed injection rates and low-resolution time in measurement instruments are required to evaluate the behavior of transient faults.

Taking into account the recommendations of the methodology discussed, and the FASST characteristics, we discarded the use of a single fault injector to make the campaign. We incorporated a logic analyzer to ensure the functions of the AFIT Even Read module, since it reduces the noise induced by the acquisition probes and also because it is able to trigger several events in the same injection. We used the Tektronix 9200 Digital Analyzing System (DAS). This device is able to perform event triggering with timestamps at 2.5 ns resolution, which is suitable for our experiment. Figure 7 shows a block diagram of the interconnection among the modules. The injector generates the reset signal and the effective error signal, and the logic analyzer is used just for capturing data.

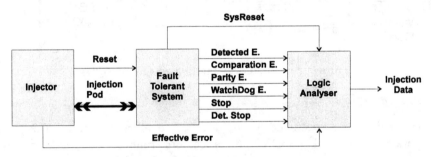

Figure 7: The injection environment

4.3. The injection campaign

The goals of the injection campaign are the estimation of the error detection coverages of the comparators, the parity and the watchdog timer included in the DPU and the calculation of the system recovery coverage. Another goal is to estimate the latency of the comparators in the detection of the error and the latency in the reconfiguration of the system. Furthermore, the time the module takes to halt once the error has been detected (in order to analyze the fail-silent characteristics) will be obtained.

In order to describe the campaign we need to define the injection attributes by means of the FARM sets [4]. The input domain is the set of faults to be injected (F set) and the activity of the system during the experiment (A set). The output domain consist of the readouts that describe the system behavior after the injection (R set) and the measures derived from the analysis of the previous sets.

4.3.1 F Set. Table 1 depicts the characteristics and the number of stuck-at injected faults according to the duration and the location of the fault. Permanent faults are active during 1.2 seconds. Transient faults are active during a random period between 100 ns and 4us. Intermittent faults are active periodically between 100 ns and 2 us in intervals between 1 and 65 ms. The injection point is randomly selected between the address bus, data bus and control bus of the master and slave processors, the host bus and the CSR bus. The connection of the AFIT IOUT signals has been done using special probes, both soldered to the vias of the FTS and connected to the processors prototyping socket.

		Injection point			
		Master processor	Slave processor	Host Bus	CSR Bus
Kind	Permanent	2640	2640	750	630
Of	Transient	2640	2640	750	630
fault	Intermittent	2640	2640	750	630
	Total:	7920	7920	2250	1890

Total injected faults:	19980

Table 1: Number, location and kind of injected faults

4.3.2 A Set. This set defines the application that is running in the system while the injection experiment takes place. A simple graphical user application is executed in parallel on two DPUs.

When one module detects an error, the system is reconfigured, isolating the faulty module and allowing the task to migrate to the other non-faulty module. The user application takes care of the establishment of recovery points, the sending of *I'm alive* messages using Futurebus+ driven interrupt messages and the use of watchdog timers. The user can trigger an artificial failure by activating an external switch which forces the cancellation of message generation. A further activation of the switch returns the system to normal behavior, simulating live insertion of the module.

4.3.3 R Set. A personal computer is responsible for controlling the whole injection campaign. This machine executes a program that makes AFIT to inject sequentially a predefined number of faults. For every experiment, after the selection of the kind of fault, its duration and the injection point, the prototype is reset and eventually the fault is injected. This program generates a log file that describes the current injected fault. When we execute this program, the analyzer already has to be ready to collect the readouts that characterize the system reaction to errors.

In the logic analyzer, we have programmed a state machine to drive data acquisition. This automaton (see Figure 8) is composed of several states that account for all the possible reactions in the evolution of a single experiment. The logic analyzer acquires new data, along with the absolute timestamp of the event, whenever a transition of the state machine takes place. The data elected to be stored in the DAS memory are the reset signal from the Futurebus+, the injection activated and effective error signal from the injection tool and the comparison error, parity error, watch-dog error and system recovered signals from the processor modules.

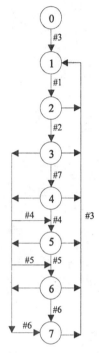

Nº	State	Actions
0	Initialisation	Wait for Reset activation
1	Reset	Activation time acquisition
2	Activated injection	Starting time acquisition
3	Effective Error	Error effective latency calculation
4	Error detected by comparison	Comparator e. detection latency calculation
5	System halted	Global error latency calculation. Acquisition of /Par and /WD
6	Error detected by the other DPU	Recovery system latency calculation
7	Experiment ended	Wait for Reset activation

	Transition triggering words							
	EEf	/Alny	/RST	/Par	/WD	Hold	/Cmp	/Rec
#1	X	X	1	X	X	X	X	X
#2	X	0	X	X	X	X	X	X
#3	X	X	0	X	X	X	X	X
#4	X	X	X	X	X	X	0	X
#5	X	X	X	X	X	1	X	X
#6	X	X	X	X	X	X	X	0
#7	1	X	X	X	X	X	X	X

Figure 8: State machine that controls the readouts

In the Reset state the state machine waits for the activation of a new experiment. When the injection takes place (assertion of signal *Activated Injection*) data is acquired and the state machine evolves to a new state depending on the trigger that has been detected (the analyzer monitors for the activation of one trigger every 2.5 ns). According to the first table of Figure 8, the detection of an error by the comparators, a system halt, a system reconfiguration or simply an assertion of the reset signal, which indicates that the experiment has ended and that a new one will proceed in a short time, can be signaled. As can be observed in the automaton, the word trigger #3, which corresponds to the detection of the reset signal activation, is enabled in every state. This is to ensure that the automaton will always return to the initial state at the beginning of the next experiment, independently of the behavior of the previous experiment.

4.3.4 The M Set. This set contains the results and conclusions obtained from the injection data analysis. The log obtained from the logic analyzer must be formatted and processed according to the following steps:
- Suppress the redundant information (captures with the same signal states).

- Eliminate the glitches (in our case, we discard the readouts with glitches shorter that 90 nanoseconds).
- Enumerate the experiments using the reset signal.
- Match this file with the log file generated by the personal computer. This establishes the system response for a specific kind of fault.
- Discard the non-effective errors (we discarded 9% of the injected faults).
- Assess the effect of the failure over the system.
- Calculate the latencies.
- Format the file to be included in a spreadsheet to facilitate the statistical study of the results.
- Classify the experiments according to the cases we want to observe in the evaluation of the system. This step is quite important since, again, it allows us to discard the invalid experiments of the campaign. Table 2 shows the set of possible behaviors of the FTAMs included in the system. The last column shows the frequency of the event.

Cod	/Par	/WD	$T_{complat}$	$T_{stoplat}$	T_{rec}	Event	%
1	1	1	0	0	0	An effective error is not propagated to the system. There is no failure	19.6
2	1	1	0	0	TR	Non-detected error (a detection coverage failure).	0.1
3	1 0 1	1 1 0	TC x x	TP	0	System failure. The error is detected but the recovery mechanisms fail.	1.9
4	1	1	TC	TP	TR	Comparison error detected	37.1
5	0	1	x	TP	TR	Parity error detected	28
6	1	0	x	TP	TR	Watch-dog error detected	2.7
7	1	1	0	TP	TR	The module is halted, however we can not guess the cause of the problem. The degradation process does not fail.	4.8
8	1	1	TC	0	0	Transient fault detected and recovered	2.4
9	1	1	TC	0	TR	System degradation due to a time overflow in the transient fault recovery process.	0
10	1	1	0	TP	0	The module is halted, however we can not guess the cause of the problem. The degradation process also fails.	3.4

TC, TP or TR means a value non equal to 0
x means do not care

Table 2: FTAMs possible evolution

In our experiment we must eliminate the cases that do not match with any of the events in Table 2, i.e. the case when a comparator error is detected while the reset signal is asserted. The use of the methodology has allowed us to detect a great deal of invalid cases, due to the noise induced by the injector and to the bad connection of the probes (we were even able to detect the open circuit of one of the analyzer probes).

Making a straightforward analysis of these cases according to the error detection and system reconfiguration capabilities, we can build the dependability predicate graph of the system [21]. Figure 9 shows the asymptotic error detection and system reconfiguration coverage of the system. We have included in the arrows the case number according to the previous table and also its frequencies.

This graph encapsulates the FASST dependability according to the fault injection campaign performed. It depicts the states of system evolution as a consequence of the faults.

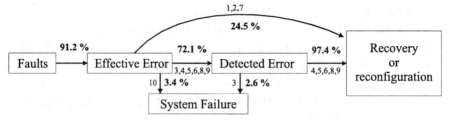

Figure 9: FASST fault-tolerance mechanisms predicate graph

One of the more important steps in the experimental validation is the measurement of the latency times of the error detection, module halt and system reconfiguration. This yields direct observation of the fail-silent characteristics of the module, and also the real-time capabilities of a simple application. The Table 3 shows the measures acquired in the injection experiment.

	Comparator	Parity	Watch-dog	Global
Error Detection	528	5242	1145	810
Module halt	6697.5	5242	1145	5170
System recovery	6,27E+08			

Table 3: Median of the latency times in nanoseconds

To conclude, the following graphs show the cumulative distribution function of the several error detection coverages versus time. These show the errors detected by the comparators, the errors detected by parity and the errors detected by the watchdog timers. Figure 10 shows a comparison of the coverages of the three error detection mechanisms. The horizontal axis shows the elapsed time from the activation of an effective error to the detection of the error. The vertical axis measures the percentage of cases where the error has been detected before the elapsed time.

The comparators exhibit the best error detection coverage and the least latency time, as could be expected, since they have been designed specially for the DPU. Practically in six microseconds they detect 90 % of detectable errors. On the other hand parity exhibits the worst coverage since many errors do not affect it. The graphic also shows the asymptotic fault detection coverage of the DPU, covering about 70 % of the injected faults.

Figure 11 shows the halt time of the DPU, i.e. the time elapsed from the moment the injected faults becomes effective until the HOLD signal of the processor is activated, thereby isolating the DPU from the system. This graph accounts for the fail-silent characteristics of the processor module. The initial low coverage of the comparators is due to the activation of the transient error detection mechanism when a comparison error is detected.

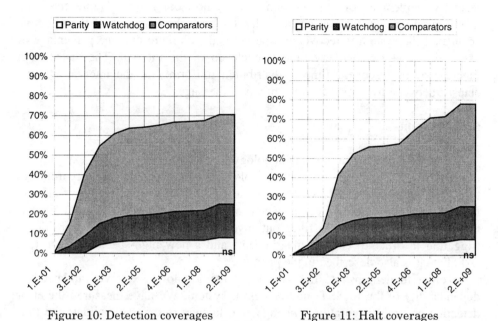

Figure 10: Detection coverages   Figure 11: Halt coverages

Figure 12 plots the percentage system recovery coverage over time. This process begins with the error detection phase. When the timer that accounts for the arrival of "I'm alive" message expires, the system reconfigures itself and the failed application is recovered.

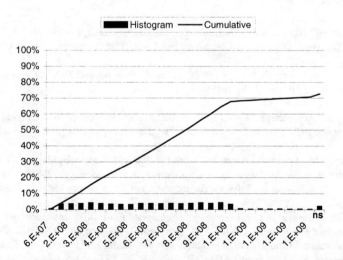

Figure 12: System recovery coverage versus time

The graph plots the frequencies of the several measured reconfiguration times, as well as the cumulative function of them, which represents the asymptotic recovery coverage of the system. The horizontal axis represents the reconfiguration latency; i.e. the time elapsed since the detection of the effective error until the system is recovered. The vertical axis represents the percentage of experiments whose recovery time is enclosed in the interval. The distribution function of the recovery time is distributed uniformly in the interval of time elapsed between two consecutive "I'm alive" messages.

5. Conclusions

We have introduced a new methodology for making the injection experiments more accurate. The basis of the methodology is to capture the data according to the fixed behavior pattern that follows the FTAMs of the system. Several state machines conduct data collecting which create a fixed acquisition pattern. It is therefore straightforward to filter out invalid experiments. We use transitional triggering in order to capture many events and a new high-speed injection tool (AFIT) that is also described in the paper.

In order to demonstrate the use of the methodology we have validated the dependability of the FASST multiprocessor system. We have measured the error detection and reconfiguration coverage, and latency in order to validate the fail-silent assumptions done in the design of the processor modules.

Future improvements of the AFIT tool under development include fitting it with new probes that exhibit low capacity at high frequencies and the design of new heuristics for the filtering out false error reading and other unexpected events.

6. References

[1]   J. Laprie. *"Dependability: basics concepts and associated terminology"*. Ed. Springer Verlag, 1992. Dependable Computing and Fault Tolerant Systems Series, number 5.

[2]   M. Hsueh, T. Tsai, R Iyer. *"Fault Injection. Techniques and Tools"*. Computer, Vol 30, n°. 4. IEEE, pp. 75-82. April 1997.

[3]   R. Iyer. *"Experimental Evaluation"*. 25th. International Symposium on Fault Tolerant Computing (FTCS-25). Special Issue Silver Jubilee, pp. 115-132. California. June 1995.

[4]   J. Arlat, M. Aguera, L. Amat, Y. Crouzet, J. Fabre, J. Laprie, E. Martins, D. Powel. *"Fault Injection for Dependability Validation: A Methodology and Some Applications"*. IEEE Transactions on Software Engineering, vol. 16, n° 2, pp. 166-182. February 1990.

[5]   P. Gil, J. Baraza, D. Gil, J. Serrano. *"High Speed Fault Injector for Safety Validation of Industrial Machinery"*. EWDC-8 (8th European Workshop on Dependable Computing). Experimental validation of dependable systems. Chalmers University of Technology, Göteborg, Sweden, April 1997.

[6]   U. Gunneflo, J. Karlsson, and J. Torin. *"Evaluation of error detection schemes using fault injection by heavy-ion radiation"*. 19th. International Symposium on Fault Tolerant Computing (FTCS-19), pp. 340-347. Chicago, MI, USA. June 1989.

[7]   J. Karlsson, P. Folkesson, J. Arlat, Y. Crouzet, G. Leber. *"Integration an Comparison of Three Physical Fault Injection Techniques"*. Predictably Dependable Computer Systems. Chapter V: Fault Injection, pp. 309-329. Springer Verlag, 1995.

[8]   J. R. Sampson, W. Moreno, F. Falquez. *"A technique for automatic validation of fault tolerant designs using laser fault injection"*. 28th. International Symposium on Fault Tolerant Computing (FTCS-28), pp. 162-167. Munich, Germany. IEEE. June 1998.

[9]   P. Folkesson, S. Svensson, J. Karlsson. *"A Comparison of simulation-based and scan chain implemented fault injection"*. 28th International Symposium on Fault Tolerant Computing (FTCS-28), pp. 284-293. Munich, Germany. IEEE. June 1998.

[10]   H. Madeira, J. Carreira, J.G. Silva. *"Injection of Faults in Complex Computers"*. IEEE Workshop on Evaluation Techniques for Dependable Systems. San Antonio. Texas. October 1995.

[11]   H. Madeira, J. Silva. *"Experimental Evaluation of the Fail Silent Behavior in Computers Without Error Masking"*. 24th International Symposium on Fault Tolerant Computing (FTCS-24), pp. 350-359. Austin, Texas. IEEE. June 1994.

[12]   H. Madeira, M. Rela, F. Moreira, J.G. Silva. *"RIFLE: A General Purpose Pin-level Fault Injector"*. First European Dependable Computing Conference (EDCC-1), pp. 199-216. Berlin, Germany. Springer Verlag. October 1994.

[13]   E. Fuchs. *"Validating the Fail-Silence Assumption of the MARS Architecture"*. Six International Working Conference on Dependable Computing for Critical Applications (DCCA-6). Grainau, Germany. March 1997.

[14]   R. D. Schlichting and F. B. Schneider. *"Fail-silent Processors: An Approach to Designing Fault-Tolerant Computing Systems"*. ACM Transactions on Computing Systems. Vol 1, nº. 3, pp. 222-238. August 1983.

[15]   G. Fabregat, C. Pérez, J.A. Boluda, R.J. Martínez and R. Munt. *"The FASST DPU Technical Description"*. FASST Project (ESPRIT P5212) Internal Report. July 1994.

[16]   FASST Project Consortium. *"FASST: Fault Tolerant Architecture with Stable Storage Technology"*. FASST Project (ESPRIT P5212) Technical Annex. 1990.

[17]   *"High-Performance I/O Bus Architecture: a Handbook for IEEE Futurebus+ Profile B"*. IEEE Standards Press. 1994.

[18]   FASST Project Consortium. *"The FASST Architecture: Overall Requirements and Specifications"*. January 1992.

[19]   R.J. Martínez, C. Pérez, G. Fabregat, J.A. Boluda, F. Pardo. *"DPU: a FB+ based fault Tolerant System"*. Open Bus Systems '95, pp. 229-236. Zurich. Switzerland. June 1995.

[20]   R.J. Martínez. *"Evaluación Experimental por Inyección Física de Fallos de la Garantía de Funcionamiento de un Sistema Multiprocesador Tolerante a Fallos"*. Tesis Doctoral. Departamento de Informática y Electrónica. Universitat de València. September 1997.

[21]   J. Arlat, A. Costes, Y. Crouzet, J. Laprie, D. Powel. *"Fault Injection and Dependability Evaluation of Fault-Tolerant Systems"*. IEEE Transactions on Computers, Vol 42, nº. 8, pp. 913-923. August 1993.

Models of Partitioning for
Integrated Modular Avionics

A Model of Cooperative Noninterference for Integrated Modular Avionics

Ben L. Di Vito*
NASA Langley Research Center
Hampton, VA 23681 USA
b.l.divito@larc.nasa.gov

Abstract

The aviation industry is gradually moving toward the use of integrated modular avionics (IMA) for civilian transport aircraft, potentially leading to multiple avionics functions hosted on each hardware platform. An important concern for IMA is ensuring that applications are safely partitioned so they cannot interfere with one another. On the other hand, such applications routinely cooperate, so strict separation cannot be enforced. We present a formal model for demonstrating the absence of unintentional interference in the presence of controlled information sharing among cooperating applications. The formalization draws from the techniques developed for computer security models based on noninterference concepts. Excerpts from the model formalization expressed in the language of SRI's Prototype Verification System (PVS) are included.

1 Introduction

The aviation industry is gradually moving toward the use of integrated modular avionics (IMA) for civilian transport aircraft. IMA offers economic advantages by hosting multiple avionics applications on a single hardware platform. An important concern for IMA is ensuring that applications are safely partitioned so they cannot interfere with one another, particularly when high levels of criticality are involved. Furthermore, IMA would allow applications of different criticality to reside on the same platform, raising the need for strong assurances of partitioning.

NASA's Langley Research Center (LaRC) has been pursuing investigations into the avionics partitioning problem. This research is aimed at ensuring safe partitioning and logical noninterference among separate applications running on a shared Avionics Computer Resource (ACR). The investigations are strongly influenced by

---

*This work was performed while the author was with VíGYAN, Inc., Hampton, VA 23666, USA.

ongoing standardization efforts, in particular, the work of RTCA committee SC-182, which is currently refining the ACR concept, and the recently completed AR-INC 653 application executive (APEX) interface standard [1].

We have developed a formal model of partitioning suitable for evaluating the design of an ACR. The model draws from the conceptual and mathematical modeling techniques developed for computer security. This paper sketches a formulation of partitioning requirements that has been rigorously formalized using the language of PVS (Prototype Verification System) [9]. A more detailed account of the model is available in report form [4]. This work was performed in the context of a broad program of applied formal methods activity at LaRC [2].

2   Avionics Computer Resource

The Avionics Computer Resource[1] (ACR) is an embedded generic computing platform, able to host multiple applications (avionics functions), while providing space (memory) and time (scheduling) protection. A software operating system is a fundamental part of the ACR platform, ensuring that the execution of an application does not interfere with the execution of any other application. Dedicated computer resources allocated to applications must not conflict or lead to memory, schedule, or interrupt clashes. Shared computer resources must be allocated in a way that maintains the integrity of the resources and the separation of applications.

The ACR operating system provides highly robust, kernel-level services that may be used directly by the application developer or serve as the basis for higher level services. To earn certification, kernel services must be developed in accordance with regulatory requirements such as RTCA DO-178B [10]. When applications having different levels of criticality reside on the same ACR, the kernel and other key ACR components must be qualified at or above the level of the most critical application.

Underlying all aspects of the kernel is partition management. The kernel manages partitions using a deterministic scheduling regime (e.g., fixed round-robin algorithm or rate monotonic algorithm); controls communications between partitions; and provides consistent time management services, low-level I/O services, and ACR-level health management services. Figure 1 shows the ACR reference architecture envisioned by SC-182 (Level A is the most critical, Level E the least).

An ACR manages all hardware resources residing within the ACR and monitors access to all hardware resources connected to the ACR. The kernel runs on the ACR hardware with sufficient control over all hardware and software resources to ensure partitions are noninterfering. As is typically required of secure systems, this access mediation must be complete, tamper-proof, and assured.

In practice, what this means is that the kernel executes in its own protected domain with the highest privilege level available on the computer. Services are re-

---

[1]The term "resource" is overloaded in this domain. In the name "ACR," resource refers to a large structure composed of processor hardware and operating system software. Most of the time, however, we use the term resource to refer to smaller entities such as memory locations.

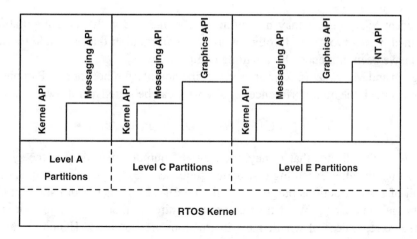

Figure 1: ACR Reference Architecture.

quested through a well-defined interface mechanism allowing users to pass parameters and receive results. Furthermore, partitions define the boundaries of resource protection. If processes or tasks are provided within partitions, ACR resource protection is not extended to enforce separation among them.

3 Formalizing Partitioning

We begin the formalization discussion by motivating the approach taken. Note that the scope of the formal models is limited to issues of space partitioning. Time partitioning and other notions of separation are not covered in this paper.

3.1 Security-Oriented Noninterference

Research in computer security has been active for many years, where three broad problem areas are generally recognized: 1) confidentiality (secrecy), 2) integrity (no unauthorized modification), and 3) denial of service. Much study has been directed at defense security needs, e.g., the "multilevel security" problem, which is primarily concerned with confidentiality. In this work the motivation comes from an operating environment where multiple users accessing a common computer system have different access permissions.

While many models have been devised to characterize and formalize security, researchers have had much success with the family of *noninterference models*. Originally introduced to address the confidentiality problem, these models can be applied to the integrity problem as well, which is the main concern in space partitioning.

Noninterference models focus on the notion of programs executing on behalf of (differently) authorized users. Each such program affects the system state in various ways as instructions are executed. Users may view portions of the system state through these programs. What noninterference means in this context is that if user v is not authorized to view information generated by user u, then the instructions executed by u's program may not influence (or interfere with) the computations performed by v's program. In other words, no information that v is able to view should have been influenced by anything computed by u.

Goguen and Meseguer [6,7] proposed the first noninterference model. Paraphrasing their model, the noninterference requirement can be stated as follows:

$$R(u, v) \supset O([[w]], v) = O([[P(w, u)]], v)$$

where $R(u, v)$ indicates that v may not view the outputs of u, $[[w]]$ is the system state that results after executing instruction sequence w, $P(w, u)$ is the sequence w with all of u's instructions purged from it, and $O(s, v)$ extracts from state s those outputs viewable by v. What this assertion requires is that v's view of the state is the same regardless of whether u's instructions are executed. Hence, u cannot "interfere" with v.

3.2 Extensions to Noninterference

After Goguen and Meseguer's original formulation, other researchers introduced variations and extensions of their model for various purposes. Important successors were the intransitive versions of noninterference formulated by Haigh and Young [8] and Rushby [12]. Roscoe, Woodcock and Wulf introduced a noteworthy formulation based on the CSP process algebra [11], which emphasizes determinism as an overriding principle.

Recently, researchers have begun to apply noninterference concepts to model the integrity of embedded control systems. Dutertre and Stavridou developed an elegant noninterference model [5] having some similarities to our own. Their model adopts a higher level of granularity, taking task execution as the basic entity. This model also takes the important step of addressing scheduling issues to capture time partitioning properties in addition to space partitioning. What the model lacks compared to ours is a provision for cooperating partitions.

Wilding, Hardin and Greve offer another model called "invariant performance" that falls in this same line of development [13]. Although couched in somewhat different terminology, their model is likewise based on noninterference ideas. They pursue a fine-grained and concrete formalism intended to model low-level hardware mechanisms as well as kernel services. Scheduling properties are an explicit part of the model. Also included is a PVS formulation of a prototype kernel known as Schultz, along with its invariant performance properties.

While the pure noninterference model is a powerful tool, its central requirement is too strong to be useful in a formalization of partitioning. The strict separation induced by this model is desirable in a security context, but is too confining in the IMA context. The reason is that cooperation and communication between ACR partitions is expressly allowed, albeit under controlled conditions.

Two types of cooperation can exist in an ACR environment: direct cooperation between partitions supported by operating system services, and indirect cooperation taking place through multiple access to avionics devices. The upshot is that it is permissible, under controlled conditions, for an application u to influence the computations of another application v, making a strict prohibition of "interference" too strong a requirement. It is possible to create a conditional noninterference model with suitable exemptions built in, but this runs the risk of exempting too much system behavior. Intransitive noninterference likewise could be used to capture exemptions. Instead, the modeling approach we have pursued takes the essence of these noninterference concepts and embeds them in a somewhat modified framework.

3.3 Modeling Partitioning

Drawing on LaRC's work with the Reliable Computing Platform (RCP) [3], our modeling approach resembles the similar technique of comparison against a "gold standard." In RCP, a comparison between a distributed implementation and a single-processor implementation was used to formalize a notion of fault tolerance. In an analogous way, we use a comparison between a federated system and an integrated system to formalize a notion of noninterference.

In both types of comparison, we start with identical application suites, we compare the effects of running applications in two different execution environments, then we try to rule out undesirable behaviors that might result when moving from the standard (assumed correct) architecture to the new (desired) architecture.

At the highest level, the following idealized method summarizes our approach:

- Given an ACR and its applications, map them into an equivalent federated system (each partitioned application in its own box).

- Model the externally visible behavior of the ACR with execution trace T_0. Assign traces $T_1, \ldots, T_n$ to the component behaviors in the federated system.

- Require that if $L(T_1, \ldots, T_n)$ is the set of feasible interleavings of $T_1, \ldots, T_n$, then $T_0 \in L(T_1, \ldots, T_n)$ is a valid consequence.

What this scheme aims to do is rule out the presence of any observable behaviors in the ACR that cannot be duplicated, at least in principle, by an equivalent federated system. In other words, if the applications were migrated from a federated to an integrated architecture, no new system behaviors (modulo minor scheduling differences) could be introduced. One consequence of this approach is the limitation that certain memory sharing arrangements cannot be directly accommodated, e.g., many of those involving multiple readers and writers. By adapting the techniques of Section 5, however, these features should be within reach.

4 Noninterference Without Cooperation

As a prelude to the discussion on cooperative noninterference, we begin with the presentation of a simpler baseline model, which assumes completely separate applications. No interpartition communication (IPC) is allowed in this baseline case. Each application computes in isolation, having access only to its own resources.

4.1 Basic Framework

There are six aspects of modeling we are concerned with, each described below. This categorization is used in the full presentation [4].

- **Representation.** A minimal set of architectural concepts is provided to represent features such as a resource name space, the system resource state, and the notion of commands.

- **Computation.** Execution of command sequences and the system's response traces form the essence of computations.

- **Separation.** Consider computation using alternative command sequences, in particular, those sequences formed by purging all commands except those belonging to a single partition. Response traces resulting from the separate execution of purged command streams are compared against segments of the integrated-system trace.

- **Requirement.** Having formed trace pairs, one from the original command stream and the other from the purged command streams, we stipulate the partitioning requirement as equality of the two traces. If this condition always holds, the same computations will always result, whether performed in integrated or separated fashion.

- **Policy.** To achieve strong partitioning, it is necessary for the ACR to properly allocate resources and enforce access to those resources according to a suitable policy. The policy and system design are chosen to ensure that the partitioning requirement is always met.

- **Verification.** Having modeled computation for the system features of interest, and captured the allocation and enforcement policy, it remains to show that the policy is a sufficient condition for the partitioning requirement. A proof is carried out to establish this result.

4.2 Model Elements

Details of the six modeling elements are presented below.

4.2.1 Representation The collective state of all applications running on an ACR is modified in response to each instruction or kernel service. State includes main memory areas allocated to applications, register bits in the processor itself, and certain devices that have memory-like semantics. Individual state elements reside in a set of locations called *resources*, denoted R. The value held by a resource is an unspecified information unit drawn from the set I. The current *resource state* is given by a mapping $S : R \rightarrow I$.

Applications compute by executing *commands*, which include ordinary machine instructions (either native, emulated, or interpreted), kernel service primitives, and possibly other operations. Each is considered an atomic operation, reading a set of arguments from the current state and writing a set of results to update the state. A command from the set K is a tuple (i, t, a, f, r), where i is the ID of the currently running application, t is the command type, a is a resource list indicating arguments to be read, f is a function with signature $f : I^* \rightarrow I^*$ representing a computation on the arguments, and r is a resource list indicating where results from function f should be written. We represent command sequences and traces by the *list* data type, semantically equivalent to that of Lisp.

4.2.2 Computation   Execution of a command to produce a new value of the system state is modeled by a function $X : K \times S \rightarrow S$. The current state is defined recursively by the cumulative application of X to a command list from K^* :

$$S(\langle \rangle) = S_0$$
$$S(C \circ \langle k \rangle) = X(k, S(C))$$

where C is a command list, k is a command, and $\circ$ denotes the sequence or list append operation.

As computations evolve, the results produced by a command sequence form a *computation trace*. A trace event, drawn from the set E, contains the values computed by the command and some identifying information as well. Construction of traces proceeds by applying the function $T : K \times S \rightarrow E$, which yields the computation event corresponding to a command's execution. The complete trace is defined recursively by the cumulative application of T to a command list from K^* :

$$D(\langle \rangle) = \langle \rangle$$
$$D(C \circ \langle k \rangle) = D(C) \circ \langle T(k, S(C)) \rangle$$

Thus, we have for a command list C two key computational products: $S(C)$ is the state after executing all the commands in C, and $D(C)$ is the trace recording all the computed results. These values describe computation within the confines of a single processor, with instructions from different partitions interleaved in the list C.

We focus on computation traces because the domain is real time control, where it is important to ensure that outputs sent to actuators are correct. State invariants fall one step short of what is needed. It is not enough to check that memory values are appropriate; what matters is what the system *does* with such values.

4.2.3 Separation   Now consider the mapping of the single processor (IMA) system into its equivalent federated system of multiple processors. Our goal is to take the same command stream and consider computation under two different architectures, integrated and federated. The method is to separate an integrated command stream into different threads of commands, one for each application (partition). Then computation is carried out separately for each individual thread.

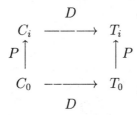

Figure 2: Trace-based partitioning requirement.

First we provide a purge function to separate the original command stream into the different threads. $P : K^* \times A \to K^*$ denotes the purge[2] function, mapping a command list C and application ID a into the appropriate subsequence of C. We overload the purge function by adding a version of it for traces. $P : E^* \times A \to E^*$ extracts those elements of a computation trace belonging to application a.

4.2.4 Requirement In the integrated system, the computation trace produced in response to a command list C is simply $D(C)$. We wish to compare portions of this trace to its analogs in the federated system.

When C is separated into subsequences based on partition, we have that the computation trace for case a is given by $D(P(C, a))$. Construct such a trace for each value a, then compare it to the subtrace found by purging the integrated trace $D(C)$. Thus the final partitioning requirement we seek has the form:

$$\forall a : P(D(C), a) = D(P(C, a))$$

The right hand side represents the computation applied to each command thread separately. Each processor in the federated system is assumed to be identical to the original, having the full complement of resources, although most will not be accessed (we hope) for a given choice of a. This formulation is similar to that of Dutertre and Stavridou [5].

Figure 2 illustrates the relationship of the various lists and traces in the manner of a classic commuting diagram, showing the familiar algebraic form of a homomorphism. In the figure we use C_0 to represent the original command list for the integrated system and $T_0 = D(C_0)$ its resulting computation trace. Then C_1 through C_n are the purged command lists and T_1 through T_n are their resulting traces.

If the access control policy of the system is working properly, then the effect of separation is invisible, yielding the same computation results as the integrated system. If, however, the policy or its enforcement is flawed in some way, one or more of the trace pairs above will differ, signaling a failure to achieve partitioning.

---

[2] The term "purge" was retained because of its historical use in noninterference models, although we now complement its selection semantics. $P(C, a)$ purges everything *not* belonging to a.

4.2.5   Policy   With the help of protection features embedded in processor hardware, the kernel enforces an access control policy on the use of system resources. We denote by the predicate $H(C)$ the condition of command list C adhering to such a policy and other well-formedness criteria. The policy and type of enforcement are system dependent; it is not possible to be more explicit about the details without considering the design features themselves.

4.2.6   Verification   Pulling together all the pieces, we can now state the theorem needed to establish that an ACR design achieves strong partitioning:

$$H(C) \supset \forall a : P(D(C), a) = D(P(C, a))$$

A proof of this conjecture for all command lists C shows that the applications will be well partitioned under ACR control.

4.3   PVS Formalization

A formalization of the baseline noninterference model was carried out using the language of PVS. This baseline assumes a simple IMA architecture for a system having a fixed set of applications, only a single type of command (machine instructions), and no interpartition communication. Assume further that each resource is accessible by at most one application, and resource allocation and access rights are static (permanently assigned).

Nearly all of the formalization necessary to capture the baseline model is unsurprising and we omit most of the details. We use the expressions do_all(cmds) to denote $D(C)$ and purge(cmds,a) to denote $P(C,a)$.

Let us now turn to the access control policy. Read and write access modes are independently supported. Each resource has an access control list (ACL) naming the applications that have access to it and in what mode(s). This degree of granularity is different from what a kernel implementation would maintain, where a range of resources would likely be assigned to one ACL.

```
access_mode:   TYPE = {READ, WRITE}
access_right:  TYPE = [# appl_id: appl_id,
                          mode: access_mode #]
access_set:    TYPE = set[access_right]
allocation:    TYPE = [resource -> access_set]
```

This scheme works to describe uses of memory and some devices. Input devices could have read-only access while output devices would be write-only.

Command lists adhering to the policy must satisfy a proper_access predicate, which requires that for every command, the application has read access to all argument resources and write access to all result resources. A predicate alloc declares the access control in effect for a given system. The following condition asserts a key requirement about alloc, namely, that a static allocation also obeys exclusivity (at most one application has access rights to each resource).

```
static_exclusive(alloc_fn: allocation): bool =
   FORALL (r: resource):
      EXISTS (a: appl_id):
         FORALL (ar: access_right):
            member(ar, alloc_fn(r)) IMPLIES a = appl_id(ar)

alloc: {p: allocation | static_exclusive(p)}
```

Finally, we arrive at the point where we must prove that enforcement of the policy is a sufficient condition for the partitioning requirement.

```
well_partitioned: THEOREM
   proper_access(cmds) IMPLIES
      purge(do_all(cmds), a) = do_all(purge(cmds, a))
```

A completely mechanical proof of the theorem well_partitioned has been constructed using the PVS theorem prover. It relies on nine supporting lemmas, the principal one being the following.

```
state_invariant: LEMMA
    proper_access(cmds) AND
    member((# appl_id := a, mode := READ #), alloc(r))
   IMPLIES
      state(cmds)(r) = state(purge(cmds, a))(r)
```

5 Cooperative Noninterference

We now consider the problem of introducing IPC services to the ACR architecture and deriving a notion of noninterference that accommodates cooperating applications. This feature is not addressed by either of the contemporary IMA models mentioned earlier [5, 13]. We draw a distinction between *resource partitioning*, protecting resources accessible to applications, and *communication partitioning*, protecting private data held by the kernel. The overall partitioning model is divided into two parts based on this distinction.

Section 5.1 describes the formalism for showing when application resources are protected from direct interference by other applications, which is an extension of the model in Section 4. Interpartition communication implemented by the kernel (or other ACR entities) presents the possibility of interference occurring within the kernel's domain. Section 5.2 develops the formalism for showing when the kernel can be considered free of flaws from this second type of interference.

We assume a basic IMA architecture having the same characteristics as before with the addition of IPC services. This leads to two classes of commands: machine instructions plus generic IPC kernel services. The exact types of communication and specific kernel services are not important for establishing resource partitioning, but they do play a role in establishing communication partitioning.

When IPC capability is added, the central problem that arises is that partitions are no longer noninterfering in the strict sense. Communicating applications do indeed "interfere" with one another. But this interdependence is intentional, and we must accept the cooperative interactions while prohibiting the unintended ones.

The primary means of achieving this goal is architectural. We observe the restriction that IPC is only allowed to occur through kernel services; no shared-memory communication is permitted. Some IPC services cause updates to application-owned resources. We incorporate constraints sufficient to keep such updates confined to one partition at a time. The net result is that we can assure that third-party partitions are protected from unintended effects during IPC activity.

Modeling this arrangement requires additional mechanisms based on the introduction of global and local portions of the system state. Local states are replicated as before to capture the separate computations of isolated processors. A global state is used to capture the computations of a part of the system we wish to hold in common for each replicated entity. The roles of local versus global will alternate for the two types of noninterference we seek to establish.

5.1 Resource Partitioning

Consider first the problem of showing that individually owned resources held by an application are shielded from direct interference. Other applications can influence resources indirectly, by sending information through IPC channels, but it should be impossible for them to access resources directly. By enforcing an access control policy on IPC services as well as processor instructions, resource partitioning can be demonstrated.

This result is obtained by replicating resource states, as before. IPC services require special treatment, however. IPC command execution draws inputs from both the resource state and the IPC state, and likewise produces outputs for both. We are not concerned with the details of IPC state updates because we only wish to compare the results produced by all the applications. As long as the same effects occur in both federated and integrated architectures, the exact nature of interpartition communication is immaterial.

This arrangement nevertheless complicates the elaboration of system computations. Resource states are now interdependent—it is no longer possible to separate the command sequences via $P(C, a)$ and then take the system's response to each separate stream. Doing so would miss the effects of IPC from an application's IPC partners. Hence, the elaboration of system computations is more intertwined, making concise mathematical notation difficult to achieve. Formalization using PVS functions, however, is readily accomplished. The definitions that follow show the replication of resource states while maintaining a common IPC state, as depicted in Figure 3.

We begin with the types representing the new state concepts. Local portions of the system state are accessed by indexing with application IDs. In addition to resource states, computation traces are kept within this structure. Traces are not part of the system state; it is simply convenient to keep a partition's trace together with its corresponding resource state.

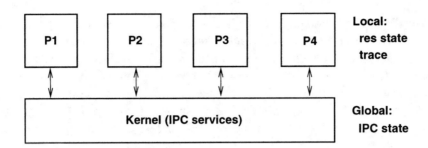

Figure 3: Global vs. local components for resource partitioning.

```
trace_state_appl:   TYPE = [# trace: comp_trace,
                               res:   res_state #]
init_trace_state_appl: trace_state_appl =
           (# trace := null, res := initial_res_state #)
trace_state_vector: TYPE = [appl_id -> trace_state_appl]
trace_state_full:   TYPE = [# local:  trace_state_vector,
                               global: IPC_state #]
```

It is also helpful to collect the local state and trace update expressions into a single update function.

```
comp_step(c: command, local: trace_state_appl,
          global: IPC_state): trace_state_appl =
   IF cmd_type(c) = IPC
      THEN (# trace := cons(IPC_event(c, res(local),
                                      global),
                            trace(local)),
             res    := res(exec_IPC(c, res(local),
                                    global)) #)
      ELSE (# trace := cons(INSTR_event(c, res(local)),
                                        trace(local)),
             res    := execute(c, res(local)) #)
   ENDIF
```

A command list is executed by the ensemble of separate processors and the common "kernel" that serves them. Each command updates the local state for one partition and, in the case of IPC commands, the global IPC state (Figure 4).

The function do_all_purge combines the roles previously served by the two functions do_all and purge. Two components are produced by this function: a vector of resource states and traces, one for each application, and a single, common IPC state. Execution of commands within do_all_purge keeps the partitions separate while allowing a common IPC state to evolve, thus ensuring that partitions receive meaningful values from their IPC operations, just as they do in the fully integrated system.

```
do_all_purge(cmds: cmd_list): RECURSIVE trace_state_full =
   CASES cmds OF
      null: (# local   := LAMBDA (a: appl_id):
                                    init_trace_state_appl,
                 global := initial_IPC_state #),
      cons(c, rest):
          LET prev = do_all_purge(rest) IN
          (# local   :=
                LAMBDA (a: appl_id):
                    IF a = appl_id(c)
                        THEN comp_step(c, local(prev)(a),
                                          global(prev))
                        ELSE local(prev)(a)
                    ENDIF,
             global :=
                IF cmd_type(c) = IPC
                    THEN IPC(exec_IPC(c,
                                res(local(prev)(appl_id(c))),
                                global(prev)))
                    ELSE global(prev)
                ENDIF
          #)
   ENDCASES    MEASURE length(cmds)
```

Figure 4: Computation in the resource partitioning model.

Access control policy in this design is identical to the baseline case. Each IPC command must adhere to the same access constraints as instruction commands. Consequently, an IPC command may access only those resources assigned to the partition requesting the IPC service. This is a reasonable restriction, and it is sufficient to ensure strong partitioning.

The main theorem for resource partitioning can be expressed as follows:

```
well_partitioned: THEOREM
    proper_access(cmds) IMPLIES
       purge(do_all(cmds), a) =
       trace(local(do_all_purge(cmds))(a))
```

This theorem has been proved in PVS with the help of some 20 supporting lemmas. The proof was more involved than the baseline case, but not overly so.

Shown below is the state invariant that holds after each command. The invariant asserts state-matching conditions for both local and global state components.

```
state_invariant: THEOREM
    proper_access(cmds) IMPLIES
       (FORALL a: state_match(a,
                    res(state(cmds)),
```

$$res(local(do\_all\_purge(cmds))(a)))) \text{ AND}$$
$$IPC(state(cmds)) = global(do\_all\_purge(cmds))$$

5.2 Communication Partitioning

The resource partitioning requirement offers assurance against direct interference caused by other applications. As long as a computation proceeds entirely within one partition, this property is sufficient to achieve independent operation. If, however, communication with other applications takes place, there are additional points of vulnerability. In particular, when data is in transit from one partition to another, temporarily being held within private ACR data structures rather than partition resources, there is a possibility of mishandling that is not covered by the previously stated requirements.

5.2.1 Inversion of System Model

Our approach is to apply the foregoing modeling framework and adapt it to the communication interference problem. What this involves is taking the traditional noninterference concept and turning it upside down. Rather than separating the applications, we choose instead to separate the IPC mechanisms within the kernel. We assume the kernel implements IPC using conventional techniques such as ports or channels. Imagine that we can separate and replicate the kernel's processing, assigning each port or channel to its own kernel "machine." Then we apply the techniques of the previous section, interchanging the roles of partitions and kernel. The partitions become the entity we hold in common while the kernel's IPC channels become the objects of separation, as if implemented by a federated system.

Application of the IPC noninterference technique requires the following steps.

- Identify the virtual IPC structures implemented within the kernel, such as ports, channels, pipes, etc. Create a vector of local states for the kernel based on these IPC structures.

- Create a global state containing the partition resources. Model computation of regular machine instructions with respect to the common global state.

- Model computation of IPC services with respect to the particular local state corresponding to the designated port, channel, etc.

- Assert that the computation results of the integrated system are the same as those of the IPC-based federated system.

From the modeling standpoint, this scheme produces a valuable dual of the traditional noninterference structure, although it may appear less intuitive. Moreover, the approach requires modeling more of the system design than is the case with resource partitioning. It is also important to note that no guarantee of functional correctness for IPC services is inherent; the method only demonstrates that the IPC structures are independent. Nevertheless, the method offers a tractable means of addressing the question of low-level interference within an ACR's operating system.

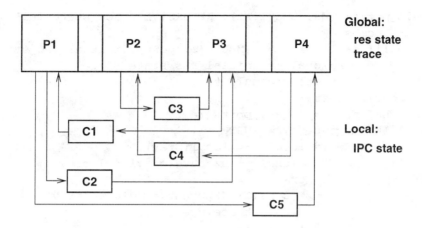

Figure 5: Global vs. local components for communication partitioning.

5.2.2 PVS Rendition   Assume a port-based IPC mechanism having the two services SEND and RECEIVE. No restrictions are placed on connectivity; ports may connect two or more partitions. Ordinary queueing behavior within the virtual channels is observed. The kernel's internal state needed to implement IPC is separated into multiple copies, one for each port in the federated system model, and the set is collected into a structure and referred to as local states (Figure 5). IPC commands operate on the global state and one of the local states. Conversely, instruction commands operate only on the global state.

The elaboration of computation is inverted from the model of Section 5.1, but otherwise works in the same manner. A composite structure containing the local and global states together with the computation trace is maintained. Only one computation trace, corresponding to the global resource state, is necessary.

```
IPC_state_vector: TYPE = [port -> IPC_state]
trace_state_full: TYPE = [# local:  IPC_state_vector,
                            global: res_state,
                            trace:  comp_trace #]
```

A command list is executed by the ensemble of partitions on one common processor and separate kernels for each port/channel. Figure 6 shows the details.

The function do_all_ports plays the same role as do_all_purge in the resource partitioning model. Three components are produced by this function: a vector of IPC states, one for each port; a single, common resource state; and a single computation trace. Execution of commands within do_all_ports keeps the IPC port structures separate while allowing a common resource state to evolve.

The main theorem for IPC partitioning can be expressed as follows:

```
well_partitioned: THEOREM
      do_all(cmds) = trace(do_all_ports(cmds))
```

This theorem has been proved in PVS with the help of five supporting lemmas. The

```
do_all_ports(cmds: cmd_list): RECURSIVE trace_state_full =
  CASES cmds OF
    null: (# local  := LAMBDA (p: port): initial_IPC_state,
             global := initial_res_state,
             trace  := null #),
    cons(c, rest):
      LET prev = do_all_ports(rest) IN
      IF cmd_type(c) = INSTR
        THEN (# local  := local(prev),
                global := execute(c, global(prev)),
                trace  :=
                  cons(INSTR_event(c, global(prev)),
                       trace(prev)) #)
        ELSE (# local  :=
                 LAMBDA (p: port):
                   IF p = port(c)
                     THEN IPC(exec_IPC(c, global(prev),
                                            local(prev)(p)))
                     ELSE local(prev)(p)
                   ENDIF,
                global :=
                  res(exec_IPC(c, global(prev),
                                    local(prev)(port(c)))),
                trace  :=
                  cons(IPC_event(c, global(prev),
                                     local(prev)(port(c))),
                       trace(prev)) #)
      ENDIF
  ENDCASES   MEASURE length(cmds)
```

Figure 6: Computation in the communication partitioning model.

proof was simpler than that of the previous models, owing to the simple nature of the IPC mechanism employed.

The overall state invariant is shown below. This invariant asserts state matching conditions for both local and global state components.

```
state_invariant: THEOREM
    res(state(cmds)) = global(do_all_ports(cmds)) AND
    FORALL p: IPC(state(cmds))(p) =
                 local(do_all_ports(cmds))(p)(p)
```

In place of an access control policy, the communication partitioning model might require assertions about how the kernel manages its internal resources, using these assertions to establish the noninterference condition. None was used here due to a highly abstract IPC design. A more realistic design and formalization would likely require such resource management constraints.

6 Conclusion

We have presented a formal model of partitioning suitable for analyzing an ACR architecture. Based in part on concepts drawn from the noninterference model used by researchers in information security, the model considers the way computations evolve in different system architectures. By defining what the system response should be in the case of a system of separate processors, the potentially interfering effects of integration can be assessed and identified.

By continuing the development begun here, more realistic model instances can be constructed and used to represent more complex systems with a variety of architectural features and specific kernel services. The PVS notation was found to be effective in expressing the model, the key requirements, and the supporting lemmas. The PVS prover was also found to be useful in carrying out the interactive proofs, all of which were completed for the designs undertaken.

In addition to IPC services, there is another area where applications may affect each other, namely, where external avionics devices are shared among multiple partitions. Allocation of such devices is typically dedicated rather than shared, but multiplexed access is possible in some architectures. For this reason, a partitioning model should accommodate this type of sharing if the need arises. We have not extended our core model to cover this case, but anticipate no problems in doing so.

Acknowledgments

The author is grateful for the cooperation and support of NASA Langley researchers during the course of this study, in particular, Ricky Butler. Discussions with Paul Miner of LaRC were also helpful in clarifying ideas. Participating in RTCA committee SC-182 has been valuable in focusing on key aspects of the avionics environment. The work of John Rushby from SRI International has likewise been useful in identifying important issues related to partitioning. Ongoing support of the PVS toolset by SRI has kept the mechanical proof activity productive.

This work was supported in part by the National Aeronautics and Space Administration under Contract NAS1-96014.

References

[1] Aeronautical Radio, Inc., Annapolis, Maryland. *ARINC Specification 653: Avionics Application Software Standard Interface*, January 1997. Prepared by the Airlines Electronic Engineering Committee.

[2] Ricky W. Butler, James L. Caldwell, Victor A. Carreno, C. Michael Holloway, Paul S. Miner, and Ben L. Di Vito. NASA Langley's research and technology transfer program in formal methods. In *Tenth Annual Conference on Computer Assurance (COMPASS 95)*, Gaithersburg, MD, June 1995.

[3] Ricky W. Butler, Ben L. Di Vito, and C. Michael Holloway. Formal design and verification of a reliable computing platform for real-time control (Phase 3 results). NASA Technical Memorandum 109140, August 1994. Earlier reports are numbered 102716 and 104196.

[4] Ben L. Di Vito. A formal model of partitioning for integrated modular avionics. NASA Contractor Report NASA/CR-1998-208703, August 1998.

[5] Bruno Dutertre and Victoria Stavridou. A model of noninterference for integrating mixed-criticality software components. In *Proceedings of Dependable Computing for Critical Applications*, San Jose, California, January 1999.

[6] Joseph A. Goguen and José Meseguer. Security policies and security models. In *Proceedings of 1982 Symposium on Security and Privacy*, Oakland, California, May 1982. IEEE.

[7] Joseph A. Goguen and José Meseguer. Unwinding and inference control. In *Proceedings of 1984 Symposium on Security and Privacy*, Oakland, California, May 1984. IEEE.

[8] J. Thomas Haigh and William D. Young. Extending the noninterference version of MLS for SAT. *IEEE Transactions on Software Engineering*, 13(2):141–150, February 1987.

[9] Sam Owre, John Rushby, Natarajan Shankar, and Friedrich von Henke. Formal verification for fault-tolerant architectures: Prolegomena to the design of PVS. *IEEE Transactions on Software Engineering*, 21(2):107–125, February 1995.

[10] Requirements and Technical Concepts for Aviation, Washington, DC. *Software Considerations in Airborne Systems and Equipment Certification*, December 1992. DO-178B, known in Europe as EURO-CAE ED-12B.

[11] A.W. Roscoe, J.C.P. Woodcock, and L. Wulf. Non-interference through determinism. *Journal of Computer Security*, 4(1):27–53, 1996.

[12] John Rushby. Noninterference, transitivity, and channel-control security policies. Technical Report CSL-92-02, SRI International, December 1992.

[13] Matthew M. Wilding, David S. Hardin, and David A. Greve. Invariant performance: A statement of task isolation useful for embedded application integration. In *Proceedings of Dependable Computing for Critical Applications*, San Jose, California, January 1999.

Invariant Performance: A Statement of Task Isolation Useful for Embedded Application Integration

Matthew M. Wilding, David S. Hardin, and David A. Greve

Rockwell Collins, Inc.
Advanced Technology Center
Cedar Rapids, IA 52498 USA
{mmwildin, dshardin, dagreve}@collins.rockwell.com

Abstract

We describe the challenge of embedded application integration and argue that the conventional formal verification approach of proving abstract behavior is not useful in this domain. We introduce invariant performance, *a formulation of task isolation useful for application integration. We demonstrate invariant performance by formalizing it in the logic of PVS for a simple yet realistic embedded system.*

1 Introduction

Integration of multiple real-time embedded applications onto a single processor is increasingly attractive because the capacity of computing devices continues to grow. The use of fewer devices reduces space and power consumption that can be very valuable in an embedded environment, and fewer device connections increase reliability. Greater integration can also simplify the development of fault-tolerant architectures.

Integration of applications poses daunting challenges as well, because integrated applications may interact. Applications that share computing resources can interfere with each other's *space* — values saved in memory by an application — and *timing* — the rate at which an application performs.

The system developer who wants to integrate an application with other applications has several concerns:

safety Can any other application in the system affect an application's performance to cause it not to meet its requirements?

security Can other applications in the system glean information that should be restricted to one application?

verification level Must each application be verified at the confidence level associated with the most critical application in the system?

verification completeness Has the verification of each application taken into account the many ways other applications might interfere with it?

These challenges can be met if the host computer system provides an encapsulation mechanism that separates applications so that they can be verified separately. This kind of mechanism, known as a "partitioning" system in the avionics community, allows not only the verification of integrated applications initially but can eliminate the need for reverification in future system configurations. An encapsulation mechanism must be no less trusted than the most trusted application in the system, so it is natural to turn to formal verification to gain a high level of confidence.

Operating system correctness statements in the literature have proved inadequate for application integration, so we have developed our own that we call *invariant performance*. In this paper we describe related work and introduce our notion of task isolation that allows separate verification of applications. We describe a small operating system and underlying hardware and a correctness statement that supports encapsulation useful for separate verification of integrated applications.

2   Verified Operating Systems

2.1   Verified Computer Systems

Machine-checked computer system proof has been used to build extremely reliable computer systems. Some examples of these involve compiled routines from the C string library targeted to the Motorola 68020 [5], microcode for the Motorola CAP processor [6], a stack of verified systems [3], verification of the "oral messages" algorithm [4, 11], code for some simple real-time systems [20], floating-point microcode [6, 17], a verified Piton [15] program [19], floating-point hardware [18], a simple scheduler [7], and partial microcode correctness of some Rockwell Collins microprocessors [13, 14].

Broadly speaking, each of these projects relates the execution of a model of a computer system with the execution of a more abstract model that describes the expected behavior of the system. This approach has also been used to establish aspects of operating system correctness. The most applicable example of the formal verification of an operating system is Bevier's verification of KIT [1, 2].

2.2   KIT

KIT ("kernel, isolated, tasks") is an operating system kernel that enforces partitioning among a set of user tasks. The kernel supports some simple communication services for interpartition messages and input devices. KIT is implemented with

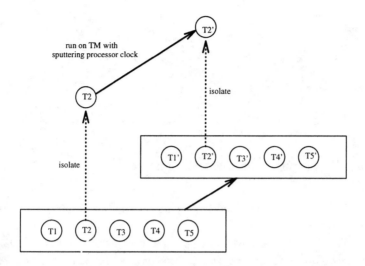

Figure 1: The KIT Correctness Theorem [2]

about 300 instructions of machine code for TM, a hypothetical machine with a simple von Neumann architecture.

KIT provides a set of user-mode tasks with the illusion that each is operating in isolation, except for the effect of interprocess communication. Each I/O device is associated with exactly one partition. Most of the verification work to establish partition isolation involves showing that KIT correctly maintains the state of the various tasks in the face of partition swapping and task execution, and that it does the right thing when there is communication with I/O devices or between partitions.

The correctness theorem relates a very detailed and realistic model of KIT executing on TM to an abstract model where tasks execute in isolation. The KIT correctness statement embodies in microcosm the appeal of formal methods. Rather than attempt to list all the things that could go wrong in a partitioned operating system (a hopeless task for all but the simplest of systems) and show that nothing undesirable occurs, one demonstrates correct functioning of the system. The KIT correctness theorem relates the execution of each partition running in isolation on an unloaded TM to its execution under KIT, and is illustrated in Figure 1. The partition running on the abstract machine used to specify KIT's behavior executes in spurts that correspond to the allocation of the CPU by the kernel at the more concrete level, and this relationship is formalized in the statement of the correctness theorem.

2.3 Invariant performance

The KIT theorem — and most of the other verification projects with which we are familiar — provides a service guarantee about a computer system. Real-time concerns are not considered in the KIT verification, but the abstract specification

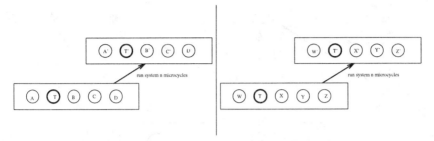

Figure 2: Invariant Performance

approach used by KIT could be extended to provide guarantees about throughput and latency.

But these properties do not suffice to allow separate verification of integrated applications. *It is unrealistic to expect application developers to verify applications against an abstract, unrealized machine model, even if the abstraction arguably characterizes "good" system behavior.* Our specification dispenses with the definition of the abstract machine altogether. We will use machine-checked proof to relate the execution of an application on a realistic model of the computer system with the application's execution when other applications are different. This approach is suggested by Figure 2: partition **T** operates without regard to the operation of the other partitions. If two kernel-controlled partition sets have identical initial kernel states and identical states for some partition **T** then the execution of the partition sets maintains the equivalence of the states of **T**.

The guarantee invariant performance makes to the application developer is that after his application is combined with other co-resident applications it will work precisely as it worked before integration. If for example the developer tests his application in a partition he can rely on the system to work identically even if other partitions are used to host other applications. This cannot be done with a conventional "abstract" description of correct system operation: the developer does not know precisely how his application will run, only that it will run just like it would run on an abstract machine described by the correctness theorem. Note that invariant performance is a very strong statement about a system, since we can predict what task is executing at each microcycle of the system's execution.

Statements of formal correctness that do not use an abstract execution model are rare. One example is the self-consistency checking work, wherein for example the operation of a processor's pipeline is specified using the same pipeline with "NOP"s inserted into the instruction stream [10]. Another is the symbolic simulation work whose objectives include regression testing of an evolving design by comparing symbolic execution of generations of designs [9].

There has been a great deal of work in the area of composing applications, most particularly related to secure systems and real-time systems. A seminal idea in security research is the notion of *non-interference*, the property that operations performed on behalf of a particular task (or "user") extracted from a system's execution history are not affected by another task [8]. A seminal idea in real-time systems

research is the *real-time scheduler*, which guarantees that each task is allocated
enough CPU time or other resource so as not to violate its deadline [12].[1] Invariant performance is a straightforward, simple policy when viewed in either of these
contexts as it requires that the operations of each task occur precisely at particular
times. A system with invariant performance exhibits both non-interference and an
unvarying schedule.

Despite its simplicity, we believe that invariant performance is the crucial property needed to allow separate verification of real-time, embedded applications since
it provides complete time and space isolation. It provides the application developer a development platform that will be unaffected by the application's integration,
thereby allowing for independent verification of real-time, embedded applications.

3 An Example Application of Invariant Performance

We demonstrate invariant performance by developing its statement on a simple,
concrete system. The system we model contains an AAMP-FV microprocessor [13]
and a partition management unit ("PMU"). The PMU maintains memory isolation
among the partitions and includes timers that allow temporal control of partitions
by the kernel. The model of the AAMP-FV we use is adapted from the instruction-
level AAMP-FV "macrolevel" model [13].

In this section we describe *Schultz*, a simple partitioning system, our formalization of invariant performance for Schultz, and an outline of the proof.

3.1 Schultz Overview

Schultz supports a cyclic schedule of noninterfering partitions. There is no explicit provision in this initial model for kernel-mediated shared resources such as
interrupt controllers. Each partition is allocated a predetermined amount of CPU
time with no interruption and has its own memory space, thereby ensuring noninterference between partitions. The Schultz kernel is responsible for initializing
the system and maintaining the partition schedule; the kernel is very simple since
there is only one shared resource, the CPU, and An unusual aspect of Schultz is
microcycle-accurate partition-starting that achieves strict temporal independence
among partitions.

Figure 3 represents the Schultz hardware configuration. The AAMP-FV and the
PMU interact in several ways:

- The accessible memory range is determined by the PMU using the processor
  user/executive line and base/limit addresses contained in memory-mapped
  PMU registers.

- For each processor memory transaction the PMU determines whether the location is currently accessible.

---

[1]A machine-checked real-time scheduling optimality proof is described in [21]

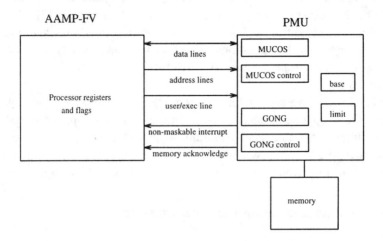

Figure 3: Schultz Hardware

- A PMU timer, the *gong timer*, generates a periodic non-maskable interrrupt ("NMI") to the processor.

- A PMU timer, the *mucos timer*, is used to generate a memory acknowledge signal to the processor when the processor writes a non-zero value to a particular memory address, the *mucos register*. As will be discussed below, this mechanism provides for strict temporal synchronization.

- Each PMU timer has a corresponding memory-mapped control register that determines whether the counter is active and, if so, the value to which the timer is set when it expires.

Our AAMP-FV model is a modification of the model of [13]. We have modified the model in order to simplify underlying proofs about code following the suggestions of [22], particularly the use of an interpreter style to facilitate code proof automation.

The Schultz PMU maintains information about the current partition executing on the processor, including its CPU time allocation, how much CPU time it has used, and the range of memory to which it has access. Expiration of the "gong" timer signals the end of the current partition's CPU allocation. The "mucos" timer signals the end of partition switch handling time and is used to time the start of a partition, thereby synchronizing the timing of partition execution to eliminate any effect of unpredictable interrupt latency — interrupts are only recognized on instruction boundaries — or early partition exits due to illegal instruction execution. The timers are free-running timers that are decremented each microcycle. When a counter reaches 0 it is reinitialized with a corresponding timer initialization value. A timer is shut off by setting the timer initialization value to 0.

```
step(system): system_state =
  LET conns = conns(system), s = processor(system), p = pmu(system) IN

  % run next instruction with protected memory and PMU-generated NMI
  LET s2 = step_processor(s WITH [(mem):=protectmem(memory(conns),p,conns),
                                  (intreg):=setint6(intreg(s), nmi(conns))]) IN

  % calculate time of instruction execution
  LET itime = step_time(s,mucosset(s2),
                        val(mucostimermod(p))>0,val(mucostimer(p))) IN

  % update connections to reflect PMU/processor operation
  LET conns2 = (# (nmi) := intreg(s2)^6 OR (val(gongtimermod(p))>0
                                            AND val(gongtimer(p)) <= itime),
                 (memory):=resetmucos(restoremem(mem(s2),mem(s),p,conns)),
                 (um) := um(s2),
                 (itime) := itime #) IN

  % update PMU state
  LET p2 = step_pmu(p,memory(conns2),itime) IN

    make_system (s2, p2, conns2)
protected_system(system,cur,finish): RECURSIVE system_state =
  IF finish<=cur
   THEN system
   ELSE
     LET system2 = step(system) IN
       protected_system (system2, cur + itime(conns(system2)), finish)
   ENDIF
  MEASURE max(0,finish-cur)
```

Figure 4: Schultz Hardware Formalization

The two PMU timers operate differently, reflecting how they are used. The gong timer signals partition switching and generates an NMI when it reaches 0. The mucos timer synchronizes the start of a partition to the correct microcycle and delays the memory acknowledge signal on non-zero writes to the mucos register until the mucos timer reaches 0.

The PMU also maintains a base/limit pair for the currently operating partition that is used to restrict partition access to memory. When a user-mode instruction writes to memory outside the range of addresses between the base and limit pair it has no effect, and when an address outside the range is read it returns 0.

We express the model and its correctness conjecture in the logic of the PVS theorem prover [16] since we intend to prove that Schultz provides invariant performance, using PVS to machine-check the proof. The PVS formalization of the Schultz hardware is presented in Figure 4. We have not provided enough information for the reader to understand this model fully. (The subsidiary functions are defined in our model but not presented in this paper, and we do not attempt here to describe the semantics of the PVS logic [16].) We present Figure 4 only to convey that we have modelled the Schultz hardware in detail to support reasoning about it.

4   The Schultz Kernel

We now introduce a partition switch signal handler that implements partitioning. The AAMP-FV assembly code is given in Figure 5. The loop initializes the PMU and schedules the next partition in the schedule.

The scheduling code maintains several data structures. A schedule of partitions is assumed at symbolic location psds. The schedule is saved using a list of length length of process state descriptors ("PSD"s), each of which represents a partition. An AAMP-FV PSD is 8 double words containing processor state values PC, TOS, LENV, and PAGE and 4 unused locations. Schultz uses 2 of the spare PSD double words to maintain the base and limit values for each partition.

The symbolic value curr is the number of the current partition in the schedule. Each time a partition switch occurs we increment curr, thereby advancing to the next partition in the schedule. The schedule is a simple, cyclic schedule, so when the value of curr reaches length it is reset to 0.

Strict time partitioning requires that partition scheduling be unaffected by what individual partitions do. This requires some effort in the face of interrupt latency, since interrupts like the partition swap interrupt are only recognized on instruction boundaries. The partition switch handler uses the PMU mucos register to guarantee strict time partitioning. Before starting a partition the mucos register is updated with a non-zero value. The memory transaction acknowledgement signal for the mucos register address is delayed until the mucos timer expires. Thus, the start of the next partition is delayed until a predictable time, as illustrated in Figure 6.

The handler also addresses another scenario: it is possible that the previous partition ended not because of a partition switch signal but rather due to the partition's execution of an illegal instruction, as illustrated in Figure 7. If this occurs then during execution of the handler the partition swap signal will be generated; and since the handler runs in executive mode the partition switch interrupt will be pending. If this happens it will occur before the mucos timer times out (since the mucos timer is designed to time out after the gong timer) so the partition switch interrupt will be pending after the mucos synchronization. The kernel executes a CLRINT instruction to clear this pending interrupt, thereby ensuring that the next partition receives its entire CPU allocation.

5   Schultz Invariant Performance

Figure 8 presents our PVS formalization of invariant performance for Schultz. Given two good initial Schultz states that have equal length schedules with a valid schedule element *i* that has identical base/limit values and processor memory that is identical for that region, then running the system will yield a state with identical memory in that region starting in either state.

The conjecture has four universally-quantified variables: sys1 and sys2, initial system states, i, a schedule element, and fin, an ending time. The hypotheses of the conjecture restrict the applicability of the conclusion to "reasonable" initial

```
ELOOP:    LIT16 0FFFFh              ;
          ASN24 exec_code           ;

          REF24 length              ; if at end of schedule, reset pointer
          REF24 curr                ;
          SUB                       ;
          SKIPT8 rpart              ;
          LIT4 0                    ;
          ASN24 curr                ;

rpart:    LIT24 psds                ; store psd table location
          REF24 curr                ;
          DUP                       ; while we've got it, set PMU num reg
          ASN24 partn               ;
          LIT4 4                    ; multiply curr pointer by 16 to get offset
          SHL                       ;
          LIT4 0                    ; make single word a double word
          ADDD                      ; calculate PSD pointer for next partition

          DUP                       ; set PMU base and limit from PSD
          LIT32 8                   ;
          ADDD                      ;
          DUP                       ;
          REFDA                     ;
          ASND24 breg               ;
          LIT32 2                   ;
          ADDD                      ;
          REFDA                     ;
          ASND24 lreg               ;

          LIT4 1
          LIT24 mreg
          ASNA                      ; write to mucos register

          LIT4 7                    ; clear pending interrupts - for example,
          CLRINT                    ; an NMI that occurred since illegal instr

          USER                      ; start user partition

          ASN24 exec_code           ; save returned value - could be partition
                                    ; signal or illegal instruction

          REF24 curr                ; increment schedule pointer
          LIT4 1                    ;
          ADD                       ;
          ASN24 curr                ;
          LIT16 ELOOP               ; calculate skip value to loop


          SKIP
```

Figure 5: Partition Switch Kernel Code

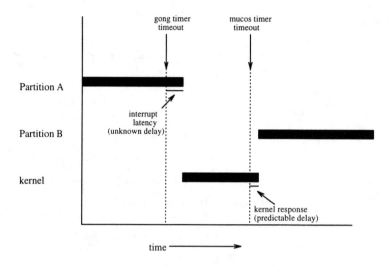

Figure 6: A Typical Schultz Partition Switch

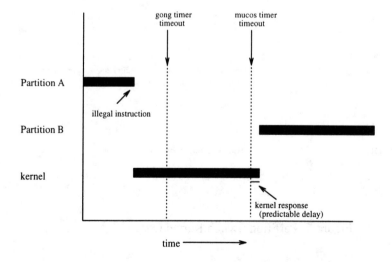

Figure 7: Partition Switch After Illegal Instruction

```
schultzip: LEMMA
  FORALL (sys1,sys2: system_state) (i: validpart) (fin: nat):
  LET m1= memory(conns(sys1)), m2= memory(conns(sys2)) IN
    initial_schultz(sys1) AND initial_schultz(sys2) AND
    length(m1) = length(m2) AND i < length(m1) AND
    psdequal(i,m1,m2) AND psdvalid(i,m1) AND psdvalid(i,m2) AND
    memoryrange(m1,base(i,m1),limit(i,m1)) =
      memoryrange(m2,base(i,m1),limit(i,m1))
    IMPLIES
      memoryrange(memory(conns(protected_system(sys1,0,fin))),
                  base(i,m1),limit(i,m1)) =
        memoryrange(memory(conns(protected_system(sys2,0,fin))),
                    base(i,m1),limit(i,m1))
```

Figure 8: Schultz Invariant Performance in PVS

states and schedule elements — the initial states have the kernel loaded, the schedule element must have identical corresponding memories in the initial states, the schedule element must actually be in the schedule, etc. The ending time at which the memories must correspond has no restriction — the conjecture must hold at all times during execution of the system.

We are currently proving this conjecture using the PVS theorem prover. There are two main lemmas needed to prove the invariant performance conjecture. The "reset" lemma guarantees that resetting the AAMP-FV with Schultz leads to a reasonable state. The "maintenance" lemma guarantees that the code in Figure 5 maintains various invariants about the system that can be used to guarantee invariant performance. We briefly sketch the proof of the maintenance lemma.

The maintenance lemma is similar to the schultzip lemma in Figure 8, except rather than assume that the two Schultz states satisfy "initial Schultz" conditions they will be assumed to have "reasonable timer values" and be "safely executing the current user partition". Reasonable timer values means that the mucos timer is greater than the gong timer value plus the maximum user instruction time plus the maximum handler execution time (excepting the write of the mucos register). Safely executing the current user partition means that the PMU is initialized with the current base/limit pair, the processor is in user mode, and the executive PSD is initialized correctly.

The proof of the maintenance lemma is by induction on the time required to complete one user partition and partition swap. The base case is when the fin value occurs before the completion of the partition swap to the next partition, which we prove by showing that the only way to modify partition i's memory is if partition i is the current partition, in which case the memory is changed identically by the two executions. The inductive case is when the fin value occurs after the switch to the next partition. We show that the execution of a partition and the partition swap code maintains each of the hypotheses of this conjecture, which together with an inductive hypothesis suffices to prove the result.

Figure 6 shows a typical partition swap, where the gong timer generates an NMI which (after whatever latency is associated with finishing the current user instruction) transitions the machine into executive mode. After setting up for the next partition the kernel then waits for the mucos timer timeout before starting the next partition. A second possibility exists for the timing of partition swapping, however: a partition can transition back to the kernel as the result of the execution of an illegal instruction, as suggested by Figure 7.

6 Summary

We are currently proving Schultz invariant performance using the PVS theorem prover. We will extend this approach to more complex partitioning systems, in particular those that allow inter-partition communication. We expect our approach to extend to this kind of system by treating the communication channel reads among the inputs to a partition, and providing only strict kernel-mediated access to these communication channels.

Theorems about computer systems that use an abstract model to specify system behavior are not especially useful for justifying the integration of embedded applications. We believe that, from the standpoint of dependable embedded application integration, invariant performance is the right property to guarantee for partitioning systems.

References

[1] William Bevier. *A Verified Operating System Kernel.* PhD thesis, University of Texas at Austin, September 1987. Also available as ftp://ftp.cs.utexas.edu/pub/boyer/diss/bevier.ps.Z.

[2] William R. Bevier. KIT: A study in operating system verification. *IEEE Transactions on Software Engineering*, 15(11):1368–81, November 1989.

[3] William R. Bevier, Warren A. Hunt Jr., J Strother Moore, and William D. Young. An approach to systems verification. *Journal of Automated Reasoning*, 5(4):411–428, December 1989.

[4] William R. Bevier and William D. Young. Machine checked proofs of the design of a fault-tolerant circuit. *Formal Aspects of Computing*, 4:755–775, 1992.

[5] Robert S. Boyer and Yuan Yu. Automated proofs of object code for a widely used microprocessor. *Journal of the ACM*, 43(1):166–192, January 1996.

[6] Bishop Brock, Matt Kaufmann, and J Strother Moore. ACL2 theorems about commercial microprocessors. In Mandayam Srivas and Albert Camilleri, editors, *Formal Methods in Computer-Aided Design – FMCAD*, volume 1166 of *Lecture Notes in Computer Science*. Springer-Verlag, 1996.

[7] Colin Fidge, Peter Kearney, and Mark Utting. Formal specification and interactive proof of a simple real-time scheduler. Technical Report 94-11, Software Verification Research Centre, The University of Queensland, April 1994.

[8] Joseph A. Goguen and Jose' Meseguer. Security policies and security models. *Proceedings of the 1982 Symposium on Security and Privacy*, May 1982.

[9] David A. Greve. Symbolic simulation of the JEM1 microprocessor. In *Formal Methods in Computer-Aided Design – FMCAD*, Lecture Notes in Computer Science. Springer-Verlag, 1998.

[10] Robert B. Jones, Carl-Johan H. Seger, and David L. Dill. Self-consistency checking. In Mandayam Srivas and Albert Camilleri, editors, *Formal Methods in Computer-Aided Design – FMCAD*, volume 1166 of *Lecture Notes in Computer Science*. Springer-Verlag, 1996.

[11] Patrick Lincoln and John Rushby. The formal verification of an algorithm for interactive consistency under a hybrid fault model. In Costas Courcoubetis, editor, *Computer-Aided Verification – CAV '93*, volume 697 of *Lecture Notes in Computer Science*. Springer-Verlag, 1993.

[12] C.L. Liu and James W. Layland. Scheduling algorithms for multiprogramming in a hard real-time environment. *Journal of the Association for Computing Machinery*, 20(1):46–61, 1975.

[13] Steven P. Miller, David A. Greve, Matthew M. Wilding, and Mandayam Srivas. Formal verification of the AAMP-FV microcode. Technical report, Rockwell Collins, Inc., Cedar Rapids, IA, 1996.

[14] Steven P. Miller and Mandayam Srivas. Formal verification of the AAMP5 microprocessor: A case study in the industrial use of formal methods. In *WIFT'95: Workshop on Industrial-Strength Formal Specification Techniques*, Boca Raton, FL, 1995. IEEE Computer Society.

[15] J Strother Moore. *Piton – A Mechanically Verified Assembly-Level Language*. Kluwer Academic Publishers, 1996.

[16] S. Owre, N. Shankar, and J. M. Rushby D. W. J. Stringer-Calvert. *PVS Language Reference (Version 2.2)*. Computer Science Laboratory, SRI International, Menlo Park, CA, Sept 1998.

[17] David M. Russinoff. A mechanically checked proof of IEEE compliance of the AMD K5 floating-point square root microcode. Available as http://www.onr.com/user/russ/david/fsqrt.html, August 1996.

[18] David M. Russinoff. A mechanically checked proof of IEEE compliance of the floating point multiplication, division, and square root algorithms of the AMD-K7 processor. Available at http://www.onr.com/user/russ/david/, January 28 1998.

[19] Matthew Wilding. A mechanically verified application for a mechanically verified environment. In Costas Courcoubetis, editor, *Computer-Aided Verification – CAV '93*, volume 697 of *Lecture Notes in Computer Science*. Springer-Verlag, 1993.

[20] Matthew Wilding. *Machine-Checked Real-Time System Verification*. PhD thesis, University of Texas at Austin, May 1996. Also available as ftp://ftp.cs.utexas.edu/pub/boyer/diss/wilding.ps.Z.

[21] Matthew Wilding. A machine-checked proof of the optimality of a real-time scheduling policy. In Alan J. Hu and Moshe Y. Vardi, editors, *Computer-Aided Verification – CAV '98*, volume 1427 of *Lecture Notes in Computer Science*. Springer-Verlag, 1998.

[22] Matthew M. Wilding. Robust computer system proofs in PVS. In C. Michael Holloway and Kelly J. Hayhurst, editors, *LFM97: Fourth NASA Langley Formal Methods Workshop*. NASA Conference Publication no. 3356, 1997. (http://atb-www.larc.nasa.gov/Lfm97/).

Acknowledgments: This work was supported at Rockwell Collins Inc. by the Defense Advanced Research Projects Agency, ARPA order D855. The views and conclusions contained in this document are those of the authors and should not be interpreted as representing the official policies, either expressed or implied, of Rockwell Collins, the Defense Advanced Research Projects Agency, or the US government.

A Model of Noninterference for Integrating Mixed-Criticality Software Components

Bruno Dutertre and Victoria Stavridou
Computer Science Laboratory, SRI International
{bruno,victoria}@csl.sri.com

Abstract

This paper examines the problem of safely integrating independent software components, of different criticality levels, in a single system. We examine the risks of interference between independent components which share common hardware resources. We propose a definition of safe integration in which only a limited form of interference is tolerated, namely a bounded performance degradation. We show how the definition can be applied to systems modeled as input-output automata, and we compare our model to other notions of non-interference and related concepts.

1 Introduction

In traditional safety-critical systems, critical functions are performed by dedicated computers running purpose-specific software. Independent functions are performed by physically separate computers and do not interfere with one another. This traditional approach is now being challenged and more integrated solutions are being proposed, such as the Integrated Modular Avionics (IMA) concept [7, 8]. In such emerging integrated systems, the hardware resource is shared between different functions and software components of mixed criticality levels may share a single processor or other hardware resource.

There is also an increased interest in developing software using off-the-shelf (OTS) components, including commercial-off-the-shelf (COTS) components and other forms of already developed software. The hope, for this approach to software development, is that developing software by integrating existing components will reduce development and maintenance costs, shorten development time, and increase productivity [3, 14]. However, the use of OTS software in high-integrity systems poses a major difficulty: key component qualities such as safety, reliability, or performance might be very difficult to establish. The internals of OTS components are rarely available for inspection, the development process might be unknown, and testing the final product is not likely to be satisfactory.

Because of these two trends, future systems may combine purpose-specific software for critical functions and OTS-based software for tasks of lower integrity. More generally, software components of different origin will coexist, performing tasks of different criticality and sharing common computing resources. Software for lower-criticality functions might not be developed to the same degree of rigor as software for critical functions, and a key issue is to ensure that the presence of lower-integrity components does not compromise the safety and reliability of the overall system. A main objective is to ensure that a piece of software whose development process might be unknown, whose performance and reliability might not be measurable, and whose design is not available for inspection will not interfere with or degrade the integrity of trusted software performing critical functions.

This paper examines the problem of ensuring that high-integrity components in an integrated system are protected from interference by other components. We assume that the high-integrity components are independent and are not intended to interact with one another or with the low-integrity components. In other words, the high-integrity components are autonomous; they perform critical functions which do not depend on any service provided by low-integrity components. In this context, the objective is to make sure that the high-integrity components behave as safely in the integrated system as they would, were they running in isolation, on separate hardware.

In Section 2, we examine the possible causes of interference between software components sharing hardware resources. We then present, in Section 3, a definition of safe integration which relates the black-box behavior of an ideal isolated component to the behavior of an integrated system which contains this component. The behavior of the two systems must be the same for all input sequences the environment may produce, modulo a limited performance degradation. Section 4 examines how safe integration can be verified when components are modeled as state machines. The integrated system can then be modeled as another state machine and we give sufficient conditions on this machine for safe integration to be achieved. Section 5 compares our noninterference model with related work on analysis of strong partitioning mechanisms for integrated systems and on extensions of security models to safety-related issues.

2   Interference between Software Components

IMA and similar systems are based on a multiprocess runtime environment. Processes which share a single processor are executing concurrently on a time-slicing basis. Process scheduling and other services are provided by a runtime environment. Communication and interaction between the processes can take place via different means which are usually implemented via shared memory. For example, the APEX interface for IMA defined in [1] supports four communication and synchronization mechanisms: semaphores, buffers, blackboards, and events, all implemented via shared memory[1].

---

[1]IMA groups processes into separate units called *partitions*. Inter-process communication via the four mechanisms above is restricted to processes which belong to the same partition. Inter-partition communication relies on a different mechanism [1].

In such systems, if two processes perform independent functions and are not intended to communicate, interference can take place through the shared resources, that is, the CPU, the physical memory, and possibly input and output devices. At least two potential sources of interference are present:

- *Data Corruption.* The nontrusted components can accidentally overwrite vital information stored in the common memory and used by the trusted components.

- *Denial of Access to Critical Resources.* The nontrusted components can prevent or delay the execution of critical functions by restricting or preventing access to a shared resource. In particular, nontrusted components can use too much CPU time or can fail to terminate or crash and hence prevent the trusted components from executing.

There is a strong analogy between these two forms of interference and two fundamental objectives of information security. Traditionally, information security aims to ensure confidentiality and integrity of sensitive data and to ensure that legitimate users are not unduly denied access to information or resources. There are clear similarities between our objectives of preventing data corruption and denial of access in a system integrating components of varying degrees of integrity and the same objectives in the security context.

The notion of secure noninterference was proposed by Goguen and Meseguer [5] to address these issues. Noninterference is the property that actions performed by a user A of a system have no effect on what another user B can observe. If user A does not interfere with user B, there is no flow of information from A to B. Similarly, we can say that a low-integrity component LO does not interfere with a high-integrity component HI if the behavior of HI is not influenced by the behavior of LO. In this sense, noninterference is an internal property of the integrated system. However, preventing internal interference may not be sufficient for safety. A nontrusted component may be able to compromise safety without internally interfering with trusted components but by accessing shared input/output channels. For example, a trusted component may be intended to control external devices such as electro-mechanical servos or actuators. In such a case, it is essential to guarantee that nontrusted components cannot have access to the same external devices. Other problems may occur if a nontrusted component is able to send messages that appear to the environment as if they originated from a trusted component or, conversely, if a nontrusted component can intercept messages destined for the trusted component.

A more general approach to ensuring safe integration is to require that the integrated system behaves like the combination of the software components running in isolation. We can establish that the integrated system is safe by comparing its black-box behavior with the black-box behavior of each of the trusted components. In the following section, we give a definition of safe integration based on this approach.

3   A Model of Safe Integration

3.1   Black-box Behavior of Systems

We consider a system integrating n independent software components, sharing a single processor. Some of these components are trusted and perform a critical function. The objective is to ensure that the global system integrating all the components is safe provided the trusted components are.

In application domains such as IMA, we can assume that the trusted components must satisfy real-time constraints. We also assume that each component is deterministic. To take execution time into account, we use a discrete time model. Assume the interface of a component with the environment is characterized by an input domain I and an output domain O. An execution of the system can be described by recording at every time $t \in \mathbb{N}$ the input event of I received at that time, if any, and the output event of O produced at time t, if any. We use the special symbol $\perp$ to denote the absence of event ($\perp \notin I$ and $\perp \notin O$). An execution of the system can then be described by two sequences $\sigma = (x_t)_{t \in \mathbb{N}}$ and $\tau = (y_t)_{t \in \mathbb{N}}$, where x_t is either $\perp$ or the input event observed at time t and y_t is either $\perp$ or the output event observed at time t.

For deterministic systems, there is only one possible output sequence τ for each input sequence σ. The black-box behavior of such a system can then be represented by a mapping F from $Seq(I)$ to $Seq(O)$, where $Seq(I)$ and $Seq(O)$ denote the set of sequences of elements of $I \cup \{\perp\}$ and $O \cup \{\perp\}$, respectively[2].

An event is the observation of input values received or output values transmitted by a system at a particular time. Events need not be atomic and a single event can represent multiple communications that occur simultaneously on different ports. However, for the remainder of this paper, the exact structure of events is not relevant. The only important property is that the event space of a software component is included into the event space of the system that contains this component[3]

3.2   Safe Integration Criteria

From the environment point of view, the system integrating all the components can also be considered as a deterministic real-time system G. The input domain I_G of G includes the input domains of the components and the output domain O_G of G includes the output domains of the components. The black-box behavior of G is characterized by a mapping F_G from $Seq(I_G)$ to $Seq(O_G)$. Let M be a trusted component of G with input domain $I_M \subseteq I_G$ and output domain $O_M \subseteq O_G$ and assume the behavior of M in isolation is defined by a mapping F_M. We can say that

---

[2]Since past or present output cannot depend on future input events, we can assume that F satisfies the following causality property: if two input sequences $\sigma = (x_t)_{t \in \mathbb{N}}$ and $\sigma' = (x'_t)_{t \in \mathbb{N}}$ are identical up to time n (i.e. $x'_0 = x_0, x'_1 = x_1, \ldots, x'_n = x_n$) then the output sequences $F(\sigma)$ and $F(\sigma')$ are also identical up to time n.

[3]More rigorously, there exists a one-to-one mapping from the event space of a component to the event space of the containing system. We use inclusion for simplicity and notational convenience.

the integration of M in G is safe if, for an external observer who can only see the events in $I_M \cup O_M$, the behavior of G is identical or sufficiently close to the ideal behavior specified by F_M.

More formally, given a sequence $\sigma = (x_t)_{t \in \mathbb{N}}$ of $Seq(I_G)$, we denote by σ / I_M the sequence obtained from σ by replacing all the events not in I_M by $\bot$:

$$\sigma / I_M = (x'_t)_{t \in \mathbb{N}} \text{ where } x'_t = \begin{cases} x_t & \text{if } x_t \in I_M \\ \bot & \text{if } x_t \notin I_M. \end{cases}$$

Informally, σ / I_M is what is observed of σ when the events in $I_G - I_M$ are invisible. Similarly, for a sequence τ of $Seq(O_G)$ we denote by τ / O_M the sequence obtained by replacing all the elements of τ not in O_M by $\bot$. The behaviors of G and M are identical with respect to events in $I_M \cup O_M$ if the following condition is satisfied:

$$\forall \sigma \in Seq(I_G) : F_G(\sigma) / O_M = F_M(\sigma / I_M).$$

In such a case, an observer who only sees events of $I_M \cup O_M$ cannot differentiate M and G: To such an observer, the two sequences σ and σ / I_M appear identical and the respective responses of G and M to σ and σ / I_M cannot be distinguished.

If the condition above is satisfied then the integration of M into G is clearly safe. However, requiring identical responses from the isolated component and the global system for all possible input sequences may be too strong a requirement in practice. The function F_M can be interpreted as the ideal behavior of component M, and in practice we can assume that G is allowed to deviate within certain limits from the ideal.

Since G performs more functions than M, a limited performance degradation, that is, a delay in producing the successive outputs, should be tolerable. We assume that a constant Δ_{out} is given which specifies how much output delay can be tolerated and we define a relation $\sqsubseteq$ between sequences as follows. If $\tau = (y_t)_{t \in \mathbb{N}}$ and $\tau' = (y'_t)_{t \in \mathbb{N}}$ are two sequences of elements of a set $E \cup \{\bot\}$ then $\tau \sqsubseteq \tau'$ if there is a bijection f from $D_\tau = \{t \mid y_t \neq \bot\}$ to the set $D_{\tau'} = \{t \mid y'_t \neq \bot\}$ such that

$$\forall t, t' \in D_\tau : t < t' \Rightarrow f(t) < f(t'),$$
$$\forall t \in D_\tau : t \leqslant f(t) \leqslant t + \Delta_{out},$$
$$\forall t \in D_\tau : y_t = y'_{f(t)}.$$

Using this notation, if $\tau = F_M(\sigma)$ is the ideal response to an input sequence σ then any τ' of $Seq(O_M)$ such that $\tau \sqsubseteq \tau'$ is also an acceptable response to σ. The same elements of O_M occur in the same order in τ and in τ' and each of these occurs in τ' no later than Δ_{out} time units after it occurs in τ.

To guarantee that the integration is safe, we can determine whether $F_M(\sigma / I_M) \sqsubseteq F_G(\sigma) / O_M$ holds for each input sequence σ the environment may produce. To satisfy this constraint, G must produce the same outputs as M and within specified deadlines. In general, it is not possible to guarantee that the deadlines are met for arbitrary input sequences. One must assume that there is a minimal delay between successive input events. Otherwise, if input events occur too frequently, G may not have enough resource to respond to them in time. We assume that a positive constant Δ_{in} gives the minimal delay between the occurrence of successive events of I_M and that another constant Δ_{in}^0 specifies the delay before the occurrence of the first event of I_M. In other words, we assume that an input sequence σ of $Seq(I_G)$ received from the environment satisfies the following constraints:

$$\forall t \in \mathbb{N} : \ \sigma_t \in I_M \Rightarrow t \geqslant \Delta_{in}^0$$
$$\forall t, t' \in \mathbb{N} : \ t < t' \wedge \sigma_t \in I_M \wedge \sigma_{t'} \in I_M \Rightarrow t' - t \geqslant \Delta_{in}.$$

We denote by Σ_{in} the set of sequences which satisfy these two conditions. The environment is assumed to produce only input sequences which belong to Σ_{in}.

Given the above assumption about the environment and the deadlines defined by the relation $\sqsubset$ we can say that the integration of M in G is safe if the following condition is satisfied:

$$\forall \sigma \in \Sigma_{in} : \ F_M(\sigma/I_M) \sqsubset F_G(\sigma)/O_M.$$

In the following section, we examine how this property can be verified when the component M and the global system G are modeled by input-output automata.

4 Proving Safe Integration

4.1 Component Model

We assume that a component running in isolation is a reactive system which is idle until input is received from the environment. Once activated by an input event, the system becomes active and starts executing and producing output events. When execution terminates, the system returns to an idle state and waits for the next input. We model such systems by a form of deterministic input-output automata which can be either in an idle state where they are waiting for input or in an active state where they are performing some computation. Any inputs submitted while the automata are in an active state are ignored. Output events are only produced during the computation steps.

This model can be used to represent systems which repeatedly perform a periodic computation, such as real-time control systems. In such cases, the input events can be assumed to be sent at regular intervals which correspond to the period of a clock. The set of input events may include a special element representing a clock tick, that carries no value and is only used to trigger a computation. This allows one to model systems that execute periodically even in the absence of input. Other systems can also be handled, where the activation events can occur at irregular intervals. For example, we can represent an emergency shutdown system by assuming that the computation is triggered when a critical event is received, without knowing when this event can occur.

More precisely, an isolated component is modeled by a state machine M of the form

$$M = (Q, q_0, I_M, O_M, W, \alpha, \beta, \delta)$$

where

- Q is the set of states and $q_0 \in Q$ is the initial state of M,

- I_M and O_M are the input and output spaces of M, respectively,

- W is a subset of Q,

- α is a total function from $W \times I_M$ to Q,

- β is a total function from Q to $O_M \cup \{\bot\}$,

- δ is a total function from Q to Q,

and the following condition is satisfied:

$$\forall q \in W, \ \delta(q) = q \ \wedge \ \beta(q) = \bot .$$

The set W is the set of idle states, where M is waiting for input from the environment. The functions α and β are the input and output functions, respectively, and δ is the transition function of M.

The transitions of the machine are determined by α and δ. The function α specifies how the state is updated when an input is received and δ represents a single computation step. We assume that reading an input is instantaneous and that performing a computation step takes one time unit. If M is in a state $q \in W$ at time t and input x is received at that time then M is in state $\delta(\alpha(q, x))$ at time $t + 1$. If $q \notin W$ or no input is present at time t then M goes to state $\delta(q)$ at time $t + 1$. Similarly, we assume that outputs are produced at the end of computation steps. If M enters a state q at time t and $\beta(q) \neq \bot$ then M produces the output value $\beta(q)$ at time $t + 1$. No output is ever produced in a state q of W, and M stays in such a state as long as no input event is received.

Given an input sequence $\sigma = (x_t)_{t \in \mathbb{N}}$ where $x_t \in I_M \cup \{\bot\}$, the machine M goes through a sequence of states $(q_t)_{t \in \mathbb{N}}$ where q_0 is the initial state of M and, for all $t \in \mathbb{N}$,

$$q_{t+1} = \begin{cases} \delta(\alpha(q_t, x_t)) & \text{if } q_t \in W \text{ and } x_t \neq \bot, \\ \delta(q_t) & \text{otherwise.} \end{cases}$$

The corresponding output sequence is $\tau = (y_t)_{t \in \mathbb{N}}$ where $y_0 = \bot$ and, for all $t \in \mathbb{N}$,

$$y_{t+1} = \beta(q_t).$$

The black-box behavior of M is defined by the function F_M which maps any input sequence σ to the corresponding τ.

A computation of M is started on reception of an input event x provided M is in an idle state $q \in W$. Once a computation is started, it is not interrupted by input events. The model does not guarantee that all computations eventually terminate or even that M will reach an idle state from the initial state q_0. However, if M is a trusted component we can make stronger assumptions about its behavior.

As indicated previously, a trusted component M is intended to execute in an environment where the first input event is received a delay Δ_{in}^0 after initialization and the subsequent events are separated by a delay Δ_{in} from each other. In this context, we can assume that M is ready to accept input before time Δ_{in}^0. Similarly, we can assume that any computation started in a state $q \in W$ at time t terminates before time $t + \Delta_{in}$.

Under these assumptions, there is a constant $\lambda_0 \leqslant \Delta_{in}^0$ such that

$$\delta^{\lambda_0}(q_0) \in W$$
$$n < \lambda_0 \implies \delta^n(q_0) \notin W.$$

The constant λ_0 is the delay for M to initialize.

Similarly, for every state $q \in W$ and every $x \in I_M$, there is a constant $\lambda(q, x) \leqslant \Delta_{in}$ such that

$$n = \lambda(q, x) \implies \delta^n(\alpha(q, x)) \in W$$
$$n < \lambda(q, x) \implies \delta^n(\alpha(q, x)) \notin W.$$

The constant $\lambda(q, x)$ is the delay for the computation triggered by x in state q to terminate.

4.2 Integrated System

Assume n independent software components are modeled by n state machines $M_1, \ldots, M_n$ as defined previously. The components share a common processor and memory space and are active alternatively under the control of a scheduling mechanism. The global system can be modeled by another state machine G whose input and output domains include the input and output domains of any machine M_i.

In every state of G, at most one of the n components is active and the behavior of G is determined by this active component. Let Q_i be the set of states of machine M_i and S be the set of states of G. A fraction of every state s of the integrated system is accessible to component M_i and this fraction corresponds to a state of Q_i. We can then assume that there is a mapping h_i from S to Q_i such that for every state $s \in S$, $h_i(s)$ is the part of s accessible by component i in the global system. If component i is active in a state s, then the behavior of G in s is the same as the behavior of M_i in $h_i(s)$: the same output is produced and the next global state s' is such that $h_i(s') = \delta_i(h_i(s))$, where δ_i is the transition function of M_i.

With respect to input events, we can no longer assume that G accepts input only when it is idle, that is, when none of the components is active. To ensure that deadlines are met, G must have the capability to interrupt the active component when urgent events are received. Also, an input received at time t may not be destined for the component active at that time. G must be able to accept such an input on behalf of a nonactive component.

As a whole, we model the integration of n components $M_1, \ldots, M_n$, where

$$M_i \;=\; (Q_i, q_0^i, I_{M_i}, O_{M_i}, W_i, \alpha_i, \beta_i, \delta_i),$$

as follows. The global system is represented by an automaton G of the form

$$G \;=\; (S, s_0, I_G, O_G, \alpha, \beta, \delta),$$

where

- S is the set of states and $s_0 \in S$ is the initial state of G,

- I_G and O_G are the input and output spaces of G,

- α is a total function from $S \times (I_G \cup \{\perp\})$ to S,

- β is a total function from S to $O_G \cup \{\perp\}$,

- δ is a function from S to S,

and the following condition is satisfied:

$$\forall s \in S : \; \alpha(s, \perp) = s.$$

As previously, α is the input function, β the output function, and δ the transition function of G. If G is in state s at time t and an input event $x \in I_G$ is received then G transitions to $\delta(\alpha(s, x))$ in one time unit. If no input is present then G only performs the computation step and enters state $\delta(\alpha(s, \perp)) = \delta(s)$ at time $t + 1$. Output values are also produced in the same way as previously. The only difference with the machine model used for isolated components is that input may be accepted at any time.

Given an input sequence $\sigma = (x_t)_{t \in \mathbb{N}}$, where $x_t \in I_G \cup \{\perp\}$ then G goes through the sequence of states $(s_t)_{t \in \mathbb{N}}$ where s_0 is the initial state of G and

$$s_{t+1} \;=\; \begin{cases} \delta(\alpha(s_t, x_t)) & \text{if } x_t \neq \perp, \\ \delta(s_t) & \text{otherwise.} \end{cases}$$

and produces an output sequence $\tau = (y_t)_{t \in \mathbb{N}}$ defined by $y_0 = \perp$ and $y_{t+1} = \beta(s_t)$. G is deterministic. For every σ, G produces a unique output sequence $\tau = F_G(\sigma)$ defined as above.

The global system G and the components $M_1, \ldots, M_n$ are related in the following way. For every component M_i, I_{M_i} is a subset of I_G and O_{M_i} a subset of O_G, and there exist a mapping h_i from S to Q_i and a subset A_i of S such that the three following conditions are satisfied:

$$\forall s \in A_i : \; h_i(\delta(s)) = \delta_i(h_i(s)) \;\wedge\; \beta(s) = \beta_i(h_i(s)),$$
$$\forall s \in S, x \in I_{M_i} : \; h_i(s) \in W_i \Rightarrow h_i(\alpha(s, x)) = \alpha_i(h_i(s), x),$$
$$h_i(s_0) \;=\; q_0^i.$$

Furthermore, the sets $A_1, \ldots, A_n$ are mutually disjoint.

The set A_i represents the set of states of G where component M_i is active. The first condition above specifies that the output of G in such a state s is the same as the output of M_i in $h_i(s)$ and that the part of the state visible to M_i is updated in G in the same way as it would be in M_i. The second condition means that an input event x relevant to M_i and received in a state s where M_i is ready for input has the same effect on $h_i(s)$ as if received by M_i.

One can think of α as the handling of interrupts by a runtime executive. If an input x is received in state s, then the current computation is interrupted, the runtime executive updates the state to $\alpha(s,x)$, and execution proceeds from there. If all interrupts are masked in a state s then we set $\alpha(s,x) = s$ for all x. States where some interrupts are masked and others are accepted can be modeled in a similar way. Also the union of the sets $A_1, \ldots, A_n$ is not necessarily equal to S; there may be states s where no component is active. This allows us to model computation steps performed by the runtime executive, such as switching execution contexts.

The transition function δ models atomic computation steps that are not interruptible and take one time unit to execute. A computation steps performed when component M_i is active may have side effects not directly visible to M_i: the function δ may modify elements of the state s which are not accessible to M_i. This provides extra generality and may be useful to model the behavior of the runtime executive. For example, the kernel may maintain a state variable to hold the active process, and the active component in state $\delta(s)$ may be different from the active component in s, that is, M_i.

4.3 Sufficient Conditions for Safe Integration

In this section, a fixed component M_i of G is assumed to be trusted. Three constants Δ_{out}, Δ_{in}^0, and Δ_{in} which characterize the task performed by M_i are given. The objective is to ensure that the integration of M_i in G is safe, according to the criterion defined in Section 3.2:

$$\forall \sigma \in \Sigma_{in} : \; F_{M_i}(\sigma/I_{M_i}) \sqsubseteq F_G(\sigma)/O_{M_i}.$$

We give several conditions on G which are sufficient to ensure that this property is satisfied. These conditions can be classified as noninterference constraints and scheduling constraints. The noninterference conditions ensure that the activity of components other than M_i does not have a visible effect on the global state as perceived by M_i. The scheduling conditions ensure that M_i is allocated sufficient CPU time so that the required deadlines are met.

The noninterference conditions are the following:

$$\forall s \in S : \; s \notin A_i \; \Rightarrow \; h_i(\delta(s)) = h_i(s),$$
$$\forall s \in S : \; s \notin A_i \; \Rightarrow \; \beta(s) \notin O_{M_i},$$
$$\forall s \in S, x \in I_G : \; x \notin I_{M_i} \; \Rightarrow \; h_i(\alpha(s,x)) = h_i(s).$$

The first constraint requires that computations performed by the runtime executive or by components other than M_i have no effect on the part of the state visible to M_i. The second constraint requires that no component other than M_i can access M_i's output interface. The last constraint requires that input events not destined for M_i have no effect on what M_i can perceive of the global state.

To specify the scheduling constraints, we need to measure the amount of CPU time allocated to M_i after a finite number of computation steps of G. Given u a finite sequence of elements of $I_G \cup \{\bot\}$ and s a state of G, we denote by $\hat{\delta}(s, u)$ the state reached by G starting from s and after the sequence u of input events has been received. The function $\hat{\delta}$ can be defined as follows:

$$\hat{\delta}(s, \epsilon) = s$$
$$\hat{\delta}(s, u.x) = \delta(\alpha(\hat{\delta}(s, u), x)),$$

where ϵ denotes the empty sequence, $x \in I_G \cup \{\bot\}$, and $u.x$ is the concatenation of u and x. The amount of CPU time allocated to M_i during the finite computation defined by s and u is denoted by $\mu(s, u)$ and it is the number of states of A_i visited between s and $\hat{\delta}(s, u)$:

$$\mu(s, \epsilon) = 0$$
$$\mu(s, u.x) = \begin{cases} 1 + \mu(s, u) & \text{if } \alpha(\hat{\delta}(s, u), x) \in A_i, \\ \mu(s, u) & \text{otherwise.} \end{cases}$$

Let B be the set of finite input sequences of $I_G \cup \{\bot\}$ which do not contain events of I_{M_i}. We denote by $\mu(s, m)$ the minimal amount of CPU allocated to M_i for all finite executions of length m, started in s, and during which no event of I_M is received:

$$\mu(s, m) = \min\{\, \mu(s, u) \mid u \in B \wedge |u| = m \,\}.$$

The scheduling constraints can be organized in two sets. The two constraints below ensure that G meets the deadlines during the initialization phase:

$$\mu(s_0, \Delta_{in}^0) \geqslant \lambda_0$$
$$\forall m \in \mathbb{N} : \delta_i^m(q_0) \in Out_i \Rightarrow \mu(s_0, m + \Delta_{out}) \geqslant m,$$

where Out_i is the set of states q of M_i such that $\beta(q) \neq \bot$ and λ_0 is the time for M_i to terminate the initial computation (cf. Sect. 3.2).

Given any global state s such that $h_i(s) \in W_i$ and any event $x \in I_{M_i}$, the second set of constraints is

$$\mu(\alpha(s, x), \Delta_{in}) \geqslant \lambda(h_i(s), x),$$
$$\forall m \in \mathbb{N} : \delta_i^m(\alpha_i(h_i(s), x)) \in Out_i \Rightarrow \mu(\alpha(s, x), m + \Delta_{out}) \geqslant m.$$

The constant $\lambda(h_i(s), x)$ is the delay for M_i to terminate the computation started in $h_i(s)$ on reception of event x.

In conjunction with the noninterference conditions, these four conditions ensure that the deadlines are met. Two constraints require that the amount of CPU time allocated to component M_i is sufficient for M_i to terminate before the deadline Δ_{in}^0 or Δ_{in}. The two other constraints are similar and ensure that the output deadlines are met: if M_i isolated produces an output after delay m then G will produce the same output before a delay $m + \Delta_{out}$.

It can be shown that if all the noninterference and scheduling constraints are satisfied then $F_{M_i}(\sigma/I_{M_i}) \sqsubseteq F_G(\sigma)/O_{M_i}$ for all input sequence σ of Σ_{in}. The proof relies on the following lemmas:

Lemma 1 *If the noninterference conditions are satisfied then for any global state s and any sequence $u \in B$, if $\mu(s, u) = m$ then*

$$h_i(\hat{\delta}(s, u)) = \delta_i^m(h_i(s)).$$

Lemma 2 *If the noninterference conditions are satisfied, s is a state of G, and u is a sequence of B then for any $m < \mu(s, u)$, there is a unique prefix $v.x$ of u such that $\alpha(\hat{\delta}(s, v), x) \in A_i$ and $\mu(s, v) = m$.*

The noninterference and scheduling constraints given above ensure that the integration of component M_i in G is safe. The model is independent of any particular mechanism for implementing these constraints. The noninterference conditions characterize the impossibility of a process to corrupt data owned by another process. Preventing such data corruption requires *space partitioning*. Typically space partitioning is achieve using memory protection mechanisms provided by hardware. If the scheduling conditions are satisfied, process M_i is guaranteed access to a sufficient amount of CPU time. Ensuring the scheduling conditions requires *temporal partitioning* that can be implemented using timer interrupts to stop and take control away from overrunning processes. The various architectural and implementation issues pertaining to both spatial and temporal partitioning are discussed at large in [11].

5   Discussion and Related Work

In critical applications, the integration of multiple functions on shared hardware requires partitioning mechanisms that provide, with high assurance, a similar level of fault containment as the federated architectures of today. The integration model presented in this paper define properties these partitioning mechanisms must achieve to ensure that non-trusted software components do not interfere with a trusted one, in a system where no intercomponent communication is intended.

As mentioned previously, there are clear similarities between safe integration and aspects of computer security and our approach is inspired from the security notions of noninterference [5, 6] and separability [10, 12]. These two concepts give criteria to guarantee that what one user does has no influence on what another user can observe. In the context of safe integration, we are more concerned with what components can do than with what they can observe and it is easy to adapt noninterference and separability to this purpose. However, in their classic forms, noninterference and separability do not address timing issues which are crucial in integrated real-time applications. Another limit of security models in our context is that they usually intend to prevent all interference while in practice some limited and controlled interference is necessary or unavoidable. The main contribution of our model is the definition of safe integration conditions involving both timing and spatial noninterference and where bounded timing interference is tolerated.

Some of the assumptions made in Sect. 3 on the behavior of software components could be relaxed. For example, it is not difficult to extend the model to include nondeterministic components. The automata-based model developed in Sect. 4 also makes particular assumptions about task execution and access to input and output. Since the possible scheduling and communication mechanisms involved can vary widely from one platform to the next, it is difficult to develop a model general enough to apply in all contexts. The details can be adjusted. The important element of the approach is the method to establish that safe integration is achieved, based on the use of mappings between global and component machines.

A more serious limitation is that our model only applies to systems where components do not communicate. In practice, most integrated systems require some form of cooperation between the different processes or tasks. We are working on extending the approach to this general case. An important issue in this more general context is ensure that there is no source of interference between processes other than via explicitly authorized communication channels. Di Vito [4] develops several partitioning models for IMA using PVS [9] where communication issues are addressed. The approach is closely related to the security notion of noninterference developed by Goguen and Meseguer [5]. Timing is ignored and only spatial partitioning is considered. In the case of cooperating processes, the partitioning requirements are based on comparing the behavior of the integrated system to the behavior of an equivalent federated system (see [4] for details). Other models are also examined with slightly different partitioning requirements. In particular a technique is developed to show that the kernel properly isolates the communication channels from one another.

Like ours, Di Vito's model is based on adapting the security concepts of noninterference and separation to integrated systems. Wilding et al. [15] propose a different approach to verifying partitioning in integrated systems. Each partition is allocated a fixed memory segment and is allocated a periodic window of CPU time on a cyclic basis. The verification of partitioning is based on comparing two systems configured identically with respect to a given partition P. The same memory segment and is allocated to P and the same global schedule is used in both systems. The partitioning mechanisms are correct if the content of the memory segment of P is the same at all time in the two systems, provided it is the same initially. This criterion addresses both timing and spatial partitioning but does not allow cooperation between partitions. The correctness criterion is specific of the detailed hardware/software model used and in particular of the adoption of a fixed scheduling. However, adapting the criterion to other scheduling policies does not seem to pose insurmountable difficulties.

Outside of the IMA context, Totel et al. [13] apply security-related notions to dependable system integration. They define an access control model for supporting object-oriented software components of multiple integrity levels in a single systems. The model includes ordinary object of a single integrity level and objects whose integrity level varies during execution. The access control policy extends Biba's model of data-integrity for multilevel security [2] and intends to ensure that data does not flow from objects of low integrity levels to object of higher integrity levels. The only exception to this rule allows a special class of so-called validation objects to upgrade data from low to high integrity levels. This model gives an approach to defining how software components of different criticality levels may cooperate safely.

The models discussed above address various aspects of a general dependable integration problem. For integrated architectures such as IMA to be acceptable in safety-critical applications one must develop mechanisms to prevent unintended interaction between components and provide high assurance that these mechanisms are adequate. As discussed in [11], there is a large space of architectural and design choices that can achieve the required partitioning. The challenge is to define models that are general enough to encompass spatial, temporal, and communication aspects. The models above address memory partitioning and to some extent temporal partitioning and intercomponent communication in the context of single-processor systems. A lot remains to be done in the areas of temporal partitioning and communication. Subtle interactions such as the impact of interrupts on timing and temporal partitioning are not yet adequately treated. It also remains to investigate the integration and partitioning issues posed by distributed systems. New risks of interference arise in such systems due to shared communication media such as avionics buses. New models need to be developed to analyze bus access conflicts and bus scheduling issues, and the impact of bus communication on the local memory and temporal partitioning defined for a single-processor hardware component of the system.

6   Conclusion

This paper proposes a model of safe integration allowing one to mix software components of different criticality levels and performing independent functions in a single system. The main principle is to ensure that the black-box behavior of the resulting integrated system does not deviate too much from the behavior of each of the high-integrity components. Based on this definition, one can derive sufficient conditions of safe integration which rely on an automata model.

The notion of safe integration and the model used are related to the two security concepts of separability and noninterference. The main differences are due to two crucial objectives: maintaining availability and responsiveness of trusted components in the integrated system. Timing issues become essential.

In future work, we envisage relating safe integration and software architecture. The main idea would be to develop software architectures for integrated systems by successive refinements, starting from a top-level description where components are isolated and by applying transformations ensuring that safe integration criteria as defined in this paper are satisfied. This approach could then be extended to cooperating components. The successive refinements would then have to ensure that no risk of interference is introduced other than via the communication channels explicitly present in the top-level description.

References

[1] Avionics Application Software Standard Interface. ARINC Specification 653, ARINC, Annapolis, Maryland, January 1997.

[2] R.R. Biba. Integrity Considerations for Secure Computer Systems. Technical Report MTR-3135, Mitre Corporation, April 1977.

[3] A. Brown, D.J. Carney, and M.D. McFalls. Proceedings of the SEI/MCC Symposium on the Use of COTS in Systems Integration. Technical Report CMU/SEI-95-SR-007, Software Engineering Insitute, June 1995.

[4] Ben Di Vito. A Model of Cooperative Noninterference for Integrated Modular Avionics. In *Dependable Computing for Critical Applications (DCCA-7)*, San Jose, CA, January 1999. This volume.

[5] J.A. Goguen and J. Meseguer. Security Policies and Security Models. In *Proceedings of the Symposium on Security and Privacy*, pages 11–20, Oakland, CA, 1982.

[6] J.A. Goguen and J. Meseguer. Unwinding and Inference Control. In *Proceedings of the Symposium on Security and Privacy*, pages 75–86, Oakland, CA, 1984.

[7] M. Morgan. Integrated Modular Avionics for Next-Generation Commercial Airplanes. *IEEE Aerospace and Electronic Systems*, 6(8):9–12, August 1991.

[8] A. Nadesakumar, R. Crowder, and C. Harris. Advanced system concepts for future civil aircraft - an overview of avionic architecture. *Proceedings of the Institution of Mechanical Engineers. Part G: Journal of Aerospace Engineering*, 209(G4), 1995.

[9] S. Owre, J. Rushby, N. Shankar, and F. von Henke. Formal Verification for Fault-Tolerant Architectures: Prolegomena to the Design of PVS. *IEEE Transactions on Software Engineering*, 21(2):107–125, February 1995.

[10] J. Rushby. Design and Verification of Secure Systems. In *Proceedings of the 8th Symposium on Operating Systems Principles, ACM SIGOPS*, volume 26, pages 54–60, November 1981.

[11] J. Rushby. Partitioning in Avionics Architectures: Requirements, Mechanisms, and Assurance. Draft technical report, Computer Science Laboratory, SRI International, October 1998.

[12] J. Rushby and B. Randell. A Distributed Secure System. *IEEE Computer*, 16(7):55–67, July 1983.

[13] E. Totel, J.-P. Blanquart, Y. Deswarte, and D. Powell. Supporting Multiple Levels of Criticality. In *FTCS-28, The 28th Annual Fault Tolerant Computing Symposium*, pages 70–79, Munich, Germany, June 1998.

[14] M.R Vigder, W.M. Gentleman, and J. Dean. COTS Software Integration: State of the Art. Technical Report 39198, National Research Council of Canada, January 1996.

[15] M. Wilding, D. Hardin, and D. Greve. Invariant Performance: A Statement of Task Isolation Useful for Embedded Application Integration. In *Dependable Computing for Critical Applications, DCCA-7*, San Jose, CA, January 1999. This volume.

Dependability Evaluation

Dependability Modeling and Evaluation of Phased Mission Systems: a DSPN Approach

I. Mura[1], A. Bondavalli[2], X. Zang[3] and K. S. Trivedi[3]

1 Department of Information Engineering, University of Pisa, Italy
{mura@rep1.iei.pi.cnr.it}
2 CNUCE/CNR, Pisa, Italy {a.bondavalli@cnuce.cnr.it}
3 CACC, Department of Electronic Engineering, Duke University, Durham NC
{xzang, kst @ee.duke.edu}

Abstract

In this paper we focus on the analytical modeling for the dependability evaluation of phased-mission systems. Because of their dynamic behavior, systems showing a phased behavior offer challenges in modeling. We propose the modeling and evaluation of phased-mission systems dependability through the Deterministic and Stochastic Petri Nets (DSPN). The DSPN approach to the phased-mission systems offers many advantages, concerning both the modeling and the solution. The DSPN model of the mission can be a very concise one, and it can be efficiently solved for the dependability evaluation purposes. The solution procedure is supported by the existence of an analytical solution for the transient probabilities of the marking process underlying the DSPN model. This analytical solution can be fully automated. We show how the DSPN models capabilities are able to deal with various peculiar features of phased-mission systems, including those systems where the next phase to be performed can be chosen at the time the preceding phase ends.

Keywords: Phased-mission, Dependability Modelling and Evaluation, Deterministic and Stochastic Petri Nets, Closed-Form Solution, Markov Chains.

1 Introduction

Many of the systems devoted to the control and management of critical activities have to perform a series of tasks that must be accomplished in sequence. Their operational life consists of a sequence of non-overlapping periods, called *phases*. These systems are often called phased-mission systems, abbreviated as PMS hereafter. Both the system behavior and the conditions of the environment in which the system is embedded may vary from phase to phase. These changes may be due to different tasks to be performed within each phase, or different stresses the system is subject to, as well as different dependability requirements and failure scenarios. In order to accomplish its mission the system needs to change its configuration over time, to adopt the most suitable one with respect to the performance and dependability requirements of the phase being currently executed. Many examples of PMS can be found in various application domains. For instance, systems for the aided-guide of aircrafts, whose mission-time is divided into several phases such as take-off, cruise, landing, with completely different requirements. Other systems alternate between operational and maintenance phases (e.g., nuclear power plants), or have missions with multiple goals such as a spacecraft meant for scientific research.

In this paper we focus on the analytical modeling for the dependability evaluation of PMS. We propose the modeling and evaluation of phased-mission systems dependability through Deterministic and Stochastic Petri Nets (DSPN). The class of DSPN models allows timed transitions with exponentially distributed firing times, immediate transitions, and includes deterministic transitions as well. Moreover, the DSPNs allow a very concise modeling of even quite complex systems, through the use of guards on transitions, timed transition priorities, halting conditions, reward rates, etc. Due to their high expressiveness, DSPNs are able to cope with the dynamic structure of the phased mission systems. The DSPN approach to the phased-mission systems offers many advantages, concerning both the modeling and the solution. Phased-mission systems are modeled with a single DSPN model representing the whole mission. This single-model approach enables us to deal with dependencies among phases caused by the sharing of architectural components. Moreover, the model of the mission can be a very concise one. The single DSPN model can be efficiently solved for dependability evaluation purposes. The solution procedure is supported by the existence of an analytical solution for the transient probabilities of the marking process underlying the DSPN model [8]. This solution only requires the separate solution of each single phase, and can be fully automated.

The main contribution of this paper lies in the proposal of the DSPN modeling approach for PMS. In this respect, it offers a suitable means for a systematic formulation and solution of PMS models, and for their sensitivity analysis. We show how well DSPN can represent the typical features of PMS that have been taken into account by the previous proposals appeared in the literature. We also point out that DSPNs models of PMS can naturally deal with the connections between solution of different phases, which has been only treated in an *ad hoc* manner in earlier approaches. Moreover, the DSPN formulation easily lends itself to automation and allows additional features of PMS to be modeled, features which are usually not considered in literature. For instance, we consider in this paper the state-dependent selection of the next phase to be executed. The exploitation of the full DSPN modeling power to include more and more features of PMS promises to be a fruitful investigation and is the subject of our on-going work.

The paper is organized as follows. Section 2 presents the class of PMS we will be dealing with. That section gives a retrospective on the different Markov chain-based models that have appeared in literature, and explains at an high abstraction level the DSPN approach in the modeling of PMS. In Section 3 we briefly introduce the mathematical background underlying the analytical solution of the DSPN models. Section 4 shows how the DSPN capabilities are able to deal with the various peculiar features of PMS, through the modeling of an imaginary though realistic example of a space application. Three different models are considered, which progressively include more and more features of PMS in a still concise, readable and easy-to-define DSPN model. In Section 5 the general theory of DSPN is specialized to PMS modeling, and an analytical solution is given for the transient probabilities of the marking process. Section 6 explains the automation procedure of the DSPN model solution, and presents the results of an evaluation aimed at assessing the probability of completing the mission for the example of space application. Finally, conclusions are given in Section 7.

2 PMS problem viewed as a DSPN

As we already pointed out, systems showing a phased behavior offer challenges in dependability modeling and evaluation. The architectural components the system utilizes during a phase are in general used in other subsequent phases, thus adding a set of dependencies among the models of different phases. Moreover, the phase changes very often reflect the occurrence of particular events that do not depend on the system state itself, but are rather triggered by time-out exceptions, or are pre-planned for the entire system life-time.

All these characteristics of PMS call for powerful modeling tools, able to capture and concisely represent these peculiar features. PMS have been widely investigated. Starting from the early studies [6, 24], which assumed fairly simple phase dependencies of system components, many works have been proposed which resort to Fault-Tree models [7, 11, 17, 23] (only for non-repairable systems) and to Markov chain models [2, 3, 5, 10, 16, 21, 22]. A different approach based on the SAN (Stochastic Activity Networks) modeling is adopted in [4], a study closely related to our investigation. To better understand the novelty of our approach, in the following we first give a brief review of the related studies that have appeared in the literature. Then, we propose the DSPN approach, in order to compare the main advantages and drawbacks of all the presented methods with respect to the new one.

2.1 Literature survey

In this section we present and compare the Markov chain-based approaches [2, 3, 5, 10, 16, 21, 22] and the one based on SAN in [4] for the dependability modeling and analysis of PMS. The most relevant aspects of the comparison are summarized in Table 1.

A key point that impacts most of the other aspects is represented by the single/separate modeling of the phases: it affects the reusability/flexibility of previously built models, the modeling of dependencies among phases and the complexity of the solution steps. The single model approaches [2, 4, 10, 21] suffer from a lack of reusability: a new model needs to be built if the behavior of the system in any phase is changed or if the phase order is changed. However, this task is considerably simpler for the SAN model of PMS than for the Markov chain based approaches. As an advantage, the single-model approach allows the exploitation of similarities among phases to obtain a compact model in which all the phases are properly embedded as in [2, 4, 10]. Conversely, the separate modeling of each phase [3, 22] allows the reuse of previously built models of the phases. Moreover, it is easier to characterize the differences among phases, in terms of different failure rates and different configuration requirements. The hierarchical approaches in [5, 16] try to combine the advantages of the single and separate modeling to keep phase models small and easy-to-define and at the same time to provide different levels of abstraction at which the mission can be described and analyzed.

The duration of phases is assumed to be fixed and known in advance in [3, 5, 10, 16]. This assumption seems to hold for a wide range of application of PMS, as for instance the space applications, where phases are pre-planned on ground. Moreover, this assumption enables an exact solution of the models through the mapping of the transient state probabilities from one phase to the next. When phases of random duration are to be considered the analysis becomes more complicated. Exponential distributions do not appear to be a suitable way to model phase durations due to their long tail behavior, while using non-exponential ones complicates the analysis and may lead to approximate solutions as in [2, 22], or may require the numerical solution of the associated set of differential equations, as in [21], or a simulative solution [4].

The treatment of dependencies among phases requires a mapping of probabilities from states of a phase to states of the next phase, and represents a relevant issue to be addressed. The single model permits representing implicitly the mapping of probabilities from one phase to another phase because phase changes and state changes are modeled together. However, this joint modeling may result in a non-homogeneous Markov model, as in [21]. On the contrary, the separate approach requires us to explicitly perform the mapping from state to state for each phase change. This job is conceptually simple but can be cumbersome and becomes a potential source of errors for large models. In [16, 22] the mapping is realized through proper intraphase matrices, whereas in [3] the mapping is carried out manually. In [5] specific submodels called *transitions* are defined to represent the intraphase behavior. Transition models permit to represent missions that may include probabilistic choices of the next phases to be performed. Therefore, while the other approaches only consider missions having a fixed linear profile, the method in [5] allows for missions with a tree configuration.

Method	Type of modeling	Phase duration	Treatment of dependencies	Mission profile	Complexity (upper-bound)
[16] (Meyer 1979)	hierarchical	fixed	intraphase matrices	chain	$O\!\left(\sum_{i=1}^{n} S_i^2 q_i t_i\right)$
[3] (Arlat 1986)	separate Markov models	fixed	by hand	chain	$O\!\left(\sum_{i=1}^{n} S_i^2 q_i t_i\right)$
[2] (Alam 1986)	single Markov models	random	implicit	chain	$O\!\left(S^2 q \sum_{i=1}^{n} t_i\right)$
[21] (Smotherman 1989)	single non-homogeneous Markov model	random	implicit	chain	$O\!\left(\left(\sum_{i=1}^{n} S_i\right)^2 q \sum_{i=1}^{n} t_i\right)$
[4] (Aupperle 1989)	single SAN model	random	implicit	chain	---
[10] (Dugan 1991)	single non-homogeneous Markov model	fixed	implicit	chain	$O\!\left(S^2 q \sum_{i=1}^{n} t_i\right)$
[22] (Somani 1992)	separate Markov models	random	intraphase matrices	chain	$O\!\left(\sum_{i=1}^{n} S_i^2 q_i t_i\right)$
[5] (Bondavalli 1997)	hierarchical	fixed	transitions	tree	$O\!\left(\sum_{i=1}^{n} S_i^2 q_i t_i\right)$

Table 1: Markov chain based methods for PMS

To carry out a comparison of the computational complexity that the various methods require, we consider the cost required to solve a phased-mission system which consists of a chain of n phases numbered $1,2,\ldots,n$. Phase i has an underlying Markov chain with S_i states and lasts for t_i units of time $i = 1,2,\ldots,n$. Both the methods in [2] and in [10] solve a unique Markov model whose state space is the set given by the union of the single state space of each phase. The size S of the unified state space is at least $\max_{i=1,2,\ldots,n} S_i$, and can be at most $\sum_{i=1}^{n} S_i$. The single Markov chain is solved n times for n phases. If the uniformization method [19] is used to evaluate the transient probability vector, the overall complexity of the solution is $O\!\left(S^2 q \sum_{i=1}^{n} t_i\right)$, where q is defined as the maximum module entry of the generator matrix of the whole Markov model. The method of Smotherman and Zemoudeh [21] requires the solution of a set of nS differential equations. The authors also adopt a Runge-Kutta solution algorithm, at a cost that can be bounded by $O\left(\left(\sum_{i=1}^{n} S_i\right)^2 q \sum_{i=1}^{n} t_i\right)$, where q is defined as above. The complexity of the solution for the method in [4] can not be compared to the other listed in Table 1, because the SAN model is to be solved by simulation. Therefore, the computational cost is affected by a number of factors, as the width of the confidence intervals, the method used for the statistical analysis, etc. The methods in [5, 16], as well as all those that adopt the separate modeling approach [3, 22], require a number of operations which is dominated by $O\left(\sum_{i=1}^{n} S_i^2 q_i t_i\right)$, where q_i is the maximum module entry of the Markov chain generator matrix of phase i. This computational complexity grows linearly with the number of phases. Therefore, the methods that use separate solution of the phase models are, in general, more efficient than the ones that use a combined model. Note that all the computational cost reported here are to be intended as upper-bounds. In fact, often the matrices obtained are quite sparse, thus allowing cheaper solution techniques [19].

2.2 The DSPN approach

DSPNs have been introduced as an extension of Generalised Stochastic Petri Nets and of Stochastic Reward Nets, to allow the modeling of events having deterministic occurrence times [1]. The set T of transitions of a DSPN can be partitioned into three disjoint sets: T^{Imm}, the set of immediate transitions, represented by a thin line, T^{Exp} the set of transitions having exponentially distributed firing times, represented by empty rectangles, and T^{Det}, the set of transitions with deterministic firing times represented by filled rectangles.

This enriched set of possible transitions offered by DSPNs allows the PMS to be represented by the general model schema shown in Figure 1. At an high abstraction level, the model of a PMS is composed of two logically separate parts: one represents the system, that is, its components and their interactions, which evolve according to the events that modify their state, and the other is the control part, which describes the phase changes. Both the parts can be modeled via DSPNs: the system part is a pure SRN submodel, that we call System Net (SN), containing only exponentially distributed and immediate transitions. The control part is represented by a DSPN submodel, the Phase Net (PhN), which contains all the deterministic transitions of the overall DSPN model and may well contain immediate transitions.

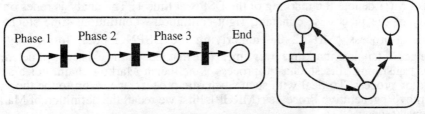

Figure 1: DSPN model of a PMS

A token in a place of the PhN model represents a phase being executed, and the firing of a deterministic transition models a phase change. The sequence of phases ends with a token in STOP place, which represents the end of the mission. The SN model describing the evolution of the underlying system is governed by the PhN:

the SN's evolution may depend on the marking of the PhN thus representing the phase-dependent behavior of the system. According to the SRN modeling rules, this phase dependent behavior is modeled by proper marking dependent predicates which modify transition rates, enabling conditions, reward rates, etc., of the overall DSPN. As we will detail in the following, the two nets can interact in various ways, and this allows the modeling of different features of PMS mentioned above. Any structure of the two nets can be considered: in particular, the PhN is not limited to have a linear structure.

The same structure of the model of a PMS can be found in the paper of Aupperle, Meyer and Wei in [4]. They used the METASAN [20] modeling tool, based on Stochastic Activity Networks, to represent both the PhN and the SN. In the SAN language, transitions are called activities. SANs allow for general distributions of activity duration, for marking dependent firing rates, and for guards on the enabling conditions of activities. Hence, SANs and DSPNs share many of the modeling features, and the work in [4] contains many interesting elements for the modeling of complex PMS. Here, we intend to apply the potentialities of DSPNs to investigate how the various aspects of PMS can be modeled. Moreover, we exploit the MRGP theory to provide an analytical solution technique for the DSPN model of PMS, and for its sensitivity analysis. The possibility of such analytical solution was not available at the time the work in [4] was proposed, and it represents a considerable step towards the definition of a systematic solution method for PMS. To guarantee the analytical tractability of the DSPN, the only constraint to be imposed on the model is the following one (although this assumption has been relaxed in some recent work [15, 18]):

Assumption 1:   at most one transition belonging to T^{Det} is enabled in each of the possible markings of the DSPN.

This condition is obviously satisfied for the DSPN model of a PMS provided that the only deterministic activities modeled are the phase durations. In this case, there is only one (and exactly one) deterministic transition enabled, which corresponds to the current phase of the system, and an elegant analytical solution can be given for the transient marking probabilities.

3   Solution of PMS via DSPN

In this section we briefly present the mathematical background underlying the analysis of a generic DSPN model. The general theory for the analysis will be tailored to the PMS problem in a subsequent section. A complete exposition of the DSPN solution approach for the general case can be found in [8, 12].

Let M(t) denote the marking of the DSPN at time t. The analysis relies on the study of the piecewise-constant, right-continuous, continuous-time stochastic marking-process $\{M(t), t > 0\}$, underlying the DSPN model, formed by the changes of tangible markings over time. Note that, due to the existence of deterministic transitions, this stochastic process is neither a Markov chain, nor a semi-Markov process. To deal with such stochastic process, we resort to the theory of Markov Regenerative Processes (MRGP). First we recall the definition of Markov renewal sequence.

Definition 1:

Let S be a discrete state space. A sequence of bivariate random variables $\{(Y_n, T_n), n \geq 0\}$ is called a Markov renewal sequence if:

1) $T_0 = 0$, $T_{n+1} \geq T_n$ $T_n \in \Re^+$; $Y_n \in S$ $n \geq 0$

2) $\forall n \geq 0, \text{Prob}[Y_{n+1} = j, T_{n+1} - T_n \leq x \,|Y_n = i, T_n, Y_{n-1}, T_{n-1}, \ldots, Y_0, T_0] =$

$$\text{Prob}[Y_{n+1} = j, T_{n+1} - T_n \leq x \,|Y_n = i] =$$
$$= \text{Prob}[Y_{n+1} = j, T_{n+1} - T_n \leq x \,|Y_0 = i] = k_{i,j}(x)$$

The matrix $K(x) = \|k_{i,j}(x)\|$ is referred as the kernel of the Markov renewal sequence. The definition of MRGP is based on Markov renewal sequences [14].

Definition 2:

A stochastic process $\{Z(t), t \geq 0\}$ is called a MRGP if there exists a Markov renewal sequence $\{(Y_n, T_n), n \geq 0\}$ of random variables such that all the conditional finite distributions of $\{Z(T_n + t), t \geq 0\}$ given $\{Z(u), 0 \leq u \leq T_n, Y_n = i\}$ are the same as those of $\{Z(t), t \geq 0\}$ given $Y_0 = i$

It is possible to show [8] that, if Assumption 1) holds, the marking process $\{M(t), t > 0\}$ of a DSPN is an MRGP. For this aim, we first define a suitable renewal sequence, as follows. Let S denote the set of tangible markings of the reachability graph of the DSPN, which is exactly the state space of the marking process $\{M(t), t > 0\}$. Let $T_0 = 0$, and consider the sequence $\{T_n, n \geq 0\}$ of time instants recursively defined. Suppose $m \in S$ is the marking such that $m = M(T_n+)$. If m is an absorbing marking, then set $T_{n+1} = \infty$. If no deterministic transitions are enabled in marking m, define T_{n+1} as the first time after T_n that a marking change occurs. If one deterministic transition is enabled in marking m, define T_{n+1} to be the time when such transition fires or is disabled. Now, define the sequence $\{Y_n, n \geq 0\}$ as $Y_n = M(T_n+)$, $\forall n \geq 0$. It can be proved that the so defined bivariate sequence $\{(Y_n, T_n), n \geq 0\}$ embedded in the marking-process $\{M(t), t > 0\}$ of the DSPN model is a Markov renewal sequence, according to Definition 1. Moreover, it is easy to show that the stochastic behavior of the marking process from time T_n onwards $\{M(T_n + t), t \geq 0\}$ depends only on $Y_n = i$, and this implies that

$$\{M(T_n + t), t \geq 0 \,|M(u), 0 \leq u \leq T_n, Y_n = i\} \overset{\text{dist}}{=} \{M(T_n + t), t \geq 0 \,|Y_n = i\} \overset{\text{dist}}{=}$$
$$\{M(T_n + t), t \geq 0 \,|Y_0 = i\}$$

where $\overset{\text{dist}}{=}$ denotes equality in distribution, and this proves that $\{M(t), t > 0\}$ is an MRGP. Let $V(t) = \|v_{i,j}(t)\|$ be the matrix defined as follows:

$$v_{i,j}(t) = \text{Prob}[M(t) = j \,|M(0) = Y_0 = i], \quad i, j \in S$$

To obtain matrix $V(t)$, which describes the transient behavior of the stochastic process underlying the DSPN, an analytical method has been proposed in [8], and here we briefly recall that. For the sake of conciseness, denote with $K * V(t)$ the matrix whose element i, j is defined as follows:

$$k * v_{i,j}(t) = \sum_{h \in S} \int_0^t dk_{i,h}(t) v_{h,j}(t-u)$$

that is $K * V(t)$ is the matrix of functions of t whose generic element is obtained with the row by column convolution of the kernel matrix $K(t)$ and matrix $V(t)$, rather than with the usual multiplication operator. According to the MRGP theory [14], the transition matrix $V(t)$ can be obtained by solving the following generalized Markov renewal equation:

$$V(t) = E(t) + K * V(t) \qquad (1)$$

where $E(t) = \|e_{i,j}(t)\|$ is the local kernel matrix defined as $e_{i,j}(t) = \text{Prob}[M(t) = j, T_1 > t \,|\, Y_0 = i]$. Solving Equation (1) to obtain matrix $V(t)$ for a general MRGP may require the use of numerical algorithms or of Laplace-Stiltjes transform. However, as we shall see in the following, the solution of Equation (1) in the case of an MRGP underlying a DSPN model for a PMS can be greatly simplified, and matrix $V(t)$ can be obtained exactly in the time domain at a limited computational cost.

4   Applications

In this section we investigate the modeling capabilities of the DSPNs, to understand what features of PMS can be represented by the high-level model in Figure 1. Different PMS characteristics will be modeled by enriching step by step the DSPN model with new interaction capabilities between the PhN and the SN. As an example, throughout the rest of the paper we will be considering a typical example of PMS: a phased-mission of an ideal space application.

4.1 Case 1: phase-dependent behavior of the SN

Consider a space application whose mission alternates operational phases as Launch, Planet, Scientific Obsevations 1 and Scientific Obsevations 2 with Hibernation phases, typically entered to maintain a low level of activity during periods of navigation. Operational phases have stringent dependability requirements, hence the system employs a set of n redundant identical processors. Processors fail and are repaired independently from each other. Processors fail with phase-dependent rates: the failure rate during hibernation phases is less than the failure rate during operational phases. The repair strategy is based on the nature of faults affecting the space-probe. Indeed, since most of the faults are of transient nature, it is possible that after a random period of time a faulty processor becomes available again. Moreover, it is also possible to reload parts of the software from ground, to recover from errors caused by design faults or by aging. Different success/failure criteria are specified for each phase. In particular, one active processor is sufficient to survive hibernation phases, but at least three active processors are needed for the operational ones.

This phased-mission system is modeled by the DSPN shown in Figure 2, where the PhN represents the sequence of phases, where $\tau_1, \tau_2, \ldots, \tau_7$ are the deterministic durations of the phases. The multiprocessor system is represented by the simple SN model in Figure 2. Transition t1 represents the failure of a processor, and transition t2 the repair of a faulty processor. The initial marking of the DSPN is

$(\#(\text{Launch}) = 1, \#(\text{Up}) = n)$, and all the other places hold no tokens at the beginning.

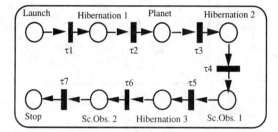 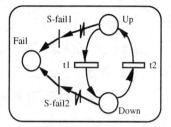

Figure 2: DSPN model of the phase-dependent multiprocessor system

The phase-dependent failure conditions are easily modeled with the proper enabling guards on the immediate transitions S-fail1 and S-fail2 and phase-dependent firing rate of transition t1. Note the variable cardinality arcs connecting places Up and Down to those transitions: as soon as the transitions are enabled, all the tokens inside the two places are moved to the place Fail. The firing rates and the guards of transitions are specified in Table 2.

transition	Hibernation	Operational	Stop
t1	$\lambda_1 \#(\text{Up})$	$\lambda_2 \#(\text{Up})$	0
t2	$\mu \#(\text{Down})$	$\mu \#(\text{Down})$	0
S-fail1	$\#(\text{Up}) = 0$	$\#(\text{Up}) < 3$	FALSE
S-fail2	$\#(\text{Up}) = 0$	$\#(\text{Up}) < 3$	FALSE

Table 2: Transition firing rates and guards for the DSPN of case 1

Several advantages are offered by the DSPN approach over previous proposals cited earlier. First, the modeling features of DSPN allow a very concise representation of PMS, compared with a Markov chain which results in huge models that readily become sources of errors in modeling. Moreover, the DSPN modeling of the PMS merges the advantages of the single model approach, together with those of the separate one. Indeed, the dependencies among phases are naturally incorporated and similarities among phases are exploited by the single model. Furthermore, the two parts of the DSPN model represent two different abstraction levels of the same PMS. The mission profile is explicitly modeled in the PhN, and can be changed to model different PMS. The different phases are very easily modified by changing the phase-dependent guard and firing rate functions.

4.2 Case 2: phase-triggered reconfigurations of the SN

Consider now another strategy to use the n redundant processors the system is equipped with. Since not all the phases have the same dependability requirements, the system could use only those processors that are actually needed to meet the dependability requirements of the current phase and keep the other ones as cold spares. This way, the unused resources will be held in a safe state to be better employed while performing critical activities. It can be assumed that a standby processor is not subject to failure.

Figure 3 shows a DSPN model for a space application performing the same mission as the PMS shown in the previous case, but employing the phase-dependent configuration policy to manage the resources of the processing system.

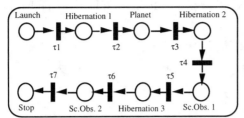 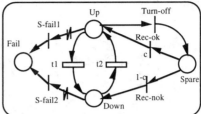

Figure 3: A DSPN model for a system with phase-triggered reconfigurations

Hibernation phases are typically the less critical phases, and two active processors is the ideal system configuration in these phases. During operational phases, a configuration with three active processors is needed to ensure adequate dependability levels. As before, the system can survive during hibernation phases even with only one active processor, and three active processors are now mandatory for the operational phases.

Due to the different configuration requirements of the different phases, several actions must be performed as the phases alternate. At the start of each hibernation phase, a reconfiguration takes place where in one of the active processor is turned off. Similarly, when a new operational phase starts, one spare must be turned on. The activation of a cold spare may succeed or fail, with probability c and $1-c$, respectively. A spare processor that fails during activation becomes a faulty processor. Those actions which must be performed at the end of a phase or when the next phase is started can be easily modeled through the guards on immediate transitions.

transition	Hibernation	Operational	Stop
t1	$\lambda_1 \#(\text{Up})$	$\lambda_2 \#(\text{Up})$	0
t2	$\mu \#(\text{Down})$	$\mu \#(\text{Down})$	0
S-fail1	$\#(\text{Up})+\#(\text{Spare}) = 0$	$\#(\text{Up})+\#(\text{Spare}) < 3$	FALSE
S-fail2	$\#(\text{Up})+\#(\text{Spare}) = 0$	$\#(\text{Up})+\#(\text{Spare}) < 3$	FALSE
Turn-off	$\#(\text{Up}) \geq 3$	$\#(\text{Up}) \geq 4$	FALSE
Rec-ok	$\#(\text{Up}) \leq 1$	$\#(\text{Up}) \geq 2$	FALSE
Rec-nok	$\#(\text{Up}) \leq 1$	$\#(\text{Up}) \geq 2$	FALSE

Table 3: Transition firing rates and guards for the DSPN of Figure 3

The guard on the immediate transition Turn-off is used to adjust the system configuration to the requirements of the phase currently being executed. Two immediate transitions Rec-ok and Rec-nok and their controlling guards model the turning-on of spare processors. The failure criteria of the different phases are accounted for by the guards on transitions S-fail1 and S-fail2. Transition rates of timed transition and guards on immediate transitions are given by Table 3. The initial marking of the DSPN is $(\#(\text{Launch}) = 1, \#(\text{Up}) = 3, \#(\text{Spare}) = n - 3)$, and no tokens in the remaining places.

It is worthwhile observing that phase-triggered reconfigurations would complicate the treatment of dependencies among phases and the mapping that it involves. Indeed, consider a change from phase i to phase j. In any marking of phase i many immediate transitions (reconfigurations) can be triggered as phase j starts, leading to different initial markings in the new phase. All those events should be accounted for by the mapping of state probability vector, which must be done at the level of the underlying marking process, and hence can be a laborious job for large models. All the separate modeling methods cited in the previous section basically deal with this issue in this tedious manner. The single model approaches in [2, 4, 10, 21] solve the dependencies problem with an implicit mapping which is embedded in the model. For our single DSPN model approach, the modeling of the mapping becomes extremely easy, in that it uses the high expressivity of the SRN paradigm.

4.3 Case 3: Mission profile depending on SN marking

Here, we consider the case when the next phase to be performed is to be chosen at the time the preceding phase ends. The dynamic choice of the mission profile may be useful while skipping phases that would risk or endanger the execution of more important activities. For instance, a secondary goal could be sacrificed if there are few available resources: these resources should be better held in a spare state in order to guarantee a reliable execution of the main goal of the mission. To the best of our knowledge, this features of PMS has been previously considered only in [5]. Here, we show how the DSPN approach can provide the flexibility to model such a dynamic behavior.

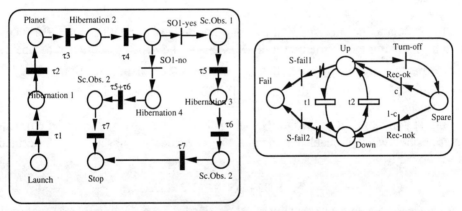

Figure 4: Mission profile dependent on the system configuration

Figure 4 shows DSPN model for this case. We assume that the secondary goal, the Scientific Obsevations 1, is to be skipped if the system has less then 4 non-failed processors. If we do not consider the place Stop, the PhN net shows a tree structure.

transition	Hibernation	Operational	Stop
t1	$\lambda_1 \#(Up)$	$\lambda_2 \#(Up)$	0
t2	$\mu \#(Down)$	$\mu \#(Down)$	0
S-fail1	$\#(Up)+\#(Spare) = 0$	$\#(Up)+\#(Spare) < 3$	FALSE
S-fail2	$\#(Up)+\#(Spare) = 0$	$\#(Up)+\#(Spare) < 3$	FALSE
Turn-off	$\#(Up) \geq 3$	$\#(Up) \geq 4$	FALSE
Rec-ok	$\#(Up) \leq 1$	$\#(Up) \geq 2$	FALSE
Rec-nok	$\#(Up) \leq 1$	$\#(Up) \geq 2$	FALSE
SO1-yes	$\#(Up)+\#(Spare) \geq 4$		
So1-no	$\#(Up)+\#(Spare) \leq 3$		

Table 4: Transition firing rates and guards for the DSPN of Figure 4

The system-dependent mission profile is easily modeled with the two immediate transitions SO1-yes and SO1-no, whose enabling conditions depend on the marking of the SN. Table 4 gives all the transition firing rates of timed transitions and the guards of immediate transitions.

5   Analytical solution

DSPN models of PMS have two properties that allow us to simplify the general expression (1) of the transient probability matrix of an MRGP:

Property 1: each of the regeneration points T_n, $n \geq 0$ is chosen as the firing time of a transition having deterministic firing duration.

Property 2: in every non-absorbing marking of the DSPN, there is always one deterministic transition enabled.

We first tailor the general theory introduced in Section 3 to the case when the PhN has a linear structure, as in cases 1 and 2 of the preceding section, and then we address the more general case (as in case 3) when the PhN has a tree structure.

5.1 Linear PhN

Let S denote the state space of the marking process of a DSPN for a PMS having a PhN with linear structure. Let $1,2,\dots,n$ be the ordered sequence of phases performed through the mission. Let t_i^{Det} be the deterministic transition having firing time τ_i which models the time the PMS spends in phase i, $i = 1,2,\dots,n$, respectively.

For any marking $\bar{m}$ of the DSPN state space S, let $D(\bar{m})$ denote the deterministic transition which is enabled in marking $\bar{m}$. Consider the subsets S_i of S defined as follows:

$$S_i = \left\{ \bar{m} \in S \mid D(\bar{m}) = t_i^{Det} \right\}, \ i = 1,2,\dots,n$$

and let C_i denote the cardinality of set S_i, $i = 1,2,\dots,n$. Owing to Assumption 1 together with the Property 2 stated above, the sets S_i are a partition of the state space S. The marking process $\{M(t), t \geq 0\}$ moves from S_i to S_{i+1}, $i = 1,2,\dots,n-1$ over time. Now, consider the continuous-time Markov chain $\{M_i(t), t \geq 0\}$ whose state transition diagram corresponds to the reduced reachability graph of the DSPN when transition t_i^{Det} is enabled, that is within the time interval $[T_{i-1}, T_i)$, $i = 1,2,\dots,n$. The state space of $\{M_i(t), t \geq 0\}$ is a subset of S, and is given by S_i. The generator matrix of $\{M_i(t), t \geq 0\}$, denoted by Q_i, can be obtained by analyzing the evolution of the SRN while staying in phase i, $i = 1,2,\dots,n$. More precisely, let $\lambda(\bar{m}, \bar{m}')$ denote the transition rate from marking $\bar{m}$ to marking $\bar{m}'$ in the reduced reachability graph. Matrix Q_i has size $C_i \times C_i$, and is defined as follows:

$$Q_i = \left\| q_{\bar{m},\bar{m}'}^i \right\| = \begin{cases} \lambda(\bar{m},\bar{m}') & \bar{m} \neq \bar{m}' \\ -\sum_{\bar{r} \in S_i, \bar{r} \neq \bar{m}} q_{\bar{m},\bar{r}}^i & \bar{m} = \bar{m}' \end{cases}, \ \bar{m},\bar{m}' \in S_i$$

Between the regeneration points T_{i-1} and T_i, $i = 1, 2, \ldots, n$, the evolution of the MRGP underlying the DSPN follows that of the simple continuous-time Markov chain $\{M_i(t), t \geq 0\}$. Therefore, for any $t \in [T_{i-1}, T_i)$, the transient probability matrix can be obtained through the exponential of the matrix Q_i.

Let us define the following branching-probability matrices which account for the branching probabilities as the deterministic transitions fire. Let Δ_i, $i = 1, 2, \ldots, n-1$ be the matrix defined as follows:

$$\Delta_i = \left\| \delta^i_{\bar{m}, \bar{m}'} \right\| = \Pr ob[Y_i = \bar{m}' \mid M(T_i-) = \bar{m}], \ \bar{m} \in S_i, \ \bar{m}' \in S_{i+1}$$

The branching-probability matrix Δ_i has dimension $C_i \times C_{i+1}$, $i = 1, 2, \ldots, n-1$. These matrices can be automatically obtained when the reachability graph is generated.

According to the partition S_i, $i = 1, 2, \ldots, n$ of the state space S, the matrices $K(t)$ and $E(t)$ can be written in block form $K(t) = \left\| K_{i,j}(t) \right\|$ and $E(t) = \left\| E_{i,j}(t) \right\|$. The block matrices $K_{i,j}(t)$ and $E_{i,j}(t)$, $i, j = 1, 2, \ldots, n$ have size $C_i \times C_j$. We emphasize that subscript i and j now denote the phase being executed and not individual markings of the DSPN. Thus $K_{i,j}(t)$ and $E_{i,j}(t)$ are submatrices of $K(t)$ and $E(t)$, respectively. They are defined as follows:

$$K_{i,j}(t) = \begin{cases} e^{Q_i \tau_i} \Delta_i u(t - \tau_i) & 1 \leq i \leq n-1, \ j = i+1 \\ 0 & \text{otherwise} \end{cases}$$

$$E_{i,j}(t) = \begin{cases} e^{Q_i t}(1 - u(t - \tau_i)) & j = i \\ 0 & \text{otherwise} \end{cases}$$

where $u(t - \tau_i)$ is the delayed unit step function defined as $u(t) = 0$ if $t < \tau_i$ and $u(t) = 1$ if $t \geq \tau_i$, $i = 1, 2, \ldots, n$. Let us observe that function $u(t - \tau_i)$ is the cumulative distribution of the deterministic firing time of transition i, for $i = 1, 2, \ldots, n$. Matrices $K(t)$ and $E(t)$ depend on time only through these delayed unit step functions because of the regeneration points $T_n, n \geq 0$ are chosen as the firing times of deterministic transitions, as stated by Property 1. Moreover, note that due to the linear structure of the PhN matrix, $K(t)$ is a block upper-diagonal matrix with only a band of non-zero blocks, and matrix $E(t)$ is a block diagonal one. These properties will be useful to simplify the general form of the transient probability matrix $V(t)$, which is the solution to matrix-equation (1). Indeed, we can solve equation (1) for matrix $V(t)$ by exploiting the block partitioning $V(t) = \left\| V_{i,j}(t) \right\|$, as follows:

$$V_{i,j}(t) = E_{i,j}(t) + \sum_{h=1}^{n} \int_0^t dK_{i,h}(x) V_{h,j}(t - x)$$

By eliminating from the summation the null blocks of matrix $K(t)$ we rewrite the preceeding expression as follows:

$$V_{i,j}(t) = E_{i,j}(t) + \int_0^t dK_{i,i+1}(x) V_{i+1,j}(t - x) =$$

$$= E_{i,j}(t) + e^{Q_i \tau_i} \Delta_i \int_0^t du(x - \tau_i) V_{i+1,j}(t - x) dx = E_{i,j}(t) + e^{Q_i \tau_i} \Delta_i V_{i+1,j}(t - \tau_i) \quad (2)$$

where the last expression comes from the fact that the derivative of function $u(x - \tau_i)$ is the Dirac impulse function at τ_i, which allows us to reduce the convolution integral to just a time shift. Observe that matrix $V(t)$ shows an upper-triangular block structure. This allows the linear system in (2) to be solved by backward substitutions, to recursively obtain all the non-zero blocks $V_{i,j}(t)$ of matrix $V(t)$, as follows:

$$V_{i,j}(t) = \begin{cases} \left(\prod_{h=1}^{j-1} e^{Q_h \tau_h} \Delta_h \right) E_{j,j}(t - \sum_{h=1}^{j-1} \tau_h) & i \le j \\ 0 & i > j \end{cases} \quad (3)$$

where the product over an empty set is intended to be the identity matrix.

It is worthwhile observing that evaluating the formula given in (3) to obtain the transient state probability matrix only requires us to derive matrices $e^{Q_h t}$, $h = 1, 2, \ldots, j$ and Δ_h, $h = 1, 2, \ldots, j - 1$. The solution of the single DSPN model is reduced to the cheaper problem of deriving the transient probability matrices of a set of homogeneous, time-continuous Markov chains whose state spaces are proper subsets of the whole state space of the marking process. Therefore, the formula (3) provides a highly effective way of solving the single DSPN model of a PMS with a linearly structured mission.

5.2 Tree-like PhN

Now, consider the case when the next phase to be performed can be chosen at the time the current phase ends, as in case 3 of Section 4. The PhN exhibits a tree-structure, with all the leaves of the tree linked to the place Stop. The solution of equation (1) is quite similar to the previous case, but it requires a little bit more notation. As before, let $1, 2, \ldots, n$ be the set of phases and $t_1^{Det}, t_2^{Det}, \ldots, t_n^{Det}$ be the corresponding deterministic transitions. Let $f(i)$ denote the forward phases of phase i in the PhN, that is the set of phases which can be performed after phase i, $i = 1, 2, \ldots, n$. For the sake of simplicity, we assume that the ordering of phases is such that $j > i$, for each $j \in f(i)$. Note that such an ordering can always be found because of the acyclic structure of the PhN.

Consider Markov chain $\{M_i(t), t \ge 0\}$, defined as in the previous subsection, and let S_i and Q_i be its state space and its transition rate matrix, respectively, $i = 1, 2, \ldots, n$. Define the branching probability matrix $\Delta_{i,j}$, $i, j = 1, 2, \ldots, n$ as follows:

$$\Delta_i = \left\| \delta_{\bar{m}, \bar{m}'}^{i,j} \right\| = \begin{cases} \operatorname{Prob}[Y_i = \bar{m}' \mid M(T_i -) = \bar{m}] & \bar{m} \in S_i, \ \bar{m}' \in S_{i+1}, \ j \in f(i) \\ 0 & \text{otherwise} \end{cases}$$

According to the partition S_i, $i = 1, 2, \ldots, n$ of the state space S, matrix $K(t)$ can be written in block form as $K(t) = \left\| K_{i,j}(t) \right\|$. Each block $K_{i,j}(t)$ has size $C_i \times C_j$ and is defined as follows:

$$K_{i,j}(t) = e^{Q_i \tau_i} \Delta_{i,j} u(t - \tau_i), \ i,j = 1,2,\ldots,n$$

Note that matrix $E(t)$ which accounts for the local evolution of the MRGP while within a phase remains unchanged. The tree-structure of the PhN still results in a block upper-diagonal form of matrix $K(t)$, but in this case more non-zero blocks may appear in each row of the block matrix. Equation (1) can be rewritten as follows:

$$V_{i,j}(t) = E_{i,j}(t) + \sum_{h=1}^{n} \int_0^t dK_{i,h}(x) V_{h,j}(t - x) =$$

$$= E_{i,j}(t) + e^{Q_i \tau_i} \sum_{h \in f(i)} \Delta_{i,h} \int_0^t du(x - \tau_i) V_{h,j}(t - x) dx = \qquad (4)$$

$$= E_{i,j}(t) + e^{Q_i \tau_i} \sum_{h \in f(i)} \Delta_{i,h} V_{h,j}(t - \tau_i)$$

The linear system in (4) can be solved by backward substitutions and a solution can be provided as follows by exploiting the acyclic structure of the PhN. Consider the unique path $p(i,j)$ linking phase i to phase j according to the tree-structure of the PhN. This path is a set of phases $p(i,j) = \{p_1, p_2, \ldots, p_r\}$, where $p_1 = i$, $p_r = j$ and $p_{h+1} \in f(p_h)$, $h = 1,2,\ldots,r-1$. Matrix $V_{i,j}(t)$ is then given by the following formula:

$$V_{i,j}(t) = \begin{cases} \left(\prod_{h=1}^{r-1} e^{Q_{p_h} \tau_{p_h}} \Delta_{p_h, p_{h+1}} \right) E_{j,j}(t - \sum_{h=1}^{r-1} \tau_{p_h}) & p(i,j) \neq \varnothing \\ 0 & \text{otherwise} \end{cases} \qquad (5)$$

Formula (5) gives an operative way to evaluate the transient probability matrix of the DSPN model through the separate analysis of the various alternative paths which compose the mission. The preceding formula (3) can be derived as a particular case of (5).

6   Automated solution of the DSPN models of PMS

To compute the reliability of the system, the probability vector $P(t)$ of each marking in SN at time t should be derived. We can obtain $P(t)$ from the transient probability matrix $V(t)$ given by Equation (5) in last section, with the equation: $P(t) = P_0 \cdot V(t)$ where P_0 is the initial probability vector of the DSPN. To numerically evaluate the transient state probability vector $V(t)$ of the DSPN models presented in the previous sections, different approaches can be considered.

A general purpose transient solver for DSPNs as TimeNET can be used for this purpose [13]. TimeNET provides many of the modeling features available under the SRN paradigm, and is able to support the proposed modeling methodology. Thus, the PMS models can be built in the TimeNET environment according to the proposed structure and solved with the transient solution algorithm based on supplementary variables [12]. Of course, in this case no advantage is obtained from the particular structure of the models, and the analytical expressions for the state probability vector can not be exploited.

In fact, in order to take advantage of the separability of the PMS model solution, a specific algorithm must be developed and implemented, to obtain from the PMS model description the matrices needed to evaluate Equations (3) and (5). The solution algorithm takes as input the DSPN model and its initial probability vector, and performs the following steps:

1) build the Markov chain subordinate to phase i, and obtain its transition rate matrix Q_i, $i = 1, 2, ..., n$;

2) build the branching probability matrix $\Delta_{i,j}$, from phase i to phase j, $i = 1, 2, ..., n-1$, $j \in f(i)$;

3) obtain the transient state probability vector of the subordinate Markov chain i at T_i, the ending time of the corresponding phase i, for $i = 1, 2, ..., n$;

4) multiply the initial probability vector and the matrices, according to the ordering given by Equation (5), to obtain the final result.

All of the steps described above only require well-known algorithms; in fact they have been implemented in most of the tools for the automated evaluation of dependability. Therefore, such tools can be used at various extents to simplify some of the steps of the algorithm. For example, it is possible to use any Markovian solver to carry out the transient analysis of the subordinate Markov chains in step 3 of the algorithm. In particular the Stochastic Petri Net Package (SPNP) [9], which supports the SRN modeling paradigm, can be efficiently used to automate all the steps of the algorithm with a limited additional programming effort.

We show now a set of experimental evaluations for the application example given in subsection 4.3, assuming the system has 4 nodes, obtained by directly implementing the four steps of the algorithm listed above. We evaluate the probability that the system succesfully completes its mission, that is the reliability of the PMS at the end of the mission time, varying the values of the relevant system parameters, that is the failure rate λ, the repair rate μ and the probability of successful spare insertion c.

Two different scenarios are analysed. In a first setting, we suppose that failure rates, repair rates and the coverage c are the same for all the phases. Then, in a second experiment, we consider different failure intensities for the different phases. The constant durations of the various phases are given (in hours) in Table 5.

Launch	Hib. 1	Planet	Hib. 2	Sc. Obs1	Hib. 3	Hib. 4	Sc. Obs2
$t_L = 48$ (2 days)	$t_{H1} = 17520$ (2 years)	$t_P = 168$ (1 week)	$t_{H2} = 26280$ (3 years)	$t_{SO1} = 240$ (10 days)	$t_{H3} = 43800$ (5 years)	$t_{H4} = 44040$ ($t_{H3} + t_{SO1}$)	$t_{SO2} = 480$ (20 days)

Table 5: Duration of the different phases (in hours)

Figure 5 shows the probability of completing the mission for different values of the failure rate λ and of the repair rate μ. The successful spare insertion probability c is fixed to the value 0.99. A threshold value has been set to 0.95. We can observe from the curves in Figure 5 that a final probability greater than such threshold can be reached only if the repair rate μ is at least one order of magnitude greater than the fault occurrence rate λ. The repair rate of faulty processors should be properly tuned by adopting the adequate fault diagnosis and recovery mechanisms to ensure a sufficiently fast repair. This same behaviour can be observed for any value of c within the interval of interest, and it is not reported here for the sake of brevity.

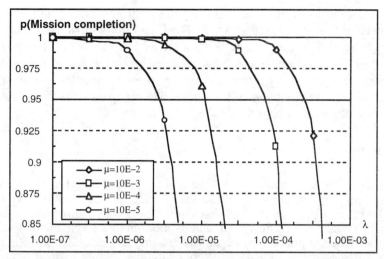

Figure 5: Probability of completing the mission for different values of fault and repair rates

In our second evaluation we consider different failure rates in the different phases. Changes of the processor failure rates are due to increased environmental stresses. Thus during the most stressing phase (Scientific Observations 2) the system is subject to an higher fault rate, while during the Hibernation phases a lower fault rate is assumed. Values assigned to the failure rate λ in the different phases are given in Table 6.

Launch	Hibernation	Planet	Sc. Obs1	Sc. Obs.2
$\lambda=10^{-5}$	$\lambda=10^{-6}$	$\lambda=10^{-5}$	$\lambda=10^{-5}$	$\lambda=10^{-4}$

Table 6: Fault occurrence rates in the different phases

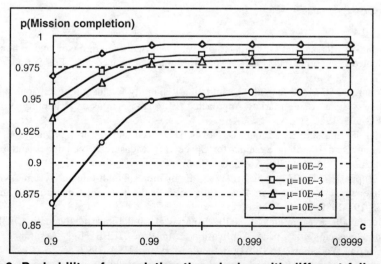

Figure 6: Probability of completing the mission with different failure rates in the different phases

Figure 6 shows the results of this evaluation for different values of the spare insertion probability c and the repair rate μ. The Figure shows that the probability of completing the mission improves rather quickly for low values of c (for any value of μ). In fact, passing from 0.9 to 0.99 it reaches acceptable values for three of the four curves. The probability of completing the mission becomes less sensitive to variations of c in the right part of the figure: passing from 0.99 to 0.9999 very slight variations can be observed.

7 Conclusions

In this paper we have shown a new method to model Phased Mission Systems reliability using DSPN. The method takes advantage of the power and expressiveness of DSPN to obtain concise and elegant models. The main advantage is the possibility to model the entire system and its mission in a single model thus automatically solving the problem of dependencies among phases. On the other hand, the method is supported by the existence of analytical solutions which can be fully automated. The solution efficiency also benefits from the splitting of Markov chains for different phases.

We have applied our method to increasingly more complete examples and shown how (well) it can deal with all the peculiar features of PMS. In particular, we have shown the case where the selection of the next phase to be performed depends on the system state (i.e., it is marking dependent).

In this paper we dealt with those PMS for which analytical solution methods have been already proposed in literature, and we have shown how naturally the DSPN approach can be used to model them. However, the DSPN modeling and in particular the underlying Markov regenerative process theory allow to further extend the class of PMS that can be modeled and analyzed. Our current work aims at relaxing the assumption of pre-fixed constant duration for phases, and at modelling PMS in which the phase durations may take more general distributions.

References

[1]   M. Ajmone Marsan and G. Chiola, "On Petri nets with deterministic and exponentially distributed firing times," in "Lecture Notes in Computer Science 266", Ed., Springer-Verlag, 1987, pp. 132-145.

[2]   M. Alam and U. M. Al-Saggaf, "Quantitative Reliability Evaluation of Reparaible Phased-Mission Systems Using Markov Approach," IEEE Transactions on Reliability, Vol. R-35, pp. 498-503, 1986.

[3]   J. Arlat, T. Eliasson, K. Kanoun, D. Noyes, D. Powell and J. Torin, "Evaluation of Fault-Tolerant Data Handling Systems for Spacecraft: Measures, Techniques and Example Applications," LAAS-CNRS November 1986.

[4]   B.E. Aupperle, J.F. Meyer and L. Wei, "Evaluation of fault-tolerant systems with non-homogeneous workloads," in Proc. 19th IEEE Fault Tolerant Computing Symposium (FTCS-19), 1989, pp. 159-166.

[5]   A. Bondavalli, I. Mura and M. Nelli, "Analytical Modelling and Evaluation of Phased-Mission Systems for Space Applications," in Proc. IEEE High Assurance System Engineering Workshop (HASE'97), Bethesda Maryland, USA, 1997, pp. 85 - 91.

[6]   J.L. Bricker, "A unified method for analizing mission reliability for fault tolerant computer systems," IEEE Trans. on Reliability, Vol. R-22, 1973.

[7]   G. R. Burdick, J. B. Fussell, D. M. Rasmuson and J. R. Wilson, "Phased Mission Analysis: A review of New Developments and An Application," IEEE Transactions on Reliability, Vol. R-26, pp. 43-49, 1977.

[8]   H. Choi, V.G. Kulkarni and K.S. Trivedi, "Transient analysis of deterministic and stochastic Petri nets.," in Proc. 14th International Conference on Application and Theory of Petri Nets, Chicago Illinois, USA, 1993, pp. 166-185.

[9]   G. Ciardo, J. Muppala and K.S. Trivedi, "Spnp: Stochastic Petri net package.," in Proc. International Conference on Petri Nets and Performance Models, Kyoto, Japan, 1989.

[10] J. B. Dugan, "Automated Analysis of Phased-Mission Reliability," IEEE Transaction on Reliability, Vol. 40, pp. 45-52, 1991.

[11] J.D. Esary and H. Ziehms, "Reliability analysis of phased missions.," in "Reliability and fault tree analysis", Ed., SIAM Philadelphia, 1975, pp. 213--236.

[12] R. German, "Transient analysis of deterministic and stochastic Petri nets by method of supplementary variables.," in Proc. MASCOTS '95, Durham, NC, 1995.

[13] R. German, C. Kelling, A. Zimmermann and G. Hommel, "TimeNET: a toolkit for evaluating non-Markovian stochastic Petri nets.," Performance Evaluation, Vol. 24, pp. 1995.

[14] V.G. Kulkarni, "Modeling and analysis of stochastic systems," Chapman-Hall, 1995.

[15] C. Lindemann, "Performance modeling using DSPNexpress," in Proc. Tool Descriptions of PNPM'97, Saint-Malo, France, 1997.

[16] J.F. Meyer, D.G. Furchgott and L.T. Wu, "Performability Evaluation of the SIFT Computer," in Proc. IEEE FTCS'79 Fault-Tolerant Computing Symposium, June20-22, Madison, Wisconsin, USA, 1979, pp. 43-50.

[17] A. Pedar and V. V. S. Sarma, "Phased-Mission Analysis for Evaluating the Effectiveness of Aerospace Computing-Systems," IEEE Transactions on Reliability, Vol. R-30, pp. 429-437, 1981.

[18] A. Puliafito, M. Scarpa and K.S. Trivedi, "Petri nets with k simultaneously enabled generally distributed timed transitions," Performance Evaluation, 1997.

[19] A. Reibman and K.S. Trivedi, "Numerical transient analysis of Markov models," Computers and Operation Research, Vol. 15, pp. 19-36, 1988.

[20] W.H. Sanders and J.F. Meyer, "METASAN: a performability evaluation tool based on stochastic activity networks," in Proc. ACM-IEEE Comp. Soc. 1986 Fall Joint Comp. Conf., Dallas TX, 1986, pp. 807--816.

[21] M. Smotherman and K. Zemoudeh, "A Non-Homogeneous Markov Model for Phased-Mission Reliability Analysis," IEEE Transactions on Reliability, Vol. 38, pp. 585-590, 1989.

[22] A. K. Somani, J. A. Ritcey and S. H. L. Au, "Computationally-Efficent Phased-Mission Reliability Analysis for Systems with Variable Configurations," IEEE Transactions on Reliability, Vol. 41, pp. 504-511, 1992.

[23] A. K. Somani and K. S. Trivedi, "Phased-Mission Systems Using Boolean Algebraic Methods," Performance Evaluation Review, Vol. pp. 98-107, 1994.

[24] H.S. Winokur and L.J. Goldstein, "Analysis of mission oriented systems," IEEE Trans. on Reliability, Vol. R-18, pp. 144-148, 1969.

Dependability Evaluation using a Multi-Criteria Decision Analysis Procedure

Divya Prasad and John McDermid
Department of Computer Science
University of York, U.K.
{divya, jam}@cs.york.ac.uk

Abstract

System dependability is a complex notion, represented by multiple attributes, and requiring diverse sources of evidence to demonstrate its achievement. This paper argues that the direct measurement of such a composite property is unlikely to be feasible, even for a single stakeholder's view of a system deployed in a specified environment. Instead, we propose an indirect evaluation procedure that is based on multiple-criteria decision analysis. The procedure is rigorous and systematic, and we illustrate it through a case study that compares alternative designs for computer assisted braking systems, to find out which of them is the more dependable. The result of the analysis is a theoretically sound, justifiable decision. The approach formalises traditional 'engineering judgement' by combining available scientific data with domain expertise, and making explicit the trade-offs within the decision.

1 Introduction

Computer systems which are responsible for critical services in any situation must be designed to be dependable. This means that despite their complexity, and the fact that they are subject to varying environmental conditions, their operation should be demonstrably safe, secure, reliable, timely, etc., as required by the application. A fundamental difficulty in quantifying dependability is that it is a composite notion — it is made up of multiple, potentially conflicting attributes, and difficult trade-offs may need to be made between these attributes. The attributes themselves are evaluated using multiple, diverse sources of evidence [8], thus compounding the problem of quantifying dependability.

This paper discusses the measurement of dependability, and highlights the role of the environment and the stake-holders in evaluating a system's dependability. We apply a result from the Theory of Measurement [4, 6] to argue that the composite notion cannot always be quantified by single numbers such as 10^{-x} failures per hour of operation. Instead, we describe dependability as a stake-holder-specific and environment-specific vector, and look for methods to compare such vectors.

Multiple Criteria Decision Analysis [5, 16] (MCDA) provides such methods, but there are specific theoretical conditions associated with their use. We investigate the conditions under which a vector of attributes can be reduced to a single number, and interpret these in the context of dependability.

In order to make the MCDA approach practically applicable to engineering problems, we propose a five-step procedure that incorporates the necessary theoretical checks, and guides engineers through the process of making a rigorous decision or evaluation. The procedure is illustrated through an extensive case-study that compares alternative designs for computer-assisted braking systems. The usefulness of the procedure and the results of the analysis are discussed, and further research directions are identified.

2 What does Dependability Really Mean?

Many authors have defined the term dependability, placing emphasis on different aspects of this complex notion. For example, Laprie [7] defines dependability as *"that property of a computer system such that reliance can justifiably be placed on the service it delivers; the service delivered by a system is its behaviour as it is perceptible by its user(s)"*. On the other hand, McDermid [9] observes that *"dependability can only be thought of as a function of a system and its environment, not as a property of the system itself, although for practical engineering purposes, we often behave as if dependability were a property of a system"*. Such definitions attempt to capture some important characteristics of the notion, but for the purpose of measurement [4, 14], it is necessary to distinguish more clearly between the entities and the attributes contributing to dependability. Hence a more useful and complete characterisation is shown in Figure 1, which depicts a system decomposition hierarchy, and the entities and attributes at each level of decomposition.

The figure shows a structural decomposition, distinguishing between: (1) Components (whose properties are given in data sheets), (2) White-box (sub-) systems (whose properties can be calculated from the properties of the constituent components), (3) Black-box systems (with some externally visible behaviour that is related to the properties of the white-box inside), and (4) Black-boxes deployed in some environment (whose behaviour is captured in terms of labels such as safety, security and reliability, which are different attributes of dependability).

Above the highest (system) level, we show that there are many different stake-holders, each of whom view the same system as having greater or lesser dependability, based on their primary concerns. A stake-holder is some individual or organisation that has to evaluate the dependability of the system, and make decisions based on this evaluation. Different stake-holders choose different combinations of labels to make up a dependability portmanteaux, and can adjust the relative importances of these labels to reflect any trade-offs they are willing to make. Thus, the definition and interpretation of dependability ultimately depends on the goals of the stake-holder(s) evaluating the system.

The diagram also helps us to recognise the 'emergent' nature of dependability,

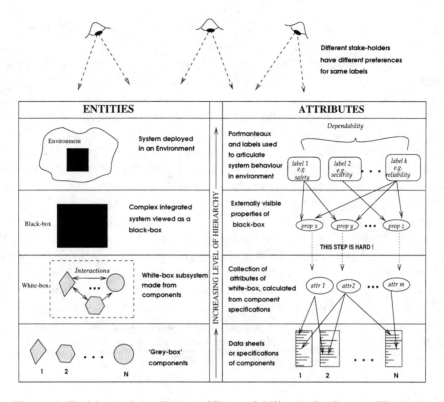

Figure 1: Entities and Attributes of Dependability in the System Hierarchy

since it only becomes visible at the highest level, when a complex integrated system is deployed in an environment, and not before this stage. Dependability is difficult to calculate from the attributes of the lower three levels. Within small sub-systems, the evaluations and decisions are more scientific as there may be physical or logical laws relating some higher-level attributes to other lower-level ones. As the complexity of the sub-system hidden inside a black-box grows, the decisions become more judgemental, since there are few laws (if any) to help in the decision-making, but merely preferences between the possible alternatives.

Dependability is thus a complex notion that encompasses more than a fixed, simplistically defined, set of attributes. We define dependability as a variable-sized vector of attributes describing overlapping desiderata, chosen subjectively by stakeholders in accordance with their particular requirements. This definition includes the wider requirements of existing definitions of dependability: justified confidence in the system, in the context of a particular environment of deployment.

3   The Role of Measurement and Decision-Making

For any ensemble of sub-systems, the prediction of an emergent property can be thought of as determining (through measurement and calculation) the properties of the 'whole' from the properties of the 'parts'. Where this is infeasible (e.g., because there is no theory to support the calculation), we would like, at the very least, to be able to compare objectively, the properties of two or more ensembles or systems, in order to choose the one that best fulfils the goals of a given stake-holder.

The problem of choosing between alternative systems is similar to many other decision problems which occur throughout the development process. At each stage, a decision could be approached by measuring the 'utility' [1] of each of the possible alternatives, and choosing the best among them. The utility of an alternative typically represents a combination of several desirable properties, or criteria, which may be met to a greater or lesser extent. We shall use the term criterion to refer to a property or an attribute which is pertinent to making a decision.

Consider the problem of choosing between two alternatives, X and Y, based on a number of criteria. In order to make a well-founded decision, consistent with the system designers' intentions, it is necessary to compare the alternatives with respect to each criterion of interest. In other words, for every property P, we need to be able to answer questions of the type "does alternative X have *more of P* than alternative Y?". Such questions can be answered without necessarily measuring (assigning a value to) the property P. The answers to these questions for all the criteria of interest must eventually be combined somehow, to give an overall conclusion to the question "is alternative X *better than* alternative Y?".

4   Measurement Theory applied to Dependability

The process of defining a scale of measurement begins by describing empirical relations between the set of all entities over which the measure is required. For any entity and its attributes, Measurement Theory [4,6,14] defines five well-understood scales of measurement. They are, in increasing order of ability to discriminate between systems: (1) nominal (simple classification with no ordering between the classes), (2) ordinal (the measure preserves order between entities), (3) interval (the measure preserves both order and distances between entities), (4) ratio (the measure has a notion of zero and preserves ratios), and (5) absolute (the measure is a count). If the property being measured is dependability, these scales could be used to answer questions such as:

(1) nominal: "Is system X *dependable?*";
(2) ordinal: "Is system X *more dependable* than Y?";
(3) interval: "*What difference in dependability* is there between X and Y?";
(4) ratio: "*How many times more dependable* is X compared to Y?";
(5) absolute: "*Exactly how much* is the dependability of system X?".

During the development stages, many related decisions must be made that contribute to properties such as dependability. For example, "*How much more reliable* will the system be if we do apply process A in contrast to not applying A?", and "Will the system be *safer* if developed using technique B as compared to using technique C?". According to the theory, the establishment and use of measures that correspond to any of the five scale types is invalid if a 'representation theorem' for that scale type is violated. There are many such theorems that provide necessary, and/or sufficient conditions for mapping the real-world entities into specific number systems. These conditions ensure that the proposed measurement mapping reflects the empirical observations expressed by appropriate observers or experts.

One of the many representation theorems for ordinal measurement (these can be found in [6]) states the conditions for mapping an empirical relation system (e.g. one expressed over the set of dependable systems being evaluated) into the numerical relation system $(\Re, >)$ — the set of real numbers with the relation 'greater than' defined over them. The conditions of this theorem can be tested by an experiment in which the set of systems are subjected to pairwise comparisons. If no two systems are found to be incomparable with respect to the relation *more dependable than*, then the theorem asserts that the set of systems can be mapped homomorphically to the numerical relation system $(\Re, >)$, thus giving an ordinal scale.

However, we know from Section 2, that dependability is a multi-stake-holder, multi-attribute concept. It is rare for any two stake-holders to have exactly the same opinion about how an arbitrary pair of systems would compare since their interests and priorities are not the same. Hence an ordinal scale measure which includes all the stake-holders' opinions is unlikely to exist. Furthermore, any individual stake-holder is unlikely to always be able to choose the more dependable system of an arbitrary pair of alternatives presented to her or him. This is because the stake-holder is having to combine mentally, a large number of attributes of dependability, and to make the necessary trade-offs where they conflict.

We conclude that dependability cannot be measured directly in $(\Re, >)$ even on an ordinal scale (which is the weakest of the useful scales of measurement). Instead, we propose that dependability can be represented (for any particular stake-holder) by a vector of attributes, and the composite property would have an ordinal scale measure in $(\Re^n, \succ)$, if we could find a suitable $\succ$ operator. This would provide an indirect measure for this stake-holder's definition of dependability. Since the activity of comparing n-dimensional vectors representing alternatives is a complex decision problem, we will use multi-criteria decision analysis to help us define this operator.

5 Multi-Criteria Decision Analysis (MCDA)

MCDA [5, 16] deals with situations where there is no obvious optimal or unanimously 'best' decision because of the large number of criteria that need to be taken into account. The decision often requires the fulfillment of conflicting objectives and hence the 'right' trade-offs must be made (e.g., in designing or choosing between systems for 'maximum' dependability). Hence, an optimal solution solution may or may not exist.

A branch of MCDA known as MAUT (Multiple Attribute Utility Theory) [17] offers methods of aggregating the multiple criteria into a single optimisation function, provided the decision-maker's preferences (between alternatives) obey certain conditions. The function which does this aggregation is known as a 'utility function' or 'value function'. Commonly studied forms of value function that can be found in the MAUT literature include the additive, polynomial, and probabilistic forms. Any value function indirectly provides the comparison operator $\succ$ over vectors of criteria.

The simplest and most well-understood value function is the additive one, where the contributions from the multiple criteria are essentially added together to determine the overall utility of each alternative. Mathematically, this is described by the following equation:

$$v(x_1, x_2, \ldots, x_n) = v_1(x_1) + v_2(x_2) + \ldots + v_n(x_n)$$

Here, v is the overall value function defined on the attributes x_i, that has been decomposed into n smaller value functions v_i. The additive value function is a powerful mechanism which breaks down a complex multi-attribute evaluation problem into smaller problems that can be solved independently. The general additive function has been implemented variously by using particular functions v_i. For example, the Analytic Hierarchy Process [15], which we will use in Section 13, uses a linear combination $v = \Sigma \lambda_i x_i$ where the constants λ_i are each greater than 0, and $\Sigma \lambda_i = 1$.

MAUT also provides representation theorems giving necessary, and sufficient conditions that relate specific preference structures to specific value functions. For example, any technique which relies on the additive value function must fulfil the condition of 'mutual preferential independence' of the criteria. This condition can be tested by investigating the nature of the trade-offs articulated by the decision maker, but we postpone a detailed discussion of this until the case study.

6   A 5-Step Decision Analysis Procedure

We present below a step-by-step decision analysis procedure [12] which has been synthesised from some of the important theoretical obligations and practical considerations of both Measurement Theory and MAUT. Questions that must be answered at each step and the results required are:

Step 1 **Identification of Decision Alternatives for Comparison and Evaluation**
Questions: What are the alternatives (entities) being compared? Are these already known or do we have to create them?
Result: The set of decision alternatives being compared and evaluated, expressed by enumeration or by describing them.

Step 2 **Definition of Evaluation Criteria and their Scales of Measurement**
Questions: What are the attributes or criteria that will be used to choose between the alternatives identified in Step 1? Can the criteria be structured into a hierarchy of high-level objectives, sub-objectives, etc., with measurable attributes at the leaves of the hierarchy?
Result: The set (expressed as a hierarchy, if possible) of criteria, with a scale of measurement defined for each of them.

Step 3 **Modelling of Preferences between Alternatives for each Criterion**
  Questions: For each criterion identified in Step 2, is there enough information to say clearly that an alternative is 'preferred', or 'equal' to another, or are they 'incomparable'? Do the preferences increase, or decrease monotonically with increasing values of each criterion?
  Result: A preference structure (consisting of n-ary relations over the set of alternatives) for each criterion.

Step 4 **Application of Representation Theorem for Proposed Value Function**
  Questions: Does there exist a multi-criteria utility or value function (for example, of additive or polynomial form) that can combine the criteria into an overall value? Do the preferences from Step 3 and the application-specific trade-offs between the criteria satisfy the representation theorem for the chosen value function?
  Result: Choice of value function, along with the validation of its representation theorem (if possible).

Step 5 **Construction of Multiple-Criteria Decision Model**
  Questions: Given the form of the value function chosen in Step 4, what are the parameters needed to completely determine the value function?
  Result: Parameters to complete the decision model, and the outcome of the decision.

Parts of the procedure may need to be repeated (refined locally or revisited in the light of insights from later steps), until a satisfactory decision model is obtained. Specific characteristics of the application problem determine which of these steps are trivial and which are hard. Step 2, in particular, may require substantial work to arrive at measurable criteria, including the resolution of uncertainty in the values of the criteria (e.g. using techniques such as Bayesian Belief Networks [11]).

7 A Case Study: Computer Assisted Braking Systems (CABS)

This case study compares the dependability of two alternative designs for a computer assisted braking system (CABS) for cars. The example paper designs (taken from [13]) are motivated by developments in the automotive industry. The comparison epitomises the difficulty of analysing and combining diverse sources of dependability evidence taken from several stages of the system life-cycle, including requirements analysis, hardware and software design, and safety case construction.

A CAB system is intended to provide braking assistance by detecting situations where the braking requested by the driver should be modified using other information from sensors. For example, if the driver 'wishes' to make an emergency stop, as inferred by the CABS (through its various sensors), then maximum braking force should be applied. What makes the system interesting from the dependability point of view, is that it improves safety via improved performance (over a hydromechanical system), but may also reduce safety due to new (different) failure modes.

The two designs (henceforth called CABS1 and CABS2) are intended to meet a common set of requirements, but differ in their software architecture. In fact, CABS2 was designed to overcome some perceived shortcomings in CABS1, and one of the goals of the analysis here is to justify the designers' belief that CABS2 is more dependable than CABS1. We will compare and contrast the two designs in detail, and use the information obtained to construct an MCDA model for evaluating them.

8   Mechanical versus Computer Aided Braking

Brakes in a car are safety-critical and any justification for introducing computers into the braking system must show that overall vehicle safety is not reduced. Before we can discuss what evaluation methods are available to ensure that this is the case, it is important to make explicit the drawbacks of existing mechanical (hydraulic) braking systems, and why it might be a good idea to computerise them.

The performance of a mechanical system is limited in terms of its response time (there is a delay between a driver's request for braking and the actual application of the brakes) and its sophistication (there is no practical way of dynamically tailoring the braking for wet or icy road conditions, emergency stops, heavy load in the vehicle etc.). These limitations of the mechanical system can be overcome by introducing electronic hardware and software components. The response time of the brakes can now be reduced to the order of milliseconds; the sophistication of the braking can be improved through the use information from various sensors. The CABS software improves the correlation between the braking that is needed, and what the system actually provides.

ID	Effect description	Risk class
a	Complete lack of braking	Catastrophic
b	Lock up (1-4 wheels, 1-2 axles)	Catastrophic
c	Unexpected application / release of brakes	Catastrophic
d	Braking response not proportional to demand	Major
e	Tardy response (time from demand to brake effect, slow rate of change in response to demand)	Major
f	Uneven braking (pressures vary "wildly" in response to constant demand)	Major
g	Unequal braking (1-3 wheels brake less or more than required)	Major

Table 1: CABS failure modes identified by Preliminary Hazard Analysis

However, the introduction of these additional components brings some new problems that did not exist in the purely mechanical system. These include:
(1) New failure modes are introduced by computerisation. Table 1 shows the results of the preliminary hazard analysis of the CAB system [13]. The failure modes

"Unexpected application of brakes" (part of failure mode **c**) and "Uneven braking" (failure mode **f**) were identified to be new to the computerised braking systems, and hence we have to take into account the additional risks they introduce.

(2) The reliability of the system might be reduced, because the electronic hardware or software systems which are used to enhance performance might themselves fail.

(3) We now have to analyse a highly complex, real-time system whose internal failure modes might have subtle, and potentially dangerous effects. The mechanical system, although limited in its functionality, was much less complex; its failure modes were more obvious and easier to analyse. There is also more theory and practical experience available in dealing with mechanical systems.

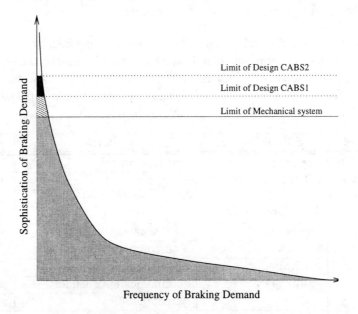

Figure 2: Limits of Mechanical and CAB Systems

The performance profile of a braking system (mechanical or CABS) can be depicted by a graph of sophistication of braking (desperation and difficulty of demand), against the likely frequency of the demand. The shape of the graph will depend on driver behaviour, and road and traffic conditions. In some countries it may typically look like Figure 2, which shows the most severe demands to have a low frequency of occurrence. The graph may look quite different in other parts of the world, (e.g. where drivers' most frequent braking requests are rather more severe!). A particular performance profile represents a subset of the input space of the braking system, and is a good example of the environment of deployment affecting the dependability of a system, as discussed in Section 2.

The lines marking the limits of the three systems help us understand their relative merits and discuss what happens in case of failures. Thus, we see that under normal circumstances the total braking available to the driver increases when using a CABS rather than a mechanical system. This assumes that the braking system cannot fail (i.e. both the hardware and software are perfect!). Since the CAB systems have more hydromechanical components than the mechanical system, and some electronic components in addition, they may be more prone to fail on any braking demand. Hence the gain in the total braking obtained by using the CABS will not be realised unless the software can compensate for some of the possible failures of the electromechanical and electronic components. The mechanical system represents a minimum acceptable baseline dependability, and we must ensure that the CABS does indeed increase the overall dependability rather than decrease it.

9   Interpretation in terms of Decision Procedure

At this point we need to relate our current understanding back to the decision-making procedure. In terms of Step 1, we have established the set of decision alternatives to be 'Mechanical', CABS1, and CABS2. Step 2, however, forms a major and creative part of this case study, and requires a lengthy analysis, which will ultimately lead to the hierarchy of criteria shown in Table 2.

Objective	Sub-objective	Criterion	Scale
Performance	degree of enhancement	anti-lock braking	ordinal
		emergency stop	ordinal
		load-compensation	ordinal
	minimal braking		ordinal
	number of sensors	ABS sensors	absolute
		load-compensation sensors	absolute
Fault Tolerance	hardware redundancy	processors	absolute
		communication channels	absolute
		output modules	absolute
	software redundancy	fall-back levels	absolute
		minimum redundancy	absolute
		extent of voting	absolute
Ease of Analysis	knowledge of failure modes		ordinal
	availability of data		ordinal
Reliability	no. of hazardous failure modes		absolute
	probability of failure	hardware	ratio
		software	ratio
Good Development Process	strength of the safety case		ordinal
	MISRA design principles		ordinal
	company procedures		ordinal

Table 2: Braking System Evaluation (Step 2) : Criteria and Scales of Measurement

This hierarchy was developed by interpreting the description of the CAB systems given in [13], using a mixture of top-down and bottom-up refinements of the meaning of dependability in the context of braking systems. Some of the high-level objectives that contribute to the hierarchy shown in Table 2 have already been identified in the previous section. They are: *Performance*, *Reliability*, *Fault Tolerance*, and *Ease of Analysis* (hereafter we will show the elements of the hierarchy in italics). Recall that the goal of the comparison is to decide which system is more dependable, so these four objectives represent an initial set of properties making up the composite notion. Now we need to identify further objectives, sub-objectives and criteria to complete the multi-criteria decision hierarchy.

The Mechanical and CAB systems have different *numbers of hazardous failure modes* — this will be a criterion under the *Reliability* branch. The objective *Ease of Analysis* includes two criteria: one to represent our *knowledge of the failure modes* of the system, and another to represent the *availability of data* about the failure modes of the system, such as hardware and software failure rates.

There are three 'added value' functions provided in the CAB systems to enhance braking performance. These are *anti-lock braking*, *emergency stop detection/enhancement*, and *load-compensated braking*, and are taken as criteria under a sub-objective representing *degree of enhancement* of braking, which is part of the *Performance* branch. Another part of the same branch is the effectiveness of *minimal braking*, to represent possible differences in the basic functionality.

10   Comparative Study of CABS1 and CABS2

The purpose of the comparative study (summarised from [12]) is to extract and characterise the criteria appropriate for evaluating the dependability of the alternative braking systems. This continues Step 2 of the decision-making procedure.

10.1   Requirements and Specifications

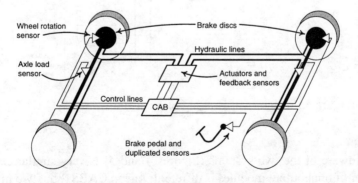

Figure 3: CABS1 Context Diagram

The two systems have very similar requirements and specifications. The braking system context for CABS1 is shown in Figure 3. We can see that CABS1 has only one load sensor on each of the two axles. CABS2 differs from CABS1 by having two sensors per axle, each positioned close to a wheel. This provides greater redundancy and potentially more information to CABS2 for carrying out the load-compensation function (and perhaps other functions).

The *number of sensors* used to enhance performance will be used as a sub-objective under the *Performance* branch of the multi-criteria decision hierarchy. The context diagrams for both designs contained sensors for the anti-lock and load compensation functions, so we sub-divide *number of sensors* into two criteria: *ABS sensors*, and *load compensation sensors*.

10.2 Hardware Architecture

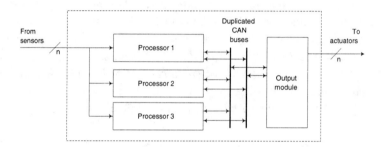

Figure 4: Structure of Braking System Hardware for CABS1

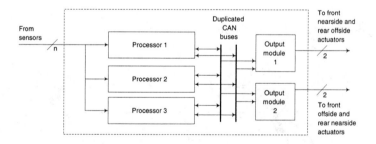

Figure 5: Structure of Braking System Hardware for CABS2

The hardware of the two systems (Figures 4 and 5) is very similar except that the number of final output modules is different: one in CABS1, but two in CABS2. Having two output modules improves the redundancy, and hence the safety of the output function in CABS2, especially as each output module controls a diagonal pair of wheels (losing a diagonal pair of brakes is less dangerous than losing either the front or rear pair). Unfortunately, this also results in a corresponding increase in the likelihood of a component failure in CABS2, since it has more components.

The *hardware redundancy* employed in the designs is a sub-objective of the *Fault Tolerance* branch of the decision hierarchy. It can be further divided into three criteria: *number of processors, number of communication channels (CAN buses), number of output modules*. The increased probability of failure due to the extra components in the second output module will be accounted for in a criterion representing the failure probability of *hardware*, under the *Reliability* branch of the decision hierarchy, through the sub-objective *probability of failure*.

10.3 Software Architecture

Figures 6 and 7 show the functional blocks in the software for CABS1 and CABS2. The main difference between the functionalities of the systems is that in CABS1, the BASIC algorithm is over-ridden by ENHANCED1 or ENHANCED2 whenever they are available, whereas in CABS2, the output of BASIC is modified by the enhanced algorithms, only if they are needed and available. Hence, in CABS1, ENHANCED1 and ENHANCED2 represent single points of failure: for example, any result generated by ENHANCED2 (whether it is correct, or not), will be used in preference to the results of ENHANCED1 and BASIC. In CABS2, on the other hand, every calculation is triplicated, and voted upon.

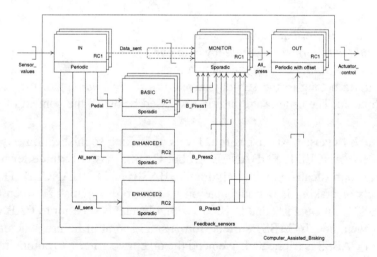

Figure 6: Functional Block Diagram of CABS1

It is not obvious how these differences of functionality and fault tolerance can best be captured in terms of measurable criteria. This is the essential difficulty of carrying out Step 2 to distinguish between the software architectures — we need a set of attributes that can characterise the different approaches employed by the systems to achieve similar goals. A lengthy analysis leads to the choice of the following three criteria which bring out the essential differences between the designs based on the software redundancy employed by them:

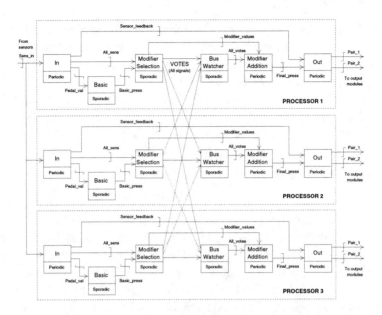

Figure 7: Functional Block Diagram of CABS2

(1) the number of *fall-back* levels of braking.
(2) the *minimum degree of redundancy* employed.
(3) the *extent of voting* used in the calculations.
These criteria belong to the sub-objective *software redundancy* of the *Fault Tolerance* branch. The criteria are briefly discussed below in the context of the two systems:

Fall-back Levels: CABS1 has four levels of braking sophistication (Hydraulic, BASIC, ENHANCED1, ENHANCED2) but CABS2 has only three levels of increasingly sophisticated braking: Hydraulic, BASIC and ENHANCED. Thus, fall-back levels of braking is not adequate on its own to distinguish between CABS1 and CABS2, as it suggests that CABS1 (with 4 levels) is superior to CABS2 (with 3 levels) even though CABS1 suffers from a single point of failure, whereas every module of CABS2 is triplicated. We need the other two criteria to complement this one.

Minimum Degree of Redundancy: This is a way of representing the minimum number of component (or module) failures that can lead to a system failure. The single points of failure in CABS1 give a value of 1 for this criterion, whereas, CABS2 has a value 2, since it requires 2 component failures before the system fails. Both CABS have triple redundancy in the calculation of BASIC braking values, and in the final processing and transmission onto the CAN bus by the OUT modules, but this is over-shadowed in CABS1 by the single point of failure.

Extent of Voting: This is the number of times that voting is employed to choose between redundant calculations. Voting is used for determining both the requirement for enhancement (represented by flags), and the values of the enhancements to braking. CABS2 generates triplicated flags for the addition of modifiers, and then each processor votes on them, but CABS1 has no redundancy for generating the flags, nor any voting to check the values resulting from the ENHANCED algorithms. The analysis in [12] calculated that a measure for the extent of voting used by CABS1 is 1, and for CABS2 it is 5.

Before leaving the topic of software architectures, we also need a criterion for the *failure probability of the software* which belongs to the sub-objective *probability of failure* under the *Reliability* branch of the decision hierarchy.

10.4 Development Process

We introduce a new high-level objective to capture the quality of the *Development Process*, including *strength of the safety case* as a sub-objective. In an industrial context, we would expect to expand this sub-objective further, assuming there were two or more full safety cases to compare. In the decision-making hierarchy developed here, we treat this sub-objective as a leaf node (criterion), entering only a value judgement for it.

Two other process related sub-objectives can be identified:
(1) extent to which the guidelines of the Motor Industries Software Reliability Association [10] (*MISRA design principles*) were followed in the development process.
(2) The extent to which the internal *company procedures* were followed. These sub-objectives could also be expanded further if more information was available, but here we treat them as leaf nodes.

11 Finishing Steps 2 and 3

So far we have only identified the criteria which will contribute to the evaluation of the braking systems. This is only a part of Step 2 of the decision-making procedure. To complete Step 2 we must also define scales of measurement for each of the criteria. Table 2 shows the hierarchy of criteria developed above with some sub-objectives themselves being leaf nodes of the hierarchy, and hence treated as criteria. The table associates each criterion with its most natural scale of measurement. The absolute scale is suggested where the criterion can be associated with a simple count. The ordinal scale is used where the criterion is much less precisely measurable. The ratio scale is used for probabilities.

Step 3 of the procedure is straightforward: all the criteria except the three under the objective *Reliability*, are of the kind 'the higher the better' (at least for the set of alternatives chosen at Step 1). In other words, the higher the value of the criterion, the more preferred the alternative is. The remaining three criteria (*no. of hazardous failure modes*, *probability of hardware failure* and *probability of software failure*) are of course of the kind 'the lower the better'. These preferences are likely to be common to most stake-holders of the braking system.

It is apparent that different stake-holders would come up with different results from carrying out the decision-making procedure, even if they started out with the same set of alternatives at Step 1. Any of, the choice of criteria, the assignment of scales of measurement to them, and the nature of the preferences could be different. Nevertheless, the model we present here attempts to include a generic set of criteria that would be of interest to most stake-holders, with varying degrees of importance.

It is instructive to relate the CABS decision hierarchy in Table 2 to Figure 1: the objectives are a particular stake-holder's view of a CABS deployed in a particular environment. The environment in this case refers to the performance profile for braking demand depicted in Figure 2. The sub-objectives of the decision hierarchy are the properties of a CAB system treated as a black-box. The criteria represent attributes that include black-box and white-box properties of the system and its components, as appropriate to each node in the decision tree.

In the next section, we investigate the theoretical validity of the model, as is required by Step 4 of the decision procedure. We try to use the simple additive value function as far as possible.

12   Is an Additive Value Function Appropriate? (Step 4)

Our ability to structure the criteria hierarchically, as shown in Table 2, and the simplicity of the preference models for the criteria considered in isolation, are both encouraging indicators for the suitability of an additive value function (at least over some parts of the model). However, this is not sufficient, and there may be some surprises in store, when we investigate the preferences over combinations of criteria. For an additive value function, we know that we have to look out for any preferential dependencies between criteria.

Preferential independence between objectives does not mean that they are not related: the real world often restricts the possible combinations of values that can be achieved simultaneously. For example, it is unlikely that a combination of very high *Fault Tolerance* and very high *Ease of Analysis* can be achieved in the same system, because fault tolerance inherently increases the complexity, and hence the difficulty of analysing the system. Preferential independence also does not imply that objectives cannot be traded-off against each other. It only means that the nature of the trade-offs between any subset of objectives, should be independent of the values of the remaining objectives. These trade-offs refer to the decision-maker's preferences for combinations of values of the objectives in that subset, and the compensation rates between them.

Sometimes, a claim of preferential independence between the sub-objectives of a particular objective can be substantiated using experimental evidence or empirical knowledge (i.e., by a descriptive approach). An example of this occurs at the sub-objective *hardware redundancy*: the criteria for computational, communications and output redundancies are mutually preferentially independent because the trade-offs between any pair of them does not depend on the value of the third. We consider this independence condition to be descriptive because it reflects our understanding of prevalent design practices.

In most cases, there may not be enough knowledge or evidence to support such a descriptive approach. Instead, a prescriptive approach may be more appropriate: we can attempt to choose objectives to be 'orthogonal' to their siblings, so that we can reasonably (and rationally) assert their mutual preferential independence. For example, the five objectives at the highest level clearly reflect such a separation of concerns, and it is reasonable to assume preferential independence between them.

The prescriptive approach may be suitable for only some of the lower levels of the hierarchy, such as the criteria under *Development Process*. On the other hand, for objectives such as *Performance* and *Fault Tolerance*, the real-life (functional or structural) interactions between their sub-objectives leave more scope for preferential dependence. For example, under *Performance*, the relative importance of the node *number of sensors* compared to the node *degree of enhancement* is not independent of the value of *degree of enhancement*, because having more sensors is of high importance only if they are used to provide enhanced braking. Otherwise, we do not care how many sensors are placed on the system.

Where there is a distinct lack of preferential independence, other value functions (e.g. a polynomial form) may be more appropriate for modelling the dependent sub-objectives. We believe that in practice, a small amount of dependency can be ignored within a sufficiently local region of the comparison space [12]. For example, additivity may hold if the comparison only included very similar alternatives (e.g. the CAB systems), but may be violated once the set of alternatives are expanded to include dissimilar entities (e.g. mechanical and CAB systems together).

In other cases where additivity does not hold, traditional domain-specific theories might be adequate and more appropriate. In other words, the local decision about the ordering of the alternatives under such an objective may be based on well-understood technical or analytical arguments, rather than being based on preferences. Another example of this is the sub-objective *probability of failure*, whose value should be calculated using probability theory from the probabilities of its children *hardware* and *software*.

Thus before we can proceed to Step 5, we need a way of eliminating the non-additive nodes in the model. This can be done by replacing the trees rooted at the non-additive nodes, by leaf nodes that represent combined (or indirect) measures of the trees they replace. For example, the evaluation of the alternatives with respect to the nodes *Performance* and *probability of failure* should be carried out by treating them as if they were leaf nodes with values calculated by the appropriate domain-specific theory (e.g. probability theory). We will not show this process in more detail, but for 'real' decisions it is an important part of completing Step 4 of the decision procedure. Here we will proceed to show how Step 5 of the decision procedure can be carried out in the knowledge that, at least the top-level objectives can be combined additively.

13   Completing the Comparison (Step 5)

The parameters needed to complete the decision model can be obtained using a
tool that implements an additive value function, such as Expert Choice [3], which
is based on the Analytic Hierarchy Process mentioned in Section 5.

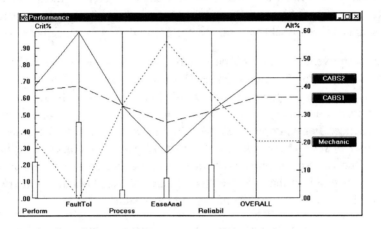

Figure 8: Braking System Comparison with Example Weights

The relative importance of the sub-objectives can be investigated using a sensitivity analysis tool as shown in Figure 8. This allows the weights of the first level
objectives to be modified interactively whilst displaying the resulting scores of the
alternatives. For example, by giving most importance to 'FaultTol', and somewhat
less importance to 'Perform' and 'Reliabil' (and hence even less to 'Process' and
'EaseAnal') as depicted by the vertical bars, we see in Figure 8 that both the CAB
systems score better than the mechanical, and CABS2 scores rather better than
CABS1 (as shown by the 'OVERALL' column on the right hand side). This result can be attributed to the lack of fault-tolerance in the mechanical system, and
the single point of failure in CABS1. The three dashed and dotted lines spanning
across the graph show the relative positions of the three systems with respect to
each objective. For example, the large vertical distance between the intercepts for
the 'EaseAnal' depicts how dissimilar the three systems are in their analysibility.

Changing the relative importance of the sub-objectives can change the relative
scores, or even reverse the order of preference between the braking systems. Hence,
a single hierarchy can be used with different weights to analyse the implications of
different stake-holders' opinions.

14   Conclusions and Further Work

The paper has argued that although it is infeasible to directly measure dependability (even for a single stake-holder), multi-criteria decision analysis provides us

with a mechanism for constructing an indirect measure from its many contributing attributes. However, this is feasible only when certain theoretical obligations are fulfiled, and we have developed a systematic decision analysis procedure that can be used to construct such a measure without overlooking the necessary theoretical conditions.

The procedure can be used for any complex multi-criteria decision contributing to dependability, since it leads to well-founded, rational, and repeatable decisions. The decision procedure does not magically dissolve the difficulty of the evaluation problem; it only renders it more tractable by making explicit the inherent conflicts and trade-offs associated with the decision. Furthermore, the analysis of any part of the problem is itself time consuming and relies on the skills of both a decision analyst and a domain expert, although the two roles are often merged. The cost of the analysis must be balanced with the benefit to be derived from it. Hence, before embarking upon such an analysis, some meta-level (possibly multi-criteria!) decisions need to be made about which of the many complex and critical decisions require rigorous decision support.

Further research based on the work described here could include:
(1) Application of Group Decision-making techniques based on several tables like Table 2, to arrive at a consensus among different stake-holders.
(2) Application of the decision analysis procedure to areas such as COTS (Commercial Off The Shelf) component evaluation and procurement, safety case construction and system certification.

In conclusion, the problem of engineering complex systems dependably is hard in essence. To recall Brooks' famous phrase [2], there is no 'silver bullet' for this problem. Instead we have to develop techniques to manage complex decisions that involve engineering judgement and expert opinion, without compromising rigour and justifiability.

15 Acknowledgements

The authors thank the following colleagues at York for many useful discussions during the development of the ideas presented in this paper: Martin Atkins, Mark Nicholson, David Pumfrey and Ian Wand. This research was initiated under the auspices of the METHOD project (Grant Number GR/J42311 of the UK Engineering and Physical Sciences Research Council).

References

[1] J. Bentham. *The Principles of Morals and Legislation*. London, 1789.

[2] F.P. Brooks. *The Mythical Man-Month: Essays on Software Engineering*. Addison-Wesley, 1995.

[3] Expert Choice Inc., 5001 Baum Blvd., Suite 650, Pittsburgh PA 15213, USA. *Expert Choice Decision Support Software*, version 9.0 edition, 1995.

[4] N. Fenton. Software measurement: A necessary scientific basis. *IEEE Transactions on Software Engineering*, 20(3):199–206, March 1994.

[5] R.L. Keeney and H. Raiffa. *Decisions with Multiple Objectives: Preferences and Value Tradeoffs*. Cambridge University Press, 1993.

[6] D.H. Krantz, R.D. Luce, P. Suppes, and A. Tversky. *Foundations of Measurement: Additive and Polynomial Representations*, volume 1. Academic Press, 1971.

[7] J.C. Laprie, editor. *Dependability: basic concepts and terminology: in English, French, German, Italian and Japanese*, volume 5 of *Dependable Computing and Fault-Tolerant Systems*. Springer-Verlag, Wien, etc., 1992.

[8] B. Littlewood. The need for evidence from disparate sources to evaluate software safety. In F. Redmill and T. Anderson, editors, *Directions in Safety-critical Systems*, pages 217–231. Springer-Verlag, 1993. Proceedings of the Safety-critical Systems Symposium, Bristol.

[9] J.A. McDermid. On dependability, its measurement and its management. *High Integrity Systems Journal*, 1(1):17–26, 1994.

[10] MISRA. *Development Guidelines for Vehicle Based Software*. Motor Industry Research Association (ISBN 0 9524156 0 7), 1994.

[11] J. Pearl. *Probabilistic Reasoning in Intelligent Systems*. Morgan Kaufmann, Palo Alto CA, 1988.

[12] D.K. Prasad. *Dependable Systems Integration Using Measurement Theory and Decision Analysis*. PhD thesis, Department of Computer Science, University of York, U.K., November 1998.

[13] D. Pumfrey and M. Nicholson. Computer assisted braking, system hazard analysis course notes. Technical report, University of York, 1995. IGDS MSc in Safety Critical Systems.

[14] F.S. Roberts. *Measurement theory, with applications to decision-making, utility and the social sciences*. Addison Wesley, 1979.

[15] T.L. Saaty. *Multiple Criteria Decision Making: The Analytic Hierarchy Process*. RWS Publications, 1992.

[16] P. Vincke. *Multicriteria Decision-Aid*. John Wiley and Sons, 1992.

[17] J. von Neumann and O. Morgenstern. *Theory of Games and Economic Behaviour*. Princeton University Press, 3rd edition, 1967.

Probabilistic Guarantees

Probabilistic Scheduling Guarantees for Fault-Tolerant Real-Time Systems

A. Burns and S. Punnekkat
Real-Time Systems Research Group
Department of Computer Science
University of York, UK

L. Strigini and D. R. Wright
Centre for Software Reliability
City University, UK

Abstract

Hard real-time systems are usually required to provide an absolute guarantee that all tasks will always complete by their deadlines. In this paper we address fault tolerant hard real-time systems, and introduce the notion of a probabilistic guarantee. Schedulability analysis is used together with sensitivity analysis to establish the maximum fault frequency that a system can tolerate. The fault model is then used to derive a probability (likelihood) that, during the lifetime of the system, faults will not arrive faster than this maximum rate. The framework presented is a general one that can accommodate transient 'software' faults, tolerated by recovery blocks or exception handling; or transient 'hardware' faults dealt with by state restoration and re-execution.

1 Introduction

Scheduling work in hard real-time systems is traditionally dominated by the notion of absolute guarantee. Static analysis is used to determine that all deadlines are met even under the worst-case load conditions. With fault-tolerant hard real-time systems this deterministic view is usually preserved even though faults are, by their very nature, stochastic. No fault tolerant system can, however, cope with an arbitrary number of errors in a bounded time. The scheduling guarantee is thus predicated on a fault model. If the faults are no worse than that defined in the fault model then all deadlines are guaranteed. The disadvantage of this separation of scheduling guarantee and fault model is that it leads to simplistic analysis; either the system is schedulable or it is not.

In this paper we bring together scheduling issues and errors to justify the notion of a *probabilistic guarantee* even for a hard real-time system. By 'probabilistic guarantee' we mean a scheduling guarantee with an associated probability. Hence, a guarantee of 99.95% does not mean that 99.95% of deadlines are met. Rather it implies that the probability of *all* deadlines being met during a given period of operation is 99.95%. Instead of starting with the fault model and using scheduling tests to see if this is feasible, we start with the scheduling analysis to derive a threshold interval between errors that can be tolerated and then employ the fault model to assign a probability to this threshold value.

To provide the flexibility needed to program fault tolerance, fixed priority preemptive scheduling will be used [13]. The faults of interest are those that are transient. Castillo *at al* [6] in their study of several systems indicate that the occurrences of transient faults are 10 to 50 times more frequent than permanent faults. In some applications this frequency can be quite large; one experiment on a satellite system observed 35 transient faults in a 15 minute interval due to cosmic ray ions [5].

We attempt to keep the framework as general as possible by accommodating 'software' faults tolerated by either exception handling or some form of recovery block, and 'hardware' faults dealt with by state restoration and re-execution. Error latencies will be assumed to be short.

Other authors have studied the probability of meeting deadlines in fault-tolerant systems. However, only some facets of this problem have been considered. For instance, Hou and Shin [9] have studied a related problem, the probability of meeting deadlines when tasks are replicated in a hardware-redundant system. However, they only consider permanent faults without repair or recovery. A similar problem was studied by Shin et al [18]. Kim et al [12] consider another related problem: the probability of a real-time controller meeting a deadline when subject to permanent faults with repair.

The rest of the paper is organised as follows. Section 2 briefly describes the scheduling analysis that is applicable to non-fault-tolerant systems. Section 3 presents the fault model and the framework for the subsequent analysis. In Section 4 the scheduling analysis for a fault tolerant system is presented. This enables the threshold fault interval (TFI) to be derived. Section 5 then uses the fault model and the TFI to assign a probability to the threshold. Conclusions are presented in Section 6.

2   Standard Scheduling Analysis

For the standard fixed priority approach, it is assumed that there is a finite number (N) of tasks ($\tau_1 .. \tau_N$). Each task has the attributes of minimum inter arrival time, T, worst-case execution time, C, deadline, D and priority P. Each task undertakes a potentially unbounded number of invocations; each must be finished by the deadline (which is measured relative to the task's invocation/release time). All tasks are deemed to start their execution at time 0. We assume a single processor platform and restrict the model to tasks with $D \leq T$. For this restriction, an optimal set of priorities can be derived such that $D_i < D_j \Rightarrow P_i > P_j$ for all tasks i, j [15]. Tasks may be periodic or sporadic (as long as two consecutive releases are separated by at least T). Once released, a task is not suspended other than by the possible action of a concurrency control protocol surrounding the use of shared data. A task, however, may be preempted at any time by a higher priority task. System overheads such as context switches and kernel manipulations of delay queues etc can easily be incorporated into the model [11, 4] but are ignored here.

The worst-case response time (completion time) R_i for each task (i) is obtained from the following [10, 1]:

$$R_i = C_i + B_i + \sum_{j \in hp(i)} \left\lceil \frac{R_i}{T_j} \right\rceil C_j \tag{1}$$

where $hp(i)$ is the set of higher priority tasks (than i), and B_i is the maximum blocking time caused by a concurrency control protocol protecting shared data.

The most common and effective concurrency control protocol assigns a ceiling priority to each shared data area. This ceiling is the maximum priority of all tasks that use the shared data area. When a task enters the protected object that contains the shared data, its priority is temporarily increased to this ceiling value. As a consequence (on a single processor system):

1. Mutual exclusion is assured (by the protocol itself).

2. Each task is only blocked once during each invocation.

3. Deadlocks are prevented (by the protocol itself).

The value of B_i is simply the maximum computation time of any protected object that has a ceiling equal or greater than P_i and is used by a task with a priority lower than P_i.

To solve equation (1) a recurrence relation is produced:

$$r_i^{n+1} = C_i + B_i + \sum_{j \in hp(i)} \left\lceil \frac{r_i^n}{T_j} \right\rceil C_j \tag{2}$$

where r_i^0 is given an initial value of C_i (although more efficient initial values can be found). The value r^n can be considered to be a computational window into which an amount of computation C_i is attempting to be placed. It is a monotonically non-decreasing function of n. Note that when r_i^{n+1} becomes equal to r_i^n then this value is the worst-case response time, R_i [4]. However if r_i^n becomes greater than D_i then the task cannot be guaranteed to meet its deadline, and the full task set is thus unschedulable.

Table 1 describes a simple 4 task system, together with the response times that are calculated by equation (2). Priorities are ordered from 1, with 4 the lowest value, and blocking times have been set to zero for simplicity. Scheduling analysis is independent of time units and hence simple integer values are used (they can be interpreted as milliseconds).

To illustrate how these values are obtained consider τ_4; r_i^0 is given the initial value of 30, r_i^1 is then just the addition of all the computation times ($30 + 35 + 25 + 30 = 120$), so r_i^2 is assigned 120. With this value τ_1 gives rise to another hit (of 30)

Task	P	T	C	D	B	R	Schedulable
τ_1	1	100	30	100	0	30	TRUE
τ_2	2	175	35	175	0	65	TRUE
τ_3	3	200	25	200	0	90	TRUE
τ_4	4	300	30	300	0	150	TRUE

Table 1: Example Task Set

and hence r_i^3 is 150. This value is then stable and hence is the required response time.

All tasks are released at time 0. For the purpose of schedulability analysis, we can assume that their behaviour is repeated every LCM, where LCM is the least common multiple of the task periods. When faults are introduced it will be necessary to know for how long the system will be executing. Let L be the lifetime of the system. For convenience we assume L is an integer multiple of the LCM. This value may however be very large (for example LCM could be 200ms, and L fifteen years!).

3   Fault Model

We assume that a single transient fault will cause just one error, and that this error will manifest itself in just a single task. With 'software' faults this is a reasonable assumption. With 'hardware' faults we are concerned with errors that manifest themselves in the processing unit (including internal busses, cache etc) rather than in memory where the error latencies may be very large. We assume that only the executing task is affected[1]. Faults that affect the kernel must either be masked or lead to permanent damage that can only be catered for by replication at the system level. To make the subsequent analysis simpler we assume perfect error recognition coverage; a probabilistic (non zero) measure of coverage could be used with a straightforward effect upon the analysis.

We make the common *homogeneous Poisson process* (HPP) assumptions that the fault arrival rate is constant and that the distribution of the fault-count for any fixed time interval can be approximated using a Poisson probability distribution. This is an appropriate model for a random process where the probability of an event does not change with time and the occurrence of one fault event does not affect the probability of another such event. A HPP process depends only on one parameter, viz, the expected number of events, λ, in unit time; here events are transient faults with $\lambda = 1/MTBF$, where $MTBF$ is the Mean Time Between transient Faults[2].

---

[1] An alternative model, namely all non-terminated tasks are affected could also have been used. This would make no fundamental difference to the analysis but would complicate the scheduling equations used in Section 4.

[2] MTBF usually stands for mean time between failures, but as the systems of interest are fault tolerant many faults will not cause system failure. Hence we use the term MTBF to model the arrival

Per the definition of a Poisson Distribution,

$$Pr_n(t) \;=\; \frac{e^{-\lambda t}(\lambda t)^n}{n!}$$

gives the probability of n events during an interval of duration t. If we take an event to be an occurrence of a transient fault and Y to be the random variable representing the number of faults in the lifetime of the system (L), then the probability of zero faults is given by

$$Pr(Y = 0) = e^{-\lambda L}$$

and the probability of at least one fault

$$Pr(Y > 0) = 1 - e^{-\lambda L}$$

Other useful values are:

$$
\begin{aligned}
Pr(Y = 1) &= e^{-\lambda L}\lambda L \\
Pr(Y < 2) &= e^{-\lambda L}(1 + \lambda L)
\end{aligned}
\tag{3}
$$

We are concerned, in this paper, with the probability of the system being schedulable. We shall write $Pr(S)$ and $Pr(U)$ to denote the probability of schedulability and unschedulability. Of course $Pr(S) = 1 - Pr(U)$.

The analysis given in the next section will determine the threshold fault interval. This gives the sustainable frequency at which faults can occur and the system still meet all its deadlines. Let this frequency be represented by the minimum time interval allowed between faults, T_F. It follows that if W is the shortest interval between fault arrivals during a mission then[3]

$$
\begin{aligned}
Pr(U) = {}& Pr(U|no\ faults).Pr(no\ faults) \\
& + Pr(U|W{\geq}T_F\ and\ there\ are\ faults).Pr(W{\geq}T_F\ and\ there\ are\ faults) \\
& + Pr(U|W{<}T_F\ and\ there\ are\ faults).Pr(W{<}T_F\ and\ there\ are\ faults)
\end{aligned}
$$

Since we are dealing with systems which are schedulable 'under no faults' we can assume $Pr(U|no\ faults)$ is zero. Also T_F has been defined so that $Pr(U|W \geq T_F)$ is zero. Hence

$$Pr(U) = Pr(U|W < T_F).Pr(W < T_F)$$

In this paper we will make the conservative assumption that $Pr(U|W < T_F)$ is one. And hence we are left with the evaluation of $Pr(W < T_F)$, i.e. the probability

---

of transient faults.

[3]To simplify notation and avoid the need to mention special cases in the remainder of the paper, we will regard the events of *no faults* and *one fault* as being subsets of the event $W{\geq}T_F$. The simplest formal mechanism to achieve this is to define W to be an improper random variable, taking the value $W{=}\infty$ when there is exactly one fault, or no faults at all, during the system lifetime. Thus W is always realised with some value, so that $Pr(W{<}T_F) + Pr(W{\geq}T_F) = 1$.

that at least two faults arrive so close together in time that they cannot both be tolerated. This is done in Section 5. Although this assumption is conservative (and hence safe) it is clearly possible to give less pessimistic values. The above formulation will allow such values to be combined with the estimates of $Pr(W < T_F)$ given in Section 5.

Issues concerned with implementing the features suggested by the Fault Model are well addressed by Fetzer and Cristian[8].

Typical Values of Key Parameters

Before proceeding with the analysis it is worth noting the ranges in value of the key parameters of the model. In most applications of interest, the "lifetime" over which a probability of failure is required is the duration of one mission. Mission times for civil aircraft are typically 3-20 hours, but for satellites 15 years of execution may be expected. The iteration periods for control loops are as short as 20ms, other loops and signals may have T values of a few seconds. Precise values for $MTBF$ are not generally known, but in a friendly operating environment perhaps 100 hours is not unreasonable. In more hostile conditions, 20 seconds may be more typical. Although T_F is derived from the characteristics of the task set under consideration, it is worth noting that very small values are unlikely (as a task will not make progress if it suffers repetitive faults), and faults spaced out beyond the LCM of the task periods will easily be catered for; hence: 200ms $< T_F <$ 5 Seconds. Table 2 summarizes these viable ranges for the key parameters (in hours and hours^{-1}).

Parameter	Range
L	$3 - 10^5$
T	$10^{-6} - 10^{-2}$
λ	$10^{-2} - 10^2$
T_F	$10^{-5} - 10^{-2}$

Table 2: Typical Values of Key Parameters

4 Schedulability Analysis for Fault Tolerant Execution

Let F_k be the extra computation time needed by τ_k if an error is detected during its execution. This could represent the re-execution of the task, the execution of an exception handler or recovery block, or the partial re-execution of a task with checkpoints. In the scheduling analysis the execution of task τ_i will be affected by a fault in τ_i or any higher priority task. We assume that any extra computation for a task will be executed at the task's (fixed) priority.

Hence if there is just a single fault, equation (1) will become [16, 2][4]:

$$R_i \;=\; C_i + B_i + \sum_{j \in hp(i)} \left\lceil \frac{R_i}{T_j} \right\rceil C_j + \max_{k \in hep(i)} F_k \qquad (4)$$

where $hep(i)$ is the set of tasks with priority equal or higher than τ_i, that is $hep(i) = hp(i) + \tau_i$.

This equation can again be solved for R_i by forming a recurrence relation. If all R_i values are still less than the corresponding D_i values then a deterministic guarantee is furnished.

Given that a fault tolerant system has been built it can be assumed (although this would need to be verified) that it will be able to tolerate a single isolated fault. And hence the more realistic problem is that of multiple faults; at some point all systems will become unschedulable when faced with an arbitrary number of fault events.

To consider maximum arrival rates, first assume that T_f is a known minimum arrival interval for fault events. Also assume the error latency is zero (this restriction will be removed shortly). Equation (4) becomes [16, 2]:

$$R_i \;=\; C_i + B_i + \sum_{j \in hp(i)} \left\lceil \frac{R_i}{T_j} \right\rceil C_j + \left\lceil \frac{R_i}{T_f} \right\rceil \max_{k \in hep(i)} F_k \qquad (5)$$

Thus in interval $(0\ R_i]$ there can be at most $\left\lceil \frac{R_i}{T_f} \right\rceil$ fault events, each of which can induce F_k amount of each computation. The validity of this equation comes from noting that fault events behave identically to sporadic tasks, and they are represented in the scheduling analysis in this way [1]. Note the equation is not exact (but it is sufficient): faults need not always induce a maximum re-execution load.

There is a useful analogy between *release jitter* and error latency. If a fault can lie dormant for time A_f, then this may cause two errors to appear to come closer together than T_f. This will increase the impact of the fault recovery. Equation (5) can be modified to include error latency in the same way that release jitter is incorporated into the standard analysis [1]:

$$R_i \;=\; C_i + B_i + \sum_{j \in hp(i)} \left\lceil \frac{R_i}{T_j} \right\rceil C_j + \left\lceil \frac{R_i + A_f}{T_f} \right\rceil \max_{k \in hep(i)} F_k \qquad (6)$$

As before, this equation can be solved for R_i by forming a recurrence relationship.

Table 3 gives an example of applying equation (6). Here full re-execution is required following a fault. Two different fault arrival intervals are considered. For one the system remains schedulable, but for the shorter interval the final task cannot be guaranteed. In this simple example, blocking and error latency are assumed to be zero. Note that for the first three tasks, the new response times are less than the shorter T_f value, and hence will remain constant for all T_f values greater than 200.

The above analysis has assumed that the task deadlines, Ds, remain in effect even during a fault handling situation. Some systems allow a relaxed deadline

---

[4]We assume that in the absence of faults, the task set is schedulable.

Task	P	T	C	D	F	R $T_f = 300$	R $T_f = 200$
τ_1	1	100	30	100	30	60	60
τ_2	2	175	35	175	35	100	100
τ_3	3	200	25	200	25	155	155
τ_4	4	300	30	300	30	275	UNSCH

Table 3: Example Task Set - T_f = 300/200

when faults occur (as long as faults are rare). This is easily accommodated into the analysis.

Limits to Schedulability

Having formed the relation between schedulability and T_f, it is possible to apply sensitivity analysis to equation (6) to find the minimum value of T_f that leads to the system being just schedulable. As indicated earlier, let this value be denoted as T_F (it is the threshold fault interval).

Sensitivity analysis [19, 14, 13, 17] is used with fixed priority systems to investigate the relationship between values of key task parameters and schedulability. For an unschedulable system it can easily generate (using simple branch and bound techniques) factors such as the percentage by which all Cs must be reduced for the system to become schedulable.

Similarly for schedulable systems, sensitivity analysis can be used to investigate the amount by which the load can be increased without jeopardising the deadline guarantees. Here we apply sensitivity analysis to T_f to obtain T_F.

When the above task set is subject to sensitivity analysis it yields a value of T_F of 275. The behaviour of the system with this threshold fault interval is shown in Table 4. A value of 274 would cause τ_4 to miss its deadline.

Task	P	T	C	D	R $T_F = 275$
τ_1	1	100	30	100	60
τ_2	2	175	35	175	100
τ_3	3	200	25	200	155
τ_4	4	300	30	300	275

Table 4: Example Task Set - T_F set at 275

5   Evaluating $Pr(W<T_F)$

We need to calculate the probability that during the lifetime, L, of the system no two faults will be closer than T_F. Two approaches are considered. The attraction of the first is that it shows that a relatively intuitive and uncomplicated approach yields upper and lower bounds on $Pr(W<T_F)$ which, for a wide range of parameter values, provide a maximum approximation error which cannot be much greater than a factor of 3 (since $\frac{\text{upper bound}}{\text{lower bound}} \approx 3$). With the second approach a more cumbersome but exact formulation is derived. Despite the inclusion of this latter exact formulation, we believe that, given that it is often rather the *order of magnitude* of the failure probability that is the primary concern (rather than an exact value), the mathematically significantly easier reasoning of the first, bounding approach retains some importance.

5.1   Upper and Lower Bounds for Evaluating $Pr(W<T_F)$

We are concerned with two faults being closer than T_F over the mission time L. Since in practice $L \gg T_F$ we can assume, without loss of generality, that L is an even integer multiple of T_F. Let *mishap* be the undesirable event of two faults indeed occurring closer than T_F i.e.

$$Pr(\text{mishap during } L) \equiv Pr(W < T_F)$$

We derive the required upper and lower bounds via the following theorems:

<u>Theorem 1</u>   If $L/(2T_F)$ is a positive integer then

$$Pr(\text{mishap during } L) < 1 + \left[e^{-\lambda T_F} \left(1 + \lambda T_F \right) \right]^{\frac{L}{T_F}-1} - 2 \left[e^{-2\lambda T_F} \left(1 + 2\lambda T_F \right) \right]^{\frac{L}{2T_F}}$$

<u>Theorem 2</u>   If $L/(2T_F)$ is a positive integer then

$$Pr(\text{mishap during } L) > 1 - \left[e^{-\lambda T_F} \left(1 + \lambda T_F \right) \right]^{\frac{L}{T_F}}$$

<u>Proof of Theorem 1</u>

Let the mission time be split into a series of 'even' time intervals with boundaries $0, 2T_F, 4T_F, \ldots, L$, as shown in Figure 1. Similarly a set of 'odd' intervals starting at times $T_F, 3T_F, 5T_F, \ldots, L-T_F$ can be defined (extending the lifetime slightly to $L+T_F$, the end point of the last odd interval, by continuing the same HPP fault model). Each set has $L/2T_F$ intervals. Let a mishap be said to lie in an interval if both of its faults occur during that interval. It follows from the geometry of these intervals that

> *mishap during L* $\Rightarrow$ *mishap in some even interval[s],*
> *or mishap in some odd interval[s]*

This property comes directly from the definition of the intervals; if a mishap (two faults closer than T_F) occurs it must lie in either an even or an odd interval[5].

$$Pr(mishap\ during\ L) \ < \ Pr(mishap\ in\ some\ even\ interval[s]$$
$$or\ mishap\ in\ some\ odd\ interval[s])$$

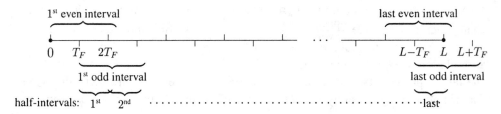

Figure 1: Definitions of *'even intervals'*, *'odd intervals'* and *'half-intervals'*

Actually the intersection of the two events on the right hand side has non-zero probability. One way that they can occur together is that a single mishap could lie in the overlap between an even and an odd interval. Call these overlaps 'half-intervals': they are of length T_F, and there are[6] $\frac{L}{T_F} - 1$ of them, respectively starting at times $T_F, 2T_F, \ldots, L-T_F$. So from the basic axioms of probability

$$Pr(mishap\ in\ some\ even\ interval[s], \ \ or \ \ mishap\ in\ some\ odd\ interval[s]) <$$
$$Pr(mishap\ in\ some\ even\ interval[s]) \ +$$
$$Pr(mishap\ in\ some\ odd\ interval[s]) \ -$$
$$Pr(mishap\ in\ some\ half\text{-}interval[s])$$

Now, given the symmetry of the construction and the HPP process assumption,

$$Pr(mishap\ in\ some\ even\ interval[s]) = Pr(mishap\ in\ some\ odd\ interval[s])$$

Hence

$$Pr(mishap\ during\ L) < 2Pr(mishap\ in\ some\ even\ interval[s])$$
$$- \ Pr(mishap\ in\ some\ half\text{-}interval[s]) \tag{7}$$

The event "mishap in a particular even interval" is independent of events in all other even intervals, and it has the same probability for every even interval. Thus

$$Pr(mishap\ in\ some\ even\ interval[s]) = 1 - Pr(no\ mishap\ in\ 2T_F)^{\frac{L}{2T_F}}. \tag{8}$$

---

[5]The difference between the two sides here is the (normally tiny since $L \gg T_F$) probability that the *second* fault of the *first* mishap occurs during $L < t \leq L + T_F$.

[6]Our term 'half-interval' *excludes* the early half of the first even interval, and the latter half of the last odd interval, since they do not arise as overlaps.

For an interval of length $2T_F$ not to contain a mishap, it is sufficient (but not necessary) that it contain 0 or 1 fault. Hence, from equation (3)

$$Pr(no\ mishap\ in\ 2T_F) > e^{-2\lambda T_F} (1 + 2\lambda T_F). \qquad (9)$$

Combining equations (8) and (9) yields

$$Pr(mishap\ in\ some\ even\ interval[s]) < 1 - \left[e^{-2\lambda T_F} (1 + 2\lambda T_F) \right]^{\frac{L}{2T_F}}. \qquad (10)$$

By a similar argument for the half-intervals

$$Pr(mishap\ in\ some\ half\text{-}interval[s]) = 1 - \left[e^{-\lambda T_F} (1 + \lambda T_F) \right]^{\frac{L}{T_F} - 1}, \qquad (11)$$

and now combining equations (7), (10), and (11) delivers the theorem statement.
□

Proof of Theorem 2

In a similar way to the previous proof, consider the series of intervals of length T_F starting at times $0, T_F, 2T_F, 3T_F, \dots, L{-}T_F$. There are $\frac{L}{T_F}$ of these, a mishap in any one of which implies a mishap during L (but not vice versa). Hence

$$Pr(mishap\ during\ L) > Pr(mishap\ in\ some\ interval[s])$$

but

$$Pr(mishap\ in\ some\ interval[s]) = 1 - Pr(no\ mishap\ in\ any\ interval)$$

Proof follows directly (as in proof of Theorem 1).
□

Both the upper and lower (exact) bounds are in mathematically non-intuitive forms, but simple approximations can be derived for most of the parameter range within which the probability of mishap is small enough to be of interest.

Corollary 3

An approximation for the upper bound on $Pr(W{<}T_F)$ given by Theorem 1 is $\frac{3}{2}\lambda^2 LT_F$, provided that λT_F, $\lambda^2 LT_F$ are small, and $L{\gg}T_F$.

Corollary 4

An approximation for the lower bound on $Pr(W{<}T_F)$ given by Theorem 2 is $\frac{1}{2}\lambda^2 LT_F$, provided only that λT_F, $\lambda^2 LT_F$ are small.

Proof of Corollary 3

The term $e^{-\lambda T_F} (1 + \lambda T_F)$ can be approximated by a Taylor series, where terms $(\lambda T_F)^3$ and beyond are ignored. Thus

$$e^{-\lambda T_F} (1 + \lambda T_F) \approx 1 - \frac{\lambda^2 T_F^2}{2}$$

Another approximation comes from noting that for small xz^2

$$\left(1 - \frac{z^2}{2}\right)^x \approx 1 - \frac{xz^2}{2}$$

where terms z^4 and higher powers of z can be ignored. Hence, under assumptions λT_F, $\lambda^2 L T_F$ small, and $L \gg T_F$, we can write

$$\left[e^{-\lambda T_F}(1 + \lambda T_F)\right]^{\frac{L}{T_F}-1} \approx \left(1 - \frac{\lambda^2 T_F^2}{2}\right)^{\frac{L}{T_F}-1} \approx 1 - \frac{L\lambda^2 T_F^2}{2T_F} \tag{12}$$

Under just the first assumptions that λT_F, $\lambda^2 L T_F$ are small we have equally

$$\left[e^{-2\lambda T_F}(1 + 2\lambda T_F)\right]^{\frac{L}{2T_F}} \approx 1 - \frac{L\lambda^2 T_F^2}{T_F} \tag{13}$$

Applying (12) and (13) to the conclusion of Theorem 1, Corollary 3 is proved.
□

Corollary 4 follows by a similar argument.

    Strictly, the bounds in Theorems 1 and 2 have only been proved here for L an even multiple of T_F. However, the realistic assumption $L \gg T_F$ allows the approximations given in the two corollaries still to extend to other values of T_F and L. In fact, where $\frac{L}{2T_F}$ *is* an exact integer, this $L \gg T_F$ assumption is not actually required, either for the derivation of the exact bounds in Theorems 1 and 2, nor for the *lower*-bound approximation of Corollary 4. For high accuracy in Corollary 4, we need only the assumption of small λT_F, $\lambda^2 L T_F$. Corollary 3 is the exception, relying on the $L \gg T_F$ assumption at one place in its derivation: the exponent to the square-bracketed term in (12) is 'out by 1' and we needed $\frac{T_F}{L}$ to be small in order to justify effectively ignoring this fact. For very short mission times, such that we do not have $L \gg T_F$, we can in fact 'retreat slightly' to a slacker upper bound for $Pr(mishap\ during\ L)$ by using 1 as an upper bound for this square-bracketed term in a modified version of Theorem 1, thus avoiding the awkward exponent $\frac{L}{T_F}-1$. Then, for positive integral $\frac{L}{2T_F}$, the resulting equivalent of Corollary 3 produces an accurate approximation $2\lambda^2 L T_F$ to this slacker upper bound on $Pr(W < T_F)$, *without* any requirement that $L \gg T_F$; i.e., under the assumptions only that λT_F, $\lambda^2 L T_F$ are small, and that $\frac{L}{2T_F}$ is a positive integer, but without now the requirement that $L \gg T_F$, the methods of this subsection are able to provide bounds on $Pr(W < T_F)$ which are approximately in the ratio $\frac{\text{upper bound}}{\text{lower bound}} \approx 4$.

    The important upper bound approximation of Corollary 3 can be written in the form $\frac{3}{2}(\lambda L)(\lambda T_F)$. It will often be the case that $\lambda T_F < 10^{-2}$; indeed this constraint allowed the approximations to deliver useful values. But λL can vary quite considerably from 10^{-2} or less in friendly environments to 10^3 or more in long-life, hostile domains. Clearly, low probability levels for this latter case will be extremely difficult to achieve by the scheduling approach defined in this paper.

	λ		
L	1	10^{-2}	10^{-4}
1	1.1×10^{-4}	1.1×10^{-8}	1.1×10^{-12}
10^1	1.1×10^{-3}	1.1×10^{-7}	1.1×10^{-11}
10^2	1.1×10^{-2}	1.1×10^{-6}	1.1×10^{-10}
10^4	1	1.1×10^{-4}	1.1×10^{-8}

Table 5: Upper bound on Non-Schedulability due to Faults.

The example introduced in Section 4 had a T_F value of 275ms. Table 5 gives the upper bound on the probability guarantee for various values of λ and L.

When $\lambda L < 10^{-2}$, λL approximates the probability of any fault happening during the mission of duration L. So, $\frac{2}{3}(\lambda T_F)^{-1}$ represents the gain that is achieved by the use of fault tolerance, under the other assumptions stated. So, for example in Table 5, when $\lambda = 10^{-2}$ and $L = 1$ the gain is approximately 10^6.

5.2   Exact Formulation for Evaluating $Pr(W < T_F)$

Unlike the bounding argument used in the last section, our exact derivation of the probability $Pr(W < T_F)$ proceeds in two stages, first conditioning on the total number n of faults seen in the lifetime L of the system. It is a well known property of the HPP process [7] that if we condition on the number n of events occurring within a specified time interval and then define $X_1, X_2, \ldots, X_n$ as ordered positions of these n points within that interval, expressed as proportions of its length, then the X_i are (conditionally given n) jointly distributed as the order statistics of an i.i.d. random sample from a uniform distribution on the unit interval $[0, 1]$. This being accepted, we now first fix u with $0 \leq u \leq 1$ and ask the question '*What is the probability, P say, that no two of these points are closer than u (conditionally given n)?*'. We can obtain the answer by n-dimensional integration. This is reported in an extended version of this paper available as a technical report [3], which says essentially that P is just the nth power of the total amount of 'slack' remaining within the unit interval after our u-separation constraint is imposed.

This solution conditional given n enables us to complete the exact derivation of the final, unconditional $Pr(W < T_F)$ relatively straightforwardly by using the 'chain rule' of conditional probability to 'uncondition on n'. Another fundamental property of the homogeneous Poisson process is that the distribution of n, the count of the number of events occurring within a fixed time interval, upon which the probabilities are conditioned, is Poisson with parameter equal to its mean, which in our case is λL. Then, working for convenience with the 'probability of *no* mishap in a time interval of length L', we have

$$
\begin{aligned}
Pr(W \geq T_F) &= \sum_{n=0}^{\infty} P_{n,\,(T_F/L)} \cdot e^{-\lambda L} \cdot \frac{(\lambda L)^n}{n!} \\
&= e^{-\lambda L} \left\{ 1 + \lambda L + \sum_{n=2}^{\lceil \frac{L}{T_F} \rceil} \left(1 - (n-1)\Big(\frac{T_F}{L}\Big) \right)^n \cdot \frac{(\lambda L)^n}{n!} \right\} \\
&= e^{-\lambda L} \left\{ 1 + \lambda L + \sum_{n=2}^{\lceil \frac{L}{T_F} \rceil} \frac{\lambda^n}{n!} \left(L - (n-1)T_F \right)^n \right\}
\end{aligned}
\tag{14}
$$

A few remarks about this exact expression   We remark firstly that (14) is essentially a function of just two arguments, λL, λT_F, rather than three (as are the bounds derived in Section 5.1). Thinking now of the function mathematically in these terms, without much concerning ourselves about physical interpretation of the arguments, if we agree to confine ourselves to the ranges $0 < \lambda L < \infty$, and $0 \leq \lambda T_F < \infty$, then we remark that the expression (14) continues to give the correct mathematical Poisson process probability at all points of this domain, including the value of 1 obtained at $\lambda T_F = 0$. (This is on the understanding that the $\lceil \infty \rceil$ occurring as the upper limit of a sum denotes a sum to infinity in the usual sense of a mathematical limit.) The purpose of stating this last point about the argument domain now to be assumed for this function is related to the practical computation problem associated with (14) which we address briefly in [3]. Note that, apart from this $\lambda T_F = 0$ case, the expression (14) represents a finite sum throughout the domain identified, although, for certain argument values, the number of terms summed can be astronomically large, which can make a simple-minded numerical computation rather slow. Moreover, some of these awkward parameter ranges may be of real practical interest to us in our application (see end of Section 3).

Note that we can use the common notation for the 'positive part function' h_+, associated with any real-valued function h, to obtain the following slightly different expression, valid throughout the argument domain we have just specified (including $\lambda T_F = 0$).

$$
Pr(W \geq T_F) = e^{-\lambda L} \left\{ 1 + \lambda L + \sum_{n=2}^{\infty} \frac{(\lambda L - (n-1)\lambda T_F)_+^n}{n!} \right\}
\tag{15}
$$

5.3   Some Numerical Results on $Pr(W < T_F)$

We decided to test the accuracy of our numerical approximations experimentally, and found that, over the physically realistic parameter ranges of concern to us, the approximations defined are extremely accurate, even at very low order in the Taylor series. This enabled us to produce Figure 2, a contour plot indicating the dependence of the *exact* value of $Pr(W < T_F)$ on its two arguments λL, λT_F. The function plotted is, in fact, the *log odds* of $Pr(W < T_F)$, chosen in order to ensure that there are some contours near each extreme, $Pr(W<T_F) = 0$ and $Pr(W<T_F) = 1$. In the top right hand corner the contours bunch too closely as the probability of a 'mishap during L' becomes *extremely* close to absolute certainty. (It is difficult to imagine a situation in which the precise values of these large probabilities would be of practical interest.) The rectangular box indicates a subdomain of the arguments over which we have also plotted the *accuracy* of our Taylor series approximation to this exact $Pr(W<T_F)$ function. The technical report[3] contains plots of the percentage inaccuracy that results from the truncation of the approximation after one or two terms.

Contours of $\log_{10}[P(W<T_F)/P(W>T_F)]$

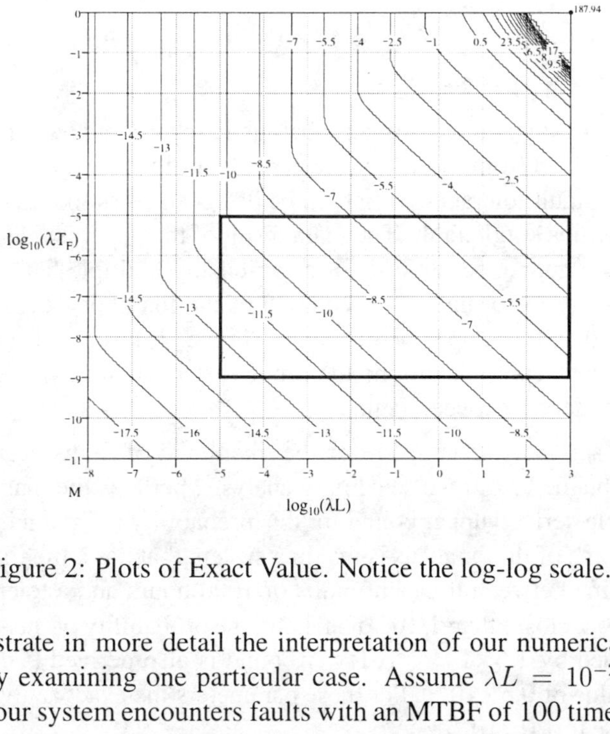

Figure 2: Plots of Exact Value. Notice the log-log scale.

We can illustrate in more detail the interpretation of our numerical results and plots briefly by examining one particular case. Assume $\lambda L = 10^{-2}$ and $\lambda T_F = 10^{-5}$. That is, our system encounters faults with an MTBF of 100 times its lifetime. It is guaranteed to be schedulable provided that it does not, during its lifetime, experience two faults separated by less than one thousandth of the lifetime duration. In such circumstances, we would clearly expect the system to be schedulable with a high probability, P say. This is a log-odds contour plot, so the proximity to the -7 contour indicates that the odds in favour of a system being schedulable with these parameter values are approximately 10^7 to 1. In fact, the bounds on the probability of schedulability, in this situation, obtained by the 'order-of-magnitude' argument of Section 5.1, are 0.4999967×10^{-7} and 1.500477×10^{-7}. The approximations to these bounds, obtained in the two corollaries in Section 5.1, are 0.5×10^{-7} and 1.5×10^{-7}, exactly. The Taylor series approximation allows, in this case, almost arbitrarily accurate calculation of the true value of P with comparatively few terms of the series. In fact we proved that all even-order partial sums, up to the 1000th-order sum, are lower bounds on P, and all odd-order partial sums, up to the 1001th-order sum, are upper bounds. With these particular arguments, the modulus of the fourth order term in the series is less than 10^{-19}, so the sum to only three terms would give an accuracy guaranteed to be better than approximately 11 or 12 significant decimal figures. To eight significant figures, the value of P is $.99948496 \times 10^{-7}$, corresponding to a log-odds very close to -7 in Figure 2 (at coordinates $(-2, -5)$). The series approximation gives first and second order Taylor approximations of 10^{-7} and $.99948495 \times 10^{-7}$, respectively. (These numbers are both exact.) See [3] for a detailed derivation of these results concerning high numerical accuracy.

6 Conclusion

We have developed the notion of a probabilistic scheduling guarantee and shown how it can be derived from the stochastic behaviour of fault events. It is reasonable to assume that a fault tolerant system will be designed so as to remain schedulable when dealing with a single fault. The main result of the paper is thus the derivation of a probabilistic guarantee for systems experiencing multiple faults. To do this it has been necessary to formulate a prediction of the likelihood of faults occurring closer together than some specified distance in time. It has also been necessary to use sensitivity analysis to determine the limits to schedulability; that is, the minimum tolerable interval between faults.

Although exact analysis is given for the likelihood of faults occurring quicker than the rate obtained from the sensitivity analysis, perhaps the main result of this paper is a simple derived upper bound for this probability (as given in Corollary 3). A typical outcome of this analysis is that in a system that has a life time of 10 hours with a mean time between transient faults of 1000 hours and a tolerance of faults that do not appear closer than 1/100 of an hour, the probability of missing a deadline is upper bounded by 1.5×10^{-7}. A lower bound is also derived (Corollary 4) and this yields a value of 0.5×10^{-7}. For these parameters the exact analysis produces a value very close to 1.0×10^{-7}.

Interestingly (and perhaps not totally intuitively) the upper, lower and exact formulations for the probabilistic scheduling guarantee all indicate that the threshold value derived from the scheduling and sensitivity analysis has a linear relationship to the probabilistic guarantee. If the threshold value T_F is halved, the probability of missing a deadline is halved. Similarly the length L of execution of the system has a linear impact.

The main obstacle to the use of some of the analysis given in this paper is the lack of empirical data concerning fault arrival times. In the future we aim to address fault clustering and less favourable fault process models. We also aim to move away from the conservative assumption that the system is unschedulable (with probability 1) when faults arrive closer than the threshold value.

References

[1] N. C. Audsley, A. Burns, M. Richardson, K. Tindell, and A. J. Wellings. Applying new scheduling theory to static priority pre-emptive scheduling. *Software Engineering Journal*, 8(5):284–292, 1993.

[2] A. Burns, R. I. Davis, and S. Punnekkat. Feasibility analysis of fault-tolerant real-time task sets. *Euromicro Real-Time Systems Workshop*, pages 29–33, June 1996.

[3] A. Burns, S. Punnekkat, L. Strigini, and D.R. Wright. Probabilistic scheduling guarantees for fault-tolerant real-time systems. Technical Report YCS.311, Department of Computer Science, University of York, 1998.

[4] A. Burns and A. J. Wellings. Engineering a hard real-time system: From theory to practice. *Software-Practice and Experience*, 25(7):705–26, 1995.

[5] A. Campbell, P. McDonald, and K. Ray. Single event upset rates in space. *IEEE Transactions on Nuclear Science*, 39(6):1828–1835, December 1992.

[6] X. Castillo, S.P. McConnel, and D.P. Siewiorek. Derivation and Calibration of a Transient Error Reliability Model. *IEEE Transactions on Computers*, 31(7):658–671, July 1982.

[7] D.R.Cox and P.A.W. Lewis. *Statistical Analysis of Series of Events*. Methuen's Monographs on Applied Probability and Statistics, London, 1966.

[8] C. Fetzer and F. Cristian. Fail-awareness: An approach to construct fail-safe applications. In *Proceedings of the 27th Int. Conf. on Fault-Tolerant Computer Systems (FTCS)*, pages 282–291, 1997.

[9] C.-J. Hou and K. G. Shin. Allocation of periodic task modules with precedence and deadline constraints in distributed real-time systems. *IEEE Transactions on Computers*, 46(12):1338–1356, 1997.

[10] M. Joseph and P. Pandya. Finding response times in a real-time system. *BCS Computer Journal*, 29(5):390–395, 1986.

[11] D.I. Katcher, H. Arakawa, and J.K. Strosnider. Engineering and analysis of fixed priority schedulers. *IEEE Trans. Softw. Eng.*, 19, 1993.

[12] H. Kim, A.L.White, and K. G.Shin. Reliability modeling of hard real-time systems. In *Proceedings 28th Int. Symp. on Fault-Tolerant Computing (FTCS-28)*, pages 304–313. IEEE Computer Society Press, 1998.

[13] M. H. Klein, T. A. Ralya, B. Pollak, R. Obenza, and M. G. Harbour. *A Practitioner's Handbook for Real-Time Analysis: A Guide to Rate Monotonic Analysis for Real-Time Systems*. Kluwer Academic Publishers, 1993.

[14] J.P. Lehoczky, L. Sha, and V. Ding. The rate monotonic scheduling algorithm: Exact characterization and average case behavior. Tech report, Department of Statistics, Carnegie-Mellon, 1987.

[15] J.Y.T. Leung and J. Whitehead. On the complexity of fixed-priority scheduling of periodic, real-time tasks. *Performance Evaluation (Netherlands)*, 2(4):237–250, 1982.

[16] S. Punnekkat. *Schedulability Analysis for Fault Tolerant Real-time Systems*. PhD thesis, Dept. Computer Science, University of York, June 1997.

[17] S. Punnekkat, R. Davis, and A. Burns. Sensitivity analysis of real-time task sets. In *Proceedings of the Conference of Advances in Computing Science - ASIAN '97*, pages 72–82. Springer, 1997.

[18] K. G. Shin, M. Krishna, and Y. H. Lee. A unified method for evaluating real-time computer controllers its application. *IEEE Transactions on Automatic Control*, 30:357–366, 1985.

[19] S. Vestal. Fixed Priority Sensitivity Analysis for Linear Compute Time Models. *IEEE Transactions on Software Engineering*, 20(4):308–317, April 1994.

Fault Detection for Byzantine Quorum Systems

Lorenzo Alvisi*   Dahlia Malkhi[†]   Evelyn Pierce[‡]   Michael Reiter[§]

Abstract

In this paper we explore techniques to detect Byzantine server failures in replicated data services. Our goal is to detect arbitrary failures of data servers in a system where each client accesses the replicated data at only a subset (quorum) of servers in each operation. In such a system, some correct servers can be out-of-date after a write and thus can return values other than the most up-to-date value in response to a client's read request, thus complicating the task of determining the number of faulty servers in the system at any point in time. We initiate the study of detecting server failures in this context, and propose two statistical approaches for estimating the number of faulty servers based on responses to read requests.

1 Introduction

Data replication is a well-known means of protecting against data unavailability or corruption in the face of data server failures. When servers can suffer Byzantine (i.e., arbitrary) failures, the foremost approach for protecting data is via *state machine replication* [Sch90], in which every correct server receives and processes every request in the same order, thereby producing the same output for each request. If the client then accepts a value returned by at least $t + 1$ servers, then up to t arbitrary server failures can be masked. Numerous systems have been built to support this approach (e.g., [PG89, SESTT92, Rei94, KMM98]).

To improve the efficiency and availability of data access while still protecting the integrity of replicated data, the use of *quorum systems* has been proposed. Quorum systems are a family of protocols that allow reads and updates of replicated data to be performed at only a subset (quorum) of the servers. In a *t-masking quorum system*, the quorums of servers are defined such that any two quorums intersect in

---

*Department of Computer Science, University of Texas, Austin, Texas; lorenzo@cs.utexas.edu. This work was funded in part by a NSF CAREER award (CCR-9734185), a DARPA/SPAWAR grant number N66001-98-8911 and a NSF CISE grant (CDA-9624082)

[†]AT&T Labs—Research, Florham Park, New Jersey; dalia@research.att.com

[‡]Department of Computer Science, University of Texas, Austin, Texas; tumlin@cs.utexas.edu

[§]Bell Laboratories, Lucent Technologies, Murray Hill, New Jersey; reiter@research.bell-labs.com

at least $2t + 1$ servers [MR97a, MRW97]. In a system with a maximum of t faulty servers, if each read and write operation is performed at a quorum, then the quorum used in a read operation will intersect the quorum used in the last preceding write operation in at least $t+1$ correct servers. With appropriate read and write protocols, this intersection condition ensures that the client is able to identify the correct, up-to-date data [MR97a].

A difficulty of using quorum systems for Byzantine fault tolerance is that *detecting* responsive but faulty servers is hard. In state machine replication, any server response that disagrees with the response of the majority immediately exposes the failure of the disagreeing server to the client. This property is lost, however, with quorum systems: because some servers remain out of date after any given write, a contrary response from a server in a read operation does not necessarily suggest the server's failure. Therefore, we must design specific mechanisms to monitor the existence of faults in a quorum-replicated system, e.g., to detect whether the number of failures is approaching t.

In this paper, we initiate the study of Byzantine fault detection methods for quorum systems by proposing two statistical techniques for estimating the number of server failures in a service replicated using a t-masking quorum system. Both of our methods estimate the total number of faulty servers from responses to a client's read requests executed at a quorum of servers, and are most readily applicable to the *threshold* quorum construction of [MR97a], in which a quorum is defined as any set of size $\lceil \frac{n+2t+1}{2} \rceil$. The first method has the advantage of requiring essentially no change to the read and write protocols proposed in [MR97a]. The second method does require an alteration of the read and write protocols, but has the advantages of improved accuracy and specific identification of a subset of the faulty servers. Furthermore, the fault identification protocol of the second method is applicable without alteration to all types of t-masking quorum systems, and indeed to other types of Byzantine quorum systems as proposed in [MR97a].

Both methods set an *alarm line* $t_a < t$ and issue a warning whenever the number of server failures exceeds t_a. We show how the system can use information from each read operation to statistically test the hypothesis that the actual number of faults f in the system is at most t_a. As we will show, if t_a is correctly selected and read operations are frequent, both methods can be expected to issue warnings in a timely fashion, i.e., while it is still the case that $f < t$. The service can then be repaired (or at least disabled) before the integrity of the data set is compromised.

As an initial investigation into the statistical monitoring of replicated data, this paper adopts a number of simplifying assumptions. First, we perform our statistical analysis in the context of read operations that are concurrent with no write operations, as observing partially completed writes during a read substantially complicates the task of inferring server failures. Second, we assume that clients are correct; distinguishing a faulty server from a server into which a faulty client has written incorrect data raises issues that we do not consider here. Third, we restrict our attention to techniques that modify the read and write protocols only minimally or not at all and that exploit data gathered from a single read only, without aggregating data across multiple reads. (As we will show in this paper, a surprising amount of information can be obtained without such aggregation.) Each of these assumptions represents an area for possible future research.

The goal of our work is substantially different from that of various recent works that have adapted *failure detectors* [CT96] to solve consensus in distributed systems that can suffer Byzantine failures [MR97b, DS97, KMM97]. These works focus on the specification of abstract failure detectors that enable consensus to be solved. Our goal here is to develop techniques for detecting Byzantine failures specifically in the context of data replicated using quorum systems, without regard to abstract failure detector specifications or the consensus problem. Lin et al. [LRM98] analyze the process of gradual infection of a system by malicious entities. Their analysis attempts to project when failures exceed certain thresholds by extrapolating from observed failures onto the future, on the basis of certain a priori assumptions about the communication patterns of processes and the infection rate of the system. Our methods do not depend on these assumptions, as they do not address the propagation of failures in the system; rather, they attempt to measure the current number of failures at any point in time.

To summarize, the contributions of this paper are twofold: we initiate the direction of fault monitoring and detection in the context of Byzantine quorum systems; and we propose two statistical techniques for performing this detection for t-masking quorum systems under the conditions described above. The rest of this paper is organized as follows. In Section 2 we describe our system model and necessary background. In Sections 3–4 we present and analyze our two statistical methods using exact formulae for alarm line placement in relatively small systems. In Section 5 we present an asymptotic analysis for estimating appropriate alarm line placement in larger systems for both methods. We conclude in Section 6.

2 Preliminaries

2.1 System model

Our system model is based on a *universe* U of n data servers. A *correct* server is one that behaves according to its specification, whereas a *faulty* server deviates from its specification arbitrarily (Byzantine failure). We denote the maximum allowable number of server failures for the system by t, and the actual number of faulty servers in the system at a particular moment by f. Because our goal in this paper is to detect faulty servers, we stipulate that a faulty server *does* in fact deviate from its I/O specification, i.e., it returns something other than what its specification would dictate (or it returns nothing, though unresponsive servers are ignored in this paper and are not the target of our detection methods). It is hardly fruitful to attempt to detect "faulty" servers whose visible behavior is consistent with correct execution.

Our system model also includes some number of clients, which we assume to be correct. Clients communicate with servers over point-to-point channels. Channels are reliable, in the sense that a message sent between a client and a correct server is eventually received by its destination. In addition, a client can authenticate the channel to a correct server; i.e., if the client receives a message from a correct server, then that server actually sent it.

2.2 Masking quorum systems

We assume that each server holds a copy of some replicated variable Z, on which clients can execute *write* and *read* operations to change or observe its value, respectively. The protocols for writing and reading Z employ a *t-masking quorum system* [MR97a, MRW97], i.e., a set of subsets of servers $\mathcal{Q} \subseteq 2^U$ such that $\forall Q_1, Q_2 \in \mathcal{Q}, |Q_1 \cap Q_2| \geq 2t + 1$. Intuitively, if each read and write is performed at a quorum of servers, then the use of a t-masking quorum system ensures that a read quorum Q_2 intersects the last write quorum Q_1 in at least $t + 1$ correct servers, which suffices to enable the reader to determine the last written value. Specifically, we base our methods on *threshold masking quorum systems* [MR97a], defined by $\mathcal{Q} = \{Q \subseteq U : |Q| = \lceil \frac{n+2t+1}{2} \rceil\}$; i.e., the quorums are all sets of servers of size $\lceil \frac{n+2t+1}{2} \rceil$. These systems are easily seen to have the t-masking property above.

We consider the following protocols for accessing the replicated variable Z, which were shown in [MR97a] to give Z the semantics of a *safe* variable [Lam86]. Each server u maintains a timestamp T_u with its copy Z_u of the variable Z. A client writes the timestamp when it writes the variable. These protocols require that different clients choose different timestamps, and thus each client c chooses its timestamps from some set $\mathcal{T}_c$ that does not intersect $\mathcal{T}_{c'}$ for any other client c'. Client operations proceed as follows.

Write: For a client c to write the value v to Z, it queries each server in some quorum Q to obtain a set of value/timestamp pairs $A = \{<Z_u, T_u>\}_{u \in Q}$, chooses a timestamp $T \in \mathcal{T}_c$ greater than the highest timestamp value in A and greater than any timestamp it has chosen in the past, and updates Z_u and T_u at each server u in some quorum Q' to v and T, respectively.

Read: For a client to read a variable Z, it queries each server in some quorum Q to obtain a set of value/timestamp pairs $A = \{<Z_u, T_u>\}_{u \in Q}$. From among all pairs returned by at least $t + 1$ servers in Q, the client chooses the pair $<v, T>$ with the highest timestamp T, and then returns v as the result of the read operation. If there is no pair returned by at least $t + 1$ servers, the result of the read operation is $\perp$ (a null value).

In a write operation, each server u updates Z_u and T_u to the received values $<v, T>$ only if T is greater than the present value of T_u; this convention guarantees the serializability of concurrent writes. As mentioned in Section 1 we consider only reads that are not concurrent with writes. In this case, the read operation will never return $\perp$ (provided that the assumed maximum number of failures t is not exceeded).

2.3 Statistical building blocks

The primary goal of this paper is to draw conclusions about the number f of faulty servers in the system, specifically whether f exceeds a selected alarm threshold t_a, where $0 \leq t_a < t$, using the responses obtained in the read protocol of the previous subsection. To do this, we make extensive use of a statistical technique called *hypothesis testing*. To use this technique, we establish two hypotheses about our universe of servers. The first of these is an *experimental hypothesis H_E* that represents a condition to be tested for, e.g., that f exceeds the alarm threshold t_a, and the second is a *null hypothesis H_0* complementing it. The idea behind hypothesis testing is to examine experimental results (in our case, read operations) for conditions that suggest the truth of the experimental hypothesis, i.e., conditions that would be "highly unlikely" if the null hypothesis were true. We define "highly unlikely" by choosing a *rejection level* $0 < \alpha < 1$ and identifying a corresponding *region of rejection* for H_0, where the region of rejection is the maximal set of possible results that suggest the truth of H_E (and thus the falsity of H_0) and whose total probability given H_0 is at most α. For the purposes of our work, H_E will be $f > t_a$, and H_0 will always be $f = t_a$. (Note that although these hypotheses are not strictly complementary, the region of rejection for H_0 encompasses that of every hypothesis $f = t'_a$, where $0 < t'_a < t_a$; therefore the rejection level of the truly complementary hypothesis $f \leq t_a$ is bounded by that of H_0. This treatment of the null hypothesis is a standard statistical procedure.)

In this paper we will typically choose t_a to be strictly less than the maximum assumed number t of failures in the system, for the reason that it is of little use to detect a dangerous condition after the integrity of the data has been compromised. The "safest" value for t_a is 0, but a higher value may be desirable if small numbers of faults are common and countermeasures are expensive.

In order for our statistical calculations to be valid, we must be able to treat individual quorums and the intersection between any two quorums as random samples of the universe of servers. Given our focus on a quorum system consisting of all sets of size $\lceil \frac{n+2t+1}{2} \rceil$, this can be accomplished by choosing quorums in such a way that each quorum (not containing unresponsive servers) is approximately equally likely to be queried for any given operation.

As in any statistical method, there is some possibility of false positives (i.e., alarms sent when the fault level remains below t_a) and false negatives (failure to detect a dangerous fault level before the threshold is exceeded). As we will show, however, the former risk can be kept to a reasonable minimum, while the latter can be made essentially negligible.[1]

---

[1]Except in catastrophically unreliable systems. Neither our method nor any other of which we are aware will protect against sudden near-simultaneous Byzantine failures in a sufficiently large number (e.g., greater than t) of servers.

3   Diagnosis using justifying sets

Our first method of fault detection for threshold quorum systems uses the read and write protocols described in Section 2.2. As the random variable for our statistical analysis, we use the size of the *justifying set* for a read operation, which is the set of servers that return the value/timestamp pair $<v, T>$ chosen by the client in the read operation. The size of the justifying set is at least $2t + 1$ if there are no faulty servers, but can be as small as $t + 1$ if $f = t$. The justifying set may be as large as $\lceil \frac{n+2t+1}{2} \rceil$ in the case where the read quorum is the same as the quorum used in the last completed write operation.

Suppose that a read operation is performed on the system, and that the size of the justifying set for that read operation is x. We would like to discover whether this evidence supports the hypothesis that the number of faults f in the system exceeds some value t_a, where $t_a < t$. We do so using a formula for the probability distribution for justifying set sizes; this formula is derived as follows.

Suppose we have a system of n servers, with a quorum size of q. Given f faulty servers in the system, the probability of exactly j failures in the read quorum can be expressed by a *hypergeometric distribution* as follows:

$$\frac{\binom{f}{j}\binom{n-f}{q-j}}{\binom{n}{q}}$$

Given that the number of failures in the read quorum is j, the probability that there are exactly x correct servers in the intersection between the read quorum and the previous write quorum is formulated as follows: the number of ways of choosing x correct servers from the read quorum is $\binom{q-j}{x}$, and the number of possible previous write quorums that intersect the read quorum in exactly those correct servers (and some number of incorrect ones) is $\binom{n-q+j}{q-x}$. The probability that the previous write quorum intersects the read quorum in exactly this way is therefore:

$$\frac{\binom{q-j}{x}\binom{n-q+j}{q-x}}{\binom{n}{q}}$$

To get the overall probability that there are exactly x correct servers in the intersection between the read and most recent write quorums, i.e., that the justifying set size $(size)$ is x, we multiply the conditional probability given j failures in the read quorum by the probability of exactly j failures in the read quorum, and sum the result for $j = 0$ to f:

$$P(size = x) = \sum_{j=0}^{f} \frac{\binom{q-j}{x}\binom{n-q+j}{q-x}\binom{f}{j}\binom{n-f}{q-j}}{\binom{n}{q}^2} \tag{1}$$

This formula expresses the probability that a particular read operation in a t-masking quorum system will have a justifying set size of x given the presence of f faults.

x	$P(size = x|f = 0)$	x	$P(size = x|f = 0)$
51	.000243	64	0.000500
52	.002922	65	7.92×10^{-05}
53	.015880	66	9.68×10^{-06}
54	.051857	67	9.03×10^{-07}
55	.114087	68	6.33×10^{-08}
56	.179687	69	3.26×10^{-09}
57	.210160	70	1.20×10^{-10}
58	.186867	71	3.05×10^{-12}
59	.128273	72	5.03×10^{-14}
60	.068649	73	5.02×10^{-16}
61	.028810	74	2.65×10^{-18}
62	.009504	75	5.89×10^{-21}
63	.002464	76	3.10×10^{-24}

Table 1: Probability distribution on justifying set sizes for Example 1

For a given rejection level α, then, the region of rejection for the null hypothesis $f = t_a$ is defined as $x \leq highreject$, where $highreject$ is the maximum value such that:

$$\sum_{x=t+1}^{highreject} \sum_{j=0}^{t_a} \frac{\binom{q-j}{x}\binom{n-q+j}{q-x}\binom{t_a}{j}\binom{n-t_a}{q-j}}{\binom{n}{q}^2} \leq \alpha$$

The left-hand expression above represents the *significance level* of the test, i.e., the probability of a false positive (false alarm).

If there are in fact $f' > t_a$ failures in the system, the probability of detecting this condition on a single read is:

$$\sum_{x=t+1}^{highreject} \sum_{j=0}^{f'} \frac{\binom{q-j}{x}\binom{n-q+j}{q-x}\binom{f'}{j}\binom{n-f'}{q-j}}{\binom{n}{q}^2}$$

If we denote this value by γ, then the probability that k consecutive reads *fail* to detect the condition is $(1 - \gamma)^k$. As shown in the following examples, k need not be very large for this probability to become negligible.

Example 1: Consider a system of $n = 101$ servers, a quorum size $q = 76$, and a fault tolerance threshold $t = 25$. In order to test whether there are *any* faults in the system, we set $t_a = 0$, so that the null hypothesis H_0 is $f = 0$ and the experimental hypothesis H_E is $f > 0$. Plugging these numbers into (1) over the full range of x yields the results in Table 1. For all other values of x not shown in Table 1, the probability of a justifying set of size x given $f = 0$ is zero.

f	$P(\text{detection})$	f	$P(\text{detection})$
1	.046772	11	.867154
2	.093352	12	.909989
3	.160471	13	.941069
4	.246231	14	.962708
5	.345534	15	.977185
6	.451337	16	.986505
7	.556213	17	.992282
8	.653732	18	.995733
9	.739333	19	.997720
10	.810618	20	.998823

Table 2: Probability of detecting $f > 0$ in Example 1

Since $P(51)+P(52)+P(53) \approx 0.019$, while $P(51)+P(52)+P(53)+P(54) \approx 0.071$, the region of rejection for $\alpha = 0.05$ is defined as $x \leq 53$; if a read operation has a justifying set of size 53 or less, the client rejects the null hypothesis and concludes that there are faults in the system. This test has a *significance level* of 0.019; that is, there is a probability of 0.019 that the client will detect faults when there are none. (If this level of risk is unacceptable for a particular system, α can be set to a lower value, thus creating a smaller region of rejection.)

Suppose that there are actually f failures in the system. The probability that this experiment will detect the presence of failures during any given read is:

$$\sum_{x=26}^{53} \sum_{j=0}^{f} \frac{\binom{76-j}{x}\binom{25+j}{76-x}\binom{f}{j}\binom{101-f}{76-j}}{\binom{101}{76}^2}$$

Table 2 shows these values for $1 \leq f \leq 20$.

Although the probability of detecting faults during a given read in this system is relatively low for very small values of f, it would appear that this test is reasonably powerful. Even for fault levels as low as 4 or 5, a client can reasonably expect to detect the presence of failures within a few reads; e.g., if $f = 5$, then the probability of detecting that $f > t_a$ in only 6 reads is already $1 - (1 - .345534)^6 = .921$. As the fault levels rise, the probability of such detection within a single read approaches near-certainty.

Example 2: Consider a much smaller system consisting of $n = 61$ servers, with a quorum size $q = 46$ and a fault tolerance threshold $t = 15$. Furthermore, suppose that the administrator of this system has decided that no action is called for if only a few failures occur, so that t_a is set at 5 rather than 0. Given $\alpha = 0.05$, the region of rejection for the null hypothesis $H_0 : f = t_a$ is $x \leq 27$. The probabilities of detecting this condition for actual values of f between 8 and 12 inclusive are shown in Table 3.

f	$P(\text{detection})$
8	.070210
9	.130284
10	.213058
11	.314905
12	.428527

Table 3: Probability of detecting $f > 5$ in Example 2

As one might expect, error conditions are more difficult to detect when they are more narrowly defined, as the contrast between examples 1 and 2 shows. Even in the latter experiment, however, a client can reasonably expect to detect a serious but non-fatal error condition within a small number of reads. For $f = 12$, the probability that the alarm is triggered within six read operations is $1 - (1 - 0.428527)^6$, approximately 96.5 percent. The probability that it is triggered within ten reads is over 99.6 percent. We can therefore reasonably consider this technique to be a useful diagnostic in systems where read operations are significantly more frequent than server failures, particularly if the systems are relatively large.

While the ability to detect faulty servers in threshold quorum systems is a step forward, this method leaves something to be desired. It gives little indication of the specific number of faults that have occurred and provides little information toward identifying which servers are faulty. In the next section we present another diagnostic method that addresses both these needs.

4 Diagnosis using quorum markers

The diagnostic method presented in this section has two distinct functions. First, it uses a technique similar to that of the previous section to estimate the fault distribution over the whole system, but with greater precision. Second, it pinpoints specific servers that exhibit detectably faulty behavior during a given read. The diagnostic operates on an enhanced version of the read/write protocol for masking quorum systems: the write marker protocol, described below.

4.1 The write marker protocol

The *write marker protocol* uses a simple enhancement to the read/write protocol of Section 2.2: we introduce a *write quorum marker* field to all variables. That is, for a replicated variable Z, each server u maintains, in addition to Z_u and T_u, a third value W_u, which is the name of the quorum (e.g., an n-bit vector indicating the servers in the quorum) used to complete the write operation in which Z_u and T_u were last written. The write protocol proceeds as in Section 2.2, except that in the last step, in addition to updating Z_u and T_u to v and T at each server u in a quorum Q', the client also updates W_u with (the name of) Q'. Specifically, to update Z_u,

T_u, and W_u at all (correct) servers in Q', the client sends a message containing $<v, T, Q'>$ to each $u \in Q'$. Because communication is reliable (see Section 2), the writer knows that Z_u, T_u and W_u will be updated at all correct servers in Q'. As before, each server u updates Z_u, T_u, and W_u to the received values $<v, T, Q'>$ only if T is greater than the present value of T_u.

The read protocol proceeds essentially as before, except that each server returns the triple $<Z_u, T_u, W_u>$ in response to a read request. From among all triples returned from at least $t + 1$ servers, the client chooses the triple with the highest timestamp.

Below we describe two ways of detecting faults by making use of the set of triples returned by the servers.

4.2   Statistical fault detection

Our revised statistical technique uses the quorum markers to determine the set S of servers whose returned values would match the accepted triple in the absence of faults, and the set S' of servers whose returned values actually do match that triple. Because of the size-based construction of threshold quorum systems and the random selection of the servers that make up the quorum for a given operation, the set S can be considered a random sample of the servers, of which $|S \setminus S'|$ are known to be faulty. Taking a random variable y to be the number of faulty servers in the sample, we can use similar calculations to those in Section 3 to analyze with greater precision the probability that f exceeds t_a.

As shown in Section 3, the probability of finding y faults in a sample of size s given a universe of size n containing f faults is expressed by the hypergeometric formula:

$$\frac{\binom{f}{y}\binom{n-f}{s-y}}{\binom{n}{s}}$$

For a rejection level α, the region of rejection for the hypothesis $f = t_a$ is therefore defined by the lowest value *lowreject* such that:

$$\sum_{y=lowreject}^{s} \frac{\binom{t_a}{y}\binom{n-t_a}{s-y}}{\binom{n}{s}} \leq \alpha$$

Again, the left-hand expression represents the parameterized probability of a false alarm.

For this method, experiments in which $t_a = 0$ are a degenerate case. The presence of *any* faults in the intersection set is visible and invalidates the null hypothesis; the probability of a false positive in such cases is zero, as the formula above confirms. Likewise, as the number of faults increases, the probability of detecting faults within one or two reads rapidly approaches certainty.

f	P(detection)	f	P(detection)
1	.564356	11	.999951
2	.812673	12	.999982
3	.920528	13	.999993
4	.966751	14	.999997
5	.986289	15	.999999
6	.994430	16	.999999
7	.997772	17	.999999
8	.999123	18	.999999
9	.999660	19	.999999
10	.999870	20	.999999

Table 4: Probability of detecting $f > 0$ in Example 3

f	P(detection)
8	.492173
9	.648616
10	.773168
11	.862716
12	.921818

Table 5: Probability of detecting $f > 5$ in Example 4

Example 3: Consider again the system of $n = 101$ servers, with a fault tolerance threshold of $t = 25$, a quorum size of $q = 76$, and $t_a = 0$, and suppose that a given read quorum overlaps the previous write quorum in $s = 57$ servers (the most likely overlap, with a probability of about 0.21). The probability of alarm on a single read operation for various values of $f < t$, is shown in Table 4. A comparison of this result with Example 1 (Table 2) illustrates the dramatically higher precision of the write-marker method over the justifying set method; see Figure 1. This precision has additional advantages when t_a is set to a value greater than 0.

Example 4: Consider again the system of $n = 61$ servers, with a fault tolerance threshold of $t = 15$, a quorum size of $q = 46$, and $t_a = 5$, and suppose that a given read quorum overlaps the previous write quorum in the most common intersection size $s = 34$ servers. The region of rejection for the null hypothesis $f = 5$, calculated using the formula above, is $y \geq 5$. The probability of alarm on a single read operation for various values of f, $t_a < f < t$, is shown in Table 5. Again, the increased strength of the write-marker method is evident (see Table 3 and Figure 2).

Like the method presented in Section 3, the write-marker technique also has the advantage of flexibility. If we wish to minimize the risk of premature alarms (i.e., alarms that are sent without the alarm threshold being exceeded) we may choose a

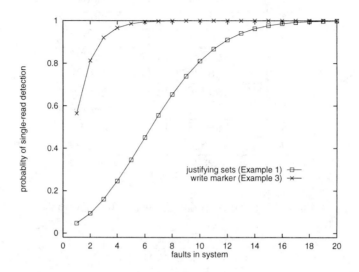

Figure 1: Comparison of methods for system with $n = 101$

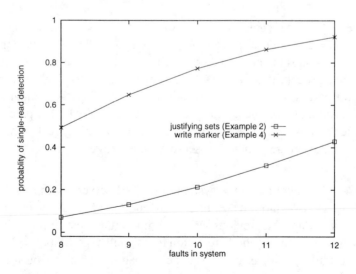

Figure 2: Comparison of methods for system with $n = 61$

smaller α at the risk of somewhat delayed alarms. In fact, the greater precision of this method decreases the risks associated with such a course: even delayed alarms can be expected to be timely.

4.3 Fault identification

The write marker protocol has an even stronger potential as a tool for fault detection: it allows the client to identify specific servers that are behaving incorrectly. By keeping a record of this list, the client can thereafter select quorums that do not contain these servers. This allows the system to behave somewhat more efficiently than it would otherwise, as well as gathering the information needed to isolate faulty servers for repair so that the system's integrity is maintained.

The fault identification algorithm accepts as input the triples $\{<Z_u, T_u, W_u>\}_{u \in Q}$ that the client obtained from servers in the read protocol, as well as the triple $<v, T, W>$ that the client chose as the result of the read operation. It then computes the set $S \setminus S'$ where $S = Q \cap W$ and S' is the set of servers that returned $<v, T, W>$ in the read operation. The servers in $S \setminus S'$ are identified as faulty.

Note that the fault identification protocol does not depend in any way on the specific characteristics of threshold quorum systems, and is easily seen to be applicable to masking quorum systems in general.

5 Choosing alarm lines for large systems

The analysis of the previous two sections is precise but computationally cumbersome for very large systems. A useful alternative is to estimate the performance of possible alarm lines by means of bound analysis. In this section we present an asymptotic analysis of the techniques of Sections 3 and 4 that shows how to choose an alarm line value for arbitrarily large systems.

Let us denote the read quorum Q, the write quorum Q', the set of faulty servers by B, and the hypothesized size of B (i.e., the alarm line) by t_a. We define a random variable $X = |(Q \cap Q') \setminus B|$, which is the justifying set size. We can compute the expectation of X directly. For each server $u \notin B$ define an indicator random variable I_u such that $I_u = 1$ if $u \in (Q \cap Q') \setminus B$ and $I_u = 0$ otherwise. For such u we have $P(I_u = 1) = q^2/n^2$ since Q and Q' are chosen independently. By linearity of expectation,

$$E[X] = \sum_{u \in U \setminus B} E[I_u] = \sum_{u \in U \setminus B} P(I_u = 1) = (n - t_a) \frac{q^2}{n^2}.$$

Intuitively, the distribution on X is centered around its expectation and decreases exponentially as X moves farther away from that expectation. Thus, we should be able to show that X grows smaller than its expectation with exponentially decreasing probability. A tempting approach to analyzing this would be to use Chernoff bounds, but these do not directly apply because the selection of individual servers in Q (similarly, Q') is not independent. In the analysis below, we thus use a more powerful tool, *martingales*, to derive the anticipated Chernoff-like bound.

We bound the probability $P(X < k)$ using the method of bounded differences, by defining a suitable Doob martingale sequence and applying Azuma's inequality (see [MR95, Ch. 4.4] for a good exposition of this technique; Appendix A provides a brief introduction). Here, a Doob martingale sequence of conditional random variables is defined by setting X_i, $0 \le i \le q$, to be the expected value of X after i selections are made in each of Q and Q'. Then, $X = X_q$ and $E[X] = X_0$, and it is not difficult to see that $|X_i - X_{i-1}| \le 2$ for all $1 \le i \le q$. This yields the following bound (see Appendix A).

$$P(X < E[X] - \delta) \le 2e^{-\frac{\delta^2}{8q}}$$

We use this formula and our desired rejection level α to determine a δ such that $P(X < E[X] - \delta) \le \alpha$. This probability value is our probability of a false alarm and can be diminished by decreasing α and recalculating δ. The value $E[X] - \delta$ defines our region of rejection (see Section 2.3).

In order to analyze the probability that our alarm is triggered when the number of faults in the system is $t' > t_a$, we define a second random variable X' identical to X except for the revised failure hypothesis. This gives us:

$$E[X'] = (n - t')\frac{q^2}{n^2} < (n - t_a)\frac{q^2}{n^2} = E[X]$$

An analysis similar to the above provides the following bound:

$$P(X' > E[X'] + \delta') \le 2e^{-\frac{\delta'^2}{8q}}$$

To summarize, these bounds can now be used as follows. For any given alarm line t_a, and any desired confidence level α, we can compute the minimum δ to satisfy $2e^{-\frac{\delta^2}{8q}} \le \alpha$. We thus derive the following test: An alarm is triggered whenever the justifying set size is less than $(n - t_a)\frac{q^2}{n^2} - \delta$. The analysis above guarantees that this alarm will be triggered with false positive probability at most our computed bound $2e^{-\frac{\delta^2}{8q}} \le \alpha$. If, in fact, f faults occur and f is sufficiently larger than t_a, then there exists $\delta' > 0$ such that $E[X'] + \delta' = E[X] - \delta$. Then, by the analysis above, the probability of triggering the alarm is greater than $1 - 2e^{-\frac{\delta'^2}{8q}}$.

In the case of the write marker protocol, we can tighten the analysis by using the (known) intersection size between Q and Q' as follows. Define $S = Q \cap Q'$, $s = |S|$, and a random variable $Y = |S \setminus B|$. Y has a hypergeometric distribution on s, $n - t_a$, and n, and $E[Y] = s(n - t_a)/n$. The appropriate Doob martingale sequence in this case defines Y_i, $0 \le i \le s$, to be the expected value of Y after i selections are made in S. Then, $|Y_i - Y_{i-1}| \le 1$, and so to set the region of rejection we can use

$$P(Y < E[Y] - \delta) \le 2e^{-\frac{\delta^2}{2s}}.$$

6 Conclusion

In this paper, we have presented two methods for probabilistic fault diagnosis for services replicated using t-masking quorum systems. Our methods mine server responses to read operations for evidence of server failures, and if necessary trigger an alarm to initiate appropriate recovery actions. Both of our methods were demonstrated in the context of the threshold construction of [MR97a], i.e., in which the quorums are all sets of size $\lceil \frac{n+2t+1}{2} \rceil$, but our techniques of Section 4 can be generalized to other masking quorum systems, as well. Our first method has the advantage of requiring no modifications to the read and write protocols proposed in [MR97a]. The second method requires minor modifications to these protocols, but also offers better diagnosis capabilities and a precise identification of faulty servers. Our methods are very effective in detecting faulty servers, since faulty servers risk detection in every read operation to which they return incorrect answers.

Future work will focus on generalizations of these techniques, as well as uses of these techniques in a larger systems context. In particular, we are presently exploring approaches to react to server failures once they are detected.

References

[CT96]   T. D. Chandra and S. Toueg. Unreliable failure detectors for reliable distributed systems. *Journal of the ACM*, 43(2):225–267, March 1996.

[DS97]   A. Doudou and A. Schiper. Muteness detectors for consensus with Byzantine processes. Technical Report TR97-230, Department of Computer Science, École Polytechnic Fédérale de Lausanne, October 1997.

[KMM97]   K. P. Kihlstrom, L. E. Moser, and P. M. Melliar-Smith. Solving consensus in a Byzantine environment using an unreliable failure detector. In *Proceedings of the International Conference on Principles of Distributed Systems*, pages 61–75, December 1997.

[KMM98]   K. P. Kihlstrom, L. E. Moser and P. M. Melliar-Smith. The SecureRing protocols for securing group communication. In *Proceedings of the 31st Annual Hawaii International Conference on System Sciences*, pages 317–326, January 1998.

[Lam86]   L. Lamport. On interprocess communication (part II: algorithms). *Distributed Computing* 1:86–101, 1986.

[LRM98]   M. J. Lin, A. Ricciardi and K. Marzullo. On the resilience of multicasting strategies in a failure-propagating environment. UT Austin TR-1998-003.

[MR95]   R. Motwani and P. Raghavan. *Randomized algorithms*. Cambridge University Press, 1995.

[MR97a]   D. Malkhi and M. Reiter. Byzantine quorum systems. *Distributed Computing* 11(4):203–213, 1998.

[MR97b]   D. Malkhi and M. Reiter. Unreliable intrusion detection in distributed computation. In *Proceedings of the 10th IEEE Computer Security Foundations Workshop*, pages 116–124, June 1997.

[MRW97]   D. Malkhi, M. Reiter, and A. Wool. The load and availability of Byzantine quorum systems. In *Proceedings of the 16th ACM Symposium on Principles of Distributed Computing*, pages 249–257, August 1997.

[Rei94]   M. K. Reiter. Secure agreement protocols: Reliable and atomic group multicast in Rampart. In *Proceedings of the 2nd ACM Conference on Computer and Communications Security*, pages 68–80, November 1994.

[PG89]   F. M. Pittelli and H. Garcia-Molina. Reliable scheduling in a TMR database system. *ACM Transactions on Computer Systems*, 7(1):25–60, February 1989.

[Sch90]   F. B. Schneider. Implementing fault-tolerant services using the state machine approach: A tutorial. *ACM Computing Surveys*, 22(4):299–319, December 1990.

[SESTT92]   S. K. Shrivastava, P. D. Ezhilchelvan, N. A. Speirs, S. Tao, and A. Tully. Principal features of the VOLTAN family of reliable node architectures for distributed systems. *IEEE Transactions on Computers*, 41(5):542–549, May 1992.

A   Martingales

In this appendix, we provide a brief introduction to martingales, which summarizes only the necessary definitions and results from the more thorough treatment found in [MR95, Ch. 4.4].

Definition 1 *A martingale sequence is a sequence of random variables* $X_0, X_1, \ldots$ *such that for all* $i > 0$,

$$E[X_i \mid X_0, \ldots, X_{i-1}] = X_{i-1}$$

Our goal in constructing martingale sequences in Section 5 is to apply the following theorem.

Theorem 1 *Let* $X_0, X_1, \ldots$ *be a martingale sequence such that for each* k,

$$|X_k - X_{k-1}| \leq c$$

where c *is independent of* k. *Then, for* $t \geq 0$ *and* $\delta > 0$,

$$P(|X_t - X_0| \geq \delta) \leq 2e^{-\frac{\delta^2}{2tc^2}}$$

The particular method that we use for constructing martingale sequences employs the notion of a *filter* over a finite sample space Ω, which is a nested sequence of event-sets $F_0 \subseteq F_1 \subseteq \cdots \subseteq F_k$ where $F_0 = \{\emptyset, \Omega\}$, $F_k = 2^\Omega$, and for $0 \leq i \leq k$, F_i is closed under complement and union. Intuitively, each F_i can be thought of as being generated by a partition of Ω into disjoint events, where F_{i+1} is generated by a more refined partition than F_i. In Section 5, each block (event) of the partition generating F_i is defined by the first i choices of servers in each of two quorums. We then apply the following theorem to construct a Doob martingale:

Theorem 2 *Let* $F_0, \ldots, F_k$ *be a filter, let* X *be any random variable, and define* $X_i = E[X \mid F_i]$, *i.e.,* X_i *is the expected value of* X *conditioned on the events in* F_i. *Then* $X_0, \ldots, X_k$ *is a martingale.*

Panel: Certification and Assessment of Critical Systems

Dependable Computing System Evaluation Criteria: SQUALE Proposal

Yves Deswarte

LAAS-CNRS -7 avenue du Colonel Roche - 31077 Toulouse cedex 4 (France)

Yves.Deswarte@laas.fr

Abstract

The SQUALE project has developed assessment criteria which aim at providing a justified confidence that an assessed system will achieve, during its operational life and its disposal, the dependability objectives assigned to it.

1. Introduction and motivation

The increasing use of computers in all industrial sectors leads to the need to specify and design computing systems which could fulfill the requirements of the targeted applications at the lowest cost. Various requirements have to be taken into account, whether functional (accuracy of the results, response time, ease of use…) or dependability requirements such as availability, confidentiality or maintainability. It is then of great importance to know if a given system is able to achieve all these requirements. Ensuring system compliance to functional requirements is not an easy task due to the fact that it is not always possible to check the system behavior in all possible conditions that may occur during its operational life. This is even more difficult for the dependability-related aspects, since it is generally not possible to exercise the system in all faulty situations, considering not only physical faults, but also design faults, human interaction faults or malicious faults.

For critical applications, i.e. those for which computing system failures could cause catastrophes, it is possible to gain a sufficient confidence in the system behavior by imposing well-suited development and validation methods which are specified in sector-specific standards: railways (CENELEC EN 50126, EN 50128 and ENV 50129), nuclear power (IEC 1880), avionics (ARP 4754 and DO 178B standards), etc. These different standards share many common characteristics, which shows the need for a generic evaluation approach, such as the one considered in the IEC 1508 standard. In the same way, when considering computing system security, there are evaluation criteria such as the TCSEC, ITSEC or Common Criteria that can help to assess the system ability to face possible threats. But all this concerns only two aspects of dependability, namely safety and security. However, it is often necessary to take into account other dependability attributes such as availability or maintainability. For instance in air or railway transportation systems, if passenger safety is essential, availability is also critical for the system profitability. It is thus of great importance to be able to check if the system achieves all its dependability requirements, not limited to safety or security.

The approach presented here is developed within SQUALE[1] (*Security, Safety and Quality Evaluation for Dependable Systems*), a European research project of the ACTS program (*Advanced Communications, Technologies and Services*). The aim of this project is to develop assessment criteria which would make it possible to gain a justified confidence that a given system will satisfy, during its operational life and its disposal, the dependability objectives assigned to it. These criteria are generic in the sense that they do not aim at a particular application sector.

2. Description of the SQUALE criteria

The SQUALE assessment framework and criteria incorporate some basic concepts from the security criteria and safety standards. Particularly:
- the roles of the different parties involved in the assessment process are defined: sponsor, developer, assessor;
- the notion of "target of dependability assessment" is introduced to specify the boundaries and the scope of the assessment;
- a process oriented assessment framework defines *confidence providing activities* which aim at giving the system the functionality and the quality necessary to fulfil its dependability objectives;
- different levels of confidence are defined to grade the importance of the dependability attributes and define the objectives to be satisfied with respect to each dependability attribute;
- different levels of rigor, detail and independence are specified for the confidence providing activities as a function of the confidence levels to be achieved with respect to each dependability attribute.

---

[1] Current SQUALE project partners are CR2A-DI (F), prime contractor, Admiral (UK), IABG (Germany), LAAS-CNRS (F), Matra Transport International (F) and Bouygues Telecom (F).

2.1 Assessment framework

SQUALE criteria application takes into account the whole system life cycle (from the definition of concepts and initial needs to the system disposal), but it does not rely on a specific life cycle model. The SQUALE assessment framework takes into account the traditional system decomposition into subsystems and components (from the definition of the high-level requirements to the realization of system components, the assembling of these components according to the architecture, and finally the integration of the overall system into its operational environment). Each step of the refinement process has to start with a hazard analysis activity that consists in identifying the set of undesirable circumstances (i.e. failures, threats, faults, etc.) that potentially have unacceptable consequences. The outputs of the hazard analysis activity should lead to: 1) the definition of the dependability objectives to be satisfied, 2) the specification of the dependability policy to be implemented to satisfy these objectives, 3) the allocation of dependability objectives to each subsystem (human, hardware, software, etc.), and finally 4) the definition of the dependability related functions to be accomplished by each subsystem.

Four *confidence providing processes* are distinguished in this general framework: dependability requirement validation, correctness verification, system dependability validation and process quality.

- *Dependability requirement validation* analyzes the dependability objectives, the dependability policy and strategies which have been chosen to fulfill these requirements and determines their suitability to counter the hazards which have been identified for the system.
- *Correctness verification* aims to ascertain that each level of the system implementation meets its validated requirements. One of its objectives is to check that the planned measures to prevent, tolerate, remove and forecast faults have been taken all along the development cycle and implemented correctly.
- *System dependability validation* checks the suitability of the dependability-related function implementation, including the effectiveness of the mechanisms implemented to counter the hazards, the ease of use of the system, the validation of fault assumptions and the analysis of side effects of the implemented system which may lead to critical situations.
- *Process quality* aims to ensure the correct application of the methods, tools and procedures which have to be used during all the development process, the operation and the maintenance of the system in order to achieve a sufficient level of quality.

2.2 Dependability profile

For a given system, the dependability requirements may apply to some or all of the dependability attributes (availability, confidentiality, reliability, integrity, safety and maintainability), and the relative importance of the attributes in a particular application may not be uniform. For instance, a safety-critical system may have safety and maintainability requirements, but the safety requirements are more significant than the maintainability requirements. In the SQUALE criteria, each attribute is assigned an expected confidence level, varying from 1 to 4, 1 being the lowest confidence level and 4 the highest one. A level 0 is also defined to indicate that nothing is required concerning this attribute. For instance, a system may be deemed to have a *dependability profile* A1, C0, R3, I3, S3, M2 which corresponds to confidence levels 1, 0, 3, 3, 3 and 2 respectively for availability, confidentiality, reliability, integrity, safety and maintainability. The dependability profile is a synthetic way to describe the dependability objectives resulting from the hazard analysis.

2.3 Confidence providing activities and assessment

For each of the four Confidence Providing Processes (CPPs), the SQUALE criteria recommend different *Confidence Providing Activities* (CPAs), and for each CPA, different methods and tools are indicated. Each CPA has been analyzed to define different levels of detail, rigor and independence with which the CPA can be applied. The level of detail can, for instance, indicate at which level of decomposition, the CPA should be applied. The level of rigor indicates how the CPA should be done and which evidence should be provided by those performing the CPA to the assessor. The level of independence indicates the relations between the developer and the person(s) performing the CPA (the assessor must always be independent from the developer). The criteria give for each CPA a mapping of the levels of detail, rigor and independence to the expected confidence levels specified in the dependability profile. The assessor checks that all required CPA have been performed in conformance with the criteria. If necessary, the assessor can also perform complementary Confidence Providing Activities, such as Penetration Testing, for instance.

References

P. Corneillie, S. Moreau, C. Valentin, J. Goodson, A. Hawes, T. Manning, H. Kurth, G. Liebisch, A. Steinacker, Y. Deswarte, M. Kaâniche, P. Benoit, *SQUALE Dependability Assessment Criteria*, LAAS Report n°98456, ACTS Project AC097, Nov. 98,182 p., also available at <http://www.research.ec.org/squale/>.

AUTHOR INDEX

Alvisi, L...379

Andriantsiferana, L...109

Arlat, J..25, 229

Avžienis, A..3

Bakken, D...149

Bensalem, S...89

Bondavalli, A. 319

Burns, A. 361

Caldwell, D. 47

Caspi, P. 89

Cristian, F...67

Cukier, M. 149

Di Vito, B...269

Dumas, C..89

Dutertre, B..301

Essamé, D...229

Fabre, J...25

Fantechi, A. 129

Fetzer, C. 67

Ghribi, B...109

Gil, P. 249

Gnesi, S. 129

Greve, D. 287

Hardin, D..287

He, Y. 3

Karr, D...149

Kopetz, H. 191

Kuntur, S. 169

Logrippo, L. 109

Malkhi, D. 379

Martín, G. 249

Martínez, R. 249

McDermid, J. 339

Millinger, D. 191

Mishra, S. 169

Mura, I. 319

Parent-Vigouroux, C. 89

Pérez, C. 249

Pfeifer, H. 207

Pierce, E. 379

Powell, D. 229

Prasad, D. 339

Punnekkat, S. 361

Reiter, M. 379

Ren, J. 149

Rennels, D. 47

Rodríguez Moreno, M. 25

Rubel, P. 149

Sabnis, C. 149

Salles, F. 25

Sanders, W. 149

Schwier, D. 207

Semini, L. 129

Serrano, J. 249

Stavridou, V. 301

Strigini, L. 361

Trivedi, K. 319

von Henke, F. 207

Wilding, M. 287

Wright, D. 361

Zang, X. 319

— *Notes* —

— *Notes* —

— *Notes* —

— *Notes* —

— *Notes* —

— *Notes* —

— *Notes* —

IEEE Computer Society Publications

The world-renowned IEEE Computer Society publishes, promotes, and distributes a wide variety of authoritative computer science and engineering texts. These books are available from most retail outlets. Visit the Online Catalog, *http://computer.org*, for a list of products.

IEEE Computer Society Proceedings

The IEEE Computer Society also produces and actively promotes the proceedings of more than 141 acclaimed international conferences each year in multimedia formats that include hard and softcover books, CD-ROMs, videos, and on-line publications.

For information on the IEEE Computer Society proceedings, send e-mail to cs.books@computer.org or write to Proceedings, IEEE Computer Society, P.O. Box 3014, 10662 Los Vaqueros Circle, Los Alamitos, CA 90720-1314. Telephone +1 714-821-8380. FAX +1 714-761-1784.

Additional information regarding the Computer Society, conferences and proceedings, CD-ROMs, videos, and books can also be accessed from our web site at *http://computer.org/cspress*

1/29/99